CHILD LAW HANDBOOK

Guide to Good Practice

Liz Goldthorpe with Pat Monro

Published with the Association of Lawyers for Children

The Law Society

This book is dedicated to Liz's son Lawrence, and Pat's daughters Kate and Lisa, whose childhoods were severely tested by having child care lawyers as mothers. . . .

ISBN 10: 1-85328-712-1
ISBN 13: 978-1-85328-712-1

Published in 2005 by Law Society Publishing
113 Chancery Lane, London WC2A 1PL

Typeset by J&L Composition, Filey, North Yorkshire
Printed by TJ International Ltd, Padstow, Cornwall

Contents

About the authors

EDITORS

Liz Goldthorpe is a child care and public policy specialist solicitor, and a well known conference speaker and tutor.

Pat Monro is a child care specialist solicitor and author of the best-selling guide *The Guardian ad Litem* (Family Law, 1995).

CONTRIBUTORS

Syd Bolton is a solicitor employed as Children's Legal and Policy Officer for the Medical Foundation for the Care of Victims of Torture.

Sarah Brooks is a self-employed children's guardian and independent social worker.

Helen Carr is a solicitor and an academic currently seconded to the Law Commission. Her specialism is housing law, although as a co-author of *Law for Social Workers* (OUP) she has some expertise in public law children act cases and community care.

David Goosey is partner at The Change Agency, a management and training consultancy, and Senior Lecturer in Advanced Social Work in the Centre for Advanced Professional Development at the University of Westminster.

Michael Griffith-Jones is a social work consultant and trainer based in London. He has acted as a children's guardian since 1985.

Penny Owston is a higher court advocate and the senior partner of Martin and Haigh. She is a member of the faculty of Nottingham Law School Centre for Law Firm Management and a graduate of the MBA programme there. She is the Law Society Council member for Lincolnshire and a member of the Standards Board.

Mark Tavender is a solicitor currently employed as Bench Legal Adviser at Bromley Magistrates' Court in south east London.

Frances Vilain is an experienced market research and commercial manager, and is Personal Assistant to Liz Goldthorpe. She has a BSc in Psychology from the University of Nottingham and over 15 years' experience in research, including project and quality management in a range of service industries.

Foreword

by the Honourable Mr Justice Munby

I am delighted – and honoured – to be asked to write the Foreword for this important and exciting book. The authors are very experienced child lawyers and they, and their contributors, have done us proud.

Their aim, modestly – too modestly – stated, is to provide a route map for busy practitioners and professionals. If this book is certainly that it is assuredly much more. It brings together a vast range of information and resources, much legal, much not. And the legal core of the book, though it is solidly grounded on legal analysis and the principles of substantive law, is founded in the practical insights and wisdom of seasoned and experienced practitioners. It is both a legal handbook and a handbook for legal practice, as the authors say, setting the framework for good practice by setting out the fundamental principles and describing the core work of the children's lawyer – safeguarding and services. If the focus is understandably on the work of lawyers, there is much that will illuminate and assist professionals in other disciplines; and if the focus, equally understandably, is on the work of solicitors and solicitor-advocates, there is much here that both the bar and the bench would do well to ponder.

It is a welcome sign of changing times that the authors put at the forefront, both of the book and of individual chapters, the increasingly important topics of human rights and diversity. In our diverse, multi-racial and increasingly pluralistic society it is good to see a book, particularly one written by and for practitioners, whose opening sentence reminds us that 'Good practice needs a solid foundation constructed with a firm grasp of applicable human rights principles and diversity issues.' Almost every chapter brings out the wisdom and importance of this observation.

The other great strength of the book is its recognition that child law extends far beyond the confines of the Children Act 1989 and that the work of children's lawyers is not limited to the Family Proceedings Court, the County Court and the Family Division. There are chapters on education, housing, mental health, the criminal justice system and the increasingly important topics of immigration, asylum and nationality as they affect children. There is welcome recognition of the fact that it is not only children in care who may be subjected to the compulsory control of the state and that the children's lawyer needs to be familiar not merely with the workings of local authorities – whether the social services, the housing or the education departments – but also, for example, with the workings of the Home Office as it bears on children caught up in the criminal justice, immigration and asylum systems. And usefully we are reminded in appropriate places of the importance of the Administrative Court, where the ever increasing volume of cases about children demonstrates the wider view that we need to take about the proper ambit of child law and the ever increasing range of professional knowledge and skills that children's lawyers need to bring to the task in hand.

All practitioners will be in debt to the authors for this ground-breaking book which will, I hope, serve as guide and friend to many.

James Munby
23 September 2005

Preface

Many things and people and a range of events and personal experiences have inspired this book. But its genesis lies principally in a long period of teaching with colleagues on the Law Society's Children Panel Qualifying Course and in the Association of Lawyers for Children.

Specialising in child law requires commitment and dedication to the belief that children, young people and their families require, and deserve, the best possible advice, representation and decision-making. Good quality legal services for them must be based on readily identifiable principles of good practice derived from a child-centred, interdisciplinary, and integrated approach. This is as important as knowledge of the law in creating good practitioners and professionals and in improving chances of good outcomes.

Children, young people and their families do not fall neatly into legal categories. Moreover, the context in which busy practitioners and professionals work is increasingly characterised by an emphasis on integrated services, and a mountain of guidance. It is not necessary, or possible, to know everything required, but increasingly critical to know how, and where, to obtain further information, support and advice, to separate out the essential elements from the sheer volume of information available and to identify the right sources against which to measure the quality of intervention in families to protect children and young people.

This book is designed to guide you to sources of further reference for other specialist areas of law, policy, practice and research that may help you in dealing with particular situations. Wherever possible, the format is geared to practical needs by listing key points or issues. This is an attempt to depart from the usual approach and serves two functions, firstly that the text should primarily be easily accessible and support actual practice by informing planning, case management and the conduct of cases in and outside court. Secondly, it seeks to summarise rather than to be encyclopaedic, and to raise awareness about the breadth of issues that need to be addressed.

It is not a comprehensive guide to either law or practice, but, in bringing together a range of information and sources, is designed to be a route map for busy practitioners and professionals. Its purpose is to set the framework for good practice by setting out the fundamental principles, to describe the core work of safeguarding and services, to outline some specialist areas that are relevant but often not known about and to indicate some sources of other good practice by which the standards of all practitioners and other professionals can be measured. It aims to reassure both practitioner and professional that there are ways of finding a path through the jungle by providing signposts to sources of further reference for other specialist areas of law, policy, practice and research.

Above all it seeks to place children and young people firmly at the heart of the work and to emphasise that lawyers in particular need to use an integrated approach to the provision of advice and representation.

The law and practice is at June 2005.

Liz Goldthorpe
September 2005

Acknowledgments

I owe a great debt of gratitude to many people who inspired this book and without whom it would never have been finished. The first of these is *Pat Monro*, whose substantial contribution has been invaluable: her long and extensive experience and expertise in various aspects of day-to-day practice has grounded the book firmly in the real world of casework.

It was also inspired by the high standards of professional practice and integrity of colleagues on the Law Society Children Panel Qualifying Course: *Michael Griffith-Jones*, children's guardian, *David Goosey*, social work consultant and *Tim O'Regan*, solicitor.

I am also deeply grateful to the small team who so freely gave of their precious time writing or contributing to the individual chapters on specialist topics – *Sarah Brooks*, *Syd Bolton*, *Helen Carr*, *David Goosey*, *Michael Griffith Jones*, *Penny Owston*, and *Mark Tavender* – as I am to those colleagues whose comments and corrections helped me avoid the worst excesses.

I should also like to thank *Mr Justice Ryder* for a long discussion that started several years ago, and the following people who kindly provided source material, or comment or professional inspiration (and often all three):

- *Lord Justice Wall*;
- *His Honour Judge Iain Hamilton*;
- *George Eddon*, Senior Law Manager, North Yorkshire County Council and Deputy District Judge (whose wit, wisdom and insightful comments made the last lap bearable);
- *Mark Powell* of Hugh James Jones, Merthyr Tydfil;
- *Angela Nield*, solicitor, for her support and encouragement;
- *Leslie Sheinman* for putting on the Children Panel course in the first place.

To *Frances Vilain*, for her organisational, research and administrative skills, calm unflappability, patience and editing prowess and to *Chris Cotter* for his endless support, love and tolerance of my many absences.

And to all my friends, family and colleagues for a continued belief that I might be justified in embarking on the project in the first place and would not drown in a sea of documents. . .

Liz Goldthorpe
September 2005

Table of cases

Table of statutes

Table of statutory instruments

Table of European conventions

Abbreviations

ACPC	Area Child Protection Committee
ACPO	Association of Chief Police Officers
AMH	adult mental health
ASBO	anti-social behaviour order
AST	assured shorthold tenancy
CAAC	Children Act Advisory Committee
CAFCASS	Children and Family Court Advisory and Support Service
CAMHS	child and adolescent mental health services
CAO	child assessment order
CCJLG	Child Care Joint Liaison Group
CPD	continuing professional development
CSA	children's services authority
CSCI	Commission for Social Care Inspection
CSO	child safety order
CYPA 1933	Children and Young Persons Act 1933
DL	discretionary leave
DTO	detention and training order
ECHR	European Convention on Human Rights
ECtHR	European Court of Human Rights
ELR	exceptional leave to remain
EPO	emergency protection order
ESO	education supervision order
EWO	education welfare officer
FGC	family group conference
FPCt	Family Proceedings Court
GAL	guardian ad litem
HP	humanitarian protection
HRA 1998	Human Rights Act 1998
IEP	individual education plan
ILR	indefinite leave to remain
IND	Immigration and Nationality Department
IPS	inadequate professional services

IRO	independent reviewing officer
ISA	information sharing and assessment
JR	judicial review
LAC	looked after child
LEA	local education authority
LSC	Legal Services Commission
LSCB	Local Safeguarding Children Board
MAPPA	multi-agency public protection arrangements
MAPPP	Multi-Agency Public Protection Panel
MHRT	Mental Health Review Tribunal
NASS	National Asylum Support Service
NGO	non-governmental organisation
NIAA 2002	Nationality, Immigration and Asylum Act 2002
OISC	Office of the Immigration Services Commissioner
OSS	Office for the Supervision of Solicitors
PAS	parental alienation syndrome
PEP	personal education plan
PII	public interest immunity
PR	parental responsibility
PRU	pupil referral unit
RCPCH	Royal College of Paediatrics and Child Health
RCP	Royal College of Psychiatrists
SCA proceedings	Special Children Act proceedings
SCIE	Social Care Institute for Excellence
SEN	special educational needs
SENDIST	Special Educational Needs and Disability Tribunal
SQMS	Specialist Quality Mark Standard
UNCRC	United Nations Convention on the Rights of the Child
UNHCR	United Nations High Commissioner for Refugees
YOT	youth offending team

CHAPTER 1

Fundamental principles and good practice

Key sources

- Race Relations Act 1976 and Race Relations (Amendment) Act 2000
- Children Acts 1989 and 2004 (and Children's Commissioner for Wales Act 2001)
- Human Rights Act 1998
- UNCRC 1990, arts 3(1), 9, 12, 19, 21, 37 and 39, and ECHR 1950
- Children Act 1989 Guidance and Regulations (1991), vols 1–10
- Protocol for Judicial Case Management in Public Law Children Act Cases (2003)
- *Good Practice in Child Care Cases*, Law Society (2004)

1.1 INTRODUCTION

Good practice needs a solid foundation constructed with a firm grasp of applicable human rights principles and diversity issues. This is the basis for all chapters, either by specific reference or by implication. The first part of this chapter contains a summary of what the key features mean for the practice of child law.

The Children Act 1989 emerged from a substantial amount of research, debate and consultation about law, legal procedure, principles and philosophy. The conduct of public law proceedings over the years, together with research findings into outcomes for children and young people, has led to inevitable comment on the legal practice standards required. This is a difficult area[1] requiring specialists: 'advocates with appropriate knowledge, experience and personal qualities'; who 'understand the work and can tackle it with knowledge, enthusiasm and sympathetic efficiency'; and 'skilled and appropriately trained . . . [with] specialist knowledge of the relevant law and practice'.[2]

Although mandatory accreditation for both solicitors and barristers has not been introduced, specialist training and extension of membership of the Law Society's Children Panel to solicitors for all parties has become widely accepted. Similar principles are being urged on the family Bar. For further discussion see [2005] Fam. Law 143.

The long awaited,[3] comprehensive Family Court is imminent, but an overall framework of good practice within which all disciplines can work effectively has yet to be fully addressed. The Children and Family Court Advisory and Support Service (CAFCASS) is still struggling with the challenge of becoming a respected, well resourced national body, and shortages of social work staff, the decrease in lawyers willing to do publicly funded work and the mirage of reliable IT systems and electronic records continue to affect the family justice system and pose challenges that undermine good outcomes for children. Many of the contributing professions feel besieged or undervalued and many are under intense pressure. Mutual support and understanding, with knowledge of the work, expertise and problems of each part of an interdisciplinary system designed to foster good outcomes for children and their families, is critical (Thorpe LJ, [2004] Fam. Law 558).

New developments include:

- Protocol for Judicial Case Management in Public Law Cases 2003;
- the new Family Justice Council and its subordinate local Family Justice Councils (from 2004);
- Her Majesty's Courts Service, a unified courts administration, responsible for all courts from the family proceedings court upwards (from April 2005);
- Children Act 2004 and integrated children's services;
- an increasingly competence-based assessment for the Children Panel;
- national core competencies and common curricula;[4]
- increasing dissemination and promotion of good practice standards and evidence-based practice by national and professional bodies and, more recently, among peer groups of professionals over the Internet.

The case for uniformity of good legal practice is 'obviously strengthened' (Thorpe LJ, [2004] Fam. Law 558) with a unified courts administration and integrated services. It is also a vital component of maintaining overall standards – all practitioners, of whatever age or experience, should have a baseline against which to measure the development of their own practice. But, above all, it is a prerequisite to providing, and improving on, service to the parties in each care case and, in particular, to the children caught up in the legal process.

This book deals mainly with solicitors' practice, and this chapter sets the framework. It first sets out the fundamental principles upon which good legal practice should be based, and secondly seeks to identify the essential components, qualities and attributes that characterise the good legal practitioner.

1.2 HUMAN RIGHTS

Human rights principles are the cornerstone of good practice for every practitioner. They are increasingly likely to place particular demands on busy specialist practitioners, not least because of:

- the speed of development of case law, with some important markers being laid down by the UK courts;
- the growing application of human rights principles to a wide range of contexts[5] affecting children and their families;
- the integrated children's services agenda.

International standards

International standards have a growing impact on UK law. The courts do not simply use the Human Rights Act (HRA) 1998, which makes the Articles of the European Convention on Human Rights (ECHR) directly applicable in domestic law, but are increasingly willing to use the UN Convention on the Rights of the Child (UNCRC), as well as judgments from other jurisdictions such as Australia and New Zealand.

The ECHR itself was not drafted to deal with children and only two of its articles are directly relevant to their developmental needs. But Convention rights apply to everyone and are given a broad interpretation and the European Court of Human Rights (ECtHR) has interpreted various Articles to impose an obligation on welfare authorities to protect children from abusive treatment. Through the HRA 1998, it is applicable in a wide range of contexts in which children are placed, or find themselves, many of which overlap with public law.

State intervention in family life, with the potential for temporary or permanent removal of a child from her parents or carers, is an extremely serious step. The ECHR principle that the more serious the interference is with family life, the more compelling must be its justification, is brought into sharp focus in public law, but subject always to the fundamental principle that the protection of the child must be paramount. The competing interests, rights and freedoms likely to arise in children's cases relate directly to these issues. The key aims of the Children Act 1989 – keeping birth families together wherever possible, and promoting contact by the child with non-custodial parents and siblings while she is living elsewhere – are therefore seen as ECHR compliant.[6]

The Act's fundamental plank – that the child's welfare is paramount – is underpinned by the ECtHR's 'skilful and dynamic interpretation':[7] since at least 1982, it has recognised that, in the final analysis, parental rights have to give way to the child's:

- 'if there is a serious conflict between the interests of the child and a parent, which can only be resolvable to the disadvantage of one of them, the interests of the child must prevail under ECHR Article 8(2)' (*Hendriks v. Netherlands* (1982) 5 EHRR 223);
- 'children in particular are entitled to effective protection' (*A* v. *UK* [1998] 3 FCR 597);

- it is necessary to strike a fair balance between the child's interests, for example to remain in public care, and both her and each of her parent's rights and interests to be reunited, but it has been repeatedly stressed that ECHR Article 8 does not entitle a parent or carer to have such measures taken as would harm the child's health and development (*Johansen* v. *Norway* [1996] 23 EHRR 33);
- a number of recent cases have stressed the crucial importance of the child's best interests, which, depending on their nature and seriousness, may override those of a parent, again specifically referring to the UNCRC as supporting the child's paramount right to protection. (See *Sahin* v. *Germany*; *Sommerfeld* v. *Germany* [2003] 2 FLR 671; *Hoffman* v. *Germany* [2002] 1 FLR 119 (but see Grand Chamber judgment on appeals 8 July 2003); *Hoppe* v. *Germany* [2003] 1 FLR 384 (contact); *Payne* v. *Payne* [2001] 1 FLR 1052; *Yousef* v. *Netherlands* [2003] 1 FLR 210 (residence and contact); *Elsholz* v. *Germany* (2002) 34 EHRR 58, [2000] 2 FLR 486, para. 52; *TP and KM* v. *UK* (2002) 34 EHRR 2, [2001] 2 FLR 549, para. 72; *Hokkanen* v. *Finland* (1994) 19 EHRR 139, para. 58 (residence); *Hoffman* v. *Austria* (1993) 17 EHRR 293 (residence).

Although not directly a part of UK law, the UNCRC (see **www.unhchr.ch**, **Treaties**) is an increasingly persuasive influence. The ECtHR has referred to it with approval and used it to fill perceived gaps in the ECHR regarding children. See *Z* v. *UK* [2001] 2 FLR 612 (ECHR Articles 2, 3 and 8 and UNCRC Article 19); *Costello-Roberts* v. *UK* [1994] 1 FCR 65 para. 35; *A* v. *UK* [1998] 2 FLR 959, para. 22; *V* v. *UK* (1999) 30 EHRR 121; *Z and Others* v. *UK* [2001] 2 FLR 603. This recognition has had a notable effect on both legislation (e.g. adjustment to procedures for trials of young children accused of serious crimes as a result of *R* v. *Secretary of State, ex p. Thompson and Venables* [1997] 2 FLR 471) and case law (e.g. reference to Article 7 in *Re H (Paternity: Blood Test)* [1996] 2 FLR 65 and application of Article 12 in *Shields* v. *Shields* 2002 SLT 579). National guidance and policies are now usually prefaced with a formal commitment to Article 12 of the UNCRC – the child's rights to express her views and be heard, although a detailed debate about genuine facilitation of children's views, voices and rights is arguably still relatively new.[8]

The UK courts are also drawing attention to UNCRC provisions when dealing with children's cases (e.g. *R* v. *Secretary of State for the Home Department, ex p. Venables and Thompson* [1997] All ER 97, at 122–123 and 151; *Re L, Re M and Re H* [2000] 2 FLR 334; *R (Williamson)* v. *Secretary of State for Education and Skills* [2005] UKHL 15; [2005] 2 WLR 590). The Administrative Court in particular is increasingly prepared to consider not only the relationship between the family and the state, but also the individual child and the state, in the context of such issues as education, housing, health, mental health, youth justice and immigration and asylum, ensuring, for example, that the prison service has a duty to consider the child's best interests (*R (D)* v. *Secretary of State for the Home Department* [2003] 1 FLR 484 at paras 65–66 and see *R (BP)* v. *Secretary of State for the Home Department* [2003] EWHC Admin 1963 para. 42. 'Family lawyers are only just beginning to appreciate that family law has anything to do with the many children who are in prisons or . . . caught up in the immigration and asylum systems . . . [and] most of us have not yet even begun to think about the possible implications . . . for those in the armed services.'[9]

In the interpretation and application of ECHR rights, there must be a victim and a public authority responsible for an alleged breach. Two basic principles of interpretation are particularly important:

- 'proportionality' and
- the 'margin of appreciation'.

Proportionality is central: interference with Convention rights must only be in accordance with the law and necessary, e.g. for the protection of the rights and freedoms of others. The margin is the degree of discretion given to an individual state in the enactment of domestic law. While rights are widely interpreted and applied to the particular facts before the court, any limitations to them, for example those applicable to Articles 8 to 11, are interpreted narrowly.

Above all, practitioners need a clear grasp of the application of ECHR Articles 6 and 8.[10] These are crucial to a consideration of whether there has been 'sufficient involvement' of both adults and children in processes affecting them so as to enable them to participate and contribute appropriately, subject to any overriding emergency need to protect a child (see e.g. social work and ASBOs in *R(M)* v. *Sheffield Magistrates' Court* [2004] EWHC Admin 1830).

Article 6

ECHR Article 6 is an *absolute* right and therefore cannot be compromised or watered down by reference to Article 8 (see *Re B (Disclosure to Other Parties)* [2001] 2 FLR 1017). It gives the right of:

- access to an independent and impartial tribunal without excessive procedural delays;
- presentation of a case and evidence under conditions that do not place the party at a substantial disadvantage compared with other parties,

subject to the recognition that neither the right of access to court, nor legal representation or public funding, is unlimited. Whilst there is no inherent right to legal representation, it may be required where the stakes are high (*Re K (Contact: Committal Order)* [2003] 1 FLR 277; *P, C and S* v. *United Kingdom* [2002] 2 FLR 631).

Cases on a child's rights under Article 6 are few as yet, but it is arguable that more direct investigation of the child's views is needed (*Re T (Contact: Alienation: Permission to Appeal)* [2003] 1 FLR 530). This is now a requirement in child protection investigations (Children Act 2004, s.53). Advocacy services must be provided to a child making a complaint (Children Act 1989, s.26A as inserted by Adoption and Children Act 2002 and see LAC (2004) 11) and, e.g., a child is entitled to attend hearings of the Special Educational Needs and Disability Tribunal even though she is not a party. But recognition of children's Article 6 rights is in its infancy with little consistent acceptance and implementation of the principle of genuine participation in decision-making processes.

Children's cases are usually regarded as complex and subject to strict timescales necessitating careful preparation and conduct, and court diligence in ensuring adherence to timetables. The domestic courts have made findings about delay (e.g. *Re D (A Child)* [2002] 2 All ER 668)[11] and the ECtHR has stated that inadequacy of resources, such as social workers or judges, is not an excuse for excessive delay. Conversely, pressure to avoid delay can in itself risk a breach of Article 6 rights, for example when the court has to consider whether to proceed with a hearing or to adjourn it to allow a parent time to prepare.

Article 8

ECHR Article 8 is very broad and has wide-ranging implications, covering respect for both *private* and *family* life – separate and sometimes overlapping concepts that may come into conflict. It places both negative and positive obligations on the state and is applicable to, e.g.

- separation of a child from her family;
- disclosure of information;
- covert surveillance and body searches.

Article 8 rights are *qualified* rights, which means they must be balanced against other rights (including other Article 8 rights). Its essential object is to protect the individual against arbitrary interference by public authorities, or to oblige the state to take positive action to prevent another individual from interfering with private or family life (see *Botta* v. *Italy* (1998) 26 EHRR 241).

It is the main Article engaged by children's cases, since the decision-making processes involved potentially have a serious effect on both family and private life. Any restrictions must be proportionate to the legitimate aim pursued (see *Olson* v. *Sweden* (1988) 10 EHRR 259; *Chassagnou* v. *France*, (2000) 29 EHRR 615, ECHR) and correspond to a 'pressing social need' (i.e. more than just 'desirable' or 'appropriate', somewhere between 'compelling' and 'imperative'). There must be adequate and effective safeguards to protect against arbitrary interference, and reasons for interference must be 'relevant and sufficient,' but there is a recognition that flexibility and the exercise of appropriate discretion are needed. (See *Olsson* v. *Sweden* (1988) 10 EHRR 259, at 283 (para. 61); *Eriksson* v. *Sweden* (1989) 11 EHRR 183, at 200–201 (paras 59–60); *Andersson* v. *Sweden* (1992) 14 EHRR 615.) Compliance with Article 8 does not only require the 'right outcome' – it also requires that the decision-making process be fair (e.g. when a local authority decides to remove a child who is placed at home under a care order).

'Family life' is a broad concept, especially in a multicultural and pluralistic society, and can depend on the facts of an individual case.[12] It is immediately obvious where it does exist, in that it applies to individual members of a family unit, including the child. But it covers a potentially wide range of relationships, does not require a biological relationship, and may not be clear in other cases (*R(L)* v. *Secretary of State for Health* [2001] 1 FLR 406): the 'existence or non-existence of "family life" is essentially a question of fact depending upon the real existence in practice of close personal ties' (*K* v. *UK* (1986) 50 DR 1991 and see *Lebbink* v. *Netherlands* [2004] 2 FLR 463). The onus on establishing its existence is always on the applicant.

'Private life' includes (*Niemietz* v. *Germany* (1993) 16 EHRR 97; *Botta* v. *Italy* (1998) 26 EHRR 241; *Pretty* v. *UK* (2002) 35 EHRR 1, [2002] 2 FLR 45):

- an 'inner circle', in which an individual may live his personal life as he chooses;
- the right to establish and develop relationships with others;
- physical and psychological integrity;
- aspects of physical and social identity; and
- a right to personal development and personal autonomy.

Critical factors include being able to interact with others to participate in community life with access to a range of social, recreational and cultural activities and encompass the emotional and developmental environment in which a child is being brought up. These principles may, for example, impose an obligation on local authorities to take positive steps to address disability issues, subject to their statutory decision-making powers and discretion to regulate their own resources (*R (A, B, X and Y)* v. *East Sussex County Council (No. 2)* [2003] EWHC Admin 167, (2002) 6 CCLR 194). This can produce unexpected results; for example, the right to tell one's story in the press can sometimes be an aspect of 'private life'.

In the conduct of care cases, careful consideration is needed in the interpretation and application of ECHR rights in terms of the paramountcy principle, the balancing exercise required between respective rights, and the evidential requirements of the Children Act 1989 and Article 8. Infringement of a parent or carer's Article 8 rights must be justified by reference to Article 8(2) and supported by evidence about the child's own rights and the issues regarding her welfare. Once the threshold criteria are established, the test for justifying the interference is to protect the child's welfare and interests, not the interests of the local authority or the public.

Article 3

The state has a positive obligation to take measures designed to ensure individuals in its jurisdiction are not subjected to torture, inhuman/degrading treatment or punishment and to prevent such breaches by one private individual against another. This particularly applies to children and other vulnerable persons, who are 'entitled to State protection, in the form of effective deterrence, against such serious breaches of personal integrity' (*A* v. *UK (Human Rights: Punishment of Child)* [1998] 2 FLR 959; *Z and Others* v. *UK* (2002) 34 EHRR 3, [2001] 2 FLR 612, at para. 73). This may arise in:

- asylum and refugee cases involving deportation or extradition to countries where there is a real risk of torture;
- severe race discrimination, which may amount to degrading treatment;
- medical treatment, mental health and secure accommodation.

Factors to consider:

- 'ill-treatment' requires a minimum level of severity to qualify;
- duration, physical and mental effects, gender, age and state of health are issues in deciding whether treatment is 'degrading';
- whether the object was to humiliate and debase the person concerned (*Price* v. *UK* (Application No. 33394/96) (2001) 34 EHRR 1285, [2001] Crim LR 916);
- conditions of detention and/or failure to improve them (*Peers* v. *Greece* (Application No. 28524/95) (2001) 33 EHRR 1192.

There is an obligation to protect the health of those deprived of liberty, and lack of appropriate medical treatment may amount to treatment in breach. For the mentally ill, assessment of whether the treatment or punishment concerned is incompatible must take into consideration their vulnerability and their inability, in some cases, to complain coherently or at all about how they are being affected by any particular treatment (*Keenan* v. *UK* (Application No. 27229/95) (2001) 33 EHRR 28).

In general terms, a human rights culture takes time to develop, but there is a growing body of case law that illustrates how public bodies have had to alter practice, procedure and policies to comply with the HRA 1998. Connections also need to be made between good practice and legislation: in particular, policies and procedures designed to achieve service improvements must be human rights compliant and reflect other equality legislation, including the Race Relations (Amendment) Act 2000.[13]

Diversity issues

Diversity is an inclusive concept that is beyond gender, skin colour and/or disability. It encompasses age, race, religious affiliation, economic class and sexual orientation. Special needs and disability issues are particularly important in many cases, because of a particular family or child's background and characteristics. Recognition and reflection of diversity in everyday practice and procedures has to be grounded in reality and understanding: making statements about 'commitment' to diversity or its 'promotion' is largely meaningless unless underpinned by a sound knowledge and value base and accompanied by a consistent approach informed by research. The Review that led to the Children Act 1989 clearly stated that 'it is important . . . to maintain the rich diversity of lifestyles which is secured by permitting families a large measure of autonomy in the way in which they bring up their children'.[14]

Britain is a multicultural society,[15] but disadvantage and discrimination characterise the lives of a wide range of black and minority ethnic groups, who experience higher levels of social and material deprivation, social exclusion and involvement in the care system.

Complex factors, which may also vary according to economic, social, cultural and religious backgrounds, are not always understood by professionals, despite:

- the duty on all public authorities to promote race equality (see Race Relations (Amendment) Act 2000);
- guidance stating this means *proactively* challenging racial discrimination and promoting good race relations;
- clear requirements in the Children Act 1989 and guidance to take account of race, culture and linguistic background.

Limited data is partly to blame, but so are misunderstandings, prejudice and lack of knowledge:

> Assumption based on race can be just as corrosive in its effect as blatant racism . . . racism can affect the way people conduct themselves in other ways. Fear of being accused of racism can stop people acting when otherwise they would . . . Assumptions that people of the same colour, but from different backgrounds, behave in similar ways can distort judgments.
> (Neil Garnham, QC to the Climbié Inquiry, 2003)

Commitment to equality in meeting the needs of all children and families, and to understand the effects of racial harassment, racial discrimination and institutional racism,[16] as well as cultural misunderstanding or misinterpretation, is essential.

Good practice must be culturally competent: this not only requires the avoidance of discrimination, but a sensitive and informed understanding that:[17]

- children from all cultures, backgrounds and circumstances are subject to abuse and neglect;
- every child has a right, regardless of background, to grow up safe from harm;
- family patterns, lifestyles and child-rearing vary across different racial, ethnic and cultural groups;
- children of mixed parentage and refugee children have specific and individual needs.

Practitioners should be aware of, and sensitive to:[18]

- ethnicity, language, religion[19], culture, gender and vulnerability relating to the child, clients and issues;[20]
- broader social factors that discriminate against black and minority ethnic people;
- the experience of racism (which differs between communities and individuals), or situations prompting claims for asylum, which may affect a child's or a family's response to assessment and enquiry processes.

Religion and culture profoundly affect an understanding of the world. Things taken for granted in one culture are alien in another, with consequences for the conduct of proceedings and the representation of clients. For example, in English law, recognition of the individual's views is seen as a critical necessity, but in some cultures these may be subjugated to the collective good. Furthermore, being from a minority ethnic group whose way of life is not respected by the majority culture can have a profound influence on the development of self-esteem. Living with racism demands different skills to resist the effect of negative stereotypes, aggression and fear.

The high proportion of females and the low number of black and minority ethnic lawyers, guardians and other professionals in this field can give rise to issues in conducting cases. But most importantly, practitioners' experience of heritage, culture, class, race and religion will differ greatly as between themselves and their clients. Many diversity issues require careful thought and planning, with advice where necessary from the Children's Guardian or other appropriate person:

- Representation of a child by guardian and solicitor may be unacceptable in some cultures, and their existence may undermine the relationship between the child and her family.
- Some cultures do not regard lawyers as independent and see them as part of 'authority', for others gender is important – a young Muslim woman, for example, should not find herself having to be represented by a male lawyer, nor, generally, should a young Muslim man have a white female lawyer.
- Having a representative or an interpreter from the same culture may have hidden consequences for communication and understanding.

- Parties from the same culture may have vastly different experiences as a result of circumstances such as marriage, education or refugee status.

Diversity includes consideration of special needs such as hearing and visual impairment, physical disability and a wide range of conditions that may affect communication, perception and cognition, with a consequential impact on instructions, advice representation and the conduct of proceedings both in and out of court. Assumptions can all too readily be made by professionals that may, for example, obstruct participation or alter expectations of behaviour, with little justification.

There are various practical consequences for the family justice system:

- In line with its general safeguarding duty, all local CAFCASS offices should identify the needs of children in their area and define and monitor the numbers of guardians in terms of their religion, race, culture and languages, to facilitate their appointment in appropriate cases or enable consultation or mentoring.
- Ethnic origin and cultural needs should be routinely recorded (but are not, arguably, a breach of the Race Relations (Amendment) Act 2000) and the availability and appointment of solicitors and guardians monitored.

Documents for use in proceedings have been singularly lacking in information about diversity. Practice, informed by valuable and ongoing research,[21] is beginning to change, but it is often hard to see the individual child in the paperwork. For example, the application form to instigate proceedings now requires a child's race/ethnic origin to be specified, but with no other details required. Inserting 'black' gives no real information about a child's heritage or needs and does not assist the courts in complying with their good practice requirements.[22]

The Judicial Case Management Protocol requires consideration of diversity issues, and provision of relevant information in:

- the composite Schedule of Issues – any diverse cultural or religious contexts (Appendix B);
- preliminary enquiries of, and instructions to, experts – any diverse ethnic, cultural, religious or linguistic contexts;
- experts' opinions – which must take into consideration any relevant factors arising from diverse cultural or religious contexts at the time, indicating the facts, literature and any other material relied upon (Appendix C, para. 1.2);
- the Case Management Questionnaire.

Implications for the legal practitioner

An up-to-date knowledge of the HRA 1998, the European jurisprudence and the relevant case law, as well as the UNCRC, is essential.[23] Human rights

11

impact on issues such as delay, case preparation, disclosure of information and access to documentation, as well as rehabilitation and any order sought regarding a child. Proceedings must be conducted with due regard to ECHR rights (HRA 1998, s.3), which requires particular attention to:

- anything likely to cause delay;
- time for preparation;
- 'equality of arms' between the parties;
- access to documentation;
- rehabilitation and ensuring any order sought regarding a child is 'legal and proportionate'.[24]

General issues as to whether the human rights of any person involved in proceedings have been breached must always be carefully considered by each practitioner, kept under review, and appropriate advice given to clients as to what further action could or should be taken, noting the following:

- the impact of human rights principles is not confined to the court process: fairness at all stages of the child protection decision-making process by public authorities is also guaranteed (*Mantovanelli* v. *France* (1997) 24 EHRR 370; *Re L (Care: Assessment: Fair Trial)* [2002] EWHC Admin 1379, [2002] 2 FLR 730);
- issues such as delay and sufficient involvement must be considered in the context of the decision-making preceding and underpinning proceedings, taking particular account of recent case law, which highlights the critical nature of the work done before the court becomes involved (*Re M (Care: Challenging Decisions by the Local Authority)* [2001] 2 FLR 1300; *Re L (Care: Assessment: Fair Trial)* [2002] EWHC Fam 1379; [2002] 2 FLR 730 and *Re G (Care: Challenge to Local Authority's Decision)* [2003] EWHC Fam 551, [2003] 2 FLR 42);
- care and judgment are always needed in taking human rights points: considering what these may achieve in the conduct of proceedings or negotiations is good practice, but using them 'inappropriately to bolster weak cases or to bring inappropriate points' is not;[25]
- the relevant *Practice Direction (Family Proceedings: Human Rights* [2004] 4 All ER 288) on citation of authorities must be observed;
- the use of ss.7 and 8 of the HRA 1998 to make applications during the course of care proceedings or free-standing applications after the making of a final care order has not been widespread.[26] Any looked after child can bring such action where it is alleged that a local authority has failed to meet its obligations to her under ECHR Article 8, for example in relation to standards in placement (see the principles stated in *Botta* v. *Italy* (1998) 26 EHRR 241). However, bringing HRA 1998 applications is not the guardian's duty (*C* v. *Bury MBC* [2002] EWHC Fam 1438, [2002] 2 FLR 868). It is generally not appropriate to bring a free-standing action when

there are family proceedings in existence within which the court can deal with HRA 1998 issues.

In order to mount effective challenges to poor practice or decision-making in the wide variety of contexts that affect children's lives, particularly in the new environment of integrated services, practitioners will need:

- a good understanding of the relationship between family law and other specialist areas of law;
- access to interdisciplinary skills and resources.

Early attention to any need for interpreters is critically important, especially in circumstances where these are required and/or will be provided free of charge (e.g. committal and domestic violence cases). The need for neutral, high quality, gender-appropriate verbatim translation or interpretation services when working with children and families whose language of normal use is not English cannot be emphasised too strongly. Practitioners should be extremely wary of using members of the client's family as interpreters. The Court Service Guide[27] contains useful guidance, pro formas, fees and details of the National Register of Public Service Interpreters who:

- have specialised in the English legal system;
- are able to translate accurately the meaning of what is being said or written from one language into another language;
- have a Diploma in Public Service Interpreting;
- are those used by the courts.

It is essential to:

- challenge assumptions, poor practice and inadequate knowledge;
- ensure all professionals carry out assessment, planning, service provision, investigations and proceedings with the fullest possible awareness of, and information about, diversity issues;
- consider the information needed by the court to address diverse cultural contexts,[28] special needs and disability issues, with particular regard to the requirements of the Judicial Case Management Protocol;
- guard against myths and stereotypes, both positive and negative; anxiety about being accused of racist or discriminatory practice should not prevent the necessary action being taken to safeguard a child: 'there can be no excuse or justification for failing to take adequate steps to protect a vulnerable child, simply because that child's cultural background would make the necessary action somehow inappropriate';[29]
- exercise humility in considering the extent of personal knowledge about different 'cultures' and to take advice whenever available;
- ensure that child or adult involved in proceedings has access to professionals with sufficient knowledge of diversity issues, who can advise

on, or carry out, the necessary work with the skills appropriate to social/cultural/circumstantial differences or backgrounds.

In certain circumstances, it may be right for assessment or enquiries to be conducted by a professional with a heritage or circumstances complementary to the child or family under consideration. But blanket assumptions that this should *always* be the case risk losing the emphasis on the child's welfare and giving wrong messages that professionals from different cultures do not have the requisite capabilities, standards and qualities.[30]

1.3   KEY PRINCIPLES FOR GOOD PRACTICE

Integrity and impartiality

The 'intellectually rigorous' partnership required between the child's solicitor and the guardian (*Re CB and JB (Care Proceedings: Guidelines)* [1998] 2 FLR 211, Wall J) applies equally between practitioners and in their relationships with other professionals. This includes challenging assumptions, exploring and analysing information with an open mind, and acting as courteous critic to fellow professionals, as well as a personal commitment and readiness to be unpopular if necessary, rather than to 'fall into line' with vested interests, or give way inappropriately under pressure.

The practice of child law centres on interrelated core principles:

- the child's paramount interests;
- treating the proceedings as 'non-adversarial';
- avoiding delay.

> The issues that have to be resolved require the most careful and sensitive handling by [those] . . . coming into contact with the child and their family. All solicitors acting in these matters have a vital role to play in ensuring that cases are dealt with justly and fairly, with the minimum of distress to the children and individuals concerned.[31]

Some elements of good practice parallel the general civil justice reforms, i.e. the principle that cases should only be conducted in a way proportionate to the likely benefit, with the court not allowing every point to be pursued and not permitting some procedural tactics. But challenges quite unlike those encountered in other fields of law can be presented by having to balance the potentially conflicting issues of freedom to instruct a lawyer of choice, the professional duty to act in the client's best interests and the need to ensure that a child's interests are paramount. The concept in the general professional conduct rules that the public interest in the administration of justice must prevail may not always prove so easy to resolve in the demands of child law practice.

Good practice and child centred representation

Principles set out here apply to all parties and should be read with Chapter 3 on child development.

Good practitioners employ a sensitive approach to negotiations and court proceedings, using careful analysis, assessment and informed judgment to identify the impact of decisions on children and adults, to identify harm or risk of harm and to test the evidence appropriately. They exercise skill in advice on, and participation in, decisions relevant to determination of where the necessary balance of disruption to family lies: finely balanced judgment is often required before and during proceedings to avoid further unnecessary disruption to family relationships and future professional work with children and families.

Crucially, the necessary skills must be deployed with a good grasp of why children's welfare is paramount, requiring a proper understanding of the overlapping areas of:

- physical, mental and emotional health and development of children and the impact of abuse and neglect on these;
- communication with children, and with clients, and the obstacles to it;
- assessment of capacity to give consent and competency to give instructions.

Central to good outcomes is the concept that a child or young person has a quite separate right to be considered as an individual. She is not a child of the state nor should she be seen merely as an adjunct of her parents or family or as an object of concern. She has a separate identity and needs that may differ depending upon physical, mental or other characteristics, and may vary with time and circumstance.

But all good professional practice is child centred, a concept founded on an understanding of children's needs, rights and welfare. The more familiar phrase is 'child *focused*', but using 'child *centred*' may be more helpful (see Chapter 3).

Each practitioner has a duty to act on the instructions of their particular client, whether local authority, parent, carer, family member, child or guardian on her behalf. But most clients, even some professionals, will not be familiar with the law and it is the duty of the practitioner to help them understand what is happening. This involves outlining the issues, the steps to be taken, keeping the client informed throughout, and explaining any delay, the effect of important and relevant documents and any changes in law, practice, policy and procedure, using a level of information and language appropriate for the individual.

The general professional conduct rules apply, and include the exercise of professional objectivity, judgment and advice to the client throughout the case. Clients have the right to put their case and care must be taken not to substitute the practitioner's own judgment on what is in the child's best interests for that of their client. In the often fraught atmosphere of child law, practitioners need to ensure that they do not become so involved in a case that personal emotions or an emotional response to the child or to any issue in the case adversely affects their judgment. This includes not pursuing a hopeless case to the extent that it adversely affects the outcome for the child. Whilst generally true that the duty to achieve and maintain proper levels of competence and care may not be breached simply by doing so (*Hartley* v. *MacDonald Glasgow Harly, The Times*, 15 May 2001), a 'particular degree of detachment and common sense [is] required . . . [you] should not be carried away by the enthusiasm, frustration and hurt of lay clients' (*Re N (Residence: Hopeless Appeals*) [1995] 2 FLR 230).

Depending on the circumstances of the case, and in the light of the practicalities, advantages and risks involved, a child's medium- to long-term welfare may be best served by her not being brought up by her natural parents, and in some cases by the child not having contact with her birth family or some members of it (Charles J in *Re R (Care: Disclosure: Nature of Proceedings)* [2002] 1 FLR 755). Dealing with these cases can demand a great deal of even very experienced practitioners, but doing the best for the client includes the ability to help the client make sense of this principle.

The individual client relationship is described in individual chapters, but includes:

- listening and taking instructions throughout;
- explaining the approach the court is likely to take and giving guidance;
- careful advice on the options/outcomes available, based on the evidence;
- objective evaluation of the evidence, especially in the early stages, to avoid, e.g. unsuccessful applications for interim orders which serve only to cause unnecessary conflict and costs;
- advising when there are reasonable grounds to contest and when it is appropriate to compromise, reach an agreement or make concessions;
- advising throughout on the consequences of the client's actions, including the consequences of failing to follow advice;
- advising the client against bringing in evidence that is irrelevant or inflammatory;
- advising on any right of appeal or human rights issue, if appropriate.

Appointing the right representative

All clients have a right to appoint a lawyer of their choice, but all practitioners should endeavour to ensure that they are competent to conduct these specialist cases. It is a requirement of Children Panel membership that practitioners do not continue with cases outside their expertise. The principles set out here apply throughout the case, bearing in mind that rigorous self assessment of capabilities, competence and fitness to act is required, taking particular account of the skills and knowledge needed for each case, and with regard to gender, race, culture and special needs.

The guardian's role is critically important for all parties and is central to the process of achieving good outcomes. Where there is no guardian appointed, the recommendations of the current Statement of Good Practice in the Appointment of Solicitors for Children should be borne in mind (see Chapter 19).

Where there is no guardian, the Law Society advises that 'the decision whether or not to accept appointment as the child's solicitor is a matter for the individual practitioner, taking into account his or her ability and competence to act and with close regard to the child's best interests'. All those in this position 'should consider seeking the advice and support of a mentor/s and once appointed, should continue to seek their assistance and guidance until the children's guardian is allocated or an independent social worker is instructed'.

Understanding the client and family

A fundamental part of child centred practice is to be fully aware of:

- the child's place in the family and family attitudes towards her;
- the family history and structure, including any members significant to the child and their roles;
- the family dynamics, and the effect of existing, past and potential adult, sibling and other significant relationships on stability and the child;
- conflicts and power relationships, and the effects of domestic abuse.

The realities of the child's and the family's life are critical to an understanding of how a case can, and should, be conducted. Asking about matters such as housing, proximity to supportive relatives and other adults, family finances, access to travel, domestic relationships and so on, can establish what obstacles to cooperation and understanding may arise and how realistic it is for a child or a member of her family to meet professional and court expectations. When acting for parents, the client's own experiences, including that of being parented, is often crucial to his or her ability to work with professionals.

It is particularly important to try and establish whether there are any other barriers to proper instructions, effective communication and participation. Anticipation of potential difficulties depends upon:

- knowing how to ask questions that may reveal hidden domestic abuse, influence exerted by other family members or special needs;
- finding out what outcome the client really wants, rather than what she says she wants (not necessarily the same), which allows soundly based advice to be given to enable the client to be realistic and to focus on

17

meeting reasonable expectations to enable good outcomes for the child;

- conducting interviews, etc. at the client's pace, allowing time to consider the options.

Avoidance of delay

All practitioners, whoever they are representing, should be committed to avoiding delay in the interests of the child. This is not only the overriding objective of the Judicial Case Management Protocol, but is also applicable to the steps taken prior to commencing proceedings.

The 'non-adversarial' approach

These proceedings, by their very nature, are clearly adversarial as the evidence to satisfy the threshold criteria must be thoroughly tested. So the requirement to be 'non-adversarial' set out in case law and guidance is frequently misunderstood. What it means in practice is that practitioners should not behave in an unduly adversarial, aggressive or confrontational manner.

It does not prevent rigorous testing of the evidence and appropriate advice to clients on conceding issues and/or contesting the case. But it requires a facilitative, rather than an antagonistic or confrontational attitude. An appropriately assertive stance is perfectly possible combined with conducting the case in a spirit of professional cooperation and treating all parties and their representatives with respect and courtesy (see Chapters 19, 21 and 22). There are sound reasons for this:

- a child's development and timespan needs prompt, effective decision-making using evidence relevant to her needs;
- children and their families are not usually involved in proceedings by choice;
- the effect of proceedings on the child and family members can be profound and long term, particularly if the proceedings are acrimonious or badly managed – practitioners' actions can, in themselves, undermine the effectiveness of measures ordered by the court;
- the 'tone' set in the early stages of a case can prove crucial to its future direction, conduct and outcome;
- proceedings are part of the child's continuing relationship with her family and of continuing personal relationships within the family;
- they are also part of the local authority's ongoing professional relationship with the child and family and guidance to other professionals stresses the need for partnership;
- however 'productive' being adversarial may appear in the short term, it may force others to adopt a similar stance, and is far more likely to lead to unnecessary acrimony, delay or cost.

Practical consequences

The court process requires the following:

- Judicial impartiality: there is Court of Appeal guidance on the test to be applied (*Locabail (UK) Ltd* v. *Bayfield Properties and Others* [2000] UKHRR 300).
- Full and frank disclosure (and see Chapter 24): 'There is the need to encourage candour from all the people involved in the proceedings, not only the professionals, but also the parents themselves, who have the most relevant information of all to impart' (*Cleveland CC* v. *F* [1995] 1 FLR 797).
- Participation in decision-making: consider:
  - legal advice and involvement of practitioners prior to proceedings;
  - any obstacles to effective participation;
  - the maintenance of an up-to-date local referral list and/or the assistance of a local authority practitioner in identifying firms with Children Panel accreditation.

Penalties for non-compliance include wasted costs orders as well as the potential for a party such as a local authority to be held liable.

Children's cases are not easy and practitioners are often under pressure while being less well remunerated than colleagues in other specialist areas of law. Child law and practice has grown considerably in complexity and legal practice varies widely, for reasons that are not always due to variations in personal experience, expertise or resources.

A breadth of knowledge and skills are required, especially in cases involving complex medical, psychiatric and psychological issues, and the rapid acquisition of knowledge and understanding of different professional disciplines and related areas of law. But it is not necessary for the lawyer to become an *expert* in other professional disciplines – it does little for personal status and good interprofessional relationships to appear to want to 'outdo' others. But it is essential to:

- know how and where to source, quickly and efficiently, good quality information and advice relevant to the lives and needs of children and families, especially a child's educational, health and developmental needs;
- understand information sharing, confidentiality and disclosure principles, partnership, and the way in which local authorities and other professional agencies operate the multidisciplinary system of child protection.

Knowledge and understanding of the relevant law, guidance and procedure and their application are not sufficient in themselves. There is often strictly no 'right' answer and the best approach often relies on acquired experience, common sense, unwritten 'rules' and an ability to learn from mistakes or misjudgments. Many of the skills required are distinct from other areas of law and the discrete approach to these proceedings has been well recognised for some time. Unlike the law, skills are rarely taught and have to be acquired with time, always bearing in mind that for the child 'it's my life you're practising with . . .'.

Arguably, the best practitioners are those who are capable of sustaining a healthy scepticism, humility and self-criticism. Displays of arrogance and overweening self-confidence are clearly misplaced, undermine the fundamental principles of good practice and damage good professional relationships. Independence, integrity and impartiality[32] are essential qualities for any good lawyer and should not be compromised, but maintaining these in the pressure of day-to-day practice is critical in proceedings when a child's future is at stake. This may take effort, but good quality advice and representation requires the ability to keep a cool head and a sense of proportion.

Representing any party requires a substantial degree of self-awareness in order to avoid imposing personal shortcomings on children and families. This does not always come easily, but good professional practice relies on a capacity to work with others, reflect on and learn from uncertainties and errors, and with a sense of continued learning in action. Each practitioner carries with them a legacy of their own experiences of childhood and parenting, the inevitable baggage of personal likes and dislikes, and prejudices: good practice means being aware of the potential effects of these and exercising consistent care in conducting cases to minimise them. The same principles apply to the practice of other professionals too.

Research[33] into a range of practice in different professions has found that what is critically valued is not so much a knowledge of one's subject, but a sense of continued learning in action and the capacity to work with, reflect on and learn from the uncertainties of the work. An essential part of good professional practice is the open-minded and active consideration of not only one's own knowledge and experiences, but those of others too. Theory, law and practice should flourish and enrich each other: the learning cycle involves reflection on concrete experiences, which leads to theorising about them, and, in turn, a testing of new ideas or concepts.

Appropriate, ongoing training in law, skills and good practice is therefore crucial for all professionals, including lawyers, however experienced. This depends on careful planning, commissioning and monitoring to ensure delivery by trainers of sufficient quality and independence, drawn from a pool of recognised and approved course providers, all of whom have 'signed up' to a common set of principles and good practice.

Finally, this can be a stressful and demanding area of work for any lawyer of whatever level of experience. Difficult situations can arise in any child care case, especially where no guardian has been allocated for the child. No one should do this work without good access to sources of formal and informal information and support, including a mentor who is a professional with sufficient understanding of the difficulties involved.

Advice can be sought from other members of the legal profession in and outside an individual's own practice or department, and, where appropriate, from professionals in other disciplines. The ALC, Resolution (formerly the SFLA) and Family Law Bar Association (FLBA)[34] can assist in finding mentors: if practitioners, they should at least be members of the Law Society Children Panel.

NOTES

1 Children Act Advisory Committee, *Annual Report 1994/5*.
2 Munby J, National Youth Advocacy Service (NYAS) lecture, February 2004.
3 See the *Finer Report* (1974).
4 For example, Core Curriculum, President's Interdisciplinary Committee 2004; Common Core of Skills, Knowledge and Competence, DfES 2004 (**www.dfes.gov.uk/commoncore/index.shtml**); Safeguarding Children Training materials, DH 2005.
5 See, e.g. 'The Child, The State and Article 8', keynote speech, Munby J, Association of Lawyers for Children (ALC) conference, November 2004.
6 But for further discussion see J. Fortin,, *Children's Rights and the Developing Law*, 2nd edn, LexisNexis (2003) and C. Henricson and A. Bainham, *The Child and Family Policy Divide: Tensions, Convergence and Rights*, York Publishing Services for the Joseph Rowntree Foundation (2005), and **www.jrf.org.uk**.
7 J. Fortin, *Children's Rights and the Developing Law* (2003), p.53.
8 See, e.g. Thorpe LJ and J. Cadbury (eds), *Hearing the Children*, President's Interdisciplinary Conference 2003, Jordans (2004).
9 Munby J, keynote speech, ALC conference, November 2004.
10 *Good Practice in Child Care Cases*, Law Society (2004), para. 2.1.1.
11 Held it was acceptable for trial of factual issues in a family case to be adjourned twice when father had not seen daughter for more than two years.
12 For a full discussion of the definition see Munby J in *Singh* v. *Entry Clearance Officer, New Delhi* [2004] EWCA Civ 1075, [2005] 2 FLR 308.
13 Note also the Solicitors' Anti-Discrimination Rules 2004 which prohibit discrimination on grounds of race, sex, sexual orientation and disability.
14 *Review of Child Care Law*, DHSS (1985), para. 2.13.
15 Nearly 6.4 million people (about 1 in 8) in England belong to ethnic minority communities.
16 Defined as 'the collective failure by an organisation to provide an appropriate and professional service to people on account of their race, culture and/or religion': Sir William Macpherson, *Stephen Lawrence Inquiry Report* (1999).
17 See *Working Together to Safeguard Children*, DH, Home Office, DfEE (1999).
18 *Ibid.* para. 7.4.
19 Religious freedom is guaranteed by ECHR, art. 9.3 subject to necessary limitations, e.g. safety, health, etc.
20 *Good Practice in Child Care Cases*, Law Society (2004), para. 2.2.1.
21 J. Brophy, J. Jhutti-Johal and C. Owen, *Significant Harm: Child Protection Litigation in a Multi-Cultural Setting*, Lord Chancellor's Department (2003).
22 See *Equal Treatment Benchbook*, Judicial Studies Board (March 2004).
23 *Good Practice in Child Care Cases*, Law Society (2004), para. 2.1.4.
24 *Ibid.* para. 2.1.1.

25 *Ibid.* para. 2.1.2; and see *Daniels* v. *Walker (Practice Note)* [2000] 1 WLR 1382, CA.

26 See, e.g. *Re M* [2001] 2 FLR 1300; and note comments of Allan Levy, QC, 'it is underused ... I am surprised there has been no test case': ALC conference, Leeds, 2002.

27 Arranging Interpreters for People with Hearing Impairment and for Foreign Languages (September 2003).

28 *Good Practice in Child Care Cases*, Law Society (2004), para 2.2.2; Law Society Guide 2004, J. Brophy *et al*, *Child Protection Litigation in a Multi-Cultural Setting*, Oxford (2003); and see Judicial Studies Board, *Race and the Courts*, **www.jsboard.co.uk/etac/race+courts.htm** (summary of different religions and associated holy days and festivals).

29 Lord Laming, *Climbié Inquiry Report* (2003), ch. 16.

30 See, e.g. Dr Nnenna Cookey, consultant paediatrician, Climbié Inquiry seminar, 2003.

31 Dame Elizabeth Butler-Sloss, Introduction to *Good Practice in Child Care Cases*, Law Society (2004).

32 See Solicitors' Practice Rules 1990, Rule 1.

33 D. Schon, *The Reflective Practitioner: How Professionals Think in Action*, New York, Basic Books (1983); F. Quinn, 'Reflection and Reflective Practice' in *Continuing Professional Development in Nursing*, Cheltenham, Stanley Thornes (1998); D. Kolb, *Experiential Learning*, New Jersey, Prentice Hall (1984).

34 See contact details in Appendix 2.

CHAPTER 2

Professional conduct and practice management

Key sources

- Solicitors Act 1974
- *The Guide to the Professional Conduct of Solicitors 1999,* Law Society
- Protocol for Judicial Case Management in Public Law Children Act Cases (2003)
- *Good Practice in Child Care Cases,* Law Society (2004)
- Children Panel: Criteria and Guidance Notes (2005) including Children Panel Undertaking
- LSC *Manual,* vol. 3 and Funding Code

2.1 INTRODUCTION

There can be few areas of legal practice more challenging than the conduct of public law proceedings, when the outcome can have such far-reaching and literally life-changing consequences for everybody concerned. This chapter deals with the general rules and good practice guidance on the relevant legal and professional duties, and should be read with the chapters on acting for individual parties.

Such issues as conflicts of interest and confidentiality that can arise in care cases can be particularly difficult to resolve, but the practitioner must have a good grasp of what constitutes good standards of professional conduct in order to understand the potential pitfalls and identify possible solutions.

2.2 GENERAL PRINCIPLES

Solicitors' Practice Rules

The aim of the professional conduct rules is to provide a safe and efficient foundation for legal practice, to provide adequate safeguards to protect the public in their dealings with the profession and to maintain the integrity of the profession in the perception of the public. They apply equally to in-house legal departments, i.e. local authorities.

The current rules (set out in *The Guide to the Professional Conduct of Solicitors 1999*, Law Society) comprise a complex mass of statutory rules, non-statutory guidance on conduct and the common law.

The Law Society has rule-making powers, which must be exercised in the public interest. The aim of its Regulation Review Working Party (set up in 1999) was to simplify the rules and make them less burdensome for solicitors and the public alike and new draft rules are currently subject to consultation with the profession.

The existing Practice Rule 1 sums up, in the form of a statutory rule, the basic principles of conduct expected from a solicitor derived from the common law:

> A solicitor shall not do anything in the course of practising as a solicitor, or permit another person to do anything on his behalf, which compromises or impairs or is likely to compromise or impair any of the following:
>
> - the solicitor's independence or integrity;
> - a person's freedom to instruct a solicitor of his choice;
> - the solicitor's duty to act in the best interests of the client;
> - the good repute of the solicitor or the solicitor's profession;
> - the solicitor's proper standard of work;
> - the solicitor's duty to the court.

This is the cornerstone upon which the other Practice Rules and regulations rest. Where two or more principles conflict, 'the determining factor in deciding which principle should take precedence must be the public interest, and especially the public interest in the administration of justice'.

This Practice Rule is to be replaced by 10 core duties overlaid with (at the moment) 21 Practice Rules. These duties are:

1. Integrity: to act with integrity towards clients, the courts, lawyers and others.
2. Independence: not to allow independence to be compromised in the face of pressure from clients, the courts or any other source.
3. Best interests of clients: to treat the interests of clients as paramount, provided they do not conflict with the practitioner's obligations in professional conduct and/or the public interest in the administration of justice.
4. Confidentiality: to keep all information about clients confidential, subject to any overriding legal obligation.
5. Conflict of interest: not to act where there is a conflict between the interests of two or more clients, or the client's and the practitioner's interests.
6. Competence: to act only where the practitioner is able to provide a competent service.
7. Fairness: to treat clients fairly, reasonably and without unlawful discrimination.
8. Client care: to maintain appropriate client care procedures, which recognise a client's right to be given information on costs which is sufficiently

clear, timely and frequent, so as to enable clients to make informed decisions.

9. Management: to operate appropriate business systems and processes to meet the practitioner's duties to clients.
10. Profession: not to behave in a way that damages the reputation or integrity of the profession.

Diversity and equality

In the context of proceedings relating to children, practitioners should be 'sensitive to issues of ethnicity, language, religion, culture, gender and vulnerability, in relation to the child, their dealings with clients and the issues in each case'[1]. Consideration should be given to the information which might be needed by the court to address cultural contexts and if necessary ensure that evidence is obtained and made available.

Avoiding discrimination: Rule 6

The Law Society is 'committed to playing a leading role in the elimination of discrimination and the promotion of equality of opportunity and diversity in all its activities as a regulator, a representative body and an employer':

- It has a new general duty at public law, in relation to its regulatory functions, to have 'due regard to the need to eliminate unlawful discrimination and to promote equality of opportunity and good relations between persons of different racial groups'.
- It has formulated an Equality and Diversity Strategy and Framework for Action with the intent that best practice permeates every area of the Society's activities.
- There are also the new Solicitors' Anti-Discrimination Rules 2004 (approved by the Law Society Council in February 2004), which go beyond current statutory requirements, anticipating the implementation of EU Employment Directives (in relation to religion and belief).

The 2004 Rules create a duty on solicitors not to discriminate and to comply with all anti-discrimination legislation from time to time in force. They also require the practitioner at all times, in professional dealings with staff, partners, barristers, other lawyers, clients or third parties, not to discriminate against any person (rule 6.01(2):

- directly or indirectly, nor victimise or harass them on the grounds of their:

  - sex (including their marital status);
  - race or racial group;
  - ethnic or national origins;

- colour;
- nationality;
- religion or belief; or
- sexual orientation;

- on grounds of disability except where, in relation to legislation, there is a specific exception or limitation preventing such discrimination being unlawful.

A principal in a firm must adopt and implement an appropriate policy for avoiding discrimination and promoting equality and diversity within the firm (rule 6.03), which must include as a minimum the provisions which appear in the Law Society's model policy.

Whilst age discrimination, which is not yet statutory, is not precluded in the Rule, the Legal Services Commission in the Specialist Quality Mark Standard (SQMS) do require participating firms to have a non-discrimination policy which precludes this (SQMS A3.1).

Consequences of breach of the professional conduct rules

Reports of the Solicitors' Disciplinary Tribunal (see the Law Society's *Gazette*) amply demonstrate the consequences of failure to comply with the Professional Conduct Rules. There are some grey areas, and categories can and do overlap, but generally:

- 'professional misconduct' is generally taken to mean breaches of the Conduct Rules, committed in the course of practising as a solicitor, e.g. failure to honour an undertaking;
- 'unbefitting conduct' includes, e.g., writing offensive letters and offensive behaviour;
- 'inadequate professional service' (IPS complaints are usually dealt with under the Consumer Redress Scheme and include delay and failure to keep the client informed);
- 'breach of duty' is one that gives rise to an action in law, e.g. in contract or tort.

The Tribunal is independent of the Law Society, but funded by the profession. There is no 'tariff' as such for breaches of the Rules and each case is dealt with on its merits. In serious cases solicitors can be struck off the Roll or at the very least have conditions imposed on their practising certificates.

Under the provisions of the Consumer Redress Scheme, which deals with IPS complaints, practitioners can be required to pay damages of up to £15,000 to clients whose complaints are upheld.

2.3 CHILDREN PANEL REQUIREMENTS

Scope of the Panel

The Children Panel covers:

- representation of children in all family proceedings where there is provision to represent children (Children Representative);
- representation of adult parties in public law proceedings under the Children Act 1989 (Adult Representative);
- representation of local authorities in public law proceedings under the Children Act 1989 (Local Authority Representative).

The eight eligibility criteria are expressed in virtually identical terms for each type of representative (except that the portfolio requirements for Children Representatives are more exacting), as follows.

Applicants must:

- demonstrate experience of representing parties/local authorities in public and private law proceedings under the Children Act 1989;
- have practised as a solicitor for at least three years and held a practising certificate throughout that period or have been a Fellow of the Institute of Legal Executives (ILEX) for three years and hold the Rights of Audience Matrimonial Proceedings Certificate;
- have attended a three-day approved training course; applications must be submitted within six months of attendance on the course;
- agree that references may be sought and that various internal checks can be made (now including Criminal Records Bureau (CRB) checks for new applicant Children Panel Representatives);
- give an undertaking (see below);
- submit the completed assessment questionnaire (the portfolio stage), together with the signed undertaking and cheque;
- have their application considered by a Law Society-appointed assessor;
- if successful, attend for an interview conducted by a solicitor interviewer and a children's guardian.

If unsuccessful at the portfolio stage, applicants will be refused membership but may appeal the decision under the appeal procedures: see below.

Transfer from one type to another is not automatic: the procedure requires applicants to submit an update of experience, continuing professional development (CPD) gained, pay a fee and attend for an interview.

Membership is normally for five years, after which reaccreditation must be applied for by completing a questionnaire detailing experience, update training and other relevant matters.

Personal conduct

Children Panel undertaking

Panel members are required to give a personal undertaking, when representing a party in proceedings covered by the Children Act 1989, as follows:

- Subject to instructing another advocate as below, they will not normally delegate the preparation, supervision, conduct or presentation of the case but will deal with it personally.
- In each case they will consider whether it is in the best interests of their client to instruct another advocate in relation to the presentation or preparation of the case.
- If it is in the best interests of their client, or necessary, to instruct another advocate, they will:
  - consider and advise their client or the children's guardian (if applicable) who should be instructed in the best interests of the client;
  - agree that, save in exceptional circumstances, any advocate who is instructed will either be:
    - another Children Panel member (approved as a Children Representative if the client is a child); or
    - a member of the Bar on their practice's approved supplier list;
  - obtain an undertaking from that advocate to:
    - attend and conduct the matter personally unless an unavoidable professional engagement arises;
    - take all reasonable steps to ensure that, as far as reasonably practicable, a conflicting professional engagement does not arise.

It is a principle of professional conduct that an undertaking given by a solicitor is personally binding on him and must be honoured. Failure to honour it is prima facie evidence of professional misconduct, which can carry serious sanctions including removal from the Panel, fines or worse.

The personal undertaking above means that the delegation of any work on a file should be carefully managed and be dealt with by properly trained, supported and supervised caseworkers. If skill, competence and 'know how' in relation to the more straightforward aspects of case preparation can safely be transferred downwards by training, coaching and mentoring arrangements, then not only will work be produced more profitably, there will be less need to instruct counsel to do the advocacy.

Conditions of membership

Panel members are required to adhere to the highest possible standards of practice, including *The Guide to the Professional Conduct of Solicitors 1999*, and any replacement and specific guidance issued from time to time. Failure to do so may lead to a complaint being made to the Consumer Complaints Service (which replaced the Office for the Supervision of Solicitors in 2004), removal from the Panel or some lesser/other sanction depending on the seriousness of the breach.

Removal from the Panel

An applicant must be a 'fit and proper person' to become and remain a member of the Panel. As the professional body approving applicants, the Law Society remains under a duty, during the currency of any membership, to investigate any matter arising which may call into question the fitness and propriety of a member of the Panel to act as such, and to take whatever action is considered appropriate at whatever stage of the investigation.

If the Law Society determines that a member of the Panel has ceased to be a fit and proper person to continue membership, or that fitness and propriety has been compromised, then it may refuse, revoke or suspend the membership or attach conditions to it. Members affected may appeal under the Law Society's adjudication procedures.

All complaints will generally be investigated by the Consumer Complaints Service .The Law Society reserves the right to suspend a Panel member whilst a serious allegation is under investigation and will give notice of such suspensions to Panel users as considered appropriate including the local courts and the CAFCASS Panel Manager. A member who is suspended can appeal to a Law Society appointed adjudicator.

2.4   DUTIES TO THE CLIENT

Client care

It goes without saying that practitioners should ensure that their clients are aware of the court's powers (*Re SW (A Minor) (Care Proceedings)* [1993] 2 FLR 609).

In the new Draft Professional Conduct Rules, Practice Rule 15 becomes Draft Rule 2, Client Relations, and is substantively the same as before. It is designed to help the lawyer and her clients to understand each others' expectations and responsibilities and to ensure that clients are given the information necessary to enable them to make appropriate decisions about how their matter should proceed.

This is particularly important when acting for 'significant others', e.g. those individuals who seek to be joined as parties to proceedings and who are ineligible for public funding. In these circumstances, the practitioner must (Draft Rule 2.02):

- identify clearly the client's objectives in relation to the work to be done;
- give the client a clear explanation of the issues involved and the options available to the client;
- agree with the client the next steps to be taken; and
- keep the client informed as to progress unless otherwise agreed.

The practitioner should also:

- agree an appropriate level of service;
- explain the solicitor's responsibilities;
- explain the client's responsibilities; and
- ensure that the client is given in writing the name and status of the person responsible for overall supervision.

Under Draft Rule 2.03, the solicitor should:

- give the client the best information possible about the likely overall cost of a matter both at the outset and, when appropriate, as the matter progresses;
- in particular, advise the client:

  - of the basis and terms of any charges;
  - if the charging rates are to be increased;
  - of likely payments which may need to be made to others;

- discuss with the client how she will pay, in particular whether:

  - the client may be eligible and should apply for public funding;
  - the client's own costs are covered by insurance or may be paid by someone else such as an employer or trade union;

- advise the client of her potential liability for any other party's costs.

Publicly funded clients

The practitioner must:

- explain the client's potential liability for her own costs and for the costs of any other party;
- discuss with the client whether her liability for another party's costs may be covered by existing insurance or whether specially purchased insurance may be obtained;
- ensure that any information about the cost is clear and confirmed in writing;

- discuss with the client whether the potential outcomes justify the expense or risk involved including, if relevant, the risk of having to pay an opponent's costs.

If it can be demonstrated that it was inappropriate in the circumstances to meet some or all of these requirements, a practitioner will not be in breach of Draft Rule 2.03.

If a client does become eligible for public funding then the requirements of the SQMS will 'kick in', which impose additional obligations in relation to funding issues, e.g. the client's duty to pay any fixed or periodic contribution assessed and the consequences of failing to do so.

Confidentiality

A solicitor:

- is under a duty to keep confidential information about a client's affairs irrespective of the source of the information; but where the client gives express consent to disclosure of information that would otherwise be confidential, this overrides the duty;
- may reveal confidential information to the extent she believes necessary to prevent the client or a third party committing a criminal act that the solicitor believes on reasonable grounds is likely to result in serious bodily harm, e.g. where an adult client discloses abuse by herself or by another adult against a child but refuses to allow disclosure;
- should consider revealing confidential information to an appropriate authority in exceptional circumstances involving children, where, e.g. the child client indicates continuing abuse but refuses to allow disclosure of this information.

It is a matter for the individual solicitor to judge whether she is required to breach client confidentiality.

The general principle is that absolute confidentiality should be maintained except in truly exceptional circumstances, but the public interest in maintaining that has to be weighed against the public interest in protecting children at risk from serious harm. Only where the solicitor believes that the second outweighs the first would she have discretion to disclose confidential information. In relation to child abuse and abduction, a breach is only justified in anticipation of a crime, i.e. where she 'strongly suspects or knows that abuse has taken, is taking, or will take place' (see *The Guide to the Professional Conduct of Solicitors 1999*, Annexes 16A and 16B).

But even if information is confidential, a lawyer may still be ordered by the court to disclose privileged information. In all cases it is the solicitor's duty, as an officer of the court, not to mislead the court (*Re B (Abduction and Disclosure)* [1995] 1 FLR 774, CA).

A solicitor is generally under a duty to allow clients unfettered access to any relevant documentary evidence that the solicitor holds, save where such evidence would adversely affect the client's physical or mental condition. Accordingly, when acting for a child, the solicitor should consider whether it is appropriate to disclose all or some of the documentation; should consult the Guardian or other professional; or seek directions from court (*Re B (A Minor) (Disclosure of Evidence)* [1993] 1 FLR 191). Where acting for several children, the extent of the access to the evidence may vary. It will be necessary to emphasise the confidential nature of the documents, and consider whether it is appropriate to give the child concerned copies. Whether the client is an adult or a child, they should be told about the circumstances in which the duty of confidentiality may be breached.

Conflict of interest

Conflict may arise where the firm has acted for a local authority or a social worker in a private law case; or on the instructions of a guardian, and is then instructed for a child/parents involving the same social worker/guardian. Information received during the course of the previous case, e.g. about a social worker's experience or a disciplinary case brought against her, may be relevant in the subsequent case. This would appear to present a conflict of interest which will be difficult to resolve.

The court has power to refuse to hear a particular advocate (Courts and Legal Services Act 1990, s.27(4)), and some further guidance can be found in case law. The basic principle is that 'justice should not only be done but should manifestly and undoubtedly be seen to be done' (see Lord Hewart CJ in *R* v. *Sussex Justices, ex p. McCarthy* [1924] 1 KB 256). (An unsuccessful party's discovery of intimate cohabitation between legal representatives 'would give rise to a grievance, in my view justified, to the effect that in part [the proceedings] had been a charade' and the court can intervene (Wilson J in *Re L (Care Proceedings: Cohabiting Solicitors)* [2000] 2 FLR 887).)

Where a firm intends to act for one party in proceedings in circumstances in which they previously acted for another party, the protection of confidential information requires a change unless it is established there is no real risk that the information is, or will become, known to those proposing to act (House of Lords in *Prince Jefri Bolkiah* v. *KPMG (A firm)* [1999] 2 AC 222). These criteria have been applied in care proceedings (see Court of Appeal in *Re T and A (Children) (Risk of Discosure)* [2000] 1 FLR 859): there is a need for all concerned to tread sensitively, but objections must be based upon more than a bona fide feeling of injustice, only sustainable by reference to a factual inquiry into whether the solicitor has access to relevant confidential information.

Careful judicial advice is as follows (Ward LJ in *Re T and A (Children) (Risk of Disclosure)* [2000] 1 FCR 659):

to endeavour so far as one possibly can . . . at times perhaps bending over back-wards, to assure the unhappy parents whose children may be removed from them and placed in care that the inquiry is thoroughly independent.

Perhaps it would be wise if solicitors would run their computer check not only when instructed but also when fresh parties are added.

Legal professional privilege

Definition

This is the privilege that attaches to communications between a lawyer and her client, described by Lord Taylor CJ in *R* v. *Derby Magistrates' Court, ex p. B* [1996] 1 FLR 513 as:

> a man must be able to consult his lawyer in confidence, since otherwise he might hold back half the truth. The client must be sure that what he tells his lawyer in confidence will never be released without his consent. Legal professional privilege is thus much more than an ordinary rule of evidence, limited in its application to the facts of a particular case. It is a fundamental condition on which the administration of justice as a whole rests.

Even where he who asserts the privilege no longer has any recognisable interest in upholding it, there are 'no exceptions to [its] absolute nature . . . once . . . established'. As such, it is 'not necessary to conduct a balancing exercise, because any such exercise must come down in favour of upholding the privilege unless . . . waived' (Lord Taylor CJ above; and see *Three Rivers District Council and Others* v. *Governor and Company of the Bank of England (No. 6)* [2004] 3 WLR 1274).

It is not the same as litigation privilege, which does not apply to children's cases. Litigation privilege is an essential component of adversarial procedure: 'in short it is one of our notions of a fair trial that, except by agreement, you are not entitled to see the proofs of the other side's witnesses' (per Lord Denning in *Re Saxton* [1962] 1 WLR 968).

In care proceedings, 'which are primarily investigative as opposed to adversarial, the notion of a fair trial between opposing parties assumes far less importance . . . The court is seeking to reach a decision, which will be in the best interest of someone who is not a direct party and is granted investigative powers to achieve that end. In these circumstances . . . such . . . proceedings . . . are so far removed from normal actions that litigation privilege has no place in relation to reports obtained by a party thereto which could not have been prepared without the leave of the court to disclose documents already filed or to examine the child' (per Lord Jauncey in *Re Saxton* [1962] 1 WLR 968).

Consider the following contrasting assertions: 'The better view is that legal professional privilege never arose in the first place, than that this court has power to override it' (*In Re L* [1997] AC 16, [1996] 1 FLR 731). 'The court's enquiry cannot be deflected, inhibited or disadvantaged by litigation privilege' (per Thorpe LJ in *Vernon* v. *Bosley* [1998] 1 FLR 304, CA).

Waiver

The privilege can be waived, e.g. when a client agrees that her correspondence with her solicitor can be disclosed to other parties.

Extent of the privilege

Under general rules of discovery, it extends to:

- communications between solicitor and client;
- communications between solicitor and counsel;
- documents produced for the purpose of assisting a solicitor in the conduct of litigation;
- reports prepared where their dominant purpose was for contemplated or actual legal action;
- reports prepared for the purpose of obtaining legal advice in existing or contemplated legal proceedings.

MATERIAL OBTAINED WITHOUT LEAVE OF THE COURT

There is no requirement to disclose statements or reports obtained without leave of the court. However, some judges have expressed a wish to see it made plain that legal representatives in possession of such material relevant to determination but contrary to the interests of their client, not only are unable to resist disclosure by reliance on the privilege but have a positive duty to disclose to other parties and the court (per Thorpe J (as he then was) in *Essex CC* v. *R* [1993] 2 FLR 826).

MATERIAL OBTAINED WITH COURT LEAVE

Where a party has been given leave to disclose documents to an expert for a report, these must be disclosed to all parties (*Oxfordshire CC* v. *M* [1994] 1 FLR 175). 'The parties owe a duty to the court to make full and frank disclosure of any material in their possession relevant to that determination. The advocate has a higher duty to the court and to the child whose interest is paramount' (per Wall J in *Re DH (A Minor) (Child Abuse)* [1994] 1 FLR 679). 'In [care] proceedings . . . where the welfare of children is paramount and thus the proceedings are essentially non-adversarial, legal professional privilege does not arise in respect of the reports of an expert based on the papers disclosed in the proceedings and which the court has given leave to a party to disclose to that expert' (*S County Council* v. *B* [2002] 2 FLR 161).

CONCURRENT CARE AND CRIMINAL PROCEEDINGS

There is a high duty of disclosure in care proceedings because the child's welfare is the court's paramount consideration. But a party in both care and criminal proceedings is entitled to refuse to disclose within the former details of experts instructed (and their reports) within the latter and is entitled to claim legal professional privilege for this (see Chapter 24).

2.5   DUTY TO THE COURT

A solicitor is entitled to take every point, technical or otherwise, that is fairly arguable on behalf of a client. But the advocates on both sides must advise the court of relevant cases. A solicitor would be guilty of unbefitting conduct if she called a witness whose evidence is untrue to the solicitor's knowledge, as opposed to her belief (*The Guide to the Professional Conduct of Solicitors 1999*, Principle 21.01).

The parties and their legal representatives owe a duty to the court to give full and frank disclosure in all children's matters and in ancillary relief applications. They must use their best endeavours:

- to confine the issues and the evidence called to what is reasonably considered to be essential for the proper presentation of their case;
- to reduce or eliminate the issues for expert evidence;
- in advance of the hearing, to agree which are the issues or the main issue (*Practice Direction*, 31 January 1995, [1995] 1 FLR 456).

A party to litigation is under a continuing obligation (see RSC Order 24) until proceedings are concluded to disclose all relevant documents, notwithstanding that discovery by affidavit or list has already been made, whenever they came into her possession unless clearly privileged from disclosure (*Vernon v. Bosley (No. 2)* [1997] 1 All ER 614).

A solicitor may be compelled to disclose confidential information, e.g. by being ordered:

- to produce envelopes of letters received from the client in order to ascertain her whereabouts from the postmarks (*Ramsbotham v. Senior* (1869) FLR Rep. 591);
- to disclose a client's whereabouts to the other party to keep her informed of the client's address, although application for disclosure of the entire file was refused (*Re B (Abduction: Disclosure)* [1995] 1 FLR 774).

The solicitor advocate

The Guide to the Professional Conduct of Solicitors 1999 deals with relevant professional issues. Solicitors who act in litigation, whilst under a duty to do their best for the client, must never deceive or mislead the court (Principle 21.01). Any solicitor acting as advocate must at all times comply with the Law Society's Code for Advocacy, before any court (Principle 21.02).

There are specific provisions regarding private communications with the judge (Principle 21.09):

- except when making an application to the court, a solicitor must not discuss the merits of the case with a judge, magistrate or other adjudicator before whom a case is pending or may be heard, unless invited to do so in the presence of the other party or their representative;
- any written communication to the court should be copied to the other party (except save where an application is being made for disclosure of information to a party without prior notice to them: *Re W (Care Proceedings; Disclosure)* [2003] EWHC Fam 1624).

A solicitor acting for any party can interview and take statements from any witness or prospective witness at any stage in the proceedings, whether or not that witness has been interviewed or called as a witness by another party (Principle 21.10).

Law Society's Code for Advocacy

Advocates have an overriding duty to the court to ensure in the public interest that the proper and efficient administration of justice is achieved; they must assist the court in this and must not deceive, or knowingly or recklessly mislead, the court.

Advocates must not engage in conduct which is:

- dishonest or otherwise discreditable to an advocate;
- prejudicial to the administration of justice;
- likely to diminish public confidence in the legal profession or the administration of justice or otherwise bring the legal profession into disrepute.

Advocates must not, in relation to any other person (including a client or another advocate), treat them for any purpose less favourably than they would treat other such persons on grounds of race, ethnic origin, gender, religion, sexual orientation or political persuasion.

Advocates must not compromise their professional standards in order to please their clients, the court or a third party, nor should they accept a brief if it would cause them to be professionally embarrassed, i.e.

- if they lack sufficient experience or competence to handle the matter, or if their experience of advocacy in the relevant court or proceedings has been so infrequent or so remote in time as to prejudice their competence;
- if they will not have adequate time and opportunity to prepare;

- if there is a risk of breach of confidence entrusted to them by another client or where the knowledge which they possess of the affairs of another client would give an undue advantage to the new client.

Advocates must promote and protect fearlessly and by all proper and lawful means the client's best interests and do so without regard to their own interests or to any consequences to themselves or to any other person (including professional clients or fellow advocates or members of the legal profession).

Subject only to compliance with the specific provisions of public funding regulations, advocates owe their primary duty to the lay client, and must not permit the legal aid authorities or professional clients to limit their discretion as to how the interests of the lay client can best be served. Advocates must act towards clients at all times in good faith.

In relation to the conduct of work, advocates must not place witnesses who are being interviewed under any pressure to provide other than a truthful account of their evidence; rehearse, practise or coach witnesses in relation to their evidence or the way in which they should give it or devise facts which will assist in advancing their client's case. Also they must not draft any documents containing:

- any statement of fact or contention which is not supported by the client or by their brief or instructions;
- any contention which they do not consider to be properly arguable;
- any statement of fact other than the evidence which in substance according to their instructions the advocate reasonably believes the witness would give if the evidence contained in the witness statement were being given orally.

Advocates must not assert a personal opinion on the facts or the law unless invited to do so by the court. They must ensure that the court is informed of all relevant decisions and legislative provisions of which they are aware, whether the effect is favourable or unfavourable towards the contention for which they argue; and must bring any procedural irregularity to the attention of the court during the hearing and not reserve such matter to be raised on appeal. They must not impugn a witness whom they have had the opportunity of cross-examining, unless they have given the witness an opportunity to answer the allegation.

Practical issues

All systems should be checked for possible conflicts, bearing in mind changes of name, wider family relationships and other proceedings. Consider also the wisdom of attending and/or chairing meetings during the course of the case.

It is possible that, if an issue were to arise about what had been said or agreed at that meeting, the solicitor may have to give evidence. This would mean being unable to continue as advocate in the case (see Chapter 25 on experts).

2.6 THE LEGAL SERVICES COMMISSION

The Funding Code

The Legal Services Commission (LSC) Funding Code, approved by Parliament, determines which cases the LSC can fund as part of the Community Legal Service. Volume 3 of the *LSC Manual* contains the details, but not the relevant Regulations.

The important sections for public law proceedings are, happily, confined to about seven pages (*LSC Manual*, vol. 3, pp. 162–168) and to Criteria 11.7, which provides that:

- legal representation will be granted in 'Special Children Act' proceedings;
- the standard criteria in s.5(4) of the Funding Code do not apply, i.e. practitioners need not address alternative funding sources, alternatives to litigation, or whether there are reasonable prospects of success.

'Special Children Act' (SCA) proceedings means (under s.2 of the Funding Code) proceedings under the Children Act 1989 (other than appeal proceedings) where legal representation is applied for on behalf of a child, a parent or person with parental responsibility (PR), for whom an application is made for an order under:

- s.31 (a care or supervision order);
- s.43 (a child assessment order);
- s.44 (an emergency protection order); and
- s.45 (extension or discharge of an emergency protection order).

This means that, generally, representation for children, parents and those with PR (including delegated PR under Children Act 1989, s.2(9)) will be granted funding without reference to means, prospects of success or reasonableness. The same applies to an application for secure accommodation (under Children Act 1989, s.25, use of accommodation for restricting liberty) where the child is not, but wishes to be, represented before the court.

Certificates granted for non-merits-tested legal representation are not normally limited as to scope short of the final hearing in the substantive proceedings, but they always bear a costs limit (note this will prevail over a court assessment of costs).

Applications for legal representation for SCA proceedings are made on a self-certification form (CLS APP 5), and provided it is made at the first available opportunity and received at the appropriate regional office within three working days from the receipt of instructions to act, costs incurred will be deemed from that date. If received by the regional office out of time, then costs can only be claimed from the date the certificate is issued.

Where practitioners are instructed to act on behalf of a number of children then the form must be submitted for each of them.

Certificates granted for such proceedings cover:

- all normal steps involved in the conduct of the substantive proceedings;
- contact on the making of an emergency protection order or interim care order (but not subsequently).

Therefore, if contact does become an issue in the course of the proceedings, necessitating an application for a Children Act 1989, s.34 order, the certificate would not cover this.

Criteria 11.7 does not apply to those applying to be or who have been joined in SCA proceedings. So a means/merits-tested application (in form CLS APP 3) will need to be completed and submitted to the regional office, together with supporting documentation including a form for applicants not in receipt of income support, income-based job-seekers' allowance or Guaranteed State Pension (CLS MEANS 1), or a form for applicants in receipt of these benefits (CLS MEANS 2).

These certificates can and do contain both scope and costs limitations. Care must be taken to operate within the constraints of the certificate as costs incurred for work done out of scope will almost certainly be disallowed on assessment.

Related proceedings

A certificate granted for representation in SCA proceedings may be granted for legal representation in related proceedings, i.e. those being heard together with SCA proceedings or in which an order is being sought as an alternative.

The certificate will not automatically cover related proceedings, i.e.

- a local authority application for refusal of contact;
- an application for a Children Act 1989, s.91(14) order; or
- an application to free for adoption that is to be dealt with in the substantive SCA proceedings:

In these cases, cover will need to be stated on the certificate or on an application made to amend.

Cover for related proceedings will thus be on a non-means/non-merits-tested basis, however 'non-related' proceedings cannot be covered on the grant of a certificate for SCA proceedings nor on an application for amendment. Cover for such proceedings, e.g. an application for a Children Act 1989, s.8 order or domestic violence injunction, should be dealt with on a means/merits-tested basis.

Other public law children cases

These proceedings (as defined in s.2.2 of the Funding Code) are subject to the standard criteria, and the general funding code, i.e. are both means and merits tested. This expressly includes:

- appeals (whether interim or final) from orders made in SCA proceedings;
- representation for parties or potential parties to SCA proceedings;
- other proceedings under Part IV or Part V of the Children Act 1989 (which would include representation of a child in private law proceedings, pursuant to the Family Proceedings Rules 1991, SI 1991/1247, rule 9.5);
- adoption proceedings (including freeing for adoption);
- proceedings under the inherent jurisdiction of the High Court in relation to children;
- applications for residence orders which, if successful, would have the effect of discharging a care order.

Applications may be refused on the following grounds:

- availability of other sources of funding;
- representation is not necessary;
- it appears unreasonable for funding to be granted, having regard to the importance of the case to the client

and will be refused if the client's prospects of succeeding on the application or appeal are poor, i.e. less than a 50 per cent chance of success.

Refusal is also possible (under s.5.4.5 of the Funding Code) if it appears unreasonable to fund representation, e.g. in the light of the existence of other proceedings or the interests of other parties in the proceedings to which the application relates. This is likely where it would be reasonable to expect the issues to be sufficiently resolved in other proceedings already in existence; or where the client's interests are such that they are likely to be adequately represented by the interests of the other party/ies, e.g. legal representation for adoptive parents is likely to be refused in circumstances where the local authority places the child and does not oppose the making of an adoption order in their favour in proceedings contested by the natural parents.

This can particularly impact on family members such as grandparents seeking residence orders (see Chapter 21).

Adoption/freeing for adoption

Where available in such proceedings, legal representation is *unlikely* to be granted for proceedings in the High Court or county court, if the application is uncontested or where the prospects of success are poor, except in the case of natural parents where the combination of the nature of the proceedings themselves, the desirability of the parents being represented and human rights principles may be sufficient to satisfy the criteria and justify granting it. Legal representation is also unlikely to be granted if it appears that the applicant has access to alternative funding sufficient to make the grant unnecessary (this may apply to foster parents supported by a local authority).

Legal representation is likely to be granted to a child who has been joined in to county court proceedings as a party.

Inherent jurisdiction (wardship)

In these proceedings, legal representation will be refused to make or support an application where the prospects of success are poor, including circumstances where the client is unlikely to obtain an order.

It is also likely to be refused:

- where orders in other proceedings (current or prospective), e.g. under the Children Act 1989, the Family Law Act 1986 or the Child Abduction and Custody Act 1985, would provide an adequate remedy;
- unless the exceptional circumstances of the case justify the use of the court's jurisdiction (e.g. sterilisation of persons unable to give informed consent);
- where the relevant child is subject to a care order (Children Act 1989, s.100);
- unless the client has sufficient interest to bring the proceedings;
- unless the issues in the case are sufficiently important or are likely to produce sufficient ultimate benefit to warrant legal proceedings (e.g. even if an order was obtained it is likely to be ineffective, possibly because the child is abroad);
- unless the particular case could not appropriately be dealt with in another way, e.g. writing a letter, involving the social services, Interpol or the port alert system.

It is likely to be refused to defend an application where the defence has poor prospects of success, perhaps because the court would have significant regard to the child's wishes as a consequence of her age and/or understanding and they are contrary to those of the applicant; or where it would otherwise be unreasonable for it to be granted in the particular circumstances, having regard to the issues in the case, the benefit to be obtained or the need for the applicant to be separately represented.

Remuneration rates and uplifts

By virtue of the enhancement provisions (see the Legal Aid in Family Proceedings (Remuneration) Regulations 1991, SI 1991/2038), a guaranteed minimum enhancement of 15 per cent is allowed on all family certificated work, where the work is done by a fee earner who is on the accredited

Specialist Panels of Resolution (formerly known as the Solicitors Family Law Association) or the Law Society's Children Panel. Higher amounts of enhancement are available if they can be justified, e.g. if a case is particularly difficult and practitioners deal with the advocacy themselves. For a Children Panel member, enhancement is available for all work done under a certificate that includes proceedings relating to children, defined as 'proceedings within which the welfare of children is determined, without limitation, proceedings under the Children Act 1989 or under the inherent jurisdiction of the High Court in relation to children'.

Conflict cases and separate representation of the children's guardian

Where separate representation of a children's guardian is necessary, CAFCASS will pay the reasonable costs of the solicitor instructed (who must be a member of the Children Panel), including any necessary disbursements and VAT. Standard terms apply and the 'reasonable costs' are the prescribed rates for such publicly funded work, at the time the work was done, together with an enhancement for 'care and control' of 15 per cent. In exceptional circumstances the enhancement can be extended up to but not exceeding 50 per cent. If practitioners wish to claim more than 15 per cent then they will need to justify this on their bill. CAFCASS can and do impose costs limits in exactly the same way as the LSC.

The Legal Help Scheme

Practitioners will very often provide legal advice and assistance to parents after intervention by the local authority but before proceedings for a public law order are issued. This can involve attendance at child protection conferences and core group meetings. This work is contracted by the LSC suppliers under the Legal Help Scheme, and clients (usually parents) must satisfy financial eligibility criteria and a merits test.

Advice and assistance must only be provided 'where there is sufficient benefit to the client having regard to all of the circumstances of the matter'. This test applies at the outset and during the subsistence of the matter but not with the benefit of hindsight. The emphasis in the Judicial Case Management Protocol on pre-proceedings work is arguably relevant here.

The LSC have announced a move to fixed fees for controlled legal help work. As before, these will be firm-specific based on a firm's own average costs, but not for long – a move to a national 'price list' is likely.

Checklist of points to note[2]

- Eligibility[3]
- Merits test
- Matter of English law
- Matter starts, matter ends and restarts
- Matter boundaries (two or more matters will count as a separate matter and must be the subject of a separate application form)
- Do not mix matters
- Disbursements: should be incurred 'when it is in the client's best interests to do so'
- Upper costs limits: £500. Apply to LSC for extension beyond that
- Paid only for work directly involved in the provision of legal services, not 'administrative matters'
- Unless the case involves a novel, developing or unusually complex point of law justifying either legal research or counsel's opinion, time spent on legal research will not be paid for as contract work
- Ensure effective and efficient case management
- Ensure correct remuneration rates are being claimed (£50.05 per hour preparation outside London and £53.10 in London – Family Rate) and disbursements accounted for
- Ensure accurate cost predictions and that clients are aware of scope and limitations of Legal Help Scheme
- Instruction/advice/action letters should contain a brief analysis of the applicable law

NOTES

1 *Good Practice in Child Care Cases*, Law Society (2004).
2 For further advice on running a publicly funded practice, see P. Owston and S. McCall, *Making a Success of Legal Aid*, Law Society Publishing (2003).
3 See *LSC Focus* 47 (April 2005) for financial eligibility upratings.

CHAPTER 3

Child development and communication issues

Key sources

- Children Act 1989, ss.1 and 17, and Children Act 2004, s.53
- *Achieving Best Evidence in Criminal Proceedings*, Home Office, LCD, CPS, DH and Welsh Assembly (2002)
- Handbooks (see Appendix 1):
  - Daniel *et al.*, *Child Development for Child Care and Protection Workers* (1999)
  - Wilson and Powell, *A Guide to Interviewing Children* (2001) and Jones, *Communicating with Vulnerable Children* (2003)

3.1 INTRODUCTION

In children's cases, it is the responsibility of the practitioner to test the evidence, but against what benchmark? The tension in perceiving children as either 'vulnerable' or 'feral'[1] is very real and reflected in much of the thinking in policy and practice.

Childhood as innocence?

Much contemporary thinking is influenced by this concept.[2] Paternalistic decision-making, especially in response to painful situations, may preserve the ideal of the child's 'inner goodness'. But it may also suppress children's views as a self-defence against behaviour and distress[3] and accusations of tainting children forever with loss of innocence. For example, in English culture many adults try to 'protect' a child from the pain of bereavement – but are they protecting only themselves? Evidence suggests children fare better if they are able to anticipate death, and helped to talk about and maintain a place for the dead person in their lives. [4]

The child as a 'naturally evil and corrupting influence'?

Alternatively, the child is seen as pleasure loving, seeking self-gratification and, from birth, demanding, wilful, impish and harbouring a potential evil, ready to emerge if she is allowed by the adult to stray from the 'appropriate' path. Such children must not fall into bad company, establish bad habits or develop idle hands, all of which enable outlets for the demonic force within – potentially destructive, not just of the child, but also of the adults.[5]

Puritanical ideas such as these gave rise to harsh child-rearing practices throughout much of the sixteenth and seventeenth centuries, which are seen periodically in contemporary society.

Risk factors

Whether a child is in the youth justice system or the subject of care proceedings, the risks to health, well-being and future prospects are largely known, and seem to be similar.[6] Social and economic disadvantage combined with troubled family lives contribute most risk to children. These factors impinge on many aspects of their lives including education, physical health and development and family and peer relationships. The risk factors affect some more than others – these children are generally the most powerless. The practitioner should be mindful of this powerful structural inequality and seek to challenge oppression.

Child centred[7] or child focused?

In *child centred* practice, work starts with the child's priorities and is concerned with the whole child. Problems are understood as functions of the wider social system and therefore the impetus for change is on adults' behaviour and systems. From this perspective, children who experience multiple problems over years are often locked into patterns of decline because the adults around them (including professionals) are unable to change their behaviour.

Child focused practice starts with the adults, who tend to be concerned with an aspect of a child's life (e.g. behaviour or abuse). Although not intending to do so, professionals soon locate 'the problem' in the child with a tendency to seek controlling solutions. The locus of attention is on the child changing to solve the problem.

The outcomes framework[8]

This describes children's needs as:

- to stay safe;
- to be healthy;
- to enjoy and achieve;
- to achieve economic well-being;
- to make a positive contribution.

Despite being based on an extensive process of consultation with children, this is not necessarily consistent with other world views (compare the importance of a single significant adult to a child in Western culture, to the many such adults in Japan).

Children's wishes, preferences, feelings, actions and needs change as they get older. Appreciation of these differences is critical to inform sound decision-making and appropriate planning, especially in contact and care cases.

Which children?

Approximately 75 per cent of cases arise as a result of parenting problems (including parental mental illness, problem drug use, domestic violence) which affect children's behaviour. Poverty and lack of housing, adequate parenting and power bring children into the legal system, yet the law says lack of resources is no excuse. The practitioner's role is not to rescue children from poverty, but to address the balance of power and ensure children's rights and needs are met.

Skills

Understanding children's development is essential to practitioner competence and confidence in working with children and families. Appreciation of developmental factors and differences makes communications with children much less tense, more fruitful and safer from errors, for all involved.

Not every professional is skilled in communicating effectively with all children. Knowing personal limitations and having the confidence and ability to access those with the requisite skills when necessary is important in achieving an accurate and comprehensive view of a child.

3.2   HUMAN RIGHTS AND DIVERSITY

The principles set out in Chapter 1 all contain a fundamental recognition of the child's separate identity and paramount needs and her basic rights to food, shelter, etc.; above all, a recognition that the child's developmental needs, timespan and circumstances require all those involved with her care and her interests to treat her in accordance with her individual characteristics set in the context of what is known about development, and taking account of gender, race, ability, heritage and so on.

It is therefore fundamental to good practice that all practitioners:

- understand the way in which children generally develop;
- place this in the appropriate context of the individual child with regard to culture, race, religion, gender, disability, etc.

There is considerable debate about the nature and extent of the difference between children and adults as discussed below: are they 'mini-adults', underdeveloped people or just 'people'? Despite the paramountcy of children's needs and rights in law, it is difficult to argue that *in reality* children have powers and influence equal to that of adults 'representing' or 'responsible for' them. But children should be regarded as having equal status. By virtue of age, children could/should be considered to be a discrete group with differing needs, composed of various sub-groups with vastly differing behaviours and capacities at different ages (e.g. infants, pre-school children, adolescents).

3.3 GENERAL

Dimensions of development: the expression of potential

When discussing a child's progress or potential, we refer to her development. The Framework for Assessment[9] measures this by seven dimensions:

- health: including growth and development, as well as physical and mental well-being;
- education: all areas of a child's cognitive development;
- emotional and behavioural development: e.g. appropriateness of response demonstrated in feelings and actions;
- identity: growing sense of self as a separate and valued person;
- family and social relationships: empathy and the ability to place self in someone else's shoes;
- social presentation: growing understanding of the way in which appearance, behaviour and any impairment are perceived by the outside world;
- self-care skills: acquisition of practical, emotional and communication competencies required for increasing independence.

Each child is an individual and develops different abilities at different rates from her twin or any other child. But observational research does elicit developmental norms, i.e. approximate ages for emerging skills and levels of understanding. These are important as parameters against which to measure the developmental factors for children with disabilities and/or special educational needs.

It is important to appreciate that this overview can obscure considerable individual differences between children. To rely on personal knowledge of children (whether family or other people's) is insufficient and can lead to misleading generalisations. A broad base of experience and knowledge is necessary, with requisite training implications for both professional and practitioner.

Stages or sequences?

Piaget's[10] theories of child development, especially cognitive growth, have been a huge influence. His argument that children develop through specific stages (see below) has been challenged – the prevailing contemporary view is of a regular sequence, a continuum – and later research has shown that children are able to develop cognitive skills younger than Piaget had suggested.

Nature or nurture?

Trying to decide which is most influential is unhelpful. Considering the interaction between what is inherited and the environment, and effects on the individual, is more useful. Two periods of child development highlight this more clearly, the first year of life and puberty:

- new-born babies do not have to be taught to move their arms and legs, to suck, to try to move, crawl or walk;
- similarly, all adolescents 'automatically' experience puberty; timing depends upon several factors, not least of which is biological programming.

However, for both groups environmental factors can inhibit, disturb or even prevent these processes. Even then, not all react in the same way to the same environments: some are almost defeated by those that stifle growth, but others are made more determined to fight.

3.4   SOCIAL AND EMOTIONAL DEVELOPMENT

Emotional development in children

This is closely related to the responses received from parents/carers. Babies are primed for attachment to warm, familiar carers, usually parents, grandparents, older siblings and key adults in early years' settings. Parents and main carers who respond and interact in ways that are:

- sensitive (i.e. able to 'tune' into the child's needs);
- warm;
- regularly available;
- reliable; and
- consistent

give a child security, building feelings of trust and safety with other human beings. A securely attached child is confident that, when anxious, her parent will respond, but is reliant on adult capacity to 'tune in' to different needs at different times.

Psychologists have long recognised that the quality of nurturing in the first year of life affects physical as well as social and emotional development. Loving relationships stimulate key hormones in the infant that influence rapid growth of neural pathways. Infants' brains are ready for this growth at birth but rate is dependent upon the quality of the relationships experienced. Recent research[11] has detected differences in brain architecture of neglected infants aged only six weeks compared to those from nurturing environments.

A sense of secure attachment to main care-givers is vital to healthy emotional development. Developing this in the early years affects development of the self – self-esteem, personality, self-identity and feelings of self-worth – and forms the basis for subsequent relationships: those who have had experience of warm attachments and positive responses become socially adept, self-assured, independent and interdependent, and higher achievers. It develops through actions and reactions of those around children, particularly parents, siblings and, increasingly, friends. Infants and young children with a sense of trust in their carers are able to internalise safety and security, allowing full access to emotions. The attachment process not only affects emotional development, but actually prompts physical changes in the brain,[12] exerting a fundamental and lasting effect upon functioning.

Pro-social behaviour, i.e. helping, cooperating, caring and being empathetic can be found in children as young as two, and persists in the absence of reinforcement – it takes a great deal to knock out entirely a child's desire and will to love. It is closely linked with a parent demonstrating clear rules, principles and emotional conviction, who also attributes pro-social qualities to

Table 3.1 Normal fears and anxieties

Age	Examples of sources of fear and anxiety
0–12 months	Loud noises (e.g. thunder), certain smells, hunger, spiders, snakes, sudden unexpected and looming objects, separation from parent from about six or eight months
1 year	Separation from parent, falling into a toilet, being injured, strangers
2 years	Many sources including loud noises, animals, darkness, separation from parent, changes in personal environment, strange peers, parents' moods
3–5 years	Masks, darkness, animals, separation from parent, noises, bodily injury
6–8 years	Supernatural beings, bodily injury, thunder, darkness, sleeping or staying alone, media events (e.g. news about child kidnapping, nuclear holocaust)
9–12 years	Tests in school, school performance, bodily injury, physical appearance, death, parental divorce
Teens	Social performance, sexuality, personal relationship, parental divorce

the child and is empathic in their care. The absence of empathy in children is a significant root of anti-social behaviour.

Normal fears and anxieties[13]

If a child is unusually worried or frightened about something, the source of the concerns should be investigated before making assumptions. For example, a four-year-old was terrified that a 'big man' was going to hurt him: the boy had seen an actor on television staring directly at him saying 'I'm coming to get you' (see Table 3.1).

3.5 COGNITIVE DEVELOPMENT

General capacities

The following are the general stages of development:

- 0 to two years: babies understand their world largely via touch and manipulating objects, or where this is not possible (e.g. in those affected by Thalidomide) via purely visual means. Babies can recognise familiar language (even sounds heard pre-birth). Their ability to form social relationships is dependent upon the actions and reactions of adult carers: but they are far from passive recipients, and demonstrate important behaviours designed to enhance social relationships, e.g. smiling.
- two to seven years: thinking processes are organised but work in one direction only, e.g. a three-year-old boy may know he has an older sister, but would not understand that his sister has a younger brother. Children may give life to inanimate objects.
- seven to 11 years: the child moves from relying on what she sees, hears, perceives to relying on logic. Children can retrace their steps, recount a familiar routine, and are capable of deduction, but need concrete objects to support their thinking. Recent research suggests this transition may come earlier than Piaget proposed and is significantly dependent upon schooling and education.
- 11 + years: the adolescent can consider hypothetical situations and can make inferences.

Piaget's stages are shown in Table 3.2.

Table 3.2 Piaget's stages

Stage	Key characteristics	Description	Some specific achievements
Sensorimotor			
0–2 years	Infant interacts with environment by manipulating objects	Learns to differentiate herself from external world; learns that objects exist even when not visible; time and space come to exist independently of her own actions; Some appreciation of cause and effect, past and future	If an object is hidden, infant will search for it; can make detours and retrace her steps to reach a goal
Pre-operational (or 'intuitive')			
2–6/7 years	Representation, mental imagery, use of speech; child can do simple reasoning, which is dominated by perception	Becomes able to represent something with something else – in speech, play, gestures, mental pictures; Egocentrism declines as starts to take account of others' perspectives	The child can represent, draw, or describe her path to a goal, narrate simple routines
Concrete operational			
6/7–11/12 years	Reasoning involves more than one idea, but applied only to objects that can be seen or manipulated	Capable of mentally undoing an action (physical or mental), so long as real or manipulable objects are involved; can relate dimensions, appreciate some objects remain the same despite changes in appearance; classify elements into hierarchies	Child can make or interpret simple map; perspective of another viewer can be appreciated

Stage	Key characteristics	Description	Some specific achievements
Formal operational			
11/12 onwards	Thinking about potential events or abstract ideas; reasoning based on purely verbal or logical statements	Can make abstract comparisons, relate any statement or element to another, deal with proportions or analogies; can construct whole belief systems, reflect on her own thinking	Adolescent can manipulate variables in a scientific experiment; can explain trajectory of rebounding ball in terms of physics, solve a geometric proof

However, Piaget's notion of young children's apparent lack of capacity for logic has been frequently challenged:

- they can reason out logical problems, and identify with another's perspective when the context of the experiment and the language in which the task is presented are made more relevant, more familiar to the everyday life of a child;
- their failure may be due instead to relatively limited memory capacity, or lack of knowledge about the subject.

Changes in understanding[14]

Ability to appreciate the nature of other people's attitudes, thoughts and feelings, and to understand that these may differ from one's own, comes in later childhood (but only if an empathic relationship between carer and child exists throughout the early years).

Older children and adolescents have expectations shaped by prior experience. They may therefore have fixed ideas about how people in authority might react to them (e.g. black teenagers' expectations of the police).

Younger children have not necessarily considered the consequence of describing adverse experiences to others. Older children may well have done so, or have attitudes already shaped by their own, or others', experiences.

Changes in memory and suggestibility

In summary, older children remember more and are far more resistant to suggestion than younger ones:

- from the age of two children can recall events they experience with rapidly increasing accuracy, especially more personally meaningful ones;
- by the age of eight children's capacity to remember (i.e. to encode, store and retrieve information) is on a par with adults;
- memory is affected by circumstances, including a child's motivation, interest level and ability to attend to the task. Maltreatment can significantly affect a child's ability to register experiences, store them in memory and later recall them when talking to an adult;
- memory capacity is significantly linked with language and communication ability: even when a child is able to remember events, there may be real difficulties in communicating them to an adult.

Communication and language development

Non-verbal communication is a far greater part of human interaction than spoken language. Babies and pre-verbal children are all social creatures and adept at gaining attention. They need encouraging interactions from adults around them, especially their parents/carers.

At what age/stage different linguistic capabilities emerge is less important than taking account of the barriers to effective communication with children. Helpful guidelines to questioning and interviewing are in Chapter 19.

Telling the truth

The younger the child is, the more likely she is to tell the truth – she has yet to learn how and what it is to lie:

- two-year-olds can demonstrate deception;
- at four to six years, children can detect and convincingly tell lies, but a 'lie' is probably any untrue statement, regardless of any intention to deceive ('I'm four, not five, you're a liar!');
- around the age of eight is the beginning of understanding that lying involves an intention to deceive, how to apply different deceptive behaviours, and assess the likelihood of being caught.

Adults are, contrary to popular opinion, very poor judges of when a child is lying. They tend to assume lack of eye contact, fidgeting, speaking hesitantly are signs of guilt; more often these are only signs of nerves.

Implications[15]

To promote accuracy of children's accounts while minimising suggestion:

- Listen to and understand the child.
- Constantly check for misunderstandings and miscommunications in both directions – a child is unlikely to correct proactively any misunderstanding.
- Convey genuine empathic concern, to a degree congruent to the child's situation.
- Adopt the perspective that the child is the expert, not the adult.
- Do not pressurise or coerce, be aware of one's expectations of compliance.
- Allow free recall, free report wherever possible.
- Specific questioning may be required to establish details but should be non-leading, and paired with open-ended questions.
- Maintain neutrality but not indifference.
- Strive to maintain an open mind, and manage any bias or presumptions held about a child's experiences.
- Keep sentences simple and avoid introducing new words for people or objects until the child has used them first.
- Take care with 'wh' questions: understanding of 'who', 'what' and 'where' is grasped earlier than 'when', 'how' and 'why'. 'Why' questions may prove especially problematic for traumatised and abused children.
- The younger the child, the shorter the interview should be.

Awareness of the impact of adult authority on a child's responses is critical. A witness usually wants to answer the direct question put to them: but for a child, their desire to please and/or comply goes much further, amply demonstrated by research.[16] When children were asked unanswerable questions such as 'which is angrier, a jumper or a tree?' or 'is red heavier than yellow?', they constructed whole strings of non-sequiturs in an attempt to give a sensible answer – if asked the same question by another child, they would probably tell them not to be so silly.

3.6 BEHAVIOURAL DEVELOPMENT

There are many different approaches to understanding children's behaviour, including:

- psychoanalytical theory based on the work of Freud and others;
- behaviourism which suggests that behaviour is learned; and
- cognitive theories derived from children's understanding of social and cultural situations.

Psychology is a social or behavioural science, not a pure one. It cannot provide incontrovertible 'rules' for what will always happen given certain circumstances, only evidence-based and statistically supported trends and tendencies.

What is probably true is that children's behaviour is determined by the interaction of a range of factors including their cognitive abilities, attachments, ability to communicate and their environment.

3.7 LITERATURE REVIEW[17]

Focused on the first three years of life, in summary, the major conclusions confirm the observations on attachment above and the following:

- All areas of learning and development are intricately intertwined; young children develop and learn holistically and their emotional and social development seem to form the bedrock for other areas.
- Parents whose own early relationships with their parents were largely negative ones, need support to overcome perpetuating such patterns and to form joyful, mutually loving relationships with their babies and small children.
- Babies are born with the ability to perceive differences in language and they can recognise the sounds used in the languages spoken in their homes.
- Between one and three years, young children grasp what is and is not culturally acceptable behaviour.
- Babies seem to be tuned to learn from, with and about, first the people and the cultural environment around them, followed by the material environment – they come into the world primed to be curious, competent learners.
- Play, in which the baby or child takes the lead and makes choices, is a process which fosters cognitive development.
- Children 'make sense' of and 'transform' knowledge, experiences and events through imaginative and creative activity.
- Language and thought are developmentally linked – each depends on and also promotes the development of the other.
- Children's developing memories and use of narrative help them make sense of their lives.
- Children want to share and express their ideas playfully through the 'hundred languages of children' (e.g. dancing, singing, talking, 'storying', music-making, painting, making and building, 'animating', puppets and other toys, dressing up, gardening, looking after animals, drawing – to list but a few).

3.8 IMPACT OF ABUSE ON DEVELOPMENT

It is difficult to separate the effects of physical, emotional or sexual abuse from those of other family problems. But it is likely that abused children and neglected children are at increased risk of having poor self-esteem, personality and behavioural problems and delayed development in several areas.[18]

'In families low on warmth and high on criticism, negative incidents accumulate, as if to remind a child that he or she is unloved.'[19]

Signs of abuse and neglect can be categorised as follows:

- physical signs, including the child's overall state;
- behavioural changes;
- developmental regression;
- what children say;
- signs of stress or fear;
- impairment of social relationships.

Some different outcomes arising from different types of abuse or neglect are set out below. But, as the comments indicate, these are not always inevitable in all children (see also 'Resilience' below).

1. Physical abuse: poor self-esteem, depression, developmental delay, behavioural difficulties, lack of educational attainment. Depends on extent and duration of abuse and, critically, on the social relationship between child and parents/carers.

2. Sexual abuse: depression, anxiety, feeling in despair, isolated and stigmatised; lack of trust, difficulties forming and maintaining social relationships, sometimes inappropriate sexualised behaviour; developmental delay (especially socially), detachment, behavioural difficulties, poor educational attainment. Depends on nature of abuse, how the abuser forces the child to keep the secret, and how it is dealt with by adults to whom a disclosure is made. Many of these problems increase when the child is removed from home. Arguably:

   (a) physical or sexual abuse simultaneously constitutes emotional abuse;
   (b) sexual abuse involving contact simultaneously constitutes physical abuse.

3. Inconsistent or chaotic care: insecure ambivalent attachments: a child is often angry and resentful of her carers, and behaviour is intensified to attract the parent.

4. Unavailable, untrustworthy and rejecting care: insecure avoidance attachments: a child anxiously avoids contact as a way of coping with her distress; distress is turned inwards resulting in an unworthy view of herself.

5. Unpredictable and rejecting care: disorganised attachments: a child feels vulnerable and out of control; becomes listless or coercive having tried but repeatedly failed to find behaviour which brings her increased care and safety.
6. Other affects of damaged attachments can include:

    (a) difficulty in giving and receiving comfort and affection;
    (b) a tendency to blame others when things go wrong;
    (c) poor peer relationships;
    (d) difficulty coping with change, which in itself often results in demanding, difficult and resistant behaviour.

When alternative placement away from the parents is deemed necessary, note the following factors:

1. Early separation from parents, especially the mother, between six months and three years is the most disruptive as it interrupts and often prevents the child's formation of attachments. Feelings of security and trust are not fully formed, and poor emotional development is dominated by anxiety in the child, compounded by the acute sense of loss.
2. If placed before the first birthday, attachments can be formed with the substitute family.
3. Research supports the assertion that parental separation affects children under six the worst. Although the main secure attachments are in place by around three, the child's still-forming sense of identity is interrupted, and links with both parents (and parents' relationships with each other) are critical to views of one's self. This has important implications for placement decisions and the nature (or quality) and frequency of contact with parents.
4. The very early attachment bond to siblings must also be considered.
5. Changing placement nearer to adolescence is likely to cause difficulties in the new family, due to the need to lose and also create attachments, and to the length of time living in a family that is deemed harmful.

'The development of social relationships occupies a crucial role in personality growth and abnormalities in relationships are important in many types of psychopathology.'[20]

Failure to thrive

Failure to thrive is defined as 'failure to grow, in terms of weight and height, and develop in a healthy and vigorous way . . . often associated with illnesses, inadequate nutrition, . . . disturbed mother-child interaction and relationships, insecure attachment, family dysfunctioning and poverty'.[21]

A range of aetiological factors can contribute:

- feeding problems;
- lack of parental understanding of children's nutritional needs;
- lack of access to support and help;
- maternal depression;
- adverse social and economic conditions.

Sometimes the following are also exhibited:

- dislike, rejection and neglect of the child;
- parental drug and alcohol misuse;
- deliberate starvation;
- fabricated or induced illness.[22]

Long-term outcomes for those who do not receive appropriate help include poor development in height, employment, attachment, educational attainment, social adjustment, sense of well-being, cognition and emotional stability.

Failure to thrive, if attended to early, has no negative long-term effects. Family support (when mutually negotiated and written down in a contract) and direct therapeutic help are effective.

Resilience

This is defined as 'normal development under difficult conditions'. Some children seem to cope with adversity better than others, associated with:[23]

- being female for pre-adolescents and male for adolescents;
- having had a secure attachment experience when younger;
- an outgoing temperament;
- sociability, good communication skills;
- possessing problem-solving skills and planning skills;
- the experience of success and achievement;
- having a capacity to reflect;
- a sense of humour.

Adverse circumstances include not only parenting difficulties, e.g. alcohol/drug use, mental health problems, domestic violence, but also the characteristics of the child herself (e.g. disability, an 'unusual' temperament), her wider family circle (e.g. lack of attachment network) and the wider community (e.g. racism, lack of community supports).

Buffers to adverse effects from negative experiences – and pointers for good practice in planning and intervention – include in the family:

- a good school experience;
- at least one good parent-child relationship;

- affection;
- clear, firm consistent discipline;
- support for education;
- long-term support/absence of severe discord.

'Stability matters enormously to separated children and should be given far higher priority in all decisions that are made about and with them.'[24]

In the wider community, factors include:

- special help with behavioural problems;
- wider support network support for vulnerable parents;
- better housing and standard of living;
- high morale school with strongly positive policies for behaviour, anti-bullying;
- range of sport/leisure activities.

Nonetheless, it is not simply a matter of checking off how many of the above factors can be put in place in order to 'achieve' resilience: there is a complex interrelationship between the factors.

3.9 PARENTING AND DEVELOPMENTAL NEEDS

What should parenting achieve?

As well as the Outcomes Framework, the preface to *Working Together*[25] states that 'all children deserve the opportunity to achieve their full potential' to achieve which:

they should be enabled to:

- be as physically and mentally healthy as possible;
- gain the maximum benefit possible from good-quality educational opportunities;
- live in a safe environment and be protected from harm;
- experience emotional well-being;
- feel loved and valued, and be supported by a network of reliable and affectionate relationships:
- become competent in looking after themselves and coping with everyday living;
- have a positive image of themselves, and a secure sense of identity including cultural and racial identity;
- develop good inter-personal skills and confidence in social situations.

If they are denied this, they are 'at risk not only of an impoverished childhood, but also more likely to experience disadvantage and social exclusion in adulthood'.

What should parenting involve?

The majority of parents safeguard and promote welfare by providing:

- basic care of physical needs and appropriate medical care;
- safety by ensuring adequate protection from harm or danger;
- emotional warmth to meet the need for emotional security as a valued being with a positive sense of racial and cultural identity;
- stimulation to promote learning;
- guidance and boundaries for the regulation of emotions and behaviour;
- stability in the family environment to enable the development and maintenance of a secure attachment to primary carers.

Parenting in context

All parents and their children function in the context of their family and wider environment. For many these aspects of life often provide support and solace, but for some little help is forthcoming. Parental problems are present in 50 per cent of the 160,000 referrals made each year.

The following factors are relevant:

- family history and functioning, including both genetic and psychosocial factors;
- wider family, including related and non-related persons or their absence;
- housing: appropriateness and adequacy;
- employment;
- income;
- family's social integration: the local neighbourhood and its impact on the child and parents;
- community resources: local services and facilities.

Good enough parenting has been variously defined. 'Good enough parenting is parenting which does not seriously prevent or hinder a child's development.'[26] "Good enough" because perfect parents do not exist. "Good-enough" parents bring up their children with success and enjoyment, even though most families meet some hard times on the way. Thus parents provide a "facilitating environment" for each child to promote his development by their sensitivity and awareness of the child's needs. Essentially this means that parents adapt their behaviour and lifestyle as far as possible for the child's well-being rather than their own and they try to put the child's needs first in all major family plans and decisions. Ordinary parents discuss their children's needs from time to time and plan for them together, and in doing so they sometimes seek advice from professionals and others.'[27]

'Good enough parents provide:[28]

- adequate verbal communication to give information and intellectual stimulation;
- sufficient physical freedom to encourage the development of the child's sensory and motor abilities;
- adequate responsiveness which balances the child's need for attention to his/her behaviour, and the needs of the parent;
- positive warmth and a loving framework.'

Parenting, difficulties and outcomes

The task of being a parent can be challenging, often involving juggling competing home and work priorities as well as trying to understand how best to meet children's needs at all stages of their development. Parents require and deserve support – asking for it should be seen as a sign of responsibility rather than as a parenting failure. Statutory and voluntary services and professionals should provide, e.g.

- universal, integrated services, especially between education, health and social services provision;
- specialist help to those who need it; and
- support, or otherwise intervening, at times of adversity or crisis.

The task can be made much harder when parents experience personal problems in caring properly for themselves as well as parenting their children, manifested, e.g. by:

- difficulty in organising their lives;
- neglecting their own and their children's physical needs;
- difficulty controlling their emotions;
- being insensitive, unresponsive, angry and critical of their children;
- children having to be separated from their families;
- attachments and bonds with their children being disrupted, distorted or not formed at all.

Adverse effects on children are less likely[29] when:

- the parental problem is mild and of short duration;
- one parent has no such problems;
- other responsible adults are involved in child care;
- the adult with the problem is in treatment;
- there is a stable home and adequate financial resources;
- there is no family violence;
- the family does not ultimately break up.

The most vulnerable children are those who:[30]

- are victims of violence, neglect or parental rejection;
- live with a number of parental problems;
- are targets of parental delusions;
- witness parent's sexual and physical abuse;
- participate (willingly or unwillingly) in the abuse of a parent;
- collude in the secrecy and concealment of parental problems.

Difficulties in parenting not only frequently disrupt relationships within the family, but may result in the loss of friendships, impact upon work and ultimately reduce the family's standard of living.

3.10   INTERVENTION

In the main, it should be the decision of parents when to ask for help and advice on their children's care and upbringing:

> Only in exceptional cases should there be compulsory intervention in family life: for example, where this is necessary to safeguard a child from significant harm. Such intervention should, provided this is consistent with the safety and welfare of the child, support families in making their own plans for the welfare and protection of their children.

> (*Working Together*)

350,000 children each year are estimated to be living in an environment of low warmth and high criticism which significantly impairs their health and development. Approximately half (160,000) are currently referred to the child protection system each year. But this system operates with the greatest emphasis on Children Act 1989, s.47 enquiries rather than planning and intervention to meet the needs of children. Investigations tend to be incident-focused, yet single incidents rarely cause long-term harm, whereas a negative environment with low warmth and high criticism is more damaging.

The immediate issue is to protect the child from future harm. For long-term benefit, if the child is to stay with the harmful care-giver, it is helpful to appreciate some of the factors which can give rise to the neglect and/or emotional abuse of children, and which therefore need to be alleviated in order to lower the risk of future neglect or abuse and ensure effective and long-lasting placement.

The link between poor outcomes for children and social and economic disadvantage has been well established in research (see Table 3.3). Less commonly, family problems may include parental alcohol and/or drug abuse or mental disorder. Long-term problems occur when parenting style fails to compensate for the ups and downs of family life.

In deciding whether intervention is necessary to protect children, agencies must consider whether the threshold of significant harm has been breached.

Table 3.3 Social and economic disadvantage and resultant poor outcomes

Common disadvantages	Families exhibit
chronic ill-health	less warmth
unemployment	less open styles of communicating
poor housing	problems managing behaviour
previous abuse of the parent	inappropriate developmental expectations
domestic violence	failure to recognise or respect individual
	and psychological boundaries

The rights of the child must be considered, but other influences on where this threshold should be drawn include:

- moral/legal questions about what is acceptable behaviour in families, which change with time and context;
- pragmatic concerns: will intervention make any beneficial difference to the child? Considerations include the severity and duration of abuse, the child's view, parent's willingness to cooperate, protective factors to increase the child's resilience;
- outcome evidence: parenting behaviour is only considered abusive when it is debilitating for the child;
- parent/child concerns: involving parents in assessing whether harm is significant and debilitating is critical to achieving best outcomes.

3.11 SIBLING RELATIONSHIPS

Siblings can form significant parts of a child's attachment network and provide support during family stress when, as a group, they struggle to cope with parental difficulties. Generally, sibling relationships help to provide resilience for children. The exception, perhaps, is when one child acts as the scapegoat in the family and experiences much less love or concern than the other siblings. She may become the subject of hostility by the other siblings and/or parents and in these circumstances is left vulnerable.

Placement decisions about siblings are fraught with complexities not least because of the shortage of suitable placements capable of caring for large groups. The evidence about continued contact between siblings is problematic and firm conclusions about contact difficult to draw.[31] But indications are that siblings placed together experience less risk in foster placements and in adoptive placements – in the latter, being placed with a sibling increases the chances of success.[32]

3.12   COMMUNICATION

Purpose

Children have a right to understand what is happening to them and to receive age-appropriate information, explanations and reassurances. This should be done in a way that facilitates their participation in decisions about their lives and enables them to express their views and to give instructions where able to do so.

Their perception of legal and other processes can be greatly coloured by the information around them, from the media, peers and family. For example, their capacity for misunderstandings about the law, the courts and what is likely to happen to them should not be underestimated: research[33] shows many believe, even at the end of a care case, that they have somehow been involved in criminal proceedings.

Successful communication must ultimately be effective and meaningful to the child and requires an understanding of how a child thinks and communicates in a given situation. A full guide to the skills involved is not possible here, but the communication and interviewing guides listed in the Key sources and Appendix 1 contain excellent tips.

Communication consists of a range of factors, and is not merely verbal. Do not assume that just because a child has special educational needs or a disability she cannot communicate – some do so extremely effectively if given the right circumstances and support.

Interviews

Knowledge about, and research into, the factors involved in successful interview techniques have developed considerably in recent years. This has been reflected in the statutory guidance, *Achieving Best Evidence 2002*, which provides comprehensive guidance for those involved in interviewing child witnesses in criminal proceedings, but is also a useful guide to interviewing children in other circumstances, including family proceedings under the Children Act 1989. It follows four stages of establishing rapport, asking for free narrative recall, asking questions and closure.

For a young child, being interviewed 'requires great courage: s/he is likely to have no idea what to expect in the process, or what the outcomes may be, but s/he still seeks acceptance and believes s/he will be listened to and believed. To interview a young child takes great knowledge and skill: knowledge of the language barriers that must be overcome . . . of what information needs to be obtained and the skills needed to access that information; and knowledge that although the interviewer may want to help, it may not always be possible . . . While the purpose and goals of . . . various professions may be very different, the process of gaining accurate information from a child is the same . . . The process of interviewing a child is very similar irrespective of the topic of the interview.'[34]

Interviews should be short and be taken at the child's pace. Although the first interview is particularly important, knowing how to communicate in a style meaningful to the child, and how to interpret her responses, takes time and effort and is unlikely to be achieved straightaway. Formal child protection interviews should only be conducted by those properly trained in the correct techniques that will also be acceptable to the court, following the detailed guidance in *Achieving Best Evidence, 2002*.

NOTES

1 Bea Campbell, ALC conference lecture, Durham 1998.
2 A. James, C. Jenks and A. Prout, *Theorizing Childhood*, Cambridge, Polity Press (1998), p.14.
3 C. Jenks, *Childhood*, London, Routledge (1996), p.73.
4 R. Haggerty, L. Sherrod, N. Garmezy and M. Rutter, *Stress Risk and Resilience in Children and Adolescents*, Cambridge, Cambridge University Press (1996).
5 C. Jenks, *Childhood*, London, Routledge (1996), p.71.
6 For example, a recent Youth Justice Board analysis of ASSET returns showed that 20% of offenders were vulnerable to harm because of other people's behaviour, 9% were considered to be at risk of suicide or self harm, 25% had special needs identified and of these 60% had a Statement of Special Educational Needs, 42% were underachieving at school with 15% currently excluded.
7 Developed at the Grubb Institute as an alternative to child focused practice.
8 Green Paper, *Every Child Matters* (2003); CfC Outcomes Framework, July 2004, and now Children Act 2004, s.10(2). See Chapter 4.
9 Framework for Assessment of Children in Need and their Families, DH, Home Office and DfEE (2000).
10 A Swiss psychologist, 1896–1980.
11 See A. Schore, *Affect Dysregulation and Disorders of the Self*, New York, Norton (2003).
12 A. Schore, 'Effects of a Secure Attachment Relationship on Right Brain Development, Affect Regulation and Infant Mental Health' (2001) 22 (1–2) *Infant Mental Health Journal* 7.
13 Extract from C. Wilson and M. Powell, *A Guide to Interviewing Children*, London, Routledge (2001).
14 Extract from D. Jones, *Communicating with Vulnerable Children*, London, Gaskell (2003).
15 See also Chapter 19 on acting for the child.
16 A. Waterman, M, Blades and C. Spencer, 'Is a Jumper Angrier than a Tree?' (2001) 14 *The Psychologist* 474.
17 See **www.dfes.gov.uk/research/data/uploadfiles/RR444.pdf**.
18 P. Barker, *Basic Child Psychiatry*, 6th edition, Oxford, Blackwell Science (1995).
19 *Child Protection: Messages from Research*, DH (1995), p.19.
20 M. Rutter, 'A Fresh Look at Maternal Deprivation', in P. Bateson (ed.) *The Development of Behaviour*, Cambridge, Cambridge University Press (1991).
21 D. Iwaniec (2000) 'From Childhood to Adulthood: The Outcome of a 20-Year Follow-up of Children who Failed to Thrive' in D. Iwaniec and M. Hill (eds),

Child Welfare Policy and Practice: Issues and Lessons Emerging from Current Research, London, Jessica Kingsley (2000).

22 Munchausen Syndrome by Proxy (fabricating physical signs in a child to substantiate false stories of illness presented to doctors/hospitals).

23 P. Fonagy, M. Steele, H. Steele, A. Higgit and M. Target, 'The Theory and Practice of Resilience' (1994) 35(2) *Journal of Child Psychology and Psychiatry* 231.

24 S. Jackson and N. Thomas, *On the Move Again?*, Ilford, Barnardos (1999).

25 Working Together to Safeguard Children, DH, Home Office, DfEE (1999).

26 M. Adcock, 'Assessing Parenting: the Context' in M. Adcock and R. White (eds), *Good-enough Parenting*, London, BAAF (1985).

27 D.W. Winnicott, *The Maturational Process and the Facilitative Environment*, New York, International Universities Press (1965).

28 A. Bentovim, 'Signficant Harm in Context' in Adcock and White, *Good-enough Parenting*.

29 H. Cleaver, I. Unell and J. Aldgate, *Children's Needs: Parenting Capacity*, DH (1999).

30 Ibid.

31 D. Quinton *et al* 'Contact between Children Placed Away from Home and their Birth Parents: Research Issues and Evidence' (1997) 2(3) *Clinical Child Psychology and Psychiatry* 393. See also N. Lowe *et al*, *Supporting Adoption: Reframing the Approach*, London, BAAF (1999).

32 C. Sellick, J. Thoburn and T. Philpot, *What works in Adoption and Foster Care?*, Barnardos (2004).

33 J. Masson and M. Oakley, *Out of Hearing: Representing Children in Care Proceedings*, Chichester, Wiley (1999).

34 C. Wilson and M. Powell, *A Guide to Interviewing Children*, London, Routledge (2001).

CHAPTER 4

Safeguarding and services

Key sources

- Local Authority Social Services Act 1970; Local Government Acts 1972 and 2000; Health Act 1999, Care Standards Act 2000
- Children Acts 1989 and 2004, Schedule 4
- Children Act Guidance and Regulations (1991), vols 1–10, DH (1991)
- National Service Framework for Children, Young People and Maternity Services, DH (2004)
- DfES, 'Every Child Matters' materials (2005), including
  - *Lead Professional Good Practice Guidance for Children with Additional Needs*
  - *Guidance on the Children and Young People's Plan*
  - *Statutory Guidance on Inter-Agency Co-operation to Improve the Well-being of Children: Children's Trusts*
  - *Statutory Guidance on the Role and Responsibilities of the Director of Children's Services and the Lead Member for Children's Services*
  - *Statutory Guidance on Making Arrangements to Safeguard and Promote the Welfare Of Children under section 11 of the Children Act 2004*

4.1 INTRODUCTION

This chapter outlines the key principles and good practice issues governing the work of safeguarding and the delivery of supportive and preventative services by a local authority and its key partners. It describes the basic structures and functions, including the changes introduced by the Children Act 2004 and other initiatives directly affecting health and education, but is not a complete guide to powers, duties or services.

The definition of 'in need' in the Children Act 1989, s.17(10) focuses on standards of health or development or disability and the provisions in the Children Act 2004 are centred on five key outcomes for children. Services have to address increasingly complex and diverse problems, encompassing poverty, social exclusion and rising levels of child mental health problems and special educational needs.

Some major structural changes are already underway which further complicate the issues practitioners may encounter in trying to get the best deals for children and families. It is critically important for all practitioners to understand the financial, legal and decision-making structures of their local model and how it fits into the national framework. Understanding how services are planned and provided in a particular area by a local authority and agencies in general and for an individual case, is a crucial element in good case management and effective representation.

Preventative services were always intended to be a central element in the local authority's safeguarding duty to children and their families (Children Act 1989, s.17) which includes its duty to take reasonable steps to reduce the need to bring care proceedings (Children Act 1989, Sched. 2 para. 7(a)(i)). This is not a safety net for use only where there is no alternative (*R* v. *Hammersmith and Fulham LBC, ex p. D* [1999] 1 FLR 642). 'The most effective way to support and protect vulnerable children is through a focus on well-developed and strong universal services . . . [but] even with the most effective forms of prevention and early intervention there will always be a need to provide specific services to the most vulnerable.'[1] Therefore effective safeguarding must mean:

- comprehensive support and services;
- measures designed either to prevent proceedings being started in the first place, or to achieve a child's successful rehabilitation by supporting families;[2]
- strategic planning, financing and provision of services in all individual cases.[3]

Artificially raised thresholds and resource-driven intervention may occur, but compensatory preventative services are then all the more critical. The combination of the pre-proceedings steps identified in the Judicial Case Management Protocol and progress towards integrated services increases the focus on prevention.

Currently, the structure, operation, practice, performance and culture of each local authority and agency differ from one area to another, with wide variations in expenditure, performance, management and record-keeping. Human and financial resources are in short supply and there is constant pressure from inspection, guidance and restructuring. Services may be universal, targeted, specialist and/or rehabilitative, and the quality and implementation of decisions and delivery depend on the level of importance, sensitivity and complexity involved, and the financial consequences. In future they are intended to be integrated, locally coordinated and preventative.[4]

From October 2005, there will be a new safeguarding duty on local authorities and their 'relevant partners', i.e. education (Education Act 2002, s.175), health, probation and youth justice, and police (Children Act 2004, s.11 (England) and s.28 (Wales) and see Chapters 5 and 6). Local authorities with social services responsibilities will be 'children's services authorities' (CSAs) (Children Act 2004, s.65), and now have a duty under Children Act 1989, s.10 to make ongoing arrangements to promote cooperation between local agencies with 'a view to improving the well-being of children', based on the five key outcomes as set out in Children Act 2004, s.10(2):

- physical and mental health and emotional well-being;
- protection from harm and neglect;
- education, training and recreation;
- the contribution made by them to society;
- social and economic well-being.

'Safeguarding' is not legally defined, but the following definition is now being used, which covers children's services and child protection:

> All agencies working with children, young people and their families take all reasonable measures to ensure that the risks of harm to children's welfare are minimised; and where there are concerns about children and young people's welfare, all agencies take all appropriate actions to address those concerns, working to agreed local policies and procedures in full partnership with other local agencies.[5]

The CSA and its relevant partners must make ongoing arrangements to ensure its functions (including any functions performed by another on its behalf) are discharged with regard to the safeguarding duty. Services and intervention should be:

- well planned around resource availability;
- founded on thorough assessment;
- based on decisions underpinned by good evidence-based practice and policy;
- founded on adequate interdisciplinary training giving professionals the opportunity to understand different perspectives and approaches, and the interrelationship of specific services.

There is a large quantity of good practice guidance (statutory if issued under National Health Service Act 1977, s.17 or Local Authority Services Act 1970, s.7), not all of which is known to professionals or properly interpreted, but practitioners should be aware of its key messages. Whilst not endorsing poor practice, it is also necessary to understand that resource delivery is often beyond the control of many of those directly involved in cases: being antagonistic and confrontational with them is pointless and undermines relationships.

This chapter overlaps with Chapter 5 on child protection work, and reference should also be made to the sections on assessments, education, housing and mental health in that chapter.

4.2   KEY PRINCIPLES

Human rights

The powers, duties and discretion afforded to public authorities are wide-ranging. However, staff are not always familiar with the implications of human rights unless principles are firmly embedded in core policies, procedures and training, and subject to regular review. Many public bodies have compliance audits of policies, procedures and practice and their lawyers highlight areas susceptible to challenge, but response is often reactive and focused on case law: see the Audit Commission Report 2003 and cases such as *K and T* v. *Finland* [2002] 2 FLR 79, [2001] 2 FLR 707; *Boultif* v. *Switzerland* [2001] 2 FLR 1228.

Prevention is supported by the local authority's duty to facilitate and coordinate service provision and therefore adequate resources by enabling others to carry out its own obligations to children in need (ECHR Article 1 and see *R* v. *Mental Health Review Tribunal and Secretary of State for Health, ex p. KB and Others* [2002] EWHC Admin 639). However, Article 8 is not an absolute right, so if the act or omission does not lead to a total failure to protect a child, it is unlikely arguments about allocation of scarce resources will succeed. Both European and domestic courts have been very reluctant to interfere in public bodies' discretion on how or what to spend on services.

In any event, Best Value may result in contracting out services to other providers, but if these are not 'public bodies', the Human Rights Act 1998 will not generally apply. An undertaking should be required from them that they will recognise the rights guaranteed by the HRA 1998: this should be a universal practice (*R (Heather)* v. *Leonard Cheshire Foundation* [2001] EWHC Admin 429 and see now Children Act 2004, ss.10, 11(2)).

Diversity

The Race Relations Acts bind public bodies, which are required to exercise their powers and duties in a non-discriminatory manner. This equally applies to decisions taken about looked after children, and to services and support under Part III of the Children Act 1989 (see *Conwell* v. *Newham LBC* [1999] 3 FCR 625, EAT). The 1989 Act (e.g. ss. 1, 22(5)(c)) and the accompanying guidance require full account to be taken of diversity.

Staff may fail to appreciate fully the impact of racism on identity and self-image, or understand racial and/or cultural identity. All too frequently, false assumptions are made about heritage, the dynamics of mixed race relationships or the issues of race and culture needs in assessment, placement and the recruitment of carers. Practitioners should actively seek to ensure that legal and professional practice demonstrates culturally competent understanding of needs and experiences; and wherever possible and appropriate, challenges miscommunication, misunderstanding, inappropriate decision-making and poor planning arising from false assumptions, stereotyping or reinforcement of it.

The experience[6] and consequences of institutional racism (see definition in Chapter 1) may also need clearer recognition and acknowledgement amongst professionals to make assessments and services more effective and appropriate. It should also be noted that, e.g., black children in particular are overrepresented in the looked after statistics.[7]

Partnership, support and protection

The principle of partnership between public bodies and families underpins the legislation and is the hallmark of good practice in all key guidance,[8] reinforced by the Children Act 2004 (ss. 10, 11 (England) and ss. 25, 26 and 28 (Wales)). But partnership does not take precedence over, nor is it a substitute for, the welfare of the child – a basic principle not always well understood. Provision of resources that are *truly* supportive of the family and protective of the child are preferable to proceedings and are more likely to be ECHR Article 8 compliant. The safeguarding duty is a shared responsibility[9] and compliance with both the 1989 and 2004 Acts requires a clear focus on a child's safety and welfare in the provision of services appropriate to her needs.[10]

Corporate parenting

Support must be given by a strong lead from members and the commitment of chief officers.[11] Guidance, reinforced by the new structures for Directors and lead members in the Children Act 2004, stresses corporate responsibility to children in need and looked after, who must have 'a fully rounded set of support and care services, in partnership with health and education'.[12]

Planning

Overall strategic planning has long been a requirement, e.g.

- local Children's Services Plans (in England, since 1997), subsumed by statutory Children and Young People's Plans 2004 (Children Act 2004, s.17 (England) and s.26 (Wales));
- Management Action Plans (MAPs) (under the Quality Protects programme): corporate plans to improve the life chances of looked after children;
- ACPC Business Plans;
- Best Value Performance Plans.

4.3   LOCAL AUTHORITIES

Structure

Flexibility in the choice of decision-making structures under the Local Government Act 2000 and extensive managerial and functions changes make identifying a 'typical' local authority difficult. But the general principle remains that decisions and actions must be taken within a system of public accountability, based on advice by politically neutral officers to elected members responsible for setting policy. The discharge of relevant functions is delegated to employed officers, usually headed by a Chief Executive. Decision-making may be by committee, cabinet or an individual with delegated powers. Local authority propriety and conduct issues are the responsibility of a monitoring officer and elected members have a national code of conduct and are expected to follow the Nolan principles.

From 1 April 2006, each local authority in England with social services responsibilities will be required to appoint a Director of Children's Services who will replace the functions of the Director of Social Services (insofar as they relate to children) and the Chief Education Officer (Children Act 2004, s.18: phased in from 2006, mandatory by 2008). In Wales there will be a Lead Director responsible for coordinating these two directorates (Children Act 2004, s.27). This does not prevent contracting out of, e.g. education, social care or legal services to private or voluntary sector providers or to other local authorities.

Safeguarding needs effective information systems, and monitoring and evaluation of outcomes to plan services strategically. But good practice is still hampered by factors such as poor record-keeping, information-sharing and cooperation, senior management failings and inadequately supported and supervised staff.[13]

Information-sharing databases will be mandatory in future (Children Act 2004, s.12 (England) and s.29 (Wales). But some areas already have Information Sharing and Assessment ('ISA') systems (formerly called Information and Referral Tracking Projects), which identify children and young people at risk, referring them to preventative services and tracking their future progress.

Social services

Local authorities with social services responsibilities (CSAs in future) usually have a committee responsible for all such functions, delegating duties and responsibilities to a Director.[14] This Director is responsible for recruiting sufficient staff to enable social services functions to be carried out under the Local Authority Social Services Act 1970. In future she will only be responsible for children's services: adult services will be transferred to a separate directorate (Children Act 2004, Sched. 2 amends Local Authority Social Services Act 1970, s.6 and the Education Act 1996).

Some decisions may be delegated to all employed social workers, e.g., permission for a looked after child to take part in external school activities. Others may require a directorate decision, such as seeking an emergency protection order or returning home a child on the Child Protection Register. Decisions with potentially high cost implications, such as the funding of residential assessments, are likely to be taken at a senior managerial level and may involve a formal decision by a panel responsible for joint planning of resources (see below).

It is important to remember that local authorities are ultimately under the political control of elected members, whose priorities may not fit with best professional practice. For example, councillors in an area with a very small ethnic minority population may be reluctant to put resources into ensuring best practice on cultural issues.

4.4 SAFEGUARDING AND SERVICE DELIVERY

Integration

Children and their families do not fit into neat departmental or agency categories. Individual children, especially the most vulnerable and at risk, need consistent, coordinated, preventative help from social services, health, education and other agencies,[15] taking account of issues such as accommodation and support for carers.

The principle of integrated services is not new, but implementation is constrained by factors such as finance, general provision for all children in need and local resources. Provision is also dependent on individual assessment, but not subject to the welfare principle, and is often service-led rather than needs-led.[16] It may also be subject to means testing (*R (Spink)* v. *London Borough of Wandsworth* [2004] EWHC Admin 2314, [2005] 1 FLR 448).

The range of local bodies responsible for general and specific areas of coordination includes:

- the Area Child Protection Committee (ACPC), to be replaced by a Local Safeguarding Children Board (LSCB) (Children Act 2004, ss.13, 14 (England) and ss. 31, 32 (Wales) by April 2006) with statutory powers and duties;
- multidisciplinary panels for joint funding arrangements (looked after children, special educational needs or disabilities);
- Multi-Agency Public Protection Panels (MAPPP) (see Criminal Justice and Court Services Act 2002, ss. 67, 68 and Criminal Justice Act 2003, ss. 325–327) dealing with high risk offenders or those requiring senior

level multi-agency cooperation: police, prison and probation services ('the Responsible Authority'), social services, health and housing must cooperate.

The Children's Trust model,[17] is designed to address multiple organisational boundaries, fragmentation of responsibilities and funding, and inconsistencies in access to services. These vary in types, but are single entities designed to provide integrated services, including youth justice and voluntary organisations. Headed by the Director of Children's Services/Lead Director, they have:

- a unified commissioning function using voluntary partnerships (Health Act 1999, s.31);
- colocated staff and multidisciplinary teams;
- common assessment processes and information-sharing protocols.

However, this is a model based on voluntary funding (arrangements are made under Health Act 1999, s.31) and does not necessarily address:

- difficulties in trying to force provision of services: there is little or no sanction against failure – the Children Act 2004, s.17 duty is general, and not owed to individuals (see *R* v. *Lambeth LBC, ex p. (Caddell)* [1998] 1 FLR 253).
- other potentially incompatible legislation, e.g. relating to special educational needs;
- cultural change in organisations rather than merely structural change;
- the inability to force a local authority to bring proceedings (*Nottinghamshire County Council* v. *P* [1994] Fam. 18, although this may no longer be compliant with a child's ECHR Article 8 rights; *Botta* v. *Italy* (1998) 26 EHRR 241);
- use of the child protection register as an artificial mechanism for prioritising service access through a child protection plan;
- cases where the threshold criteria may be satisfied simply due to a lack of services.

Maximum information should be obtained on the availability and cost of services, and the following considered:

- Has an adequate, holistic and culturally competent assessment been done?
- Have any special issues such as disability been considered?
- Has the widest range of providers been explored, including the private and voluntary sector?
- Is a package of support required that needs joint planning?

Public bodies must act under the general guidance of the Secretary of State (including the exercise of any discretion) and in accordance with any directions given under Local Authority Social Services Act 1970, s.7(1) as amended by NHS and Community Care Act 1990, s.50. Breaches are only permissible where there are good reasons, but that does not mean there is freedom to take a substantially different course (see *R* v. *Islington LBC, ex p. Rixon* [1997] 1 CCLR 119; *R* v. *Cornwall County Council, ex p. LH* [2000] 1 FLR 236 and see application to Children Act 2004, s.17 in *R* v. *Lambeth LBC, ex p. K* [2000] 3 CCLR 141). In certain circumstances a local authority may be directed under 'general guidance' to take a particular course of action, cause an inquiry to be held (Children Act 1989, s.81), or, if the complaint relates to accommodation for a child, cause an inspection to take place (s.80).

Decisions on services must be informed by assessment that complies with guidance. Once identified, an individual's particular needs must be met by appropriate services (*R* v. *Wigan Metropolitan Borough Council, ex p. Tammadge* (1998) 1 CCL Rep 581, subject to means: see *(R) Spink* v. *Wandsworth LBC* [2005] FLR 448). Mandatory and advisory guidance is not always implemented consistently, but can be used to challenge the adequacy of service delivery. Practitioners should also be aware of:

- up-to-date case law, particularly relating to accommodation (*R (G)* v. *Barnet LBC; R (W)* v. *Lambeth LBC; R (A)* v. *Lambeth LBC* [2003] UKHL 57, [2003] 3 WLR 1194 HL and see Chapter 14 on housing), and offers of funding (*R* v. *Hammersmith and Fulham LBC, ex p. D* [1999] 1 FLR 642);
- shifts in previous judicial reluctance to allow challenges via judicial review (*R* v. *Kingston upon Thames RBC, ex p. T* [1994] 1 FCR 232; *R* v. *London Borough of Brent, ex p. S* [1994] 1 FLR 203; *R* v. *London Borough of Barnet, ex p. B* [1994] 1 FLR 592), particularly in the light of the 2004 Act and new safeguarding and cooperation duties (e.g. *Re T (Judicial Review: Local Authority Decisions Concerning Child in Need)* [2003] EWHC Admin 2515);
- the possibility of human rights challenges under ECHR Article 8 (see HRA 1998, ss. 6 and 7 and see e.g. *R* v. *Hammersmith and Fulham LBC, ex p. D* [1999] 1 FLR 642; *Botta* v. *Italy* (1998) 26 EHRR 241).

4.5   FINANCES AND RESOURCES

General

User-friendly, consultative services that focus on the needs of children and their families, rather than on organisational needs, require adequate resources, subject to discretion (ECHR Article 1, see Chapter 1). But these are stretched, pooled funding is not universal and the spending on, and respective costs of, services can differ substantially from one authority or agency to another. Some of this is due to central underfunding of services.[18] But lack of money is not always the cause: some authorities fail to plan strategically and, e.g., lack assessments of children in need.[19]

Local authority finances

A local authority has general powers to:

- do anything designed to facilitate or support any of its functions (Local Government Act 1972, s.111);
- do anything it considers likely to achieve, e.g., an improvement in the social well-being of the area, with power to give financial assistance to achieve this (Local Government Act 2000, s.2(1), (4)).

LSCBs are expected to have much wider-ranging responsibilities than ACPCs, which were concerned exclusively with child protection, but may well not be given sufficient resources to implement these.

Local authority powers and duties are strictly controlled by a detailed statutory and financial regime and the doctrine of *ultra vires*. The Best Value regime (under the Local Government Act 2000, s.3) requires demonstrating value for money in service provision, underpinned by increased financial scrutiny, regular monitoring and inspection regimes, and new powers to intervene in failing authorities.

Discretion is allowed in carrying out statutory duties and powers as a local authority sees fit, as long as its decisions are taken in accordance with the law and general local government ground rules. This has been widely interpreted by the courts and the ECHR 'margin of appreciation' is of particular relevance where expenditure is concerned.

Since the welfare principle (Children Act 1989, s.1) does not apply to any Children Act 1989 Part III powers and duties:

- competing resource considerations can outweigh a child's welfare (*Re M (Secure Accommodation Order)* [1995] 1 FLR 418);
- limited resources can drive intervention: it is all too common to find the threshold criteria for proceedings being satisfied because services are simply not available.

Internal finances are usually managed by a system of cost centre management, with departmental or team 'budget holders'. Finding out 'who, how, when and if', *before* applying to court for leave, especially for a high level of expenditure, is essential. The frontline worker almost never holds the purse strings, nor may the immediate line manager, even for relatively straightforward matters. Decisions with potentially high cost implications, such as funding residential assessments, are likely to be taken by a senior manager or the Director.

Complex financial and administrative systems and competitive internal budgets often militate against effective interdepartmental and/or interagency resource allocation. The protectionist 'territorial' approach between some departments, agencies and authorities is not assisted by complex financial recoupment arrangements that impact on children's services, particularly for those with multiple needs. Pooling scarce resources is not universal and relies on voluntary arrangements.

Multidisciplinary bodies exist in various guises such as Advisory Panels, budget focus groups, joint committees, implementation management groups or corporate parent groups. These usually hold the purse strings and the real decision-making power, so find out which is the relevant group for the case.

For resolution of disputes between authorities and agencies about responsibility for children, particularly those who are disabled or have special educational needs, some limited assistance can be found in case law on the interpretation of 'designated local authority' (Children Act 1989, s.31(8)) and 'ordinary residence'. But definitive answers for every case are limited and recourse may be needed to arguments on principles.

Public bodies are organisationally complex and employees will not necessarily know the answers, but consider who:

- is responsible for decisions and who supervises them;
- takes financial decisions for individual provision;
- is the budget or cost centre manager;
- has the power to overrule or overturn decisions?

and, is there an avenue of appeal/complaint which will not of itself cause the child further unreasonable delay?

If staff involved are not giving clear information on these issues, it is possible to use the procedure contained in Freedom of Information Act 2000, s.1, to require the local authority to provide copies of its policies, procedures, etc. (but not documents relating to identified individuals, which is regulated by the Data Protection Act 1998) (see Chapter 24 for further information on disclosure generally).

Even with sufficient funds, there are limitations on what can be provided: the level of loss, disruption, abuse and/or neglect some children suffer can result in damage that may present challenging behaviour and, in some cases, almost intractable difficulties. Some placement breakdowns are beyond the control of even the best local authority, or the carers they employ.

Alternative dispute resolution in the form of family group conferences, specialist child care mediation, or conciliation, arbitration or mediation has been suggested.[20]

4.6 HEALTH

Health agencies and professionals, including the private and voluntary sector, are often the first to be aware of family difficulty in caring for children.[21] Many staff (e.g. GPs, health visitors, midwives and practice nurses) are in the most readily-accessed primary care services, but consistency, availability and entitlement are not uniform, and boundaries are not largely coterminous with social care.

The NHS is undergoing major change,[22] with an emphasis on primary care, clinical excellence and evidence-based practice. Improvements to services target:

- screening programmes for women and children;
- mental health;
- an enhanced role for midwives.

Monitoring of standards include a national Children's Taskforce responsible for ensuring the changes reflect children's views and improve outcomes for the vulnerable, and National Service Frameworks (NSFs), which set standards.[23] For example, the Children's NSF[24] sets out protocols for treatment and access to locally coordinated services, echoing the language of social care changes, emphasising integrated services ('local children's networks') linking with education and social care.

The NHS in England is a framework of trusts responsible for providing acute and community health services. This includes Strategic Health Authorities, with Primary Care Trusts as the focal point for joint working with social care, and regional or national Acute Trusts managing hospitals, and Mental Health Trusts providing more specialist services.

The NHS in Wales[25] has primary, secondary, tertiary and community care within a National Public Health Service framework giving advice and guidance on child protection, Local Health Boards coterminous with the 22 local authorities in Wales (with a statutory duty to work together) and a Health Commission Wales, responsible for specialised services.

The safeguarding role

The responsibilities of *all* those providing health services, including primary care, adult mental health (AMH) and child and adolescent mental health (CAMH), under safeguarding duties (Children Act 2004, s.11 (England) and s.28 (Wales) as from 1 October 2005) are set out in statutory guidance,[26] and include agreements to provide a full clinical service for child protection in each area, including access by health professionals to expert advice; and designated professionals (senior paediatrician and senior nurse) to lead on safeguarding in each Trust providing professional advice to other professionals and to social services departments.[27] Their job descriptions should include:

- representing the local health service on the ACPC/LSCB;
- regular contact with named Trust professionals;
- promoting and influencing skilled professional involvement in child protection processes in line with ACPC/LSCB protocols;

- promoting and influencing relevant training;
- participating in case reviews under *Working Together*.[28]

Wherever overall responsibility for local services lies, that body must take the strategic lead in planning safeguarding services with the local authority. Commissioners of services should ensure service specifications include clear service standards for safeguarding consistent with local ACPC/LSCB procedures (Children Act 2004, s.11 (England) and s.28 (Wales)).[29]

Consent, capacity and disclosure

There is an excellent guide available for professionals covering a wide range of situations,[30] including children, learning disabilities and those in prison, which provides a model documentation including policies and forms for use with patients.

Chapter 15 has a brief overview of confidentiality, but several guides are available covering a range of health services.[31]

4.7   EDUCATION

Services may range from general education services to those specific to special educational needs or disability, such as educational psychologists or specialist teachers. Specialist therapies (e.g. speech and language, physiotherapy) are normally provided by the health trust. The education sector is seen as the future hub of provision for integrated services, with 'extended schools' and multidisciplinary teams in schools providing common assessments and early intervention on a preventative basis.

Education has a separate safeguarding duty (Education Act 2002, s.175), and only has cooperation duties under the 1989 Act (save for the new general duty to cooperate with assessments) (Children Act 2004, s.22). This applies to schools, LEAs and governors and there should be a Designated Teacher in every school.

4.8   PROBATION

The new safeguarding duty may have implications for information-sharing over, e.g., substance misuse or anger management programmes.

There is a revised risk assessment designed to take account of children for probation, but offenders who may pose a serious community risk should be the subject of risk assessment and management through the local Multi-Agency Public Protection Panel.

4.9 PRACTICAL ISSUES

Access to services

Early intervention on the basis of clear information from good assessment is preferable. Where this is not possible, obtain an assessment of entitlement to services and push for provision to be put in place. The longer a family is without supportive services, the greater the likelihood of protective intervention, and increasing pressure from the child's developmental timescale.

There are specific programmes targeted at particular groups, such as Sure Start (England), which provides help for families with children under four years in areas of high need, and Home-Start, which provides help from trained volunteers at home for young families under stress and with one or more children aged under five years.

Carers

Carers now have enhanced rights and are entitled to a holistic assessment of their needs, taking account of leisure and respite (see the Carers (Equal Opportunities) Act 2004, Carers (Recognition and Services) Act 1995 and Carers and Disabled Children Act 2000). Public bodies have a duty to help local authorities in planning and providing services that might assist carers in caring and continuing to care.

This should include consideration of kinship carers. The interrelationship of benefits with other payments can impact adversely on finances, but there is a little known system of 'direct payments' available (see Community Care (Direct Payments) Act 1996). Specialist advisers in welfare rights may be able to sort out the complexities. But get this advice well before proceedings start, or as soon as possible thereafter: the court will want clear information to ensure, e.g., that placements are properly financially supported.

Confidentiality and information-sharing

At present, relevant provisions are contained in the Data Protection Acts and other legislation, with the main guidance issued in 2004.[32] Further guidance is awaited in the wake of the Children Act 2004.

4.10 PROFESSIONAL PRACTICE STANDARDS

Inspection

In England, under the Health and Social Care (Community Health and Standards) Act 2003 this is now the responsibility of:

- the Commission for Social Care Inspection (CSCI) (which replaces the work of Social Services Inspectorate, SSI/Audit Commission Joint Review Team and the National Care Standards Commission); and
- the Commission for Healthcare Audit and Inspection (CHAI) (responsible for inspecting all health services in England, including independent provision; in Wales NHS bodies are governed by the Healthcare Inspectorate Wales and the private sector by Care Standards Inspectorate for Wales (CISW));[33]

who have a legal duty to cooperate (and are to be amalgamated in 2005).

CSCI has a legal duty to safeguard and promote not only children's welfare, but also their rights, and hosts a Children's Rights Directorate.[34] A new Inspection Framework (Children Act 2004, ss. 20–24 (England) and s.30 (Wales)) will carry out Joint Area Reviews of all children's services and settings (also subject to a unified Annual Performance Assessment), based on 42 key judgments for overall performance, including safeguarding procedures, and five outcomes. All inspection reports are public documents available on the Internet.

Social care registration

The General Social Care Council (GSCC) in England, and the Care Council for Wales, are now the independent statutory bodies for the registration, regulation and training of social care workers (see the Care Standards Act 2000). Codes of practice are available and all social workers and guardians should have applied for registration by December 2004.

Research and evidence-based practice

Further information and advice on practice and research is in statutory and advisory guidance issued by government departments and the NHS. Specialist professional bodies, such as the Royal Colleges, are also helpful sources of good practice guides. Relevant bodies include:

- Social Care Institute for Excellence (SCIE) (evidence-based practice via knowledge reviews and resource guides);[35]
- National Institute for Clinical Excellence (treatment and care recommendations;[36]
- National Electronic Library for Health;[37]
- National Knowledge Service for Health and Social Care (knowledge for patients and staff based on research, data and experience);[38]
- government public service information;[39]
- CAFCASS (digest of research, evaluation and best practice).

NOTES

1   Inter-agency position statement on vulnerable children by ADSS and partner agencies, 2004.
2   *Working Together to Safeguard Children*, DH, Home Office, DfEE (1999), para. 1.9.
3   See, e.g. Care Plans Circular LAC 99.
4   See 'Every Child Matters, Change for Children' at **www.everychildmatters.co.uk**. See also various DfES guidance, e.g. *Lead Professional Good Practice Guidance for Children with Additional Needs* (July 2005); *Statutory Guidance on the Role and Responsibilities of the Director of Children's Services and the Lead Member* (2005); *Statutory Guidance on Making Arrangements to Safeguard and Promote the Welfare of Children under section 11 of the Children Act 2004* and *Guidance on the Children and Young People's Plan* (2005); *Statutory Guidance on Inter-Agency Cooperation to improve the Well-being of Children: Children's Trusts* (2005); *Cross-Government Guidance – Sharing Information on Children and Young People* (consultation draft, August 2005, due for publication in December 2005); and new version of *Working Together to Safeguard Children* (consultation draft, July 2005).
5   Safeguards Review 2002; Green Paper, *Every Child Matters* (2003).
6   'Experiencing Ethnicity: Discrimination and Service Provision' at **www.jrf.org.uk/knowledge/findings/foundations/914.asp**.
7   Studies from Gale in 1963 and Brophy *et al.* in 2003, see e.g. British Agencies for Fostering and Adoption (BAAF), Barnados, etc.
8   *Working Together*, para. 1.10, and see Children Act 1989, ss.27 and 47.
9   *Working Together*, paras 1.10 – 1.13.
10 See Children Act 1989, s.17 and findings of the Rikki Neave Inquiry.
11 *Working Together*, para. 1.10.
12 Secretary of State for Health, September 1998; Government Response to the Children's Safeguards Review, November 1998; Quality Protects.
13 Joint Reviews of Powys Council, 1999 and Torbay Council 2001; Climbié Inquiry, January 2003.
14 Varying titles and responsibilities include 'Social Services', 'Personal Services', 'Education and Social Services', 'Children, Families and Schools'.
15 *Working Together*, para. 1.12.
16 *Climbié Inquiry Report*, para. 17.62.
17 See **www.doh.gov.uk/childrenstrusts**.
18 *Report of Chief Inspector SSI for Wales to Health and Social Services Committee*, Welsh Assembly (March 2001).
19 See Joint Review of Torbay Council (2001).
20 See Thorpe LJ and E. Clarke (eds), *Divided Duties: Care Planning for Children within the Family Justice System*, Jordans Family Law (1998).
21 *Working Together*, para. 3.18.
22 See **www.modern.nhs.uk** and **www.cgsupport.nhs.uk**.
23 For example, *National Service Framework for Hospital Services*, April 2003.
24 Children, Young People and Maternity Services 2004 for children under 19 (England only): **www.doh.gov.uk**.
25 See **www.wales.nhs.uk**.
26 *Working Together*, paras. 3.18–3.53.
27 *Ibid.*, para. 3.21, but see criticism in *Climbié Inquiry Report*.
28 *Working Together*, ch. 8.
29 *Ibid.*, para. 3.20.

30 See **www.doh.gov.uk/consent**.
31 For example, NHS Code of Practice on Confidentiality, DH (2003); Confidentiality and Disclosure of Information: General Medical Services (GMS), Personal Medical Services (PMS), and Alternative Provider Medical Services (APMS) Code of Practice, DH (2004); Responsibilities of Doctors in Child Protection Cases with Regard to Confidentiality, RCPCH (2004).
32 DCA, *Public Sector Data Sharing: Guidance on the Law* (2003) and *A Public Sector Toolkit on Data Sharing* (2004).
33 See *Working Together To Safeguard Children*; *Procedure for Responding to the Alleged Abuse of Children in Regulated Services*, CISW (2003).
34 **www.rights4me.org.uk**.
35 **www.scie.org.uk**.
36 **www.nice.org.uk**.
37 **www.nelh.nhs.uk**.
38 **www.nks.nhs.uk**.
39 **www.direct.gov.uk**.

CHAPTER 5

The multi-agency child protection system

Key sources

- *Challenge of Partnership in Child Protection*, DH, SSI (1995)
- *Working Together to Safeguard Children* (1999) and supplements
- Framework for Assessment of Children in Need and their Families, DH, Home Office and DfEE (2000)
- *Achieving Best Evidence in Criminal Proceedings* (2002)
- Protocol between CPS, Police and Local Authorities in the Exchange of Information in the Investigation and Prosecution of Child Abuse Cases (2003)
- *What to Do If You are Worried a Child is Being Abused*, DH (2003)
- *Safeguarding Children in Education*, DfES (2004)
- *Guidance on Investigating Child Abuse and Safeguarding Children*, ACPO and Centrex (2005)

5.1 INTRODUCTION

> If a child is not safe at home, he cannot be protected by casework.[1]

Understanding how the multidisciplinary child protection system works is essential to good practice. The Children Act 2004 encourages partnership working and increases accountability, but an integrated, common approach is some way off[2] and each agency will differ in its decision-making approach. This chapter covers child protection investigations, but overlaps with the preceding chapter on services.

The national statutory guidance framework (issued under Local Authority Social Services Act 1970, s.7) for inter-agency case management and good professional practice is based on:[3]

- *Working Together*;[4]
- the Framework for Assessment;
- the Children Act Volumes of Guidance.

These must be followed unless there are exceptional reasons for diverting from them, which can be appropriately justified. It is essential that all practitioners have ready access to them and to any statutory guidance issued under the Children Act 2004.

Important advisory guidance is contained in:

- *What To Do If You Are Worried a Child is Being Abused;*[5]
- *Safeguarding Children in Education;*[6]
- local Area Child Protection Committee (Local Safeguarding Board) policies and procedures (Children Act 2004, ss.13–16 (England) and ss.31–34 (Wales) from April 2006) and the agency specific individual documents based on these (see below).[7]

Do not assume all professionals know what guidance actually says: mistaken interpretation and assumptions have all been highlighted in inquiries and the conduct of investigations is still marred by confusion in roles and responsibilities. Use guidance where necessary to support, or to test, decisions: see Appendix 1.

Note, however, that guidance:

- is no substitute for informed professional judgment based on good evidence and research;
- must be firmly supported by good quality training and supervision;
- cannot cover all eventualities: common sense is required.

The investigation of crime against children is as important as the investigation of any other form of serious crime.[8] But decisions not to prosecute cases of alleged child abuse and neglect are common and levels of conviction not high. Differences in the criminal and civil standards of proof and the different focus on the defendant's behaviour in prosecutions, and the child's interests in care cases, can create misunderstandings. Any suggestion that serious allegations in civil cases require a higher standard of proof, have been firmly scotched (Court of Appeal in *Re L and U* [2004] EWCA Civ 567, [2004] 2 FLR 263).

5.2 HUMAN RIGHTS AND DIVERSITY

Statutory guidance states as a matter of course that it reflects the principles in the UNCRC, and takes account of Convention rights. Social services staff are generally aware of the existence of ECHR rights but few have any real awareness of UNCRC rights. The principal aim of the Children Act 1989 is to keep birth families together, and to promote contact by the child living elsewhere, subject to the fundamental principle that it must be compatible with the protection of the child. Medium- to long-term welfare may be best served by the child not being with her natural parents in the light of the practicalities, advantages and risks involved and, in some cases, by not having contact with her birth family or some members of it.

Local authorities are bound by the requirements of fairness mandated by ECHR Article 8 (see Chapter 1) and the quality of child protection decision-making is increasingly scrutinised (*Re M (Care: Challenging Decisions by Local Authority)* [2001] 2 FLR 1300; *Re L (Care: Assessment: Fair Trial)* [2002] EWHC Fam 1379, [2002] 2 FLR 730; *Re G (Care: Challenge to Local Authority's Decision)* [2003] EWHC Fam 551, [2003] 2 FLR 42; *X Council* v. *B (Emergency Protection Order)* [2005] 1 FLR 341). This must also apply to collective decision-making: other agencies and individuals have a 'collective responsibility and a collective duty to act fairly' (*Re L (Care: Assessment: Fair Trial)* [2002] EWHC Fam 1379, [2002] 2 FLR 730). With the wider application of the safeguarding duty, this raises implications for all key agencies involved in investigations. All too often, a pattern of lack of investigation, communication and cooperation can have a significant influence on the course of events (*E* v. *UK* [2003] 1 FLR 348).

Decision-making must therefore be founded on:

- correct and complete information, 'an indispensable prerequisite for . . . striking a fair balance between the interests at stake' (*Sahin, Sommerfeld, Hoffmann* v. *Germany* [2002] 1 FLR 119);
- careful assessment of the impact of any proposed measure on parents and child, with consideration of possible alternatives prior to her removal (*Venema* v. *Netherlands* [2003] 1 FLR 551);
- sufficient involvement of parents, carers and children (*W* v. *UK* (1987) 10 EHRR 29; *McMichael* v. *UK* (1995) 20 EHRR 205; *TP and KM* v. *UK* [2001] 2 FLR 549; *Re G (Care: Challenge to Local Authority's Decision)* [2003] EWHC Fam 551, [2003] 2 FLR 42; and, for children, see *Eriksson* v. *Sweden* (1989) 12 EHRR 183 (private law case));
- detailed information and reasons, to enable effective participation and access to adequate appeal processes (*KA* v. *Finland* [2003] 1 FLR 696).

'Sufficient involvement' can be judged by whether, in the particular circumstances, (*Re M (Care: Challenging Decisions by Local Authority)* [2001] 2 FLR 1300) and given the serious nature of the decisions to be taken, parents have been involved in the process as a whole, (*Mantovanelli* v. *France* (1997) 24 EHRR 370) sufficiently to provide requisite protection of their interests. If not, this will constitute a failure to respect family life and intervention cannot be regarded as 'necessary' within the meaning of ECHR Article 8 (*R* v. *UK* [1988] 2 FLR 445; *W* v. *UK* (1988) 10 EHRR 29; *P C and S* v. *UK* [2002] 2 FLR 631). Matters overall must be assessed (*Scott* v. *UK* [2000] 1 FLR 958) and regard had 'to all circumstances' (*Buchberger* v. *Austria* (2003) 37 EHRR 13, ECHR). Exclusion from meetings or from access to documents may be so significant as to make the whole proceedings unfair, (e.g. *Re M (Care: Challenging Decisions by Local Authority)* [2001] 2 FLR 1300) or not (*Scott* v. *UK* [2000] 1 FLR 958; *C* v. *Bury MBC* [2002] EWHC Fam 1438, [2002] 2 FLR 868).

ECHR Article 8 is the key, but Article 6 rights clearly apply directly to the conduct of proceedings, and to an (implied) right of access to a court or tribunal, (*Golder* v. *UK* (1979–80) EHRR 524) and a hearing within a reasonable time. These factors must be taken into account in decision-making, bearing in mind:

- the 'exceptional diligence' required to comply with the principle that delay is likely to prejudice the child's welfare (*H* v. *UK* (1988) 10 EHRR 95; *Hokkanen* v. *Finland* [1996] 1 FLR 289);
- the appropriate timescale, depending on the complexity of the case;
- the principle of 'equality of arms' (fair balance between the parties, which covers, e.g. disclosure);
- the reality of participation in child protection processes.[9]

Facilitation of children's voices, views and rights requires a commitment to UNCRC Article 12. The need to provide information and consultative processes facilitating children's wishes and feelings is clear, and this is now mandatory in child protection investigations (Children Act 1989, s.47(5) as inserted by Children Act 2004, s.53). Identifying how they can be assisted in participating and given information is not a new task,[10] but has only recently received wider attention:[11] age and maturity are important factors and the judiciary are willing to regard 16 and 14 (per HHJ Tyrer in *Re S (Contact: Children's Views)* [2002] 1 FLR 1156) as old enough to participate in proceedings, but perhaps not to approve the appointment of a solicitor as guardian for a young child wishing to do so (*Re N (Residence Order: Procedural Mismanagement)* [2001] 1 FLR 1028).

Children much younger can contribute their views, but ways to facilitate this are only just beginning to be accepted.

Authorities have a wide margin of appreciation: whilst the scope of any discretion given must be indicated (*Silver* v. *UK* (1983) 5 EHRR 347; *Malone* v. *UK* (1984) 7 EHRR 14; *Ames* v. *UK* (1986) 8 EHRR 123), flexibility in child protection is recognised as both inevitable and permissible (*Olsson* v. *Sweden (No. 1)* (1989) 11 EHRR 259; *R* v. *UK* [1988] 2 FLR 445; *C* v. *Bury MBC* [2002] EWHC Fam 1438, [2002] 2 FLR 868 para.56). But the potential effect of processes on family relationships, particularly those between parents and children (*K and T* v. *Finland* [2000] 2 FLR 79, [2001] 2 FLR 707; *Boultif* v. *Switzerland* [2001] 2 FLR 1228), makes it even more important to scrutinise the adequacy of procedural and other safeguards designed to protect the child and effective participation by her and her family, and the arrangements for contact.

There are certain fundamental principles of good practice (see Munby J in *Re L (Care: Assessment: Fair Trial)* [2002] EWHC 1379, [2002] 2 FLR 730), but courts may be very reluctant to find the acts or omissions of a social worker in intervention prior to proceedings in breach of the Convention (Court of Appeal in *Re V (Care: Pre-birth Actions)* [2004] EWCA Civ 1575; [2005] 1 FLR 627).

Judicial review is not appropriate to prevent a local authority commencing emergency protection or care proceedings unless exceptional *(Re M (Care Proceedings: Judicial Review)* [2003] 2 FLR 171), but failure or refusal to bring such proceedings could arguably now be challenged, despite the pre-HRA 1998 case law to the contrary (see positive obligations in *Botta* v. *Italy* (1998) 26 EHRR 241; *Nottinghamshire CC* v. *P* [1994] Fam 18, [1993] 2 FLR 134). Where a child is looked after by a local authority, but it is refusing to start proceedings, the Independent Reviewing Officer may be able to assist.

Child protection intervention requires judgments about the adequacy of parenting. Comparisons with a 'similar child' (Children Act 1989, s.31(10)) further add to the likelihood of difficult issues arising about, e.g. cultural and religious practice, or what constitutes 'good enough' parenting for a child with special needs/disability. The principles in Chapter 1 are of particular importance here.

There are also human rights implications for the disabled, whether children, adults or carers. ECHR Article 8 may impose obligations to take positive steps to improve their situation: disability too often cuts them off from what the able-bodied take for granted (Munby J in *R (A, B, X and Y)* v. *East Sussex CC (No. 2)* [2003] EWHC Admin 167, (2002) 6 CCLR 194).

5.3 PARTNERSHIP, PARTICIPATION AND CHILD CENTRED PRACTICE

Agencies must work in partnership with family members, particularly parents and children, and facilitate their maximum involvement in *all* stages of planning and decision-making to comply with the strong emphasis on this in law and guidance. Combined with openness and honesty at investigation and conference stages, this is seen as critical to sound decision-making and to good outcomes for the child. However, research indicates some parental confusion about how agreements are reached about plans,[12] professionals often fail to distinguish between passive acceptance/compliance and true partnership, and some need to overcome 'a mindset and culture' (*Re L (Care: Assessment: Fair Trial)* [2002] 2 FLR 730).

All stages of the decision-making process require a transparency and fairness (Munby J in *Re L (Care: Assessment: Fair Trial)* [2002] 2 FLR 730), with:

- documents made openly available,
- crucial meetings conducted openly with parents (or children who are able to take part) who wish to attend or be represented;
- a written agenda circulated in advance;
- full, balanced, clear, accurate, agreed and disclosed notes/minutes of all relevant conversations/meetings;

- an obligation to ensure individual difficulties do not prevent full participation (e.g. where capacity to understand is limited (Munby J in *Re G
(Care: Challenge to Local Authority's Decision)* [2003] 2 FLR 42; *Kutzner*
v. *Germany* (26 February 2002, ECtHR, unreported)).

Correct and complete information (*Sahin* v. *Germany* [2002] 1 FLR 119)
must be supplied to both adults and children. However, careful thought and
planning is needed: 'sharing' information may not be enough to facilitate
sufficient involvement in and throughout the process, and vulnerability,
disability and disadvantage and the way in which intervention and professionals themselves may be seen must be accounted for (Munby J in *Re G
(Care: Challenge to Local Authority's Decision)* [2003] 2 FLR 42).

Information and reports should be supplied to family members in sufficient time for them to digest, understand and, if necessary, take advice on the
contents.

Critically, partnership cannot take precedence over, nor is it a substitute
for, the welfare of the child. Where safeguarding is necessary, then compulsory intervention, as part of a carefully planned process, will always be the
appropriate remedy: local authorities should not be inhibited from seeking
appropriate court orders by the idea that partnership must be pursued at all
costs.[13] This principle is much misunderstood by professionals, who risk
operating on a rule of optimism and accepting explanations that are least
discrediting to parents.[14]

In cases of chronic neglect and/or non-compliance, professionals' individual 'tolerance thresholds' can become raised to the point that professionals will 'live with' a situation that, if it had existed at the time of initial
referral, would have led to immediate intervention. Those representing
children must be prepared to challenge this where appropriate.

Some still find this difficult in relation to children, but 'whilst children
want professionals to be sympathetic, supportive and optimistic, they want
straight-talking, realism and reliability and not as it is sometimes seen
"bullshit and false promises"' [15]

5.4 PLANNING AND JOINT WORK

Pre-proceedings

The Judicial Case Management Protocol requires documentation and 'sufficient information about the local authority's case' to be filed with the initial
application and, for the most part, the presumption is that the local authority
has carried out all the assessments and investigations necessary to start
proceedings.

Once proceedings begin, they tend to take on a life of their own, so
sensible and sensitive negotiations with the local authority in advance are

crucial. Public funding can be used for this purpose, and may cover attendance at child protection conferences.[16] Alternative advocacy services may also be available and are subject to national standards.[17]

Planning

The ideal is a traceable, well documented and well planned path from initial referral to final order, beginning with an initial assessment, followed by strategy discussions, investigations, core assessment, conference and child protection plan, leading to an interim care plan for the proceedings.

Good practice includes:

- consistent, cross-professional acceptance of the paramountcy principle in all agencies' and individuals' practice;
- consistent strategies on budgets and services;
- proper interagency negotiations about resource provision, or well thought-out contract specifications, resulting in practical and effective child protection services;
- regular and effective monitoring and audit of child protection procedures;
- consistent professional knowledge and training, including realistic evidence-based intervention based on recent research.

Joint working

Never assume that, just because agencies and individuals are apparently working together, this is based on a common set of values and good practice principles. Consensus on cooperation cannot always be taken for granted, but a lack of it is not always obvious.

Apparent consensus may mask unspoken/hidden/unacknowledged tensions:

- decision-making, especially in conferences, may not be firmly rooted in the same level, or 'ownership', of common purpose, commitment, language, perception, knowledge or understanding, or even research;
- unfamiliarity with child protection procedures or lack of regular experience may influence contributions;
- failure to acknowledge mistrust/misunderstanding, personal attitudes and experiences, lack of managerial support or training may affect decisions;
- the 'rule of optimism' or a 'divided loyalty' syndrome may affect views expressed, especially when family members are present; some professionals are more closely involved with families and for longer, so, e.g. adult psychiatrists, GPs, health visitors and teachers may not always achieve balance and objectivity, and fail to acknowledge or understand the effects of this.

5.5 INFORMATION-SHARING[18]

The basic principles are the overriding need to safeguard the child; and the duty of full and frank disclosure in care proceedings.

Information must also be held securely by all agencies (*Re M (Challenging Decisions by Local Authority)* [2001] 2 FLR 1300). However, it is all too easy to assume that the interests of all the agencies involved in working together in a child's interests are the same – in practice, there are sometimes real tensions and constraints in disclosing information (Lawson J in *Re M (Care Proceedings: Disclosure: Human Rights)* [2001] 2 FLR 1316).

Currently, local authorities can legally request information from specified authorities, who are required to cooperate (i.e. other local authorities, education or housing authorities and NHS bodies, see Children Act 1989, ss.27 and 47). Anyone can disclose information to such authorities in relation to crime (Crime and Disorder Act 1998, s.115) and the importance of information-sharing is stressed in statutory guidance.[19] Advice is available,[20] but clearer guidance is awaited in the wake of the Children Act 2004.

Data protection officers are responsible for dealing with information issues, and each local authority and NHS body should have a framework for intra- and interagency information-sharing. This includes a 'Caldicott guardian',[21] responsible for safeguarding and governing the use of personal information, who should have knowledge of child protection law, guidance and practice and an understanding of the overriding principle of protecting the child.

Immigration/refugee status

Guidance[22] is available on procedures for local authorities to obtain information on an individual's status (including a child in need) when contacting the Home Office Immigration and Nationality Department (HO IND), to ensure compliance with data protection requirements and on the HO IND's duty of confidentiality.

Education

Parents and older pupils are entitled to access school records (see Education (School Records) Regulations 1989, SI 1989/1261). But this does not authorise or require the disclosure of any information in relation to child protection: these records are exempt from the statutory disclosure provisions (i.e. Data Protection Act 1984: the Education (School Records) Regulations 1989 exempt manual records), but may be required in proceedings.

Records and record-keeping

Good, accurate, records are essential, but most major inspection and inquiry reports highlight poor case recording as an obstacle to planning and decision-making. Coherent information and systems management in and between key agencies lack clarity and consistency and current arrangements have not been exemplary despite (or perhaps because of) computer systems.[23] But there are plans to introduce electronic social care and health records: the former are to replace current Assessment Framework and LAC records by December 2005 through the Integrated Children's System.

All records and reports should be objective, based on evidence and distinguish between fact, observation, allegation and opinion. Good record-keeping requires obvious, but often neglected, noting of dates, events and action taken and signatures.

5.6 SAFEGUARDING AND COOPERATION

The Area Child Protection Committee or Local Safeguarding Children Board

The ACPC[24] is responsible for overseeing the child protection system in each area. Its replacement, the LSCB, will have statutory membership, functions and procedures (under Children Act 2004 and Regulations to be published). But, in essence, both are an interagency forum made up of representatives from all local agencies with a role in child protection, including social services, police, health, education and probation.

Responsibilities include:

- a proactive role in local safeguarding and cooperation arrangements;
- establishing and monitoring local procedures and related training;
- promoting effective interagency working relationships;
- raising wider community awareness of safeguarding;
- conducting Part 8 case reviews on child deaths or concerns about inter-agency working where a child is harmed or dies;[25]
- complaints, and general review of individual cases (so concerns about individuals and agencies can be raised with the ACPC/LSCB).

Social services/children's services authorities

Social work staff have some difficult people and circumstances to deal with, are often the target for criticism, and their sense of vocation underestimated. They exercise state power in significant decisions about children's removal from their family, placements and future, which should rarely be taken in isolation. They need (see *Arthurworrey (Lisa)* v. *Secretary of State for Education and Skills* [2004] PC 268, Care Standards Tribunal):

- professional confidence based on good training, managerial support and administrative systems for recording and managing information;
- a broad knowledge of human development, parenting and caring abilities, environmental stresses and diversity, and the law;
- good decision-making skills and professional judgments;
- a good understanding of different professional perspectives/approaches.

Police

Emergencies

Chapter 6 has details of police powers, but note that police protection powers are often exercised by ordinary officers, not specialist Child Protection Unit officers. Police should usually obtain legal advice and always consider whether action is required to safeguard other children.

Child protection

Specialist teams of specifically trained officers (the 'Child Protection/Family Protection Unit') work jointly with social workers and should clarify the basis for criminal investigation, and any processes relevant to other agencies, including timing and methods of evidence gathering. Efforts are still needed to raise the status of this work in the force generally.

Information-sharing

Police have a common law power to disclose information for the prevention, detection and reduction of crime. Safeguarding requires their commitment to:

- sharing information where necessary;
- the attendance of officers at child protection conferences who are fully informed about the case, experienced in risk assessment and the process;
- checks on criminal records and sex offender registers.

As regards the police's use of 'soft intelligence' (i.e. information held by police pursuant to a series of complaints not resulting in criminal prosecution) criticism has led to national changes.[26]

Other agencies are expected to share information 'to enable the police to carry out their duties', but statutory cooperation (Children Act 1989, ss.27 and 47) does *not* specify police so full reciprocity with the police is not possible.

The CPS should be consulted about evidence gathered during a criminal investigation, which will normally be shared in the child's interests.

Protocols exist for the exchange of information between CPS, police and local authorities and for dealing with requests for exchange of information in police records (to avoid the need for court applications in domestic abuse and child protection cases).[27]

Joint investigations

The Climbié Inquiry demonstrated the importance of understanding clearly the respective agency roles/responsibilities/boundaries, especially between police and social services. The police:

- are the lead agency for the purpose of a criminal investigation;
- have a duty to carry out prompt, efficient, thorough and professional investigations into allegations of crime;
- have guidance on their new safeguarding duty;[28]
- must respond to information from social services and decide what further action it might be necessary to take.

Obtaining clear, strong evidence will always be in a child's best interests, reducing the likelihood of having to give evidence in criminal proceedings.

Children Act 1989, s.47 enquiries may run concurrently with police investigations and may produce information relevant to decisions for both agencies. The most common joint investigations concern direct allegations of sexual abuse, all cases of serious assault and persistent abuse and may be more likely for domestic violence (see criminal offence under the Domestic Violence, Crime and Victims Act 2004).

Both police and social services may contribute to criminal and/or civil proceedings – ACPC/LSCB protocols should provide guidance on the conduct of the respective investigations, supported by comprehensive training. Both agencies need to work together to create a planned, coordinated basis for future support and help to the child and family.

Health

A named doctor and nurse ('designated health professionals') responsible for child protection issues should be in all major health settings. This is reinforced in NSF Standards, which require:

- interpreting services;
- contemporaneous, clear, accurate, comprehensive hospital care records;
- adequate support and supervision for staff;
- staff and service users able to report incidents affecting a child's safety.

Health staff, especially those working in Accident and Emergency (A&E) departments and minor injury centres should:[29]

- know how to make enquiries of the child protection register in accordance with local procedures;

- have access to specialist paediatric advice at all times (which should also be available to all wards caring for children);
- know where and how to access sources of information and advice, including from designated health professionals;
- have access to advice and discussion on child welfare concerns with other professional colleagues/managers;
- never delay emergency action to protect a child;
- have access to good interpreters and/or the *Emergency Multilingual Phrasebook* for A&E staff;[30]
- where a child is in hospital, consider, discuss and agree how best to ensure her safe transfer when she is fit for discharge, with other core agencies.

General practitioners can provide helpful information, often crucially for children not in formal education, but their attendance at conferences is not high (timing and payment are obstacles) despite guidance.[31] Primary Care Trusts' safeguarding duty may change that.

Education[32]

The 2004 guidance[33] sets out the specific roles and responsibilities of the education service and practitioners should be aware of relevant local policies and procedures – for general discussion, see Chapter 13.

Pupils are owed a moral responsibility, a general duty of care and a direct safeguarding duty (Education Act 2002, s.175). School staff are in a unique position to identify and help abused children. More child protection referrals come from schools than from any other source, so they, and professionals from local education authorities (LEAs), are likely to become involved in providing information about a child to social services. There are statutory duties and responsibilities on the independent sector (Education Act 2002, s.157), maintained special schools and boarding schools.

Schools and LEAs must follow local authority and ACPC/LSCB policies and procedures. All staff have a role to play in child protection: it should not be assumed that junior/administrative staff have nothing to contribute – their observations can be just as valuable as those from more senior staff. A lunchtime or playground supervisor, or a caretaker, may well see and hear a child in less guarded moments than staff involved in more formal curriculum duties (see, e.g. the role of the school caretaker in *Z* v. *UK* [2001] 2 FLR 612).

There must be a 'designated teacher' in each school, known to staff and pupils, with responsibility for:[34]

- liaising with social services and other agencies in cases of actual/suspected abuse;
- making referrals or discussing issues with investigating agencies according to relevant local ACPC/LSCB/LEA procedures;

- detailed recording of concerns, including agency contacts, identifying those involved, the source and the action taken;
- ensuring they have appropriate, practical in-service training.

The guidance also provides that:

- child protection investigations must *not* be carried out by schools or LEAs;
- staff must report all concerns to the designated teacher, who must inform social services about allegations or suspicions;
- no school/LEA should warn people of pending investigations by social services or police in case the investigation is prejudiced, but parents need to be kept informed during an investigation; the only restriction on this is when the school may wish to await the outcome of a police/social services investigation.

Allegations against staff [35]

All schools should have clear recruitment, vetting and reporting procedures, and an environment that encourages pupils and staff to make truthful reports of any inappropriate behaviour. Any incident where there are grounds to believe staff/volunteers have crossed the boundary of acceptable behaviour should be reported and pupils should not feel inhibited from so doing.

Probation

A register of 'risky adults' is maintained in some areas to facilitate the protection of children with whom a known or suspected abuser might associate in the future. The multi-agency public protection arrangements for community management of high risk offenders include probation staff. Staff are also involved in substance misuse and anger management programmes.

Armed services [36]

Where there are investigations relating to the children of serving personnel, a representative of the relevant service will be involved. Each service has the support of social work staff and the lead organisation is the Soldiers, Sailors, Airmen and Families Association (SSAFA) Forces Help (UK).

Service bases overseas can carry out investigations, exercise police protection powers (via military police) and make emergency protection applications, but cannot take care proceedings. A child who needs legal protection beyond the life of emergency measures must be returned to the UK and the jurisdiction of the relevant local authority.

5.7   CONDUCT OF CHILD PROTECTION INVESTIGATIONS

Referrals[37]

Child protection services should be well signposted locally,[38] and all allegations, from whatever source, taken seriously.

The Framework for Assessment has a 'Referral and Initial Information Record'. Feedback should be provided as far as possible to helpline staff and to the referrer (where there is an initial needs assessment or no further action), on what action has been taken (in a manner consistent with respecting the confidentiality of child and family).

Section 47 enquiries

These should determine whether safeguarding action is needed and should include consideration of the potential needs and safety of any siblings, other children in the household and children in other households where there may have been contact with the person under investigation.

At the same time, the police need to establish facts about any offence committed against a child, and to collect evidence.

Several sources of potentially relevant information can be identified, all of which have a duty to assist, but are not always considered. Housing services can provide information on possession proceedings, action by environmental health, etc. Fire and ambulance services can be crucial: there should be information protocols with Chief Officers. The police can provide information on convictions and cautions: it is important they do not determine what is important or not, so the information should come through the specialist child protection officer.

Specific protocols exist for the investigation of particular cases, such as sudden infant death[39] or fabricated illness, and these enquiries should have specialist advice from well trained police and medical personnel.

Strategy discussion

A strategy discussion should take place whenever there is reasonable cause to suspect significant harm, either following a referral or, e.g. following an emergency or notification of concerns about significant harm.

Social services (via a team manager/senior social worker) should convene a discussion immediately with police, and other appropriate agencies.[40] Its purpose is:

- to agree whether to initiate s.47 enquiries;
- to commence/complete a core assessment (unless application for an emergency protection order (EPO) is justified);

- to identify relevant tasks and timescales for each professional and agency, and agree what further help or support may be necessary.

Depending on the child's needs and the urgency of the situation, it can be an actual meeting, or a series of telephone conversations. In complex types of maltreatment/neglect, the former is likely to be the most effective. If circumstances are very complex, several discussions may be needed to consider the conduct of enquiries. The location should be convenient for key attendees and those attending should include:

- sufficiently senior agency staff able to contribute, and to make decisions, including the referring agency, the child's nursery/school and health workers;
- a senior doctor where medical examination is necessary/has already taken place;
- the responsible medical consultant where the child is a hospital patient or receiving services from a child development team;
- a senior ward nurse if the child is an in-patient.

Consider also obtaining the advice and/or attendance of additional professionals with expertise in the particular type of suspected maltreatment/neglect to enable complex information to be presented and evaluated, and the attendance of the local authority's solicitor.

Information provided should be verified at source, and presented in a clear and comprehensible format. If authorisation of disclosure is in doubt, it is best to obtain express consent unless contrary to a child's welfare, e.g. where information is needed urgently and delay in obtaining it may not be justified, or where seeking consent may prejudice a police investigation or increase the risk of harm to the child.

The principal tasks of the strategy discussion are to:

- share available information;
- agree the conduct and timing of any criminal investigation;
- decide on the most appropriate timing of parental participation and the effect on the conduct of any police investigations;[41]
- decide whether s.47 enquiries should be initiated or continued;
- plan enquiries and decide whether a core assessment should be initiated or continued;
- identify further information needed about the child and family and how to obtain it.

If grounds justify enquiries, decisions should be made on their conduct identifying tasks, timing, responsibilities and purpose of the enquiries, including:

- any medical treatment needed;
- further information about the child and family;

101

- interviews;
- core assessment;
- immediate and short-term safeguarding action required;
- provision of interim services and support;
- safe discharge of a child in hospital;
- information to be shared with the family and how (unless this may place a child at risk of significant harm or jeopardise police investigations);
- any legal action required, including further action where emergency powers have been exercised.

All information shared, all decisions reached, and the basis for this, should be clearly recorded by all parties to the discussion and recorded with the actions taken on the Strategy Discussion Record,[42] which should be sent to all relevant professionals and agencies. Decisions should be kept under review.

Relevant considerations include the race and ethnicity of the child and family, and how this should be taken into account in enquiries, and whether an interpreter will be needed; and the needs of other children who may be affected, e.g. siblings and other children in contact with alleged abusers.

Interviews, assessments and examinations

Investigations should usually include interviews with parents and/or carers, and observation of the interactions between them and the child, and with those personally and professionally connected with the child and parents and/or carers.

Following the Climbié Inquiry, children's wishes and feelings must be ascertained and given due consideration in child protection investigations (Children Act 1989, s.47 as amended by Children Act 2004, s.53). Children are a key, and sometimes the only, source of information about what has happened to them: accurate and complete information is essential for safeguarding and for any criminal proceedings.

Clarity about the nature and extent of any harm suffered or whether a criminal offence has been committed may not be available and the timing and handling of interviews with victims, families and witnesses can have important implications for the collection and preservation of evidence. The way in which they are conducted can also play a significant part in minimising any distress caused to children, and increasing the likelihood of maintaining constructive working relationships with families.

Therefore, it is important that:

- even initial discussions with children minimise distress;
- the child should be seen separately;
- leading/suggestive communication is always avoided;
- time and opportunity are given to children to develop sufficient trust to

communicate, especially if they have communication/learning difficulties, are very young or have mental health problems.

Achieving best evidence

Achieving Best Evidence in Criminal Proceedings[43] contains essential guidance:

- assessments must inform investigation and take the Assessment Framework as a guide for considering the child in her family context;
- assessment may need to happen prior to an investigation, particularly if the child has no previous or current involvement with social services or other agencies;
- early specialist assessments are advisable where there are any signs of confusion, or potential difficulty in participating, giving a reliable account of events or giving a statement at all.

Achieving Best Evidence also sets out general factors to consider in setting up witness interviews, including the child's ability and willingness to talk within a formal interview setting; the levels of cognitive, social and emotional development, past experiences and any apparent clinical or psychiatric problems which may affect the interview; and the child's competency to give consent to the interview and medical examination.

It gives detailed advice on talking to children and other vulnerable witnesses: how to avoid 'leading' them, whilst also not stopping free recall and emphasising the need for interviewers to have the necessary experience and expertise to evaluate responses or to make a referral to a specialist.

Exceptionally, a joint enquiries/investigation team may need to speak to the child without the knowledge of the parent or carer, e.g. where a child would be threatened or otherwise coerced into silence; where there is a strong likelihood that important evidence would be destroyed; or where a competent child does not wish the parent to be involved.

Full participation in the enquiry process may need to be facilitated by communication aids or interpreters, if a child or parent is disabled or speaks a language other than that spoken by the interviewer.

If a child is unable to take part because of age or understanding, 'alternative means of understanding her perspective should be used', including observation where the child is very young or there are communication impairments.

Framework for Assessment

The Framework for Assessment contributes a structure for collection and analysis of information obtained. Assessments (covered in more detail in Chapter 8) should include:

- a core assessment of the child's needs and the capacity of their parents or wider family network adequately to ensure their safety, health and development, building a picture of the child's situation from as many sources of information as possible;
- specific professional examinations/assessments of the child (medical/developmental checks, assessment of emotional/psychological state, etc.).

Professionals should make every effort to get willing cooperation and participation by explaining and justifying actions, and demonstrating that the investigation is being done in a way that will help the child.

Consent

Consent to examination or treatment in investigations or provision of services is a matter for the medical professional concerned, not anyone else. Helpful and comprehensive guidance on consent issues is available.[44]

5.8   CHILD PROTECTION CONFERENCES

See the Local Government Act 1972, s.112. Multidisciplinary meetings to discuss individual cases are either *initial* or *review* conferences.

Initial child protection conference

This is convened in an emergency, or where s.47 enquiries conclude that a child is at continuing risk of suffering, or is likely to suffer, significant harm. It is normally held within 15 days of the end of the last strategy discussion. Its tasks must include deciding:

- whether the child is at continuing risk;
- what steps must be taken to protect her;
- whether registration is appropriate and in which category.[45]

    If protection is required, tasks are:

- drawing up the inter-agency child protection plan;
- allocation of a key social worker;
- identification of a 'core group' to develop and implement the plan, with timescales;
- establishing how the child and family should be involved in planning;
- identifying what further assessments are required;
- a contingency plan.

    The core group[46] is led by the key worker (responsible for a written record of action agreed, decisions taken and updating the plan) and should include the child, if appropriate, family members, and professionals and foster carers in direct contact with the family. Its tasks include:[47]

- meeting within 10 working days and sufficiently regularly to facilitate action and outcomes;
- ensuring the child's best interests always take precedence over those of other family members, especially where there are conflicts of interest;
- developing, refining and monitoring the child protection plan, providing reports for conferences;
- arranging for the provision of appropriate services whilst awaiting completion of any specialist assessment(s).

Convening and preparation

Any agency or professional may initiate a conference, but the social services department (or NSPCC) is responsible for setting it up, and should provide a written report summarising and analysing assessment information.

Where there are concerns that an unborn child may be at future risk of significant harm, there may be a pre-birth conference. This has the same status and procedure, but the involvement of midwifery services is vital.[48]

Full and effective participation of all professionals and, as far as possible, that of the child and family members needs careful planning: the role of the independent Chair is crucial, and a model agenda is available.[49]

Conference Chairs may decide to exclude a family member altogether when, with a little planning, it would be possible to involve them, e.g. by meeting with the Chair separately or being present for only part of the meeting. Practitioners need to be aware of this and, where appropriate, challenge decisions to exclude and suggest ways in which the client's views can be available to the conference.

Attendance, participation and representation

The child's welfare is the overriding factor: guidance[50] stresses full participation of children and parents at all stages of the child protection process, particularly at conferences. It also gives advice on arrangements to facilitate this attendance and on the exceptional circumstances in which they may be excluded.

Those attending should be there because they have a significant contribution to make. Parents, family members (including the wider family) and 'significant others' should be invited to attend, as far as possible, for the whole of the conference and helped to participate fully, unless, in the Chair's view, their presence would preclude a full and proper consideration of the child's interests.

Parents and family

Local authority practice and policies on conference conduct and attendance have been the subject of several challenges. The days of banning lawyers from attending or refusing to provide parents with minutes should now be long gone (see *R* v. *Cornwall CC, ex p. LH* [2000] 1 FLR 236). A procedure on justified exclusion is perfectly permissible, but blanket bans on attendance of parents/solicitors are unlawful. Parents or their solicitors should be allowed to attend, and the parent is entitled to the minutes on the part she attended (*R* v. *Cornwall CC, ex p. LH* [2000] 1 FLR 236).

Failure to invite parents to attend is not necessarily unfair or unreasonable (*R* v. *Harrow LBC, ex p. D* [1990] 3 All ER 12, [1990] 1 FLR 79, but see *Re M (Care: Challenging Decisions by Local Authority)* [2001] 2 FLR 1300), but ECHR compliance and their personal knowledge of the child dictate that every encouragement should be given to them, and to members of the wider family.

Parents should be given information about sources of help and advice, and told that they may bring an advocate, friend or supporter.[51] If these are not lawyers, they need to be 'people who can be seen to be independent of the local or other public authority, but equally people who can win the trust and confidence of both "sides"'.[52] The Chair should make the role of the supporter clear before the meeting: this will probably be covered in the local ACPC/LSCB procedures.

Child or young person

Children or young persons should also be encouraged, depending upon age and understanding, and provided it will not be a detrimental experience. The views of those not present should also be represented. Practitioners acting for children should ensure that, preferably, the guardian gives the child's views, or alternatively the practitioner should do so.

Exclusions

Participation of family members has to be carefully planned and the effect of factors such as allegations of organised abuse, domestic violence or sexual abuse taken into account. There must be a ACPC/LSCB policy on attendance and participation,[53] but it is for the conference Chair to decide on its implementation in each individual case. The Chair may consider it necessary (in what should be exceptional circumstances) to exclude either/both parents or other family members from part or all of the conference, e.g. where:[54]

- one of them is the alleged abuser;
- there is a high level of conflict between the family members;

- adults and/or a child who wish to make representations to the conference may not wish to speak in front of each other;
- information is to be shared about an ongoing police investigation.

But reasons must be given and social workers must ensure the conference has family background information and parents' views on the issues,[55] regardless of who attends. If possible, the individual should be excluded from part, rather than the whole, of the meeting.

Professionals and other relevant personnel

The guidance does not set a quorum for a child protection conference, although local ACPC/LSCB procedures may impose one. There should be sufficient information and expertise available to enable the conference to make an informed decision.[56]

Professionals and others involved with the child and/or family, including those who know the child and/or have reported the suspected abuse, or have been involved in inquiries, such as the police, should attend.

This should include staff from health and education (the teacher with the best knowledge of the child, accompanied by the headteacher, if the school deems appropriate). They should be involved in preparation of the interagency child protection plan, and their role and contribution stated clearly in that plan.[57]

Where a child has been injured, the relevant file, including all X-rays and other medical notes and reports, should be available at the conference and presented by a health professional with sufficient ability and understanding to do so.

The children's guardian should be notified and given the option to attend conferences and statutory reviews (Wall J in *Re M (A Minor) (Application for a Care Order)* [1995] 3 FCR 611 at 634). Attendance is a matter for her professional judgment and discretion, taking into account the potential for compromising independent status in the eyes of the parents or the appropriateness of witnessing local authority deliberations, even as an observer.

Others who may helpfully attend include foster carers (current or former); NSPCC or other voluntary organisations; and an armed services representative, if there is a service connection.

Legal representation

The relevant, up-to-date Law Society guidance must be followed: local ACPC/LSCB procedures are likely to cover this.

Practitioners from the firms representing parents and child should be invited, to assist their client to express their views and participate in the conference and to speak on their behalf, subject to the Chair's permission (clarify their role with the Chair beforehand[58] to avoid any misunderstandings).

Details of the local authority lawyer's role are in Chapter 22 but general principles are:

- where other parties are present, she should not use their ability to attend without the other party's lawyer being present to unfair advantage;[59]
- she attends as a legal expert, not a full participant;
- lawyers acting for other parties cannot object to her presence.

Alternative advocacy services

The role of alternative advocacy services is not explored in *Working Together*, but the Judicial Case Management Protocol emphasises the importance of clear pre-proceedings preparation and European and domestic case law emphasises the importance of informed participation in decision-making in order to comply with ECHR Articles 8 and 6. Regulations, guidance and national standards govern local authority duties to arrange advocacy for children making representations/complaints. The Legal Services Commission recognises that public funding should be more focused on earlier processes than proceedings.[60]

Guidance and standards for lay and specialist advocates in several settings is available, but compliance with professional guidance and rules for any lawyer takes precedence over any protocol. Such supporters/advocates may be involved in the early stages of involvement with a case, followed by representation from a specialist legal practitioner. This raises the potential for confusion and conflict unless care is taken in communicating information and ensuring consistency. Local authority practitioners should assist in resolving these issues.

Information and reports

Social services should[61] provide a written report summarising and analysing the information obtained during initial assessment, to include:

- a chronology of significant events;
- information about the child's health and development;
- information on the capacity of the parents and other family members to protect the child and promote her development;
- the wishes and feelings of the child, parents and other family members;
- analysis of the implications of the information obtained for the child's future safety.

Parents should be provided with a copy of reports in advance, i.e. in sufficient time to consider the contents, not as they are walking into the conference.

The Chair

The Chair plays a pivotal role in establishing 'an ethos in which openness and honesty can thrive',[62] ensuring the conference 'focuses on the child as the primary client whose interests must transcend those of the parents and other carers when there is any conflict,'[63] and in clarifying the role of lawyers attending conferences.

Conferences are inquisitorial and should be conducted reasonably, without aggression. Any difficulties should be raised with the Chair. If the Chair cannot resolve the difficulty, a complaint can be referred to an inter-agency panel.[64]

Minutes

The child protection conference embraces a range of difficult cases that may never enter the family justice system and it is 'absolutely essential that there should be the fullest cooperation between the two systems in those cases where both are involved'.[65]

Increasingly, many conferences do not result in proceedings. Since the prime purpose is to enable professionals and the family to share information and concerns, to consider registration, and to formulate an outline care and protection plan together, it is arguably a therapeutic process, rather than a legal one, and does not follow the forensic processes familiar to lawyers. It is neither a 'pre-trial review' nor a dress rehearsal for court proceedings.

The Judicial Case Management Protocol may help to curb the all too common practice of automatically appending case conference minutes to statements or applications. Minutes are not usually taken by social work professionals and are not necessarily accurate or detailed records of discussions (especially taking into account the hidden tensions referred to above). Minutes are disclosable (*Re L (Care: Assessment: Fair Trial)* [2002] EWHC Fam 1379, [2002] 2 FLR 730), but their wholesale use as reliable first-hand evidence to support or refute facts should be discouraged.

Decision and recommendations

Conference makes *recommendations*, but its only formal *decision* is whether to register the name of the child on the child protection register. This is not binding upon the local authority, but is a recommendation for action. It should not, therefore, consider the planning/conduct of s.47 investigations or decide whether court proceedings should be initiated: it may *recommend* consideration of court action, but initiation is for the local authority.

Registration on the child protection register

The test for registration is 'Is the child at continuing risk of significant harm?'. This conclusion can be based *either* on observed harm, coupled with the likelihood of future harm, *or* on the outcomes of assessments, coupled with professional judgment that the child is likely to suffer harm.[66]

Whatever the chosen category,[67] the decision must be based on evidence of harm or likelihood of harm to the *individual* child, for example:

- to justify registration for emotional abuse, there must be sufficient information about persistent/severe emotional ill-treatment/rejection likely to have a severe adverse effect on a child's emotional and behavioural development;
- medical/psychological evidence may not be essential if there is an assessment by a relevant professional;
- lack of attendance from the child's school/GP may add to the risk that registration would not be justified;
- evidence of physical abuse of a sibling is not sufficient to justify registration in another category (*R* v. *Hampshire CC, ex p. H* [1999] 2 FLR 359);
- if parents are unable/unwilling to work in partnership with agencies, that does not necessarily mean either is likely to harm their child, but the lack of cooperation in itself may be a factor to be taken into account when deciding whether or not to register a child;
- simultaneous registration under two or more categories should be the exception rather than the rule; in particular, the 'emotional abuse' category should only be used as a second category where emotional abuse is a major concern in its own right, not just the inevitable consequence of other harm;[68]
- the fact that the court has declined to make findings in relation to alleged abuse does not prevent a child protection conference treating the same allegations as the basis for registration (*North Yorkshire CC* v. *S and S* [2005] EWCA Civ 316).

Recording the name of alleged or known abusers

ECHR Articles 6 and 8 require fairness, i.e. giving a party an opportunity to know the case against him and allowing him to be heard, so careful consideration is required when deciding to put the name of an alleged abuser on the main, or a supplementary register. This will be unfair and unreasonable if the procedure denies that person all opportunity of advance warning of its intention, or of prior consultation, or of being heard to object, or of knowing the full circumstances surrounding the decision (*R* v. *Norfolk CC, ex p. M* [1989] 2 All ER 359; and *R* v. *Harrow LBC, ex p. D* [1990] Fam. 133, [1990] 1 FLR 79) as will removal of a foster parent's name from the approved list without giving an opportunity to answer allegations.

A child protection review conference must:

- be held within three months of the initial conference and at regular inter-vals of not more than six months throughout the child protection process;
- review the child's safety, health and development;
- explicitly consider the current level of risk to the child and review arrangements for her protection or deregistration;
- review the child protection plan.

A conference to deregister a child should have the same quorum and decision-making procedure as for registration.[69]

Distinguish between reviews held by a responsible authority and confer-ences: if a conference considers wider issues affecting the child's plan, it is part of a review (see Review of Children's Cases Regulations 1991, SI 1991/895, regs 2, 3).

The reasons for deregistration are that the child:[70]

- is no longer at continuing risk of significant harm, and does not require safeguarding by means of a child protection plan;
- the family have moved permanently to another area; or
- the child has reached the age of 18 or died.

Family group conference[71]

Non-court-based processes may provide assistance in the case, particularly family group conferences, which are a growing area of social work practice. They can be a useful tool to avoid the issue of proceedings or can be recom-mended by the court to take place during the course of proceedings, where appropriate.

The conference is a decision-making forum focusing on the child's welfare. The wider family, and sometimes friends, meet and are given information by the relevant agencies on the child's needs and the reasons why a decision is required. They are given time on their own to make a decision that promotes and safeguards the child's welfare. In care proceedings, this may be helpful in:

- identifying family/community supports to make it safe for a child to live with her parents; or
- identifying a placement in the wider family if the child cannot do so; or
- where a kinship placement is not possible, allowing the wider family to support the plan for the child.

Adult clients should be strongly advised and encouraged to attend any such conference, bearing in mind family members or family friends who have not been invited, yet may have something to contribute.

In some areas of the country, mediation may be used, although this is at present unusual and will, for obvious reasons, not be suitable for some cases.

NOTES

1　Dr R. Kempe.
2　See 'Every Child Matters – Change for Children' programme at **www.everychild matters.gov.uk**.
3　No single document despite recommendations of *Climbié Inquiry Report* (2003) and see quantity of 'Every Child Matters' guidance.
4　*Working Together to Safeguard Children*, DH, Home Office, DfEE (1999), under revision in 2005. See supplementary guidance *Safeguarding Children Involved in Prostitution*, DH (2000), and *Safeguarding Children in Whom Illness is Fabricated or Induced*, DH (2002); and see also All Wales Child Protection Procedures (2004).
5　DfES (2003), advisory only, but replaces Appendix 5 of *Working Together* and supplements *Medical Responsibilities: Guidance to Doctors, and Guidance for Senior Nurses*, etc.
6　DfES (2004).
7　London and Wales have policies and procedures applicable to a much wider area.
8　Lord Laming, *Climbié Inquiry Report* (2003).
9　See J. Hunt and A. McLeod, Last Resort, Child Protection, Courts and Children Act, HMSO (1999).
10　R. Sinclair, 'Involving Children in Planning their Care: Research Review' (1998) 3 *Child and Family Social Work* 137.
11　'Hearing the Children', President's Interdisciplinary Conference 2003, Jordans (2004).
12　B. Lindley, *On the Receiving End*, Family Rights Group (1994).
13　Children Act Advisory Committee Report (1992).
14　R. Dingwall, J. Eekelaar and T. Murray, *The Protection of Children: State Intervention and Family Life*, Oxford, Blackwell (1983).
15　D. Platt and D. Shemmings, *Making Enquiries into Alleged Child Abuse and Neglect: Partnership with Families*, Pennant (1996).
16　'General Family Help' in LSC *Manual*, vol. 3 p. 3C-153, para. 20.8(3).
17　See (statutory) National Standards for the Provision of Children's Advocacy Services, DH (November 2002) and LAC(2004)11; and (advisory only) B. Lindley and M. Richards, *Protocol on Advice and Advocacy for Parents (Child Protection)*, University of Cambridge, for Department of Health (2002).
18　See *Working Together* and Appendix 1 of *What to Do If You are Worried a Child is Being Abused*, DH (2003); see also *Cross-Government Guidance – Sharing Information on Children and Young People*, DfES (consultation draft August 2005).
19　See *Working Together*.
20　Appendix 3 of *What To Do If You're Worried a Child is Being Abused* and *Data Sharing for Public Authorities*, DCA (2002).
21　See *Implementing the Caldicott Standard into Social Care*, HSC 2002/003, LAC(2002)2; *Protecting and Using Patient Information, A Manual for Caldicott Guardians*, NHS Executive, DH (1999) and further information at **www.doh.gov.uk/ipu/socialcare/caldicott.htm** or **www.doh.gov.uk/ipu/confiden**.
22　Guidance to Local Authorities on Contact with Home Office Immigration and Nationality Department (December 2003).
23　Chief Inspector Social Services, December 1993; SSI Inspection Overview 1995; DH 'Quality Protects Management Information' (October 2000).
24　See individual and national websites at **www.dfes.gov.uk**.
25　For further details see Part 8 of *Working Together*.

26 The Bichard Inquiry led to a Statutory Code of Practice on police information management (in force May 2005) and national IT system for police information-sharing (IMPACT): see Home Office Progress Report (December 2004) at **www.homeoffice.gov.uk**.

27 Being piloted in London, Manchester, Merseyside and Lancashire, see **www.dca.gov.uk**.

28 Children Act 2004 and see *Guidance on Investigating Child Abuse and Safeguarding Children*, ACPO and Centrex (2005). See also *Guidelines on Investigating Infant Deaths*, ACPO (2002); *Guidance on Investigating Domestic Violence*, ACPO and Centrex (2004); *Complex Child Abuse Investigations: Inter-Agency Issues*, Home Office and DH (2002), Welsh Assembly (2003).

29 See *Working Together*, para. 5.4.

30 In 36 languages, endorsed by the British Association for Emergency Medicine, intended for initial assessment until trained interpreter contacted, Red Cross and DH (2003).

31 See Y. Carter and M. Bannon, *The Role of Primary Care in the Protection of Children from Abuse and Neglect*, Royal College of General Practitioners (2002) at **www.rcgp.org.uk/corporate/position/childprotection.pdf**.

32 See **www.teachernet.gov.uk/childprotection** with examples of good practice and model policies.

33 *Safeguarding Children in Education*, DfES (2004).

34 Reinforced in *Safeguarding Children in Education*.

35 New guidance is due and staff help is available from the Investigation and Referral Support Coordinators network; also from **www.lg-employers.gov.uk/conditions/education/allegations**.

36 See *Working Together*, paras 3.89–3.96, and see Defence Council Instruction (Joint Service) (DCI(JS)), Ministry of Defence. See also Armed Forces Act 1991, ss.17–23 (and Tri-Services Bill 2004).

37 See *Working Together,* paras 5.12–5.17.

38 See Local Authority Social Services Letter LASSL(2004)7.

39 *The Kennedy Report, Sudden Unexpected Death In Infancy, A Multi-Agency Protocol for Care and Investigation*, Royal Colleges of Pathologists, Paediatrics and Child Health (2004); *Guidelines on Investigating Infant Deaths*, ACPO (2002); *Sudden Unexpected Deaths in Infancy: A Suggested Approach for Police and Coroner's Officers*, Foundation for the Study of Infant Deaths (2002); **www.sids.org.uk/fsid/**.

40 See *Working Together*, para. 5.12.

41 *Complex Child Abuse Investigations: Inter-Agency Issues*, Home Office and DH (2002), Welsh assembly (2003) and at **www.homeoffice.gov.uk/docs/child_abuse_guidance.pdf**.

42 DH (2002).

43 *Achieving Best Evidence in Criminal Proceedings: Guidance for Vulnerable or Intimidated Witnesses Including Children*, Home Office, LCD, CPS, DH and Welsh National Assembly (2002).

44 **www.doh.gov.uk**.

45 See *Working Together*.

46 *What To Do If You are Worried a Child is Being Abused*, para. 52.4.

47 See *Working Together*, paras 5.79 and 5.91 and *What To Do If You are Worried a Child is Being Abused*, para. 52.

48 *What To Do If You are Worried a Child is Being Abused*, para. 50.

49 See pro-forma agenda, *Challenge of Partnership in Child Protection*, SSI (1995).

50 *Working Together*, paras 5.57–5.58; *Challenge of Partnership*, ch. 2; Children Act Guidance, vol. 3, para. 8.16.

51 *Working Together*, para. 5.57.
52 Munby J, NYAS lecture, February 2004.
53 *Working Together*, para. 4.18.
54 *Ibid.* para. 5.5.8.
55 *Report of the Inquiry into Child Abuse in Cleveland* (1987), p.246.
56 See *Working Together*, para. 5.55.
57 See *Working Together*, paras 3.12–3.13 and Framework for Assessment of Children in Need and their Families, DH, Home Office and DfEE (2000), paras 5.41–5.50.
58 Law Society Family Law Committee guidance, *Attendance of Solicitors at Child Protection Conferences* (June 1997).
59 *Arrangements for Handling Child Care Cases*, Association of Council Secretaries and Solicitors in Local Government: Child Care Law Joint Liaison Group (2004).
60 LSC Consultation, 2004.
61 *Working Together*, para. 5.61.
62 *Challenge of Partnership*, para. 7.16.
63 *Working Together*, para. 6.30.
64 See *Working Together*, para. 5.72.
65 Thorpe LJ in *Re M (Disclosure)* [1998] 1 FLR 734, which concerned the Family Proceedings Rules 1991, SI 1991/1247, rule 4.23(2) to material to be disclosed at a case conference.
66 See *Working Together*, para. 5.64.
67 See *Working Together* for details and bear in mind selection of categories may vary with time and professional understanding.
68 See *Safeguarding Children in Education*, DfES (2004).
69 *What To Do If You are Worried a Child is Being Abused*, para. 67.
70 *Working Together*, para 5.93.
71 For further information see **www.frg.org.uk**.

CHAPTER 6

Emergency powers

Key sources

- Children Act 1989, Part V
- Family Law Act 1996, s.42; Protection from Harassment Act 1997 ss.3–5; Domestic Violence, Crime and Victims Act 2004
- *Working Together* (1999), para. 5 as amended by *What To Do If You Are Worried A Child is Being Abused*, DH (2003), para. 22
- *Family Law Protocol*, Law Society (2002)
- HO Circular 44/03: *Duties and Powers of the Police under the Children Act 1989* (replaces HO Circular 54/1991)
- *Domestic Violence: A Resource Manual for Healthcare Professionals*, DH (2000)
- Hague Conference on Private International Law Permanent Bureau, *Guide to Good Practice* (2003)
- President's Guidance (Liaison between Courts and British Embassies and High Commissions Abroad) [2004] Fam Law 68
- *Policy for Prosecuting Cases of Domestic Violence*, CPS (2005)

6.1 INTRODUCTION

Emergency situations may arise before or during the course of proceedings. Wherever possible, these will require immediate action by some or all of those acting for parties. This chapter sets out the available remedies, but additional Law Society guidance is available (see Appendix 1).

Also covered are:

- the emergency situations that may lead a local authority to put in place protective measures for a child;
- the remedies available if a child is removed from its care;
- professional guidance on sudden infant death investigations;
- domestic abuse remedies and guidance in outline only (this topic in specific contexts is also in Chapters 8 and 9 on assessment and contact, but a detailed account of private law remedies is outside the scope of this book).

6.2   HUMAN RIGHTS AND DIVERSITY

Proportionality applies and courts should be aware of the limits to the proper use of *ex parte* emergency applications and orders. (See Ryder J in *Haringey LBC* v. *C (A Child), E and another intervening* [2004] EWHC Fam 2580; *X Council* v. *B (Emergency Protection Orders)* [2004] EWHC 2015, [2005] 2 FLR 47, [2004] 1 FLR 341.)

Considerable care and sensitivity are required in intervention, but especially so when dealing with the particular circumstances of children and families from different cultures, or with prior adverse experiences (e.g. asylum seekers/refugees), or special needs.

6.3   THE ROLE OF THE STATUTORY AGENCIES

Emergency action

Neglect, as well as abuse, can pose such a risk of significant harm to a child that urgent protective action is needed. This might be necessary as soon as a referral is received, or at any point in involvement with children and families as more is learned about their circumstances. The necessity for action to safeguard other children in the same household (e.g. siblings), the household of an alleged perpetrator or elsewhere, should always be considered.

If there is reasonable cause to suspect the child is suffering, or is likely to suffer significant harm, an agency with statutory child protection powers, i.e. social services, police or NSPCC, should act quickly to secure her immediate safety.

Planned emergency action normally occurs following an immediate strategy discussion between police, social services and other agencies as appropriate. Where *immediate* action is necessary to protect a child, this discussion should take place as soon as possible afterwards to plan next steps.

In some cases, a parent taking action to remove an alleged perpetrator or his agreeing to leave the home may be sufficient to secure a child's safety. In others, it may be necessary to ensure the child remains in, or is removed to, a safe place, either on a voluntary basis or by obtaining an emergency protection order (EPO). If the child's removal is necessary, a local authority should wherever possible (unless her safety is otherwise at immediate risk) apply for an EPO, and not rely on police protection powers (see below). Courts should make magistrates available out of hours, rather than expecting the local authority to rely on the police.

Responsibility for emergency action lies with the local authority in whose area a child is found. It must consult any other authority looking after her or that has her on its child protection register and is only relieved of its responsibility if the other authority explicitly accepts responsibility, which should be confirmed in writing.

Emergency action addresses only immediate circumstances and should be followed quickly by s.47 enquiries as necessary. The agencies primarily involved with the child and family should then assess the child and the family's circumstances and agree action to safeguard the child in the longer term and promote her welfare. If there is an EPO, social services need to consider quickly whether to initiate legal proceedings, or let the order lapse so the child returns home.

Legal advice should be obtained before initiating legal action:

- 'no emergency action . . . should be taken without first obtaining this' and it must be 'available 24 hours a day';[1]
- 'no legal proceedings should be initiated unless [it] has been given . . . there should be sufficient legal staff available [to advise conferences and meetings as required] . . . the Head of Service [should] ensure appropriate arrangements . . . [for] access to out of hours legal advice';[2]
- it 'should always be sought when time allows'.[3]

If the social worker considers that a criminal offence may have been committed against a child, she should involve the police as soon as possible, unless there are exceptional reasons not to do so, and consider with them and other relevant agencies how to safeguard the child. She should see the child (as part of safeguarding decisions) (Children Act 2004, s.53(3)), acknowledging that the police have the lead role in investigating crime.

Strategy discussion

Its purpose, composition and conduct should follow the model set out in Chapter 5, and consider s.47 enquiries and core assessment, and EPO application (unless appropriate alternative arrangements have been made with the authority where the child normally lives).

Tasks must include agreeing what immediate and short-term action is required to safeguard the child, and should include considering:

- how to secure the safe discharge of a child in hospital;
- what further action is required where the child is subject to an EPO or police protection;
- consent issues: consent should be obtained unless information is needed urgently and delay may not be justified, and/or seeking it may prejudice a police investigation or increase risk of harm to the child.

Role of health staff and police

The general safeguarding roles of key agencies are dealt with in Chapter 5, but the following points are particularly important here.

Health staff, especially those working in Accident and Emergency (A&E) departments and minor injury centres have a crucial role and should:[4]

- have ready access to specialist paediatric advice and designated professionals;
- obtain a full history, including details of previous admissions to hospital;
- never delay emergency action to protect a child;
- always discuss and agree safe transfer on discharge with other core agencies.

The police must:[5]

- respond to information from whatever source;
- decide what further action is necessary;
- take full responsibility for prompt and efficient criminal investigations;
- usually obtain prior legal advice, especially when an EPO is being sought;
- always consider any safeguarding action required for other children in the same household (e.g. siblings), in the household of an alleged perpetrator or elsewhere; the nature of the abuse is a key determinant and if a child's life is in danger, then immediate action should be taken;
- discuss the basis for any criminal investigation, and any relevant processes, including timing and methods of evidence-gathering.

Sudden infant death

The roles of both police and social services are critical in cases of unexplained baby deaths. The huge variance in practice and the high profile cases involving Sally Clarke, Trupti Patel and Angela Cannings in 2003 led to recommendations for a consistent national approach to the conduct of investigations to be made compulsory. Details of a professional multi-agency protocol are contained in the Kennedy Report,[6] which sets out in detail the respective professional roles of paediatrician, pathologist and police.[7]

6.4   POLICE POWERS

Police protection powers

In addition to their criminal investigation duty, police have powers to ensure the immediate protection of children believed to be suffering from, or at risk of, significant harm by taking them into police protection (Children Act 1989, s.46) or applying for an EPO.

These are exercised inconsistently, not well understood and the relationship with EPOs is subject to poor practice: all local authorities should have arrangements to enable out-of-hours applications for EPOs to be made quickly. Recent research showed:[8]

- wide variations in use, e.g. with teenagers;
- human rights issues arising from the shortage of appropriate facilities at police stations and appropriately trained officers (the custody officer may be the only person who is available at night);
- a lack of record-keeping and protocols between police and social services;
- extensive use of police protection powers at social services request, with monitoring of this dependent on the duty Inspector;
- some court endorsement in preference to emergency or out-of-hours EPO hearings;
- their use for very urgent matters in areas where out-of-hours applications were not the norm and an EPO could not be obtained by the end of the working day.

Home Office guidance[9] was revised in light of the Climbié Inquiry to give greater clarity about when and how police should use these powers (it also advises on EPOs, abduction and recovery, powers of entry, and refuges for children at risk). This Circular covers:

- the meaning and interpretation of significant harm;
- the meaning and use of reasonable force;
- that there is no right to enter and search premises to remove a child without a warrant unless one of the grounds under Police and Criminal Evidence Act (PACE) 1984, s.17 is satisfied (here, entry to save life and limb);
- not exercising the power until the investigating officer has seen the child and assessed her circumstances (save for circumstances indicating an imminent threat to the child's welfare);[10]
- the circumstances of any release from police protection (the decision should occur only following discussion with the relevant personnel in the social services department and should be recorded).

The main provisions of the Circular are contained in the paragraphs below.

The powers should only be exercised in exceptional circumstances, i.e. if insufficient time to seek an EPO or for reasons relating to the child's immediate safety (the principle being that wherever possible, courts should make removal decisions).

For example, an EPO cannot be obtained pre-birth, regardless of risk, and 'police protection is the appropriate way to ensure the child's safety immediately after birth'. This is a temporary measure: social services should ensure that accommodation pursuant to Children Act 1989, s.21 is provided or an EPO applied for as soon as possible post-birth.

Save in exceptional circumstances the child should be seen and her circumstances assessed by the police before exercising police protection powers.

The powers are time-limited: a police constable (in the armed forces, a military police officer overseas) may, for up to 72 hours, remove a child to suitable accommodation and keep her there or prevent her removal from a place where she is being accommodated.

The constable must also (Children Act 1989, s.46(3)):

- notify the local authority in whose area the child was found and that in which she is ordinarily resident;
- tell the child why the action has been taken and what further action may be taken, if she is capable of understanding (see below);
- take reasonably practicable steps to discover her wishes and feelings;
- take reasonable steps to inform the following of what action has been taken and may be taken:

    – the parents;
    – anyone with parental responsibility;
    – anyone with whom the child was living before the action was taken;

- ensure the child is moved into local authority accommodation;
- secure that the case is inquired into by the 'designated officer'.

The 'designated officer' at the police station is the person to whom all cases must be referred, whose role is to:

- inquire into the matter;
- decide whether or not to seek an EPO on behalf of the local authority, with or without its agreement;
- do what is reasonable in all the circumstances to safeguard or promote the child's welfare, having regard to the length of the police protection;
- allow such contact as he considers reasonable and in the child's best interests with:

    – the parents;
    – anyone with parental responsibility;
    – any person with whom the child was living before she was taken into police protection;
    – any person with a contact or access order (i.e. under the Children Act 1989 or preceding legislation);
    – anyone acting on behalf of any of those persons.

Guidance on contact is in the Circular, which states that any issues should, wherever possible, be jointly agreed with social services and recorded.[11]

Information

The information which must be supplied to social services, and should be given to the child and to her parents, is specified and police should:

- ensure, as far as possible given the child's age, that the child understands what steps need to be taken to ensure that she is safe;
- explain his role, what has been done and what is going to happen/may happen next, and who else is involved in helping and supporting the child;
- use the *Achieving Best Evidence*[12] guidelines in any full interview with the child as a possible victim of crime.

The child or young person

Police, especially the investigating officer, are required to communicate with the child, keeping her informed throughout and taking account of her wishes and feelings as part of the decision-making process. Particular discretion should be exercised with older children.

However, being taken into police protection can be a bewildering or even traumatic experience, causing fear, confusion and distress – the circumstances may affect even the most mature young person, or result in failure to understand what is being said. Officers should use the new Home Office leaflets (there are also leaflets for parents, guardians and carers) to help explain in simple terms why the police need to protect the child, to help her understand what is happening and what will happen to her and to reassure her that she is not in any trouble.

Accommodation

In practice, a child is unlikely to remain in police protection for more than a few hours, while the notified local authority finds accommodation for her. A police station is not considered 'suitable accommodation' and the child should not be taken there 'except in exceptional circumstances, such as a lack of immediately available local authority accommodation, and then only for a short period'. Whilst there, 'every effort' should be made to ensure she is 'physically safe and comfortable and has access to food and drink and toilet and washroom facilities'.

If the child has to stay with relatives or other appropriate carers, basic appropriate checks must be made (e.g. Police National Computer, sex offenders register and child protection register). Responsibility for the risk assessment lies jointly with the police and social services, but the investigating officer should ensure that the necessary arrangements do not place the child at further risk.

Emergency protection orders application

Applications for an EPO (under Children Act 1989, s.46(7)) without waiting for a local authority request should be made in 'rare circumstances'. Every effort should be made to consult with the local authority beforehand, and contact made with the local Justices Clerk for advice on the process.

6.5   CHILD ASSESSMENT ORDERS

The local authority should make all reasonable efforts to persuade parents to cooperate with Children Act 1989, s.47 enquiries. If, despite this, parents continue to refuse access to a child for the purpose of establishing basic facts about her condition – but concerns about her safety are not so urgent as to require an EPO – a local authority may apply for a child assessment order under Children Act 1989, s.43.

The court may direct parents/carers to cooperate with an assessment of the child, the details of which should be specified. The order does not take away the child's own right to refuse to participate in an assessment, e.g. a medical examination, so long as she is of sufficient age and understanding.

The order must specify the date by which the assessment is to begin and has effect for a maximum of seven days from that date. This means that arrangements for the assessment (location, personnel, etc.) must be firm, since there is no power to keep the child away from her parents after this period expires.

A court may treat the application as an application for an EPO, if satisfied there are grounds, and that it ought to make that order instead.

6.6   EMERGENCY PROTECTION ORDERS

Legal basis

EPOs should only be made where there is a risk of significant harm during the period of the emergency. The intervention may be proportionate but local authority efforts must be directed to the aim of reunification when circumstances permit this.

Although emergency measures may be taken to remove a child from immediate danger, they must be properly justified by the circumstances, otherwise there may be a breach of ECHR Article 8. An *ex parte* order should be for no longer than necessary (*Venema* v. *Netherlands* [2003] 1 FLR 551: *P,C and S* v. *UK* [2002] 2 FLR 631; *K and T* v. *Finland* [2001] 2 FLR 707; see also Munby J's analysis in *X Council* v. *B (Emergency Protection Orders)* [2004] EWHC Fam 2015, [2004] 1 FLR 341).

The order:

- may last for no more than eight days initially, and may be extended for a further seven days;
- authorises the applicant to remove the child, or prevent her removal (but the child must be returned as soon as it is safe to do so, even if the order is still in force);
- acts as a direction to anyone in a position to do so, to comply with the order to produce the child;
- gives the applicant parental responsibility.

Practice issues

An application for an EPO can be *ex parte* or on short notice, but should be made on one day's notice unless this would place the child at immediate risk of harm. If an order is made *ex parte*, a copy of the application must be served on the respondents within 48 hours.

There is no provision for appeals (which was accepted by the ECtHR in *Covezzi and Morselli* v. *Italy* (2003) 38 EHRR 28) and judicial review proceedings to prevent a local authority commencing emergency protection or care proceedings are not appropriate (*Re M (Care Proceedings: Judicial Review)* [2003] 2 FLR 171), save in an exceptional case, nor is *habeas corpus* (*Re S (Habeas Corpus)*; *S* v. *Haringey LBC* [2004] 1 FLR 590). Application can be made to discharge the EPO, not to be heard until after 72 hours, by a parent, the child, anyone with parental responsibility, or the person with whom the child was living at the time (but not if they were given notice of the application and were present) (Children Act 1989, s.45(11)).

Courts do not commonly list a review hearing and, given the short period of the order, it may be wiser to concentrate the preparation of the case on the next stage of the process, i.e. the application extension of the EPO or for an interim care order.

The court may impose an exclusion requirement, or accept an undertaking; issue a warrant for a police officer to accompany the person authorised by the court to enter and search for the child; require a person having information about the child's whereabouts to disclose it; or give directions as to medical or psychiatric examination or other assessment of the child, who may, if of sufficient understanding, refuse to submit to this (Children Act 1989, s.44(7) mirrors s.38(6) and see analysis by Munby J in *X Council* v. *B (EPOs)* [2005] 1 FLR 341. (This is subject to power under the inherent jurisdiction to override a *Gillick* competent child's wishes) (*South Glamorgan CC* v. *W and B* [1993] 1 FLR 574, also referred to as *Fraser* competent).

Research

A 2004 research study[13] included pertinent findings on the circumstances leading to EPOs, with neglect as a major precipitating factor and non-cooperation with statutory agencies a major feature. Parental mental illness and/or learning difficulties also led to intervention, but domestic abuse did not, although present in many cases. Some were very complicated family situations, and there were few, if any, risk assessments.

This research raises issues about the removal of new-born babies, the experience and approach of magistrates and concerns about the way in which applications are made and the support, advice and representation available to the child and parent/carer.

Removal of new-born babies

Removal of new-born babies is deemed to be an extremely harsh measure, requiring 'extraordinarily compelling reasons' (see Chapter 1), and careful advance assessment of the impact on parents. The possibility of abduction may cause concern, but consideration must be given to:

- the availability of hospital security measures;
- pre-birth planning;
- breast-feeding mothers;
- the circumstances of removal;
- involvement of a guardian (especially where adoption is already the care plan).

Experience and approach of magistrates

Few magistrates outside major cities have substantial experience of EPOs, and should have the assistance of a guardian (and the child should have a solicitor, if possible). Magistrates should consider and test the evidence for removal carefully and should consider the difficulties in representation for parents given short notice and the lack of documentation and time and the need to put forward evidence to counter allegations being made.

Applications by social services

Careful consideration, with legal advice, should be given to:

- definitions of what constitutes a real emergency;
- whether the application is effectively being used as a last resort or not;
- whether alternative steps could be taken on a voluntary basis;
- the potential for an EPO setting an inevitable course towards proceedings and compulsion without further consideration, rather than partnership;
- the level at which some decisions need to be taken, and ratified by legal advice;
- the written evidence required and, if urgent action is needed, how quickly it should be taken.

Notwithstanding the need for haste, the evidence presented needs to be accurate and balanced; this is especially important in an *ex parte* application where the evidence will not be challenged.

Alternatives

Using proportionality principles, it might be justifiable to consider a child assessment order under the Children Act 1989, s.43, but this needs seven days' notice and is designed for a situation where parents cannot agree to assessment but will not interfere with it. Also, s.20 accommodation may be considered, but this option is intended to be voluntary.

Armed forces

Where a child of serving personnel is overseas, applications for an emergency order for her removal are made by a designated person to a commanding officer (this may change in future, see Tri-Services Bill 2004). The grounds for making the order are contained in Armed Forces Act 1991, ss.17–23 and mirror those for EPOs at home.

If a child protection conference decides that it is not in the child's best interests to return to the service family home, she will be placed in the care of an appropriate local authority social services department in the UK. The order made in the overseas command remains in effect for 24 hours following her arrival. During this period, the relevant local authority must decide whether to apply to the UK court for a further order.

It is the duty of the responsible person (through the service authorities, particularly the Soldiers, Sailors and Airmen and Families Association (SSAFA) Forces Help, the armed forces social work service based in each British forces area) to help parents return home to the UK to facilitate their participation in all proceedings and decisions affecting their child.[14] Where armed forces are being deployed elsewhere for operational reasons, this may give rise to particular issues and require particularly sensitive handling.

6.7   EXCLUSION ORDERS

An exclusion requirement may be included in an EPO (Children Act 1989, s.44A(2)) or in an interim care order (s.38A(2)). This allows an alleged perpetrator to be removed from the home instead of the child being removed.

The conditions require the court to be satisfied there is reasonable cause to believe that exclusion of the person from the child's home will mean that:

- significant harm, or the likelihood of it, to the child will cease; or
- enquiries will cease to be frustrated; and

- another person living there is able and willing to give the child the care which it would be reasonable to expect a parent to give, and consents to the exclusion requirement (orally or in writing).

The exclusion may:

- require a person to leave the home where he is living with the child;
- exclude him from a defined area (Children Act 1989, s.38A(3));
- have a power of arrest attached (s.38A(5)), which gives a constable power to arrest the person if he has reasonable cause to believe there is a breach of the exclusion requirement;
- be replaced by an individual's undertaking (which courts may accept if made in the same form, s.44B(1)), but there is no power to attach a power of arrest.

The exclusion (or undertaking) ceases to have effect if the child is removed from the house from which the person was excluded for a continuous period of 24 hours (Children Act 1989, s.38A(10)).

6.8   RECOVERY ORDERS

A recovery order (Children Act 1989, s.50) is designed to secure the return of a child who is in care, in police protection or subject to an EPO and has been removed or kept away from the relevant agency.

This order (in form C29) operates as a direction to any person who is in a position to do so, to produce the child on request to an authorised person (i.e. any constable, any person authorised by the court, or any person authorised by those with parental responsibility under an EPO or care order, to exercise that power), who is then authorised to remove the child. It requires any person who has any information on the child's whereabouts to disclose them, if asked to do so, to a constable or officer of the court. It authorises a constable to enter any premises specified in the order and search for the child, using reasonable force if necessary. The court may only specify premises if it appears to it there are reasonable grounds for believing the child to be on them.

An application (in form C1 and supplement C18) can only be made by:

- a person with parental responsibility;
- the designated officer if the child is in police protection; or
- the local authority if the child is abducted while subject to a care order, an EPO or is in police protection (Children Act 1989, s.50(4)).

Where a child is subject to an EPO, all pre-existing orders remain in force, e.g. a residence order. The child's parents retain their right to apply for orders for the child's return. If the child is accommodated, it is for those with parental responsibility to apply for an order for her return, although a local authority may seek an order for her protection.

Application (on form C1 with C18) must be to the Family Proceedings Court (under Children (Allocation of Proceedings) Order 1991, SI 1991/1677, art. 3(1)) unless it is made as a result of a court-directed investigation, in which case the application must be made to that court, or where there are other public law proceedings pending, it must be made to that court.

The respondents are each person whom the applicant believes has parental responsibility, the child, and the person whom the applicant believes is responsible for taking or keeping the child (under Family Proceedings Court (Children Act 1989) Rules 1991, SI 1991/1395, rules 7, 4.7); a local authority providing accommodation for the child, and any person with whom the child was living at the time the proceedings were commenced.

The application can be made *ex parte* (rule 4.4(4)(a)); if made by telephone, it must be filed within 24 hours and copies served within 48 hours after the order is made. It must be served with the Notice of Proceedings one day before the date fixed for directions or the hearing (rule 4(1)(b), form 6). Once filed and served, the matter is listed for hearing or directions, and the procedure thereafter is the same as for a care order application.

6.9   REMOVAL FROM THE JURISDICTION

There are restrictions on removal from the jurisdiction where a care order is in force. The local authority may remove the child from the UK for up to one calendar month, but the child may not be removed from the UK for more than one calendar month without either the consent of every person with parental responsibility or the leave of the court. The local authority may not arrange for the child to live outside England and Wales without the leave of the court, granted only when the child (if she has sufficient understanding) consents, and each person with parental responsibility has consented, or their consent dispensed with (Children Act 1989, s.33(7), Sched. 2 para. 19).

A court may include a provision in a residence order prohibiting removal for any period.

If removal is without permission, a recovery order may be enforceable in New Zealand (under New Zealand Guardianship Act 1968) and Australia (under Australian Family Law Act 1975, s.68). The local authority with a care order can apply under the Hague Convention to the Department for Constitutional Affairs for assistance in recovering the child (under Child Abduction and Custody Act 1985); or to the central authority of the contracting state, or directly to a court in the country to which she has been removed (Hague Convention, Arts 8 and 9).

6.10 PORT ALERT SYSTEM

The port alert system may be triggered by any person concerned about possible imminent removal of a child from the UK (but not the Channel Isles or the Isle of Man) (see Interpretation Act 1878, s.5 Sched. 1). Concerned local authorities may seek assistance from the police, who will alert all police forces and notify immigration officers of details of the child at risk. A Practice Direction (*Practice Direction (Children: Removal from Jurisdiction*) [1986] 1 All ER 983 at 984B) and a Home Office Circular 21/1986 describe the system.

Before police will act, they must:

- be contacted through the applicant's local police station;
- be provided with a copy of any court order concerning the child showing the child's legal status;
- be satisfied the threat is real and imminent;
- receive detailed information about:

    - the applicant;
    - the child;
    - the person likely to remove her;
    - the likely destination and arrival time, and port of embarkation;
    - the grounds for the port alert;
    - the person to whom the child should be returned if found.

An immigration officer has no power to detain a person intent on removing a child, and must refer the matter to the police.

6.11 THE ACCOMMODATED CHILD

The local authority does not have parental responsibility for a child accommodated under Children Act 1989, s.20. If it fears she may be removed from the UK, it can apply for a prohibited steps order, an EPO, an interim care order or possibly request to have the child removed into police protection.

6.12 OTHER PROTECTIVE MEASURES AND ISSUES

Passports

The local authority may register an objection to the provision of a passport to a child with the Passport Department at the Home Office without court leave.

Where there is an order prohibiting/restricting a child's removal from the UK or the Isle of Man, the court may require relevant UK passports to be surrendered. Further, it will notify the Passport Office to prevent the issue of any replacements.

The High Court, under its inherent jurisdiction, may order the surrender of a foreign passport, although it cannot prevent the issue of another passport by a foreign state (*Re A-K (Foreign Passport: Jurisdiction)* [1997] 2 FLR 569).

Where a parent refuses to disclose her whereabouts, or they are not known, and she is understood to be a foreign national, it is possible that her passport will be with the Home Office. Information should be sought, through the court, of the Home Office in order to ascertain the status of the parent and the whereabouts of her passport.[15]

Non-disclosure of address

Where there is thought to be a risk of removal of a looked after child, the local authority has the right to accommodate her at an address not disclosed to the parents (Children Act 1989, Sched. 2 para. 15).

6.13 DOMESTIC ABUSE

Context, definition and response

Violence in the home, domestic violence or abuse as commonly defined, is the physical, emotional, psychological or sexual abuse inflicted on a man or woman by their partner and is now a crime under the Domestic Violence, Crime and Victims Act 2004. Statistics indicate that 80 per cent of women, and 8 per cent of men, experience this abuse.

When persistent, it should be considered as a form of emotional abuse and a child protection issue: it is an issue for about 33 per cent of children on child protection registers.[16] According to a recent study,[17] 38 per cent of people who reported domestic violence also reported problems relating to their children.

It is good practice for any professional to ask sufficient questions and to carry out sufficient assessment of a given emergency situation, to establish wherever possible whether domestic abuse is a contributing or precipitating factor, and a wide range of professional guidance in this crucial area is available (see Chapter 8).

Consequences for children and young people

Children witness domestic violence in the home either directly or indirectly. They may be in the room as it takes place, or elsewhere, and can hear or see the consequences of the violence; they may try to intervene and get hurt in the process, or themselves be hit or beaten, sexually and emotionally abused.

Its impact can be enduring and severe and have long- and short-term consequences, leading to a variety of mental health problems. Children may:

- experience feelings of guilt, fear and often blame themselves or get angry for not protecting their mothers;
- internalise this distress and get depressed, become withdrawn and anxious, and suffer low self-esteem;
- externalise these feelings and become aggressive, violent or display difficult behaviour;
- experience problems with sleep, bed-wetting, disrupted or shortened attention spans, problems with school and schoolwork;
- display somatic distress such as tummy aches or not feeling well and not wanting to go out or to school.

Exposure to hostility and conflict in the home is a major risk factor for child mental health problems, particularly for conduct disorder in boys:[18]

- boys are more likely to externalise and develop aggressive behaviour, identifying with the aggressor;
- girls occasionally become aggressive but are more likely to become depressed and withdrawn;
- children exposed to severe prolonged violence, from which they cannot escape, cope by dissociating, either to specific triggers or more generally: they may appear detached and emotionally inaccessible, and do not reveal feelings, especially fear;
- severe humiliation and shame in childhood have an impact on adult relationships and may act as precipitants to violence in adult life.[19]

The definition of harm (Children Act 1989, s.11 as amended by Adoption and Children Act 2002, s.120) now includes 'impairment suffered from seeing or hearing the ill-treatment of another'. Children who have lived in a domestic abuse situation may become the subject of care proceedings, in addition to being caught up in the conflict between their parents. A finding of fact made in the care court, or in family proceedings, will be relied on in proceedings in the other court.

Contact

Practitioners must be aware of the core principles applied by the court for contact in domestic violence cases, which include ensuring that decisions are child centred and benefit the child.[20] These are (per the Court of Appeal in *Re L, Re V, Re M, Re H (Contact: Domestic Violence)* [2000] 2 FLR 334; *Re G (Domestic Violence: Direct Contact)* [2000] 2 FLR 865):

- the need for a heightened awareness of the consequences on children of exposure to domestic violence between parents or other partners;
- as a matter of principle, it is not a bar to contact but it is one factor in a delicate balancing exercise of discretion;
- where an allegation of domestic violence is made which might affect the outcome, it should be adjudicated on and found proved or not;
- in the interim, prior to adjudication, the court should give particular consideration to the likelihood of harm to the child if contact orders are granted or refused, including the safety of the child and residential parent before, during and after such contact.

Civil remedies

The victim has a choice of civil remedies under Family Law Act 1996, s.42 or the Protection from Harassment Act 1997. Compensatory damages can be awarded under the 1997 Act, but there is a two-year limit on sentences for breaches of injunctions (Protection from Harassment Act 1997, s.3(2)). There is nothing to stop concurrent applications under both Acts, but these should be issued in the same court, consolidated and tried by the same judge with experience in both family and civil jurisdictions (see Court of Appeal guidance in *Lomas* v. *Parle* [2003] EWCA Civ 1804, [2004] 1 FLR 812). Non-molestation orders may be made, providing protection against violence and abuse.

Criminal remedies

Every police force has a Domestic Violence Unit, which gives advice and takes action where necessary. The conduct of criminal proceedings is a matter for the police and the CPS, and the victim has little control over the process. They are likely to require more extensive preparation and take longer than committal proceedings in the family justice system. Therefore, committal applications should be issued promptly after the alleged breach and listed without delay. There must be good communication between the different courts responsible for sentencing and findings, especially with regard to the availability of transcripts of judgments.

However, the new Domestic Violence, Crime and Victims Act 2004 introduces significant changes and additional remedies for use against a violent partner, which in turn may reduce the necessity for intervention by a social services department. The 2004 Act:

- extends the availability of restraining orders under the Protection from Harassment Act 1997: they may be made on conviction or acquittal for any offence where the court considers that it is necessary to do so;

- makes breach of non-molestation orders under the Family Law Act 1996 a criminal offence;
- makes common assault an arrestable offence (by amendment of the Family Law Act 1996, s.42);
- includes (by amendment of the Family Law Act 1996) in 'associated persons' those who 'have had an intimate personal relationship with each other which is or was of significant duration' (which allows those who have never married/cohabited to seek protection).

The 2004 Act is complemented by a code of practice requiring all victims to be given all advice, information, support and protection needed and an independent Commissioner for Victims.

Rehousing

People experiencing domestic abuse are defined as homeless and women who are pregnant, have dependent children, are vulnerable or threatened with homelessness because of an emergency are designated as in priority need. Where homeless persons have dependent children, housing authorities must refer to social services those who are ineligible for homelessness assistance or who are intentionally homeless, provided the person consents (Homelessness Act 2002, s.12). If homelessness persists, any child in the family could be in need. If social services decide the child's needs would be best met by helping the family to obtain accommodation, they can ask the housing authority for reasonable assistance in this and it must respond.

Concurrent proceedings

It is not unusual for cases to generate concurrent proceedings in different criminal, civil and family courts dealing with different incidents and/or offences. Practitioners need to exercise careful control over this and follow judicial guidance on the interrelationship between the respective Acts and the management of concurrent proceedings (see *Lomas* v. *Parle* [2003] EWCA Civ 1804, [2004] 1 FLR 812, which supplements *Hale* v. *Tanner* [2000] 1 WLR 2377, [2000] 2 FLR 879).

Therapeutic programmes

Courts often make referrals to anger management programmes (widely available), although more extensive emotional management programmes might be more effective in helping some offenders to resolve the distorted, often obsessive, emotional attachments that give rise to violence.

See Appendix 2 for useful telephone numbers and contact details for use in emergencies.

NOTES

1 Recommendation 36 of the *Climbié Inquiry Report* (2003).
2 *Arrangements for Handling Child Care Cases*, Association of Council Secretaries and Solicitors and Solicitors in Local Government: Child Care Law Joint Liaison Group (2004).
3 See *Keeping Children Safe: The Government's Response to the Victoria Climbié Inquiry Report* and the Joint Chief Inspectors' Report, *Safeguarding Children*, DfES, DH,Home Office (2003).
4 *Working Together to Safeguard Children*, DH, Home Office, DfEE (1999), para. 5.4, and Lord Laming, *Climbié Inquiry Report* (2003), recommendations 64–90.
5 *Climbié Inquiry Report* (2003), recommendations 91–108.
6 *Sudden Unexpected Death in Infancy, A Multi-Agency Protocol for Care and Investigation*, Royal College of Paediatrics and Child Health and Royal College of Pathologists (2004).
7 *Ibid.*, App. II, III and IV respectively, and see Avon Protocol and Metropolitan Police Protocol for London (Project Indigo) which has specially trained police officers and health professionals.
8 J. Masson *et al.*, *Emergency Intervention in Child Protection*, University of Warwick (2004); J. Masson, M. Winn Oakley and D. McGovern, *'Working in the Dark' The Use of Police Protection*, University of Warwick (2002) and see [2004] Family Law 882.
9 *Duties and Powers of the Police under Children Act 1989*, HO 44/2003 (September 2003), cancels HO 54/1991.
10 Home Office Circular 2003(44), para. 16.
11 *Ibid.*, para. 46.
12 *Achieving Best Evidence in Criminal Proceedings*, Home Office, LCD, CPS, DH and Welsh National Assembly (2002).
13 J. Masson *et al.*, *EPOs, Court Order for Child Protection Crises*, University of Warwick (2004), a study of 86 families and 126 applications; and see [2004] Fam Law 882.
14 *Working Together*, para. 3.93.
15 Protocol from the President's Office (Communicating with the Home Office) [2004] Fam Law 608.
16 T.E. Moffitt and A. Caspi, 'Violence Between Intimate Partners: Implications for Child Psychologists and Psychiatrists' (1998) 39 *Journal of Child Psychology and Psychiatry* 137.
17 P. Pleasance *et al.*, 'Family Problems – What Happened and to Whom: Findings from the LSRC Survey of Justiciable Problems' [2003] Fam Law 497 and 822.
18 M. Rutter and D. Quinton, 'Parental Psychiatric Disorder: Effects on Children' (1984) 14 *Psychological Medicine* 853.
19 K. Browne and M. Herbert, *Preventing Family Violence*, Chichester, Wiley (1997).
20 For a summary of the issues see Dr Sturge and Dr Glaser, 'Contact and Domestic Violence: The Expert's Court Report' [2000] Fam Law 615.

CHAPTER 7

Secure accommodation orders

Key sources

- Children and Young Persons Act 1969, s. 23
- Children Act 1989, s.25
- Family Proceedings Rules 1991
- Children (Secure Accommodation) Regulations 1991 and Children (Secure Accommodation) (No. 2) Regulations 1991; Children (Homes and Secure Accommodation) (Miscellaneous Amendments) Regulations 1996
- Children Act Guidance and Regulations (1991), vol. 1, para. 5.1, and vol 4, para. 8.5
- Circular LAC(92)13

7.1   INTRODUCTION

This chapter should be read in conjunction with Chapter 16 on criminal issues and Chapter 15 on mental health.

Caution has repeatedly been expressed against seeing secure accommodation as the solution rather than a temporary opportunity or respite within which solutions may be sought. It is not a benign intervention. For many young people it not only does not help, but rather it increases their difficulties and causes further harm. More practice ideas and strategies, which are properly resourced, are needed as alternatives. 'Criminalisation' of secure accommodation increases the likelihood that young people 'at risk' whose admission is a consequence of their difficult life experiences and related to inadequate services, policy and practice, will be further stigmatised and their different needs neglected.[1]

The statistics show:

- a great shortage of places but a rising number of applications and orders;
- a significant proportion of the care population in young offender institutions originates from secure accommodation (See statistics in *R (Howard League for Penal Reform)* v. *Secretary of State for the Home Office* [2002] EWHC Admin 2497, [2003] 1 FLR 484);
- over 25 children have died in prison since 1990 – arguably these young people should, at the very least, have been looked after in secure accommodation.

7.2   HUMAN RIGHTS

Relevant ECHR Articles include Articles 3, 5, 6 and 8 (see Chapter 1).

Every child deprived of liberty must be treated with humanity and respect for dignity, and in a manner which takes into account the needs of a person of her age, and separated from adults unless it is considered in the child's best interests not to do so (see UNCRC Article 37(c) cited by Munby J in *R (Howard League for Penal Reform)* v. *Secretary of State for the Home Office* [2002] EWHC Admin 2497, [2003] 1 FLR 484).

A number of essential safeguards should be observed in *all* settings in which children live away from home, including secure units. These include[2] children feeling valued and respected and their self-esteem promoted, and staff trained in all aspects of safeguarding, alert to children's vulnerabilities and risks of harm, and knowledgeable about how to implement child protection procedures.

Safeguarding duties are also imposed on those owning, or responsible for, places with secure units under Children Act 1989 s.87(1) and Children Act 2004, s.11 (England) and s.28 (Wales).

Despite being the sole Member State to lock up children outside criminal or mental health provisions, the UK is unlikely to breach Convention rights if proper procedures are followed, although there is greater emphasis on the need to protect these rights (*Re C (SAO: Representation)* [2001] EWCA Civ 458, [2001] 2 FLR 169 and see *R (Howard League for Penal Reform)* v. *Secretary of State for the Home Office* [2002] EWHC Admin 2497, [2003] 1 FLR 484). An application for an order is not a criminal charge within the meaning of ECHR Article 6, but the child's minimum rights are set out in Article 6(3).

For the purpose of ECHR Article 5, orders restrict liberty, but will usually fall within the definition of lawful detention for the purpose of educational supervision. The UK courts have found the provisions of the Children Act 1989 to be Convention compliant in this respect, noting that the court, at any level, must have the requirements of Article 5(1)(d) in mind when considering the relevant criteria. It is taken as read that the child will receive some form of education in the secure unit as 'educational supervision' is part of the local authority's exercise of parental rights for the benefit and protection of the looked after child (*Koniarska* v. *UK (Admissibility Decision)* (Application No. 33670/96, 12 October 2000, unreported, ECtHR). Therefore, as long as the purpose of the order is broadly educational, there will be no breach even if the child is over 16 and is not required to undergo full-time education (*Re K (Secure Accommodation Order: Right to Liberty)* [2001] 1 FLR 526). However, where there are no secure education facilities available, and the child is detained in prison as a result, there may be a breach (*DG* v. *Ireland* (2002) 35 EHRR 33, ECHR: breaches of Articles 5(1) and 5(5), but not of Articles 3, 8, or 14).

The courts have stated that the most appropriate remedy in most cases will be judicial review because the application can be combined with human rights points and requires permission to issue the relevant proceedings (*S* v. *Knowsley BC* [2004] 2 FLR 716).

7.3 DEFINITION OF SECURE ACCOMMODATION

It is for the court to decide whether accommodation is 'secure' as a question of fact, i.e. to use the more natural meaning, accommodation 'designed for, or having as its primary purpose' the restriction of liberty (*Re C (Detention: Medical Treatment)* [1997] 2 FLR 180).

However, any practice or measure that prevents a child from leaving a room or building of her own free will may be deemed to constitute 'restriction of liberty'. For example, locking her in a room, or part of a building, to prevent her leaving voluntarily is covered by the statutory definition, but other practices which place restrictions on freedom of mobility, e.g. creating a human barrier, are not so clear cut.[3] Examples include a maternity ward secured by a key/pass system (*A Metropolitan Borough Council* v. *DB* [1997] 1 FLR 767).

The High Court also has power, under its inherent jurisdiction, to direct that a child be detained as an in-patient at a clinic (which is not secure accommodation) for treatment of anorexia nervosa, using reasonable force if necessary (*Re C (Detention: Medical Treatment)* [1997] 2 FLR 180).

7.4 POWER OF THE LOCAL AUTHORITY

The local authority has a power to detain a child in secure accommodation without court authority for a maximum of 72 hours either consecutively or in aggregate, in any period of 28 consecutive days (subject to some flexibility to take account of weekends and public holidays) (Children (Secure Accommodation) Regulations 1991, SI 1991/1505, reg. 10(1), (3)). But the same grounds as for a court order must be satisfied (see below) and under Children Act 1989, s.20 a person with parental responsibility has the right to remove the child.

The local authority also has a duty to take reasonable steps designed to avoid the need for children within its area to be placed in secure accommodation (Children Act 1989, Sched. 2, para. 7(c)) Restricting a child's liberty is a serious step, which must be taken only when there is no genuine appropriate alternative. It must be a 'last resort', in the sense that all else must first have been comprehensively considered and rejected, and never:

- because no other placement was available at the relevant time;
- because there are inadequacies in staffing;

- because the child is simply being a nuisance or runs away from her accommodation and is not likely to suffer harm in doing so; or
- as a form of punishment.

In considering the potential use of secure accommodation, there must be a clear view of the aims and objectives, which can be fully met by those providing it.[4]

7.5 RESTRICTIONS

The restrictions on the use of secure accommodation do not apply to a child detained under the Mental Health Act 1983. The spirit of the Children Act Guidance indicates secure accommodation should be used for children subject to care orders who need compulsory mental health treatment, but this has been ignored in some cases (see *R* v. *Kirklees MBC, ex p. C* [1993] 2 FLR 187 and further discussion in Chapter 15). Nor do the restrictions apply to a child detained under Children and Young Persons Act 1933, s.53 (punishment of specified grave crimes).

The following cannot have their liberty restricted in any circumstances:

- a young person over 16 accommodated under Children Act 1989, s.20(5);
- a child who is the subject of a child assessment order and kept away from home for that purpose.

Secure accommodation can be used, with modified criteria, for a child remanded to local authority accommodation by a criminal court under Children and Young Persons Act 1969, s.23, and also for a child detained under powers in Police and Criminal Evidence Act 1984, s.38(6) but the grounds are that any accommodation other than that provided for the purpose of restricting liberty is inappropriate because the child is likely to abscond from such accommodation, or the child is likely to injure herself or other people if she is kept in any such accommodation (Children (Secure Accommodation) Regulations 1991, SI 1991/1505, reg.6(1)).

A child who is a ward may not be placed in secure accommodation without a direction from a judge exercising the wardship jurisdiction.

Age of child

A child under 13 may not be placed in secure accommodation without authority from the Secretary of State. An accommodated child who has reached 16 can only be placed in secure accommodation if the order was made prior to her sixteenth birthday and extends beyond that date (*Re G (Secure Accommodation Order)* [2001] 1 FLR 884).

7.6 APPLICATION OF SECURE ACCOMMODATION ORDERS

Grounds

The grounds for making a secure accommodation order (Children Act 1989, s.25(1)) are that the child has a history of absconding, or will be likely to abscond and, if she absconds, is likely to suffer significant harm or likely to injure herself or others.

The words 'likely to abscond' should be construed as for 'likely' in Children Act 1989, s.31, i.e. in the sense of a real possibility that cannot be sensibly ignored having regard to the nature and gravity of the feared harm (per *Re H and R* [1996] 1 FLR 80, HL and see *S* v. *Knowsley BC* [2004] 2 FLR 716). In, e.g. *Re D (Secure Accommodation Order)* [1999] Fam Law 311, the criteria were made out on evidence and the court was obliged to make an order, but made it for one day only since the local authority wanted the order as a deterrent only and intended to make an open unit placement.

The child must be released once the criteria no longer exist: a continued detention in such circumstances can only be challenged by an application for *habeas corpus* (*LM* v. *Essex CC* [1999] 1 FLR 988).

Court

An order may be made by the family proceedings court, county court or High Court. The youth court may make an order by virtue of Criminal Justice Act 1991, s.60(3) (Children (Secure Accommodation) Regulations 1991, SI 1991/1505, reg.6(1)(b)) where the child is accommodated by the local authority following an order made in criminal proceedings.

Once the criteria are satisfied, the order must be made and the court's discretion is limited to fixing the maximum duration (Johnson J in *Re A (SAO)* [2001] Fam. Law 806).

Length of the order

In remand cases, the maximum length of the order will be the period of remand, and no order may last beyond 28 days. In non-remand cases, the court may make an order on the first occasion for three months. This includes any period of a prior interim order. It is not tied to this period and must consider what is necessary in the circumstances (*Re W (A Minor) (Secure Accommodation Order)* [1993] 1 FLR 692). An order for a further period not exceeding six months at any one time can be made thereafter.

An order made before the child's sixteenth birthday can be made for a period going beyond that birthday without breaching Children Act 1989, s.20(5) (*Re G (Secure Accommodation Order)* [2001] 1 FLR 884). The maximum period allowed should be ordered only when necessary and not as a matter of course (*Re W (A Minor) (Secure Accommodation Order)* [1993] 1 FLR 692). The order runs from the date on which the order is made not, in the case of a child who has absconded, from the date of placement (*Re B (A Minor) (Secure Accommodation)* [1994] 2 FLR 707).

Interim orders

Interim orders may be made on any adjournment of a hearing under Children Act 1989, s.25(5). The criteria are the same as those for a final order under s.25(4), which does not set a minimum period. There would seem to be no reason why a court should not always make its order under s.25(4) (Munby J in *Re G (Secure Accommodation Order)* [2001] 1 FLR 884), despite a previous suggestion that an interim order may be made where the grounds are made out, but not so as to justify the full length of the order being sought (Connell J in *Hereford and Worcester CC* v. *S* [1993] 2 FLR 648).

Evidence and reasons

These are family proceedings, but also proceedings of 'last resort' (see above) so hearsay evidence is admissible, but every effort should be made to obtain psychiatric evidence where relevant (*Oxfordshire CC* v. *R* [1992] 1 FLR 648). Evidence must be adduced showing that all possible efforts have been made to find alternatives and keep the child in that placement.[5] Evidence should be rigorously tested by all the parties since the serious issue of the child's liberty is at stake.[6]

The court must give reasons for its decision (Family Proceedings Rules 1991, SI 1991/1247, rule 21).

Local authority's role

Once made, such a placement should be for only so long as is necessary and unavoidable. The order is permissive only and does not *compel* detention: it may have a short-term usefulness in breaking a pattern of absconding (*W* v. *North Yorkshire CC* [1993] 1 FCR 693). Children should not be retained in security simply to complete a predetermined assessment or treatment programme.[7]

The local authority must formally review the placement within a month and every three months thereafter. A panel, comprising at least three members who are a senior social services manager without direct responsibility for the case, a councillor and an independent individual, often from an organisation such as Voice for the Child in Care, must consider whether: the criteria are still met, such a placement continues to be necessary and whether any other description of accommodation would be appropriate, and should consider whether any assessments or therapeutic work needs to be undertaken by the allocated social worker or the unit.

The unit staff social worker and parents are invited to the meeting and the panel are required to take into account the wishes and feelings of the child, parent, anyone with parental responsibility, the independent visitor and anyone else the panel considers should be consulted, including anyone who has had care of the child.

The local authority's role during the currency of an order and its duties to review the continued legality of a placement reliant on a secure accommodation order can be challenged by way of judicial review which is, in most cases, likely to be the most appropriate procedure (Charles J in *S* v. *Knowsley BC* [2004] EWHC Admin 491; [2004] 2 FLR 716).

The local authority (or those responsible for managing the accommodation) must ensure that a case record is kept of the placement as follows (Children (Secure Accommodation) Regulations 1991, SI 1991/1505, reg.17, as amended by Children (Homes and Secure Accommodation) (Miscellaneous Amendments) Regulations 1996, SI 1996/692, reg.3):

- the child's name, date of birth and sex;
- the care order or other statutory provision under which she is kept there, and particulars of any other local authority involved;
- the date and time of placement and name of the officer authorising it;
- all persons informed of it;
- any court orders and directions with regard to it;
- all reviews in respect of it;
- the date and time of any occasion on which the child is locked on her own in any room, other than her bedroom during usual bedtime hours, the name of the person authorising this, the reason and the date and time when she ceased to be locked in that room;
- the date and time of discharge, and her subsequent address.

7.7 THE CHILD OR YOUNG PERSON

Application of the welfare principle

The welfare principle is relevant and important, but not the paramount consideration, and the Children Act 1989, s.1 criteria are not applicable (*Re M (Secure Accommodation Order)* [1995] 1 FLR 418). The court's role is to decide whether the evidence shows that the agency making the application should be given the power to take such a serious step.

The role of the children's guardian is not to advise the court solely on welfare considerations, but also on criteria and merits of an order. The court must give reasons for departing from the guardian's recommendations (*Re W (A Minor) (Secure Accommodation Order)* [1993] 1 FLR 692).

Representation in court

Natural justice requires notice to the child of the application (*Re AS* [1999] 1 FLR 103, and *LM* v *Essex CC* [1995] 1 FLR 988). Liberty is at stake, therefore proper legal representation is required (applying *J* v. *Merthyr Tydfil BC* [1997] Fam. Law 522). It is wrong to rely on an unsworn written statement which is not open to challenge in the absence of instructions. It is wrong not to hear evidence as there will be no record of findings of fact. It was held in *Re C (Secure Accommodation Order: Representation)* [2001] 1 FLR 857 that it is not outside a reasonable exercise of justices' discretion to proceed with a hearing even though, due to an oversight, the child's solicitor did not have one day's minimum notice of the application. The solicitor and her client had time at court to discuss the application.

It is wrong not to appoint a guardian unless there are highly unusual circumstances. The use of a children's guardian is appropriate in specified proceedings, but the appointment ends once proceedings conclude; it is then a matter for the local authority under its s.17 duties to safeguard and promote the welfare of the child in need (but this is not justiciable under judicial review: *A.* v. *Lambeth LBC* [2001] EWHC Admin 376, [2001] 2 FLR 1201).

Right to be present in court

The court can allow the child to be present if it is satisfied that it is in her interests to do so, but this may not always be interpreted generously (*Re W (Secure Accommodation Order: Attendance at Court)* [1994] 2 FLR 1092). However, before making an order, the court should allow the child to be present or the lawyer representing her to have the opportunity to take instructions (*Re AS (Secure Accommodation Order)* [1999] 1 FLR 103).

7.8 PRACTICAL CONSIDERATIONS

Practitioners will probably only have a few hours' notice of an appointment to act for a child on a secure accommodation application and should:[8]

- consider how instructions will be obtained and confirm the arrangements for the child's attendance at court;
- try to ensure the child is brought to court as early as possible in order to allow time for the taking of instructions;
- through liaison with the court ensure that the matter is heard promptly to avoid unnecessary waiting time, particularly if the court facilities are inadequate;
- check in advance with the court and the secure unit to ensure that children will not be kept in cells before the hearing, nor be admitted to the court through the cells, and make representations as necessary;

- assess initially whether the child is of sufficient age and understanding to give instructions;
- ensure continuity of representation for all parties, since the orders are frequently made after adjournment and such continuity for the child is vital.

Practitioners should also consider the following:

- What enquiries have been made to find alternative accommodation?
- Is the recommendation for an order to achieve an assessment of the child?
- Is the proposed accommodation suitable?
- What is the programme of work? When will it be available and is it tailored to this child's needs?
- What are the restraint provisions?
- What are the staff qualifications?
- What psychological and/or psychiatric help will be available to the child? In most establishments, such advice is available to the staff on a consultation basis; so how often are the consultants actually on the premises, will they be willing to see her, and on what basis?
- Are reports from the establishment produced as a matter of course, and by whom? (These are not automatic: sometimes it is suggested no report can be prepared during the first few weeks, but if an interim order is made, a report will be required for the final hearing.)
- Who will be writing the report on which the local authority will rely? (Reports prepared by unqualified staff may not be helpful if a final or further order needs to be challenged.)
- Will the unit manager or key worker attend court on request, or only on a witness summons?
- Make sure arrangements are made for the child to attend the hearing (Sometimes a social worker or staff member decides against, without consulting the child's lawyer.)
- Has a mobility programme started (part of the programme leading to a child moving to an open unit, or back into the community) and if not, why not, and when will it start? A careful check is needed because if she has not been out of the secure unit at all prior to a hearing, it may be argued that she would be likely to abscond if an order is not made, as she has not been tested away from the unit.
- Has the local authority provided details of alternative available accommodation? (It should not assume that an order will be made.)

As the children's guardian and solicitor will be discharged if a final order is made, consider seeking an interim order wherever possible to ensure continued representation. If there is likely to be a considerable delay in that appointment, consider making an application for leave to instruct an expert to prepare a report for the final hearing, as the assessment of the local authority case for a final order is beyond the competence of a solicitor.

Plans should be made sufficiently well in advance for discharge, but if the child cannot immediately be accommodated at home or elsewhere, it is arguable that permitting her to remain on the same premises is lawful, provided that it is made clear to her and the adult with parental responsibility that the child can leave freely.[9]

NOTES

1   See T. O'Neill, 'Locking up Children in Secure Accommodation: A Guardian Ad Litem's Perspective' [1999] 11(4) *Representing Children* 289.

2   *Working Together to Safeguard Children*, DH, Home Office, DfEE (1999), para. 6.5.

3   Children Act Guidance, vol. 4, para. 8.10.

4   Children Act Guidance, vol. 4, para 8.5.

5   M. Walker, 'Foster Care: An Alternative to Secure Accommodation?' [2003] *Childright* 194 and note that grants are available to recruit and retain specialist foster carers.

6   *Good Practice in Child Care Cases*, Law Society (2004), para. 6.1.4.

7   Children Act Guidance, vol. 4, para. 8.5.

8   *Good Practice in Child Care Cases*, para. 6.1.

9   R. White, A. Harbour and R. Williams, *Safeguarding Young Minds*, 2nd edn, Gaskell (2004).

CHAPTER 8

Assessments

Key sources

- Children Act 1989, s.38(6), s.43
- Special Educational Needs and Disability Act 2001
- Arrangements for Placement for Children (General) Regulations 1991 and Review of Children's Cases Regulations 1991 (as amended by the Children Act (Miscellaneous Amendments) (England) Regulations 2002)
- Fostering Services Regulations 2002
- Circulars LAC (2002) 16 and LAC (99) 29
- Protocol for Judicial Case Management in Public Law Children Act Cases (2003), App. F and App. C
- *What to Do If You are Worried A Child is Being Abused*, DH (2003), App. 1

8.1 INTRODUCTION

Assessment is:

- a regular, continuous process undertaken by all professionals in reaching individual and joint decisions;
- a key skill that underpins all good evidence-based practice and all decision-making, right from the first contact with an individual.

Thorough and sound assessments of various kinds are required to identify needs, and for the progression and ultimate disposal of each case. They are a fundamental and continuous part of planning a care case, and make all strategy meetings, interviews, conferences, plans, placements and reviews much more effective by assessing, e.g:

- a child in need;
- circumstances – by a police officer taking emergency measures;[1]
- family/parenting;
- mother and baby;
- residence /accommodation;
- kinship/foster care;
- leaving care;
- psychiatric, psychological or mental health;

- physical health;
- special educational needs;
- risk;
- age (e.g. of runaway children or refugees);
- disabled child's needs;
- child's needs/circumstances in private law cases.

Assessments should provide a clear evidential basis for professional judgments and decisions, so they must be sound, culturally competent and fully informed, including adequate data from all agencies of the child's needs, the parents' capacity to respond to those needs, including their capacity to keep the child safe from significant harm and the wider family circumstances,[2] and with systematic reference to relevant current research.[3]

Information may already be available from various sources that should be brought together to obtain a holistic picture of a child and her family, and to reach an informed decision based on assessment of the full range of issues.

Repetition and duplication should be avoided,[4] hopefully assisted by the requirements to cooperate with the new Common Assessment Framework.[5]

The catalyst for assessment and planning has all too often been the issuing of proceedings, with the children's guardian and child's solicitor prompting the process and public funding certificates as the cost provider. However, since the introduction of the Judicial Case Management Protocol, the courts 'acknowledge and encourage inter-disciplinary best practice and in particular pre-application investigation, assessment, consultation and planning by statutory agencies (including local authorities) and other potential parties.'[6] Assessment must be considered throughout the court process, at first and allocation hearings, pre-hearing review, the case management conference and in checklists, issues to be addressed and timetabling.

Consider:

- What type of assessment is proposed?
- Who is to carry it out and how?
- What criteria are being used?
- Does it, or should it, involve treatment?
- Is it properly part of a planning process?
- Is it enough, or are other assessments required?[7]

8.2 HUMAN RIGHTS AND DIVERSITY

Human rights

Intervention in family life is a draconian measure, and requires an analysis of whether satisfactory arrangements can be made which truly safeguard the child's welfare and are supportive of the family without the necessity for proceedings. However, since it is currently not possible to force a local authority to provide services following assessment, the threshold criteria may be satisfied in default.

A care order must be based on sufficient and relevant reasons: the ECtHR has made it clear that any order related to the public care of a child should, first, be capable of 'convincing an objective observer that the measure is based on a careful and unprejudiced assessment of all the evidence on file, with the distinct reasons for the care measure being stated explicitly'. (*KA* v. *Finland* [2003] 1 FLR 696).

Whatever the urgency, it is the duty of the public authority to establish that a careful assessment of the impact on parents and child of the proposed care measures, as well as of the possible alternatives to taking the child into public care, was carried out prior to placing a child in emergency care (*K and T* v. *Finland* [2001] 2 FLR 707; *KA* v. *Finland* [2003] 1 FLR 696).

Removal of a baby at birth, with no provision for an assessment of parenting ability, may breach the ECHR Article 8 rights of the mother and child, even where an emergency protection order is justified. The viability of supervised contact periods with the mother, for example, should first be assessed (*P, C and S* v. *UK* [2002] 2 FLR 631; *K and T* v. *Finland* [2002] 2 FLR 79; *Venema* v. *Netherlands* [2003] 1 FLR 552; *Haase* v. *Germany* [2004] 2 FLR 39).

Applications for assessment (under Children Act 1989, s.38(6)) potentially engage both ECHR Articles 6 and 8 (*Re G (Interim Care Order: Residential Assessment)* [2004] 1 FLR 876). To comply with Article 8 a local authority must satisfy itself that sufficient assessment has taken place before ruling out rehabilitation or placement with relatives, even where the facts are not disputed and adoption is the preferred option in the care plan.

Diversity

The importance of a culturally competent and accurate understanding of a child's identity and circumstances cannot be overstated.[8] Despite research,[9] information gathered in assessment on the ethnic background of children and carers often does not fulfil Children Act 1989 requirements. Sometimes 'vague and unsophisticated',[10] it may be absent altogether: 'although many professionals are aware that it is essential to take account of race and culture . . . they are often at a loss to translate this into practice'.[11]

Working Together states:

- assessment should maintain a focus on the individual child's needs;[12]
- all children have the same fundamental care needs;
- cultural factors neither explain nor condone acts of omission or commission that place a child at risk of significant harm;[13]
- baselines for assessing parental capacity and a child's development needs should be the same irrespective of race.

The range of cultures and behavioural patterns included in 'good enough parenting' is so wide, generalisations may be meaningless and potentially damaging to an effective assessment of the child's needs. It is critical to guard against myths, stereotypes and assumptions, – both positive and negative.[14] 'Anxiety about being accused of racist practice should not prevent the necessary action being taken to safeguard a child. Careful assessment – based on evidence – of a child's needs, and a family's strengths and weaknesses, understood in the context of the wider social environment, will help to avoid any distorting effect of these influences on professional judgements.'[15]

Inconsistent interpretation of 'good enough parenting' is matched by the varying degree to which assessments address and analyse cultural/religious diversity. Research[16] shows a deficit in professional ability to address differing cultural and social contexts in child protection. Cross-cultural assessments lack documented analysis of the relevance of diverse cultural contexts and transparency and consistency in the treatment of these issues.

Disability

Disabled children are far more likely to be subject to multiple assessments by health, education and social services than non-disabled children. Chapter 3 of the Framework for Assessment Practice Guidance sets out how assessments should be carried out and used positively with disabled children.

8.3 STATUTORY GUIDANCE

Framework for Assessment and Practice Guide

Agencies must follow this key statutory guidance for all initial and core assessments, which stresses the importance of effective assessment as key to safeguarding and a holistic, multidisciplinary, inter-agency approach to achieve improvements in a child's life (*R* v. *Nottinghamshire CC, ex p. AB and SB* [2001] EWHC Admin 235; *Re T (Judicial Review: Local Authority Decisions concerning Child in Need)* [2003] EWHC Admin 2515).

The Framework for Assessment is a systematic approach and its operation must be based on a good understanding of child development and research evidence. The following records must be kept:

- referral and initial information record;
- initial assessment and core assessment records.

Chapter 4 of the Practice Guidance has information about practice materials, evidence-based publications and training resources and materials.

Approach and methodology

Appendix 1 of *What To Do If You are Worried a Child is Being Abused*[17] contains a list of questionnaires and scales to evidence assessment and decision-making, including adult[18] and adolescent[19] well-being. Some have also suggested that a new model of assessment is needed, 'rooted in child-focused, empowering practice, rejecting of class bias and giving greater prominence to inherent benefits of kinship placements, while incorporating a framework for risk assessment.'[20]

Assessment must provide sufficient, accurate and full information on which to base effective safeguarding judgments and plans, support the task of parenting and underpin any conference child protection plan. It is not an end in itself, but aims to establish a realistic plan of action and should be carried out with the individual, her carer or family members. To be reliable it must be comprehensive, i.e. it must:

- obtain and record the fullest information about the individual;
- take a comprehensive history;
- identify *all* relevant extended family members;
- consider the role of all responsible carers, residential/custodial staff;[21]
- identify the nature of perceived issues;
- take account of all other assessments conducted/to be conducted, e.g. health, special educational needs, etc.;
- follow relevant national and professional guidance;
- obtain and use information from existing previous files;[22]
- consider race, culture, heritage, language, religious belief and practice;
- consider reasonable standards (e.g. of parenting) in the individual's society (see, e.g. *Re T (Minors) (Custody: Religious Upbringing)* [1981] 2 FLR 239 (Jehovah's Witness); *Re H (Minors) (Wardship: Cultural Background)* [1987] 2 FLR 12 (Vietnamese); *Re R (A Minor) (Residence: Religion)* [1993] 2 FLR 163 (Exclusive Brethren sect); *Re J (Specific Issue Order: Muslim Upbringing and Circumcision)* [1999] 2 FLR 678);

using the support of interpreters, translators or advocates as necessary.

The reasons for the assessment and its purpose should be set out.[23] A manager should approve all social services assessments and resulting action plans in writing, confirming the child and her carer have been seen and spoken to.[24]

Disclosure

Information subject to the Data Protection Act 1998 can be shared if it is necessary for the exercise of a statutory or other public function exercised in the public interest (e.g. s.17 assessment or s.47 enquiry); and the pursuit by the person sharing the information for a legitimate purpose, except where prejudice to the rights and freedoms or legitimate interests of the data subject make this unwarranted.[25]

8.4   TYPES OF ASSESSMENT

Initial assessment

This brief assessment of a child referred to social services must:

- be completed within seven days;
- always evaluate risk;
- determine, once concluded, whether the child is in need;
- decide the nature of any services required;
- be recorded, with findings and an initial analysis and decisions arising, with reasons and action taken;[26]
- lead to a discussion about whether a further, more detailed core assessment is required.[27]

It should gather and analyse information following the Framework for Assessment based on up-to-date interviews with child and family members, separately and together as appropriate, using appropriate communications assistance as necessary (e.g. translators, expertise in non-verbal communications for the disabled),[28] information obtained from professionals and others in contact with the child and family, and existing records, previous assessments and other historical information.

It should also be carefully planned in collaboration with all those involved with the child and family, clarifying:

- who is doing what;
- the timing of the different assessment activities;
- when and what information is to be shared with parents

and indicating where specialist assessment is required by, e.g. paediatricians, speech therapists, educational psychologists, child and family psychiatrists.

Each area of need and resulting action should be determined with constant regard to the child's welfare and safety, i.e.[29]

- Is the child in need within the meaning of Children Act 1989, s.17?
- Is the child being adequately safeguarded from significant harm?
- Are the parents able to promote the child's health and development?
- Is action required to safeguard and promote the child's welfare?
- Is it suspected that this child is suffering, or is likely to suffer, significant harm (within the meaning of Children Act 1989, s.47)?

Research identified common pitfalls, including failure to give sufficient weight or attention to, e.g. information from family, friends and neighbours or what children say, how they look and how they behave.

Detailed questions to address this are in *Working Together*, focusing on the professional's reaction to different sources of information and to presenting behaviour, family circumstances and personal safety and importantly to the risks of:

- inadequate access to, or communication with, a child;
- assumption, prejudgment and misinterpretation;
- overlooking relevant support for the child or family;
- failing to see the situation from the child's perspective;
- failing to record information adequately or accurately, or check discrepancies in the facts;
- failing to reach evidence-based decisions or to record the reasons for decisions/ actions taken in response.

The child should[30] be observed and communicated with in a manner appropriate to her age and understanding, and have her views ascertained and understood (as statutorily required by Children Act 2004, s.53).

This will usually require seeing the child in the absence of her carers. Chapter 3 has further information on communication and essential factors to consider.

Core assessment[31]

This is an in-depth assessment where there is suspected or likely harm. Depending on individual circumstances, it can take place at any time, before or after a child protection conference, but preferably before proceedings. It should be carried out within a maximum of 35 working days and by day 42 of the Judicial Case Management Protocol.

It should begin by focusing on information identified during the initial assessment and cover all relevant dimensions in the Framework of Assessment. The core assessment should be considered in any strategy discussion, with decisions taken about who should do it and when, what further information is required and how it is to be obtained and recorded. It should be as wide as possible, encompassing other professionals' contributions of information and specialist knowledge and be written up in a Core Assessment Record.

Similar general principles apply as with the initial assessment above, including, e.g.

- interpreters;
- alternative means of understanding the child's perspective, including observation where children are very young or where they have communication impairments;
- direct communication with the child and family;

- gathering current and historical information from prior involvement of professionals or other assessments.

Decisions about significant harm are complex and must concentrate on harm that has occurred or is likely to occur to the child as a result of maltreatment, to inform future plans and the nature of services required. The assessment should involve separate interviews with the child,[32] and with parents and/or carers, and observation of interactions between parents and children.

The aim is to assess the child's understanding of her situation and the nature of her relationship with each significant family member (including all care-givers) and to assess the relationships of all the adults with the child and each other, including the wider family, and the social and environmental factors impacting on them, using relevant tools/methods.

Information should be gathered from as many relevant sources as possible, including other specific professional examinations or assessments of the child (e.g. medical/developmental checks, assessment of emotional or psychological state).

The assessment should also involve interviews with those personally and professionally connected with the child and her parents or carers.

Records of the assessment and any decisions taken must be kept, including careful, detailed, legible, timed, dated and signed notes with any unusual events recorded. A distinction should be drawn between events reported by the carer and those actually witnessed by others, including professionals. Any relevant information must be recorded in the chronology.

Concluding findings should be analysed with managers and other professionals to enable the child's circumstances to be understood and to inform:

- the interim care plan and future plans;
- decisions about services to be provided;
- what further work is required to complete the assessment;
- what monitoring may be needed over time, with milestones for progress, e.g. on a child's health and development set out in a plan.

If assessment occurs after registration, it should focus on areas arising from the conference and recommendations as developed by the Core Group.

Specialist assessments

Specialists/experts may be asked to undertake specific assessments and many have to be commenced by a lead health practitioner (a consultant paediatrician, or possibly the child's GP). They may include paediatricians, speech therapists, educational psychologists, physiotherapists, occupational therapists as well as child psychologists (who assess the child's developmental progress, see Chapter 25).

It may not be possible to complete some of these within 35 days, or they may not be required until later, particularly when the child's needs are very complex. But they should not be allowed to delay the core assessment's findings.

Training of social workers must equip them with the confidence to question the opinion of professionals in other agencies when conducting their own assessment of the child's needs.[33]

Parenting and family assessments

The commonly accepted theoretical framework describes parenting as a relationship affected by factors:

- in parents (especially their personalities and own experiences of being parented);
- in the child (e.g. vulnerability or resilience); and
- in living circumstances (e.g. poverty, isolation or the couple's relationship).

A distinction must be made between:

- family assessments in everyday clinical practice (e.g. as part of intervention in parenting behaviour);
- assessments by social workers and guardians in court proceedings;
- professional mental health opinions (based on previous/current clinical involvement with the family); and
- independent expert opinions by mental health professionals ordered by the court.

Parenting and family assessments must prioritise the child's welfare and how the parent–child relationship is experienced from the child's perspective. If the parent has mental health issues, the prognosis of her disorder is only one element of a much wider assessment – parenting capacity should not be provided by psychiatrists based solely on this one factor. Traditional psychological tests, devised to measure intelligence and personality, are only indirectly applicable to parenting capacity.

Expert parenting assessments

These address all aspects of the parent–child relationship that impact on the child's welfare and therefore are more inclusive than risk assessments of child maltreatment.

They should address:

- the ability to parent *this* child;
- the interaction of all members of the family with each other;
- the role and contribution of each family member;

- the developmental needs of the child;
- the quality of the child's attachments.

They should also focus on any issues likely to impact on parenting such as any parental or carer mental illness,[34] substance misuse or domestic violence, and fully address the tension between these and the child's developmental needs and timescale. Not all cases involving these factors lead to core assessment, even where families are experiencing difficulties in all three Framework for Assessment domains[35] but the implications for any child must always be assessed,[36] and a firm finding of fact in a causation hearing leads to the need for one (*Re S (Care Proceedings: Split Hearing)* [1996] 2 FLR 773).

Risk assessment

All child protection assessments involve some assessment of risk, but each should consider:

- previous or current history of abuse (physical, sexual or emotional) of an adult or child;
- whether any violence has increased in intensity, frequency or severity;
- whether the abuser is making verbal threats, frightening/intimidating friends, family members or neighbours;
- specific information on other children in the household (including any in attendance part-time), with their ages, health and well-being.

Specific risk assessments may be necessary with regard to:

- substance misuse;
- domestic abuse;
- mental health issues;[37]
- convicted/remand prisoners returning to live in the community or at home.

Assessment is not the same as prediction. Predicting future behaviour is more likely to be accurate over the short term, but never over the longer term because changes in mental state, psychological and physical environment will affect risk.

Simple checklists and general assessment tools are not adequate, especially for psychiatrists.[38] Potential for violence can only be determined by:

- explicitly recording essential information;
- coordinated, systematic and focused assessment, involving multidisciplinary specialist team skills and information;
- at minimum, identifying the nature of the risk, its degree, persons at risk, associated potential and protective factors and warning signs, and actions in response;

- compiling a full patient history, noting such factors as deliberate self-harm, substance misuse, reluctance to accept help, past violence, with precipitating factors and contemporaneous mental state;
- addressing mental state, supplemented by other information sources and noting any gaps in documentation;
- obtaining previous clinical records to establish past management and previous interventions.

Offenders

The Multi-Agency Public Protection Panel (MAPPP)[39] can offer advice about risk assessment and management of registered sex offenders, violent or serious offenders. Agencies have a duty to cooperate with multi-agency public protection arrangements (MAPPA) (Criminal Justice Act 2003, ss.325–327) and the role of the prison service is defined. The probation service has an assessment system for offenders (OASYs), which includes assessment of risk to children.

Mental health

Royal Colleges guidance contains advice on questions to be considered with regard to mental health, including:

- the effects of parental illness on a child;
- any risk that may require referral to child protection agencies;
- the child's own need for assessment of developmental and health status;
- the child's presentation at school;
- the availability of alternative carers;
- whether a child's health/well-being may be significantly affected, taking into account who is caring for her and whether the patient is too emotionally unavailable, or too ill and preoccupied, to attend to her needs.

Royal College of Psychiatrists practice guidance can be used to judge the quality of an adult psychiatrist's assessment, which should include:

- a comprehensive psychiatric and family history;
- establishing any patient responsibility for, or contact with, dependent children and their whereabouts;
- checking other agency involvement (e.g. child protection register);
- asking about the parental relationship, exploring any homicidal/suicidal thoughts, behaviour towards/ideas about the child, and any presentation of injury to her;
- stated diagnosis and likely prognosis;
- treatment required and probable duration;

- impact of the difficulties on functioning and on ability to meet the child's needs;
- implications for the child's welfare and safety if there is no formal diagnosis that the condition is untreatable;
- support required for a parent to meet the child's needs and safety;
- whether the child's health visitor has been alerted, and her help sought in making appropriate support plans.

The guidance also emphasises the need to consult child care professionals if there are any concerns about child safety and welfare and evidence of:

- persistent negative views about a child;
- ongoing emotional unavailability, unresponsiveness and neglect;
- inability to recognise a child's needs and to maintain appropriate parent–child boundaries;
- ongoing use of a child to meet a parent's own needs;
- distorted, confusing or misleading communications with a child or abnormal thinking/behaviour;
- ongoing hostility, irritability, criticism or inconsistent and/or inappropriate expectations of the child.

Domestic abuse

Effective intervention requires a holistic approach, and the involvement of domestic abuse experts, such as experienced voluntary sector workers, to ensure a comprehensive assessment of needs, risks and protective steps.[40]

Professional medical guidance (i.e. from the Royal College of Psychiatrists and Royal College of General Practitioners) states that routine enquiries about past and current abuse should be made during clinical assessment. This means asking sensitive questions about domestic abuse and providing information on, e.g. victim safety, mental illness and local resources. All reported cases require risk assessment.

The assessment should consider the history of abuse of the parent and child, whether violence has increased in intensity, frequency or severity and whether the abuser is making verbal threats, is frightening or intimidating friends, family or neighbours.

The assessment should also cover specific information on children in the household, e.g. ages, health and well-being.

Working Together recommends[41] that professionals check whether domestic abuse has occurred whenever child abuse is suspected, consider the impact of this at all stages of assessment and ask direct questions about domestic abuse.

Young abusers[42]

Distinguishing between normal childhood sexual development and experimentation and sexually inappropriate or aggressive behaviour can cause problems and expert professional judgment may be needed, based on knowledge about normal child sexuality.

Whether the abuse is sexual or physical, relevant considerations include:

- the nature, extent and context of the abusive behaviour;
- the child's development and family and social circumstances;
- the need for services, focusing on the child's harmful behaviour as well as other significant needs; and
- the risks to self and others, including other children in the household, extended family, school, peer group or wider social network.

Diminishing the risk involves ending opportunities for further abuse, acknowledgement by the abuser of the behaviour and acceptance of responsibility, and an agreement to work with the relevant agencies.

Health assessments

On entering care, a child must have a holistic health assessment, which should involve parents, and a health plan as part of the care plan.[43]

Other assessments may be needed in the case of, e.g. the needs of carers of the severely mentally ill (see the Carers and Disabled Children Act 2000),[44] of the chronically sick and disabled, of children with a certain level of special educational needs (see Chapter 13) or relevant and eligible young care leavers (see Chapter 11).

8.5 CHILD ASSESSMENT ORDERS

A child assessment order (CAO) under the Children Act 1989, s.43 is to enable an assessment of a child's health or development, or of the way in which she has been treated. The court may specify the terms of the order, and what contact the child should have with the parents or others during its currency (Children Act 1989, s.43(7),(10)).

The application constitutes specified proceedings (under Children Act 1989, s.41) but not family proceedings (as defined in s.8(4)), and the court has no power to make any s.8 orders instead. However, the court can treat it as an application for an EPO (Children Act1989, s.43(4)).

All reasonable efforts should be made to persuade parents/carers to cooperate with s.47 enquiries. If they continue to refuse access to a child for the purpose of establishing basic facts about her condition, but concerns about her safety are not so urgent as to require an EPO, an application may be made for a CAO. The court may direct them to cooperate with an assessment of the child, the details of which should be specified.

The order does not take away the child's own right to refuse to participate in an assessment, e.g. a medical examination, so long as she is of sufficient age and understanding.[45] Consent to a CAO should be sought from a child of sufficient maturity and understanding.

8.6   ASSESSMENT DURING PROCEEDINGS

Considerations for the court

The court has wide general powers (under Family Proceedings Rules 1991, SI 1991/1247, rule 4.14) to make directions for the conduct of assessment during proceedings, including submission of evidence such as expert reports. Therefore, the court can direct a party to commission, obtain a report and pay for it. It can invite parties to act jointly and bear equal costs.

In considering who is best placed to do it, any party proposing to ask the court for permission to instruct an expert must set out why the expert evidence cannot be obtained through a core assessment or by the children's guardian.[46]

Necessity for court leave

Leave of the court must be obtained before documents filed in the proceedings are disclosed, if a child who is the subject of the proceedings is to be examined and/or assessed, and unless the evidence is to be filed in accordance with relevant directions.

Direction for assessment

When making an interim care order, the court (under Children Act 1989, s.38(6)) may direct the local authority to make an assessment to provide information necessary for the court's decision.

The dividing line between the court's functions and the local authority's functions is that a child in interim care is subject to the local authority's control and the court has no power to interfere with its decisions save in specified cases (*Re C (Interim Care Order: Residential Assessment)* [1997] 1 FLR 1).

A direction for assessment at a Mother and Baby Unit is within the court's jurisdiction, provided that independent assessment is considered appropriate to best promote the child's welfare, even if separation at birth is sought (see *Re C (Interim Care Order: Residential Assessment)* [1997] 1 FLR 1, HL).

The local authority can be directed to arrange and fund either a home-based or residential assessment, but parents/mature children cannot be compelled to participate. It is a matter for judicial discretion, taking into account any financial implications for the local authority (see *Re C (Interim Care Order: Residential Assessment)* [1997] 1 FLR 1, HL).

Where the local authority seeks on financial grounds to argue against an order, it must file detailed evidence well in advance of the hearing, and demonstrate efforts made to seek alternative funding from health/education sources. A residential assessment can be directed even where a local authority asserts that placement would cost its entire annual budget (*Re C (Residential Assessment)* [2001] EWCA Civ 1305, [2001] 3 FCR 164).

A residential placement is 'within the context of a series of simultaneous assessments designed to illuminate the court's ultimate conclusion'; so the court has broad power of determination concerning the process suitable to the child (per the Court of Appeal in *Re B (ICO: Directions)* [2002] EWCA Civ 25).

Preconditions

As regards the imposition of preconditions (*Re M* [1998] 2 FLR 371), the process must be for assessment and not treatment and must not be contrary to the child's best interests, taking the wide- and long-term view of them. They must be necessary to enable the court properly to reach its decision and not be unreasonable in requiring the local authority to fund them.

Other considerations

A residential assessment is not confined to the child alone but applies to the whole family unit.

Treatment is to be distinguished from therapy (which is outside the ambit of Children Act 1989, s.38(6)). Directions for a residential treatment programme to include supervision and assessment of a child's care were over-turned where the primary focus was the mother's emotional problems and drug addiction and little dispute that the primary aim was treatment. But the court observed it was possible for the programme to satisfy s.38(6) even if it included a large element of therapy, with the aim of initiating change (see the Court of Appeal in *Re D* [1999] 2 FLR 632).

What the court sees as assessment may well be experienced by the family as therapy; where psychotherapeutic engagement with the family over an extensive period is an essential element, it may be legalistic and artificial to label the first period of admission as assessment and the second as therapy (*Re G (Interim Care Order: Residential Assessment)* [2004] 1 FLR 876). It is probably an abuse of process to make an interim care order where the main purpose is to enable parents to receive therapy.

Where there is an inexpensive acceptable option it should be directed.

Consent of child

If the child is of sufficient understanding to make an informed decision, she may refuse consent (Children Act 1989, s.38(6)). If so, the High Court in the exercise of its inherent jurisdiction has power to override the refusal if it is in the child's best interests (*South Glamorgan CC* v. *W and B* [1993] 1 FLR 574).

Payment

In *Calderdale Metropolitan Borough Council* v. *S* [2004] EWHC 2529, Bodey J accepted that a specialist report can, and on some occasions, should be comprised within a local authority's core assessment and/or should be part of its own basic case.

Where an apportionment of cost is appropriate it should generally be on a pro rata or proportionate basis, i.e. each party paying equally towards the cost.

The funding of assessments under Children Act 1989, s.38(6) was reviewed by Ryder J in *London Borough of Lambeth* v. *S, C, V and J and the Legal Services Commission* [2005] EWHC 776 (Fam) in which the judge rejected the submission of the LSC that such funding was beyond its powers.

Following the decisions in Calderdale and Lambeth, the LSC has issued revised guidance on its position in relation to experts, and the costs of treatment, therapy and training. This appears in *Focus* 48 (August 2005) and will be contained in Part D (Narrative and Guidance) in the next release of the LSC Manual, vol. 1, The guidance is effective from 25 July 2005.

The LSC will not fund the costs of treatment or expenses in relation to therapy, training or other interventions of an educative or rehabilitative nature.

The LSC discourages applications for prior authority in public law Protocol cases unless the expense is exceptional, i.e. in excess of £5,000 per funded client.

NOTES

1   Unless exceptional circumstances, there must be a compulsory assessment prior to taking a child into police protection: HOC 44/2003 and see *Climbié Inquiry Report* (2003), para 13.17 and recommendation 91.
2   *What to Do If You are Worried a Child is Being Abused*, DH (2003), para. 5.
3   See H. Bretherton, 'How do We Know What We Are Doing? Evidence Based Policy and Practice for CAFCASS' [2003]1 *Family Court Journal*.

4   See *Keeping Children Safe: The Government's Response to the Victoria Climbié Inquiry Report* and the Joint Chief Inspectors' Report, *Safeguarding Children*, DfES, DH, Home Office (2003).

5   Children Act 2004, s.22: partial implementation 2005/2006, full by 2006/2008, and see 'Every Child Matters – Change for Children' materials at **www.everychild matters.gov.uk**.

6   *Practice Direction (Care Cases: Judicial Continuity and Judicial Case Management)* [2003] 2 FLR 719.

7   See, e.g. *Good Practice in Child Care Cases*, Law Society (2004) and requirements on local authority lawyers.

8   See, e.g. the cases of Tyra Henry, 1997; Victoria Climbié, 2003.

9   J. Brophy *et al.*, *Significant Harm: Child Protection Litigation in a Multi-Cultural Setting*, Lord Chancellor's Department (2003).

10 *Learning from Past Experience – A Review of Serious Cases Reviews*, DH (2002).

11 Practice Guidance to the Framework for Assessment of Children in Need and their Families, DH, Home Office and DfEE (2000) (35 pages on assessment of black children in need and their families).

12 *Working Together to Safeguard Children*, DH, Home Office, DfEE (1999), para. 7.25.

13 *Ibid.*, para 6.7.

14 See e.g. *Climbié Inquiry Report* (2003), ch. 16, interpretation of marks on child's body.

15 *Working Together*, para 7.26.

16 J. Butt and K. Mirza quoted in J. Brophy *et al.*, *Significant Harm*.

17 DfES (2003).

18 R.P. Snaith, *Irritability, Depression, Anxiety*, IDA (1978).

19 P. Birleson, *Self Rating Scale for Depression in Young People* (1980).

20 See C. Talbot and P. Kidd, 'Special Guardianship Issues Re Family Assessment', [2004] Fam Law 273.

21 See *What To Do If You are Worried A Child Is Being Abused*.

22 See *Lauren Wright Inquiry Report* (2001).

23 President of the Family Division Guidance Court Business (September 1997).

24 *Climbié Inquiry Report* (2003) Recommendation 25 and para. 4.152.

25 See Appendix 3 to *What to Do If You are Worried a Child is Being Abused*.

26 *Initial Assessment Record*, DH and Welsh Assembly.

27 Framework for Assessment, para. 3.9.

28 *What To Do If You are Worried A Child Is Being Abused*, para. 16.3 and *Working Together*, para. 5.13.

29 *Working Together*, paras 5.13 and 5.15.

30 See *What To Do If You are Worried A Child Is Being Abused*, para. 16.2 and Working Together, para. 5.13.

31 See *What To Do If You are Worried A Child Is Being Abused*, para. 33 and *Working Together*.

32 *Working Together*, para. 5.34.

33 *Climbié Inquiry Report* (2003), Recommendation 37 and para. 5.138.

34 See *Patients as Parents* (2002), and *Child Abuse and Neglect: The Role of Mental Health Services*, Council Report CR120, Royal College of Psychiatrists (April 2004) and further details in Chapter 15 on mental health.

35 *Assessing Children's Needs and Circumstances: Impact of Assessment Framework* (March 2003).

36 *Working Together*, para. 2.22.

37 See Council Report CR120, Royal College of Psychiatrists (April 2004).

38 *Good Medical Practice in the Psychiatric Care of Potentially Violent Patients in the Community*, Report CR80, Royal College of Psychiatrists (2000).

39 See **www.homeoffice.gov.uk** and LASSL (2004)2734.

40 *Domestic Violence, Break The Chain, Multi-Agency Guidance*, Home Office (2002), para. 2c, see **www.homeoffice.gov.uk/docs/index.html**.

41 *Working Together*, para. 6.41.

42 *Ibid.*, para. 6.35.

43 Children Act (Miscellaneous Amendments) (England) Regulations 2002, SI 2002/546; LAC (2002)16 and *Guidance on Promoting the Health of Looked After Children*, DH (2002).

44 And see guidance on **www.carers.gov.uk/carersdisabledchildact2000.htm**.

45 *Working Together*, para. 5.42.

46 Protocol for Judicial Case Management in Public Law Children Act Cases, LCD (2003), App. C.

CHAPTER 9

Contact in public law proceedings

Key sources

- Children Act 1989
- Contact with Children Regulations 1991
- *The Care of Children: Principles and Practice in Regulations and Guidance*, DH (1990)

9.1 INTRODUCTION

The local authority's duty to encourage contact between the child who is looked after and her birth family is enshrined in the Children Act 1989 and the courts have repeatedly endorsed this principle. 'It is the right of a child to have a relationship with both parents wherever possible . . . It is underlined in the United Nations Convention on the Rights of the Child and endorsed in the Children Act 1989' (*Re R (A Minor) (Contact)* [1993] 2 FLR 762 at 767, per Butler-Sloss LJ).

The duty is statutory: local authorities must promote contact between a looked after child and all those connected with her 'unless it is not reasonably practicable or consistent with the child's welfare'. Firmly linked to this is the issue of reunification: 'if contact is not maintained reunification becomes less likely and recognition of this has to underpin all considerations in planning for a child'.[1]

The importance of continuing contact cannot be overestimated:

- only a minority remain looked after on a long-term basis;[2]
- most will return to live with their parents or other members of their birth families or move to independence;
- foster care research has demonstrated that contact is the 'key to discharge' for children's return home;[3]
- even after adoption, children and their birth families are likely to have some form of contact at some point;[4]
- contact and links with friends and family are a major preoccupation of young people looked after.[5]

9.2   HUMAN RIGHTS

The UN Convention on the Rights of the Child (UNCRC) specifies that any child separated from one/both parents has the right to maintain personal relations and direct contact with both on a regular basis except where contrary to her best interests.

Following removal, the primary aim of intervention must be, initially, an attempt at reunification as the first and natural choice except in the clearest of cases (see Chapter 1). Removal is to be seen as a temporary measure only and local authorities have a positive duty to take measures to facilitate family reunification 'as soon as reasonably feasible' (*K and T* v. *Finland* [2000] 2 FLR 79, [2001] 2 FLR 707; *Boultif* v. *Switzerland* [2001] 2 FLR 1228. Whatever the nature of the abuse, assessment for reunification must still be considered, together with all other concurrent planning issues.

9.3   THE LOCAL AUTHORITY'S ROLE

Duty of those with parental responsibility

A parent or person with parental responsibility has a legal obligation to keep the local authority informed of her address and it is an offence (punishable with a level 2 fine) for the parent of a child in care not to disclose this.

Local authority duties

The local authority must (under Children Act 1989, Sched. 2 para.15) promote contact with parents, relatives, friends and people connected with the child and notify parents and those with parental responsibility as to where the child is living, unless this will prejudice her welfare. The local authority must allow the child reasonable contact with (s.34(1)):

- her parents/guardian;
- anyone with a residence order made before the care order;
- anyone with care of the child by virtue of an order made under the court's inherent jurisdiction.

The local authority has discretion to provide expenses payments to the child, parents, relatives, friends, etc. in order to promote contact where hardship would otherwise be caused and the circumstances warrant it (Sched. 2 para.16).

Care of Children guidance

The Care of Children guidance states that there are unique advantages for children in experiencing normal family life in their own birth family; every effort should be made to preserve home and family links. When out-of-home care is necessary, active steps should be taken to ensure a speedy return home.

Siblings should not be separated when being looked after, unless part of a well thought-out plan based on each child's needs. Family links should be actively maintained through visits and other forms of contact. Both parents are important even if one is no longer at home; fathers should not be over-looked or marginalised.

The wider family matters as well, especially siblings and grandparents. Continuity of relationships is important and attachments should be respected, sustained and developed.

Change of home/care-giver/social worker/school almost always carries some risk to the child's development and welfare. Time is a crucial element in child care and should be reckoned in days and months rather than years.

'Reasonable' contact is 'agreed between [all] parties' (*Re P (Minors) (Contact with Children in Care)* [1993] 2 FLR 156) and without agreement is 'objectively defined', i.e. not at the discretion of the local authority.

The Guidance considers how this might take place. Visits by the parents to the child in her foster/residential home or in the family home are the most common form: this provides continuity for the child and opportunities for parents and carers to meet. If family reunification is the plan, visits should be in the family home at the earliest possible stage: this has the advantage of maintaining links with the neighbourhood to which the child will be returning. However, other venues may have advantages for some children and in some circumstances, e.g. outings.

Whatever the venue, the aim should be to ensure privacy, and a welcoming and congenial setting, encouraging parental participation in the child's daily life by, e.g. preparing tea, clothes shopping or putting a child to bed.

Contact at the interim stage

The first weeks are likely to be crucial to the success of the relationship between parent, social worker and the child's carers and to the level of future parent-child contact. Patterns can be set which it may be difficult to change. Parents should be involved in preplacement assessment and planning wherever possible.

Emergency admissions require special care to minimise distress for the child and provide reassurance to parents about their continuing role in the child's life. Early visits and meetings should be encouraged even though parents may need help to cope with the child's distress and their own. These considerations, subject to necessary safeguards for the child, are equally important in emergency protection.[7]

The same principles should arguably apply to contact during child assessment orders and police protection (although in the latter case this is at the discretion of the designated officer).[8] There should be sufficient planning for contact by the time of the first hearing, giving adequate consideration to the guidance above.

Managing and reviewing contact

There are many types of contact:

- face to face;
- by phone;
- letters and cards;
- videotape or exchange of photographs;
- emails or faxes.

The local authority's duties continue after the care order is made. At each review, contact and discharge of the care order must be discussed: without active planning and support for carers, children and birth families, contact in foster care can diminish significantly over time.[9]

The local authority must keep in contact with the looked after child, particularly important when contact with the birth family is not frequent, and must appoint an independent visitor when the child has not been visited by a parent or person with parental responsibility for 12 months (Children Act 1989, Sched. 2, para.17).

Under the Review of Children's Cases Regulations 1991, SI 1991/895, Sched.1, the local authority must review the child's case once within the first three months of placement, and then at six-monthly intervals, to discuss the care plan, the child's progress, and to give the child information, including her right to apply to court under Children Act 1989, s.34 for a contact order or a variation of an existing order.

Reviews are now chaired by an independent reviewing officer (IRO) (see Chapter 11), who must also:

- monitor the review and negotiate to effect a change in contact arrangements if not satisfied with them;
- refer the case to CAFCASS as a last resort (Adoption and Children Act 2002, s.26(2A); potentially particularly important for children held in secure accommodation and penal establishments;
- ensure that the child knows how to use the local authority complaints procedure (under Children Act 1989, s.26), and is aware of her right to have an advocate to speak for her and support her.

9.4   CONTACT FOR CHILDREN IN CUSTODY

It seems clear that such contact arrangements are very unsatisfactory,[10] and it has been argued that a national directive should be issued requiring local authorities to interpret their duties under Children Act 1989, Sched. 2 Pt 2 para.10 much more expansively and seriously, and that the Children Act 1989 should be amended to require local authorities to take proper steps to promote contact between the child and her family and others, wherever she is accommodated.[11]

At present the legislative provisions do not apply to children in custody. However, whilst the 1989 Act does not confer any duties or powers on the Home Secretary or Prison Department, local authority functions, powers and duties (particularly Children Act 1989, ss.17 and 47) apply to all children in prison establishments, including Young Offender Institutions (subject to the necessary requirements of imprisonment) (*R (Howard League for Penal Reform)* v. *Secretary of State for the Home Department* [2003] 1 FLR 484).

9.5   POLICE PROTECTION

When a child is in police protection, the designated officer must decide what contact to allow with the child's parents, anyone with whom she was living immediately before the police intervened, and any person with a contact order, or any person acting on their behalf. The officer must decide what contact is reasonable, and in the child's best interests (Children Act 1989, s.46(10)).

A lawyer acting on behalf of a parent could argue that he or she is entitled to contact; however, access is unlikely to be granted if the parent has been refused on the ground that contact is not in the child's best interests. But the child or young person ought to be offered the opportunity to seek legal advice.

9.6   THE COURT'S ROLE

Duty to consider contact

Before making a care/supervision order the court must consider the contact arrangements made/proposed and invite the parties to comment. This applies to both final and interim orders, and therefore in theory on each renewal.

The Judicial Case Management Protocol requires this to be addressed in the initial social work statement (Appendix B), the interim care plan and the final care plan (Appendix F).

The court has power to make orders regarding contact in all situations where the child is in care: it may make directions about the type or amount to be allowed; impose conditions; make orders even where no relief is sought, and can use family assistance orders to force local authorities to facilitate contact at a distance (*Re E (Family Assistance Order)* [1999] 2 FLR 512).

An interim care order theoretically gives no advantage to any party and should not prejudice the final outcome, so the court's approach when making such orders will be that, save only in circumstances of exceptional and severe risk, contact should be maintained pending final hearing (*A and M* v. *Walsall MBC* [1993] 2 FLR 244).

Leave to terminate contact

An order under Children Act 1989, s.34(4) should be refused where there is a possibility of reunification (*Re L (Sexual Abuse Standard of Proof)* [1996] 1 FLR 116). It is only justified if the probable need to terminate contact is foreseeable (*Re T* [1997] 1 All ER 65) and, once made, implementation is an administrative decision.

Care plans

Contact must be for the child's benefit and balanced against her long-term welfare. Two categories of contact applications should be distinguished, one asking for contact as such, another which effectively attempts to set aside the care order by frustrating the care plan (*Re B (Minors) (Care: Contact)* [1993] 1 FLR 543).

Relevant issues (as set out by the Court of Appeal in *Re E (A Minor) (Care Order: Contact)* [1994] 1 FLR 146) are:

- it is wrong to place too much emphasis on the care plan (i.e. the test in *Re B (Minors) (Care: Contact)* is correct);
- if the benefit of contact outweighs the disadvantages of disrupting the local authority's long-term plans, so be it – that is a proper discharge of the duties placed on courts by Parliament;
- there is a presumption in favour of continuing parental contact (Children Act 1989, s.34(1));
- even when the statutory criteria are satisfied, contact might well be of singular importance to the child's long-term welfare.

Orders for no contact

Such an order is not appropriate because the parties should attempt to reach an agreement under the Contact with Children Regulations 1991, SI 1991/891. It may be preferable for the court to make 'no order for contact', leaving it to the local authority to decide what contact, if any, should take place (*Re CN* [1992] 2 FCR 40).

Without an order, the local authority must allow reasonable contact under Children Act 1989, s.34(1).

The court has no power to prohibit a local authority from allowing contact to a looked after child subject to a care order (*Re W (Section 34(2) Orders)* [2000] 1 FLR 502). Where there is agreement, the 1991 Regulations provide the means to enlarge a pre-existing positive order without unnecessary returns to court, i.e. the local authority can alter the details/nature of contact, e.g. by allowing staying contact (Thorpe LJ in *Re W (Section 34(2) Orders)* [2000] 1 FLR 502).

Refusal of contact ordered by the court

An authority may refuse to allow such contact if satisfied it is necessary to do so in order to safeguard or promote the child's welfare and the refusal is decided upon as a matter of urgency and does not last for more than seven days.

The tension between courts and local authorities

When there is a full care order, the local authority cannot be directed to provide a particular placement/services or be subjected to conditions, but the court does have residual powers (under Children Act 1989, s.34) and can frustrate care plans: 'Parliament has given the courts, not local authorities, the duty to decide on contact' but local authority proposals must 'command the greatest respect and consideration from the court' (*Re B* [1993] 1 FLR 543).

When a judge approves a care plan, it is wrong to make orders for contact inconsistent with local authority recommendations (per the Court of Appeal in *Re D and H (Minors) (Children in Care: Termination of Contact)* [1997] 1 FLR 841. But, in contact applications the child's welfare is paramount and parental contact can be ordered if in the child's best interests even if the long-term care plan envisages eventual termination of such contact (in *Berkshire CC v. B* [1997] 1 FLR 171).

The court may indicate what might be the appropriate level of contact, but should not use the word 'expect' – local authority discretion is subject to statutory provisions (see *Re L (Minors: Care Proceedings: Contact)* [1998] 3 FCR 339; Children Act 1989, s.34(1)(a), Sched. 2 para.15(1)(c)). Once a contact order is made, it is an administrative decision as to whether or not it is acted upon.

9.7   CONTACT UNDER A CHILD ASSESSMENT ORDER

Where it is proposed to keep a child away from home under such an order, it must contain such directions as the court thinks fit with regard to contact during her absence from home (Children Act 1989, s.43(10)).

Although the child's welfare is the court's paramount consideration, the court is not required to apply the welfare checklist as the application is under Children Act 1989, Part V. This distinction is probably academic, as any court applying the welfare principle is likely to have regard to the matters set out in the checklist.

9.8   CONTACT UNDER AN EMERGENCY PROTECTION ORDER

When a court makes an EPO, the applicant must allow the child reasonable contact with the same people as specified above for a child in police protection (Children Act 1989, s.44(13)), but subject to any order the court may make (s.44(6)).

'Reasonable' implies contact agreed between the local authority and the parents or, if no agreement, contact which can be regarded as objectively reasonable (*P (Minors) (Contact with Children in Care)* [1993] 2 FLR 156).

9.9   RELEVANT RESEARCH

Since 1980, all studies have consistently shown that the best predictor of reunification from care is the maintenance of contact links, and that frequent contact between parents and children is an essential part of successful rehabilitation.

The following (not an exhaustive list) are important aspects of such contact:[12]

- the first six months are the most crucial;
- arrangements and support are the most difficult and time-consuming aspects of social work with children in placement;
- commitment of carers to contact visits;
- placement of children near parents' homes;
- placement of siblings together;
- written plans;
- influence of resources on visits;
- flexibility;
- preparatory work with parents;
- planning contact activities geared to the child's current developmental stage;
- overnight contact is essential to reunification.

BAAF publications re-emphasise[13] that contact for children in foster care is universally accepted; that social workers still struggle to accommodate the wishes of separated parents and that there can be risks to a child's welfare.

The purpose of contact needs to be evaluated to:

- maintain relationships;
- reassure children they have not been abandoned;
- reassure children that their own family is safe and well;
- assess parenting skills and the parents' motivation;
- assist children and families to develop better ways to interact and communicate.

9.10 PRACTICAL CONSIDERATIONS

Local authority practitioners need to reinforce research messages to social workers.

Children's guardians and practitioners need to remind themselves not only of the child's wishes and feelings and the rights of other parties, but also the important research messages.

Parents' representatives need to ensure their clients have the best opportunity to achieve reunification and should encourage them to maintain contact: 'it cannot be in the interest of the child and is no service to parents to allow them to drift to the periphery of a child's life, without reminding them of the possible implications of this course to the plan for their child and his/her relationship with them'.[14]

The issue of contact with other parties, siblings and other adults significant to the child must also be considered – a requirement in proceedings in any event.[15]

Arrangements for contact

Ascertaining the child's wishes and feelings in relation to proposals is essential. The arrangements must be watertight and in writing.[16] Arrangements often fail due to difficulties over, e.g. payment for travel, an escort to accompany the child, the venue, which may be closed at the time that contact ought to happen, or where foster carers go away at weekends.

Contact is often supervised when this is not necessary. The practitioner should closely question the social worker on the proposed arrangements, and must not assume that they will be satisfactory. The details should be included in the care plan. If they are amended at court, an amended care plan should be prepared and signed in the usual way.

Foster carers may refuse to agree to contact in their home because they have not been given accurate or detailed enough information about the family, and may be apprehensive for no sound reasons. New foster carers may be more resistant to contact arrangements.

Types of contact

The balance between the child's need for stability, roots and identity and maintaining existing relationships must be borne in mind: indirect contact may be an appropriate substitute for direct contact. Parental acceptance of permanence of the care plan is likely to be a relevant factor in settling contact arrangements. It is often suggested that there should be a period of no contact while a child settles in to a new placement – this should be closely scrutinised. It may not be necessary, particularly where a parent is cooperating with the planned placement.

Consider also the need for the child to be protected from the risk of harm, emotional or physical or otherwise, during contact. The parents' rights may well be overridden by, e.g. domestic abuse (see guidelines in *Re L; Re V; Re M; Re H (Contact: Domestic Violence)* [2000] 2 FLR 334).

NOTES

1 Children Act Guidance, para. 2.33.
2 S. Milham, R. Bullock, K. Hosie and M. Haak, *Lost in Care: the Problems of Maintaining Links between Children and their Families*, Aldershot, Gower (1986).
3 D. Fanshel and E.B. Shinn, *Children in Foster Care: A Longitudinal Investigation*, New York, Columbia University Press (1978).
4 C. Thomas and V. Beckford with M.A. Murch and N. Lowe, *Adopted Children Speaking*, London, BAAF (1999).
5 See J. Timms and J. Thoburn, *Your Shout*, NSPCC (2003).
6 *The Care of Children: Principles and Practice in Regulations and Guidance*, DH (1990).
7 *Ibid.*, vol. 3, para. 6.10.
8 See HOC 44/2003 and Chapter 6.
9 A. Bilson and R. Barker, 'Parental Contact with Children Fostered and in Residential Care after the Children Act 1989' (1995) 25(3) *British Journal of Social Work* 367.
10 B. Goldson, *Vulnerable Inside – Children in Secure and Penal Settings*, Children's Society (2002); report by HM Inspector of Prisons for England and Wales, *Young Prisoners: A Thematic Review* (1997).
11 C. Lyon, *Child Abuse*, 3rd edn, Family Law (2003).
12 See *Contact: managing visits to children looked after away from home*, BAAF (1993); J. Tresiolotis, *Prevention and Reunification in Child Care* (1993).
13 J. Tresiolotis *et al.*, *Developing Foster Care* (2000) and *Signposts in Fostering: Policy, Practice and Research Issues* (1999).
14 Children Act Guidance, vol. 3 'Family Placements' para. 6.38 and vol. 4 'Residential Care', para. 4.38.
15 Protocol for Judicial Case Management in Public Law Children Act Cases, LCD (2003), App. F.
16 Children Act Guidance.

CHAPTER 10

Care plans

Key sources

- Special Educational Needs and Disability Act 2001
- Adoption and Children Act 2002, s.118
- Arrangements for Placement Regulations 1991
- Children Act Guidance and Regulations (1991), vols 3 and 4, paras 2.43–2.62
- Circulars LAC (98)20, LAC (99)29, and LAC (2000)13
- *Planning and Providing Good Quality Placements for Children in Care*, DH (2001)
- Protocol for Judicial Case Management in Public Law Children Act Cases (2003)

10.1 INTRODUCTION

This chapter should be read with Chapter 4 on safeguarding and services, Chapter 5 on child protection, Chapter 8 on assessments, and Chapter 9 on contact.

Planning is a process that consists of four components:

- enquiry;
- consultation;
- assessment; and
- decision-making.

10.2 HUMAN RIGHTS

The human rights and diversity principles set out in Chapter 3 on child development and Chapter 19 on child centred representation are directly relevant.

Planning for a child needs to be started early, be comprehensive, culturally competent and focused on the individual child's needs. It should be possible for a child to identify what decisions have been taken and the rationale for them. Above all, it should involve the child in the process: all too often, children do not even know what a care plan is, let alone who is responsible for it.[1]

The Children Act 1989 emphasises that delay in making decisions for children may be prejudicial and in recent years the judiciary have been taking steps to ensure that delays in planning for children are minimised.

10.3 TIMING AND TYPES OF PLANS

A care plan for a child is relevant:

- at the disposal stage of care proceedings, if the threshold criteria have been established;
- during the course of the proceedings, when the court is considering whether or not to make an interim care order;
- for a child who is looked after, but who is not the subject of proceedings.

Different types of plans

Sequential planning

Sequential planning is no longer used – waiting until care proceedings are concluded before taking steps to plan for the child would now be regarded as poor social work practice, as it delays final placement for the child.

Twin track/parallel planning

Two options for the child are considered:

- rehabilitation within a strictly time limited framework, or
- adoption outside the family.

Enquiries proceed on a 'twin track', i.e. both options in parallel, so the court can be presented with well-researched options in order to prevent delay. 'Such a course requires an approach from local authorities which breaks the mould of sequential planning' (Bracewell J in *Re D and K (Care Plan: Twin Track Planning)* [1999] 2 FLR 872).

Concurrent planning

Concurrent planning was first developed in 1981 by the Lutheran Social Services in Seattle, USA, with the aim of speeding up placement of children into permanent families, to prevent drift and delay. It means permanence planning involving both the birth family as well as the substitute family. The at risk child is placed with a foster family, while the social work team works concurrently with the birth family to address the causes of the child's removal, and sustain contact with a view to eventual rehabilitation.

At the same time, social workers attempt to find and assess other members of the extended family who might take the child or support the birth family if they were reunited. If efforts to reunite fail within a tight timescale, the child remains with the foster family as an adoptive placement.

Judicial guidance[2] recommended that:

- it was incumbent on guardians and local authorities to ensure twin track, and not sequential, planning to avoid delay in proceedings and placement;
- it must be made clear to parents at the outset that options are being considered;
- courts should be proactive and issue necessary directions and liaise with connected persons such as Directors of social services, Chairs of panels and guardian managers;
- pilot schemes should be undertaken, as in the USA, to recruit specially trained foster carers able to work with parents to reunify but in the event that this fails, to be prepared to adopt the child.

In the mid-1990s the first projects started in England: the Goodman Project, launched in Manchester in 1998; Coram Family, an independent adoption agency in London, taking families from the London Boroughs of Camden and Islington, and concurrency planning by a team in Brighton and Hove Social Services Department.

A Protocol was agreed between the Inner London and City Family Proceedings Court and the Coram Concurrent Planning Project that required:

- identification of the concurrent planning intention in the supplement to the application for a care order;
- appointment of the child's solicitor within 24 hours of the application;
- publicity leaflets about the Project to be exhibited to the initial social work statement;
- where a party wishes to instruct an expert, to identify why an expert opinion in respect of parenting issues is required over and above the professional opinion provided by the Project.

A 1993 evaluation of the work carried out by the schemes, which involved 24 concurrent planning placements,[3] and 68 children, concluded that cases moved faster to permanence and involved the children in fewer moves between carers; children did not show any evidence of harm on developmental and relationship measures; and it was possible to say with confidence that it worked well for the children in the study.

10.4 STRUCTURE AND CONTENT OF CARE PLAN

Guidance

The contents of the care plan should be as follows: [4]

- the child's identified needs (including those arising from race, culture, religion or language, special educational or health needs) and how they might be met;
- aim of the plan and timescale;
- proposed placement, with type and details;
- other services to be provided to the child and/or family by the local authority or other agencies;
- arrangements for contact and reunification;
- support in the placement;
- likely duration of placement;
- contingency plan, if placement breaks down;
- arrangements for ending the placement (if made under voluntary arrangements);
- who is to be responsible for implementing the plan (specific tasks and overall plan);
- specific detail of the parents' role in day-to-day arrangements;
- extent to which the wishes and views of child, parents and anyone else (including representatives of other agencies) with sufficient interest in the child have been obtained, acted upon and reasons supporting this or explanations of why the wishes/views have been discounted;
- dates of reviews.

The care plan should also include arrangements for:

- input by parents, child and others into ongoing decision-making process;
- notifying the responsible authority of disagreements or making representations;
- health care (including consent to examination and treatment);
- education.

About one quarter of looked after children are disabled.[5] These children tend to be placed in residential care more often than non-disabled children, and to remain away from home for longer periods.

The care plan must show that what is proposed is the best way to meet the particular child's assessed needs, paying particular attention to any physical or other characteristics in the environment, which may exacerbate the impact of the child's impairment.

Further guidance issued in 1999[6] supplements the original 1998 guidance[7] and is specific to those children who are the subject of court proceedings. It was approved by the President of the Family Division and is binding on local authorities. The mature child should have her own copy. The plan should be considered at statutory reviews. Practitioners need to advise clients, parents and mature children of the statutory review procedure which should now assume greater emphasis.

The plan in proceedings is a distinct and separate formal court document, which must stand on its own. It should not be presented as a sworn statement or affidavit or be incorporated into a local statement of evidence. It should not inappropriately duplicate information in such statements, such as the child's history and evidential aspects of proceedings, nor contain the welfare checklist, nor references to other documents.

Care plans, although incomplete, may sometimes be needed at an interim stage in care proceedings. This will not necessarily represent the local authority's final views by the time of the final hearing. The first page under 'type of hearing' must clearly distinguish between interim plans for interim hearings and a complete care plan for the final hearing.

The last and separate page should include the full name and professional position of the person who has prepared the plan – normally the social worker allocated to the case, although a range of other people within the local authority and from other agencies may have contributed to it, as may have the child, her family and the children's guardian.

The last page should also include the full name(s) and professional position(s) of person(s) endorsing the plan (this is only needed for the care plan prepared for the final hearing).

10.5 COURT REQUIREMENTS FOR THE CARE PLAN

'The local authority care plan should, so far as is reasonably possible, accord with [Children Act Guidance] paragraph 2.62 of Volume 3 as to its form and content' (*Manchester City Council* v. *F* [1993] 1 FLR 419).

Before a care order is made (per Wall in *Re J (Minors) (Care Plan)* [1994] 1 FLR 253) the care plan must be subject to vigorous scrutiny. If foster carers are identified, evidence about them should be in the plan. A properly constructed plan is essential to enable the court to make its decision: the plan should enable parties to focus on relevant issues and thereby save court time and costs.

10.6 CARE PLANS AND EDUCATION

Local authorities must[8] ensure all looked after children have a personal education plan (PEP) and establish and maintain a protocol for sharing relevant information about the care and education of children.

Except where the child is placed in an emergency, the arrangements for suitable placement should include suitable education, and no placement should be made without the education element being satisfactorily sorted out.

Where placement has to be made in an emergency, and education has not been secured, or where education provision breaks down, the local authority must secure an education placement within 20 school days.[9]

The plan's educational component should be informed by special educational needs and disability law (see the Education Act 1996 as amended by the Special Educational Needs and Disability Act 2001), and statutory guidance,[10] which strengthen the right to mainstream education for children.

Under the Disability Discrimination Act 1995, service providers must:

- take reasonable steps to change practice, policies and procedures which make it impossible or unreasonably difficult for disabled people to use a service;
- provide auxiliary aids or services enabling disabled people to use a service;
- overcome physical barriers by service provision through a reasonable alternative method.

For definitions of special educational needs and/or disabilities see Chapter 13.

Access to education for children and young people with medical needs must be detailed in the care plan.[11]

Reviews

The social worker retains responsibility for case management and the statutory review process, of which the PEP is a part. The PEP will normally be reviewed concurrently with the care plan, i.e. within 28 days/three months/six months, etc. However, reviews can take place at any time in response to arising needs, relevant changes or at the young person's request. Significant decisions about education should not take place without reviewing the PEP and this must involve the child.

Using the statutory review cycle underpins the minimum of six-month reviews of the PEP and highlights the link between the PEP and the care plan. However, the logistics of this may prove impractical where, e.g. a child's statutory reviews coincide with school holidays, especially the summer vacation. If so, local authorities should make arrangements for the PEP to be reviewed at least every six months and for the results to go to the care plan review.

10.7 CARE PLANS AND CARE LEAVERS

For a teenage child, the care plan may well need to consider arrangements for leaving care. Changes to arrangements for those living in and leaving care have been aimed at developing life skills and clarifying responsibility for financial support:[12] note the provisions on pathway plans in the Children (Leaving Care) Act 2000 and Children (Leaving Care) (England) Regulations 2001, SI 2001/2874, and see Chapter 11 for further details.

10.8 CARE PLANS AND ADOPTION

Where the facts of the case remain in dispute up to the final hearing, choice of placement may significantly depend on findings of fact. It is in these cases where it is likely to be most difficult to carry out much, if any, of the detailed preparatory work for a placement prior to the final hearing. However, even here it should normally be possible, within the care plan, to explain the principal steps needed before an adoptive placement could be made, and give estimated timescales for each of the key steps.

This would include those cases where it is necessary to timetable therapeutic work with a child before preparing her for placement.

A well-managed case will avoid this situation arising; where it is unlikely that the parties will be able to agree the facts, a causation hearing should be fixed early on in the proceedings. Even where facts are not disputed and the preferred option is adoption, it is important that the local authority satisfies itself that sufficient assessment has taken place to rule out rehabilitation or placement with relatives (e.g. under a Children Act 1989, s.8 residence order). Local authority procedures should facilitate the process of finding an adoptive placement – how much progress can be made before final hearing will depend on a range of factors, including the overall timescale of the proceedings.

Where adoption is the preferred option, the following issues should be addressed during the care proceedings:[13]

- The local authority should take steps to coordinate information between the team responsible for the care proceedings and those responsible for family finding and allocate responsibilities for carrying out the necessary work.
- The BAAF Form E (details about the child) should be completed as far as possible, including obtaining from the parents relevant medical and other details.
- The adoption panel should consider the case, with a view to making a recommendation on whether adoption is in the child's best interests. The local authority should have identified the key steps and timetable,

including family finding and any necessary therapy, and issues of contact (for inclusion in the care plan) which would lead to an adoptive placement, if the court made a care order.

- The care plan should include a contingency plan for use in specified circumstances if the preferred option for adoption cannot be achieved. Consideration should be given to whether a freeing application is appropriate.

It is not appropriate for there to have been introductions between the child and the prospective adopters, or confirmation by the agency of the panel's recommendations before the final hearing.

10.9   CONSIDERATIONS FOR THE PRACTITIONER

Does the care plan represent an authoritative statement about the child's needs?

Does the care plan fully reflect the dimensions of the child and family's race, culture, religion and language? Relevant guidance is in Circular LAC (98) 20[14] and information from research should be used (see below).

Does it deal with the best way of responding to those needs?

Consider in particular:

- Are there details of how the local authority will provide services to promote and protect the child's welfare whilst she is the subject of a care order?
- Is it clear where the child will be in two, four, six, eight, ten or 12 months' time?
- Who will be responsible for her?
- Is the strategy identified in the plan for change able to achieve the objectives?
- Are the timescales suggested in the plan ones that support the child's development?
- What will happen to the child before any placement is made?
- Are the objectives suggested in plan supported by the local authority's track record?

Is the involvement of other agencies needed?

To what extent is input from a range of services other than social services relevant (e.g. health and education)? It is important that agreement on service provision is reached before the making of any final order.

Placement outside the area?

Where the proposed placement is outside the area of the local authority bringing the proceedings, what discussion has taken place and agreement reached between authorities on the provision of appropriate services to meet the child's needs? Have the details been included in the care plan?

How many plans?

A separate care plan is needed for each child who is the subject of care proceedings. Some of the information for siblings may be similar or identical; other material may be different because the distinct characteristics of each child must be addressed, together with the way in which the plan proposes to meet each child's needs.

The practitioners acting for the parents and child will wish to scrutinise the care plans for each sibling, and to draw the attention of the court to any important differences between the respective plans reflecting individual needs.

Who has endorsed the plan?

One or more relevant senior officers within the local authority should endorse the plan for the final hearing, to indicate the authority's commitment to it. Consider whether the budget holder has endorsed it, and where a placement outside the extended family is planned, has the Family Placement Section been advised of the plan and approved the timescales and plans for placement?

If the care plan is for adoption, has the proposal been to the Permanency Panel for a recommendation, followed by a decision by the Adoption Agency decision-maker? Without this decision, there can be no valid plan.

Should a senior manager attend court to give evidence in relation to the wider considerations that may have influenced the choice of care plan, such as the overall aim of plan or selection of particular placement or other resource?

Practitioners should consider whether there is any research material that will inform their consideration of the plan.[15]

10.10   AMENDMENT OF THE CARE PLAN

If the plan is amended in the course of proceedings orally or by hand-written amendment, a new complete typewritten document properly signed by relevant personnel must be lodged at court and served (by court direction if necessary).

10.11   REVIEWING IMPLEMENTATION

Reviews must take place within a statutory framework (see the Review of Children's Cases Regulations 1991, SI 1991/895). Circular LAC (98) 20 reiterates the importance of providing an oversight of the implementation of the care plan within this framework.[16]

Monitoring individual children's care plans through the reviewing system will also generate management information about any difficulties, such as lack of key services or other inputs, which may have contributed to delay in implementing the plan. Information may usefully inform the children's services planning process.

10.12   CHALLENGING THE CARE PLAN DURING CARE PROCEEDINGS

If the court disagrees with the care plan, it has limited options available (*Re T (A Minor) (Care Order: Conditions)* [1994] 2 FLR 423). There is no power to impose conditions on a final care order nor to require the local authority to place the child in a given setting (Children Act 1989, s.100(2)(a) prohibits this). It is the court's duty to scrutinise the care plan and, if it disagrees with it, it can refuse to make the order sought by the local authority. The circumstances in which such refusal is likely should be rare (*Re KDT* [1994] FCR 721).

Parliament has given local authorities the responsibility for decisions concerning a child who is the subject of a care order and the discretion to carry out post-care order responsibilities. Thus, neither the court nor the guardian has any function once the care order is made (*Re CN* [1992] 2 FCR 40). The time must come when the court withdraws from exercising further control over the child and passes it to the local authority. Accordingly, the court will be acting beyond its powers if it makes a care order subject to court review in six months' time (*Re B (A Minor) (Care Order Review)* [1993] 1 FLR 421) and cannot attach an injunction to a public law Children Act order as a means of frustrating the local authority care plan for reunification (*Re S and D (Children: Powers of Court)* [1995] 2 FLR 456). Nor can the court make a series of interim care orders over an indefinite period: this is an artificial use of the power to make such orders, which are restricted to cases where the courts are not in a position to dispose of applications for care orders (*Re L* [1996] 1 FLR 116).

10.13 CHALLENGING THE CARE PLAN POST PROCEEDINGS

Changes

There are a number of avenues available if the local authority changes the care plan after the final care hearing. Generally, the court process is not applicable until the complaints procedure has been exhausted (see *R* v. *Royal Borough of Kingston upon Thames, ex p. T* [1994] 1 FLR 798), although this does not apply to Human Rights Act 1998 applications. The children's guardian should not use judicial review to mount such challenges: the proper forum is within the care proceedings when the full merits of the plan can be considered (*Re L (Care Proceedings Human Rights Claims)* [2003] EWHC Fam. 665, [2003] 2 FLR 60).

Consider the following steps:

- issuing an appeal out of time against the original order: this is difficult (see *Re FB* [1999] 1 FLR 713) but it is a matter of court discretion;
- making a residence order application;
- making an application to discharge the care order under Children Act 1989, s.39;
- making an application for contact, when the court can look again at the care plan (under s.34; *Re B* [1993] 1 FLR 543);
- making an application for permission to apply for judicial review;
- making a freestanding human rights application under Human Rights Act 1998, s.7;
- encouraging the court to 'name and shame' (see *Re F; F* v. *Lambeth LBC* [2002] 1 FLR 217);
- making a complaint under Children Act 1989, s.26;
- a referral to the Commissioner for Children (Wales) or the Children's Rights Director under the Care Standards Act 2000 (note that the English Children's Commissioner cannot consider individual cases);
- requesting the Independent Reviewing Officer to investigate;
- suing the local authority for a failure of care (*Barrett* v. *Enfield LBC* [1999] 2 FLR 426; *C* v. *Flintshire CC* [2001] 2 FLR 33; *Z and others* v. *UK* [2001] 2 FLR 612);
- a complaint to the Secretary of State (Children Act 1989, s.84(1)).

10.14 FAMILY GROUP CONFERENCES[17]

This model of planning for a child's future ensures that children and their families are centrally involved in decisions that affect their lives. Family group conferences (FGCs) originated in New Zealand in the 1980s as an alternative to more conventional decision-making processes – they are central to the legal process there. They were introduced in Scotland in 1999.

Their importance as a planning tool has now been recognised by inclusion in the Judicial Case Management Protocol Checklist for court consideration at the case management stage. This means that the local authority, in theory, has a maximum of 60 days from commencement of the proceedings to consider making a referral for an FGC.

The FGC aims to ensure state intervention in family life is kept at the minimum level compatible with ensuring promotion of the child's welfare. Research consistently shows that in over 90 per cent of cases, families make plans that agencies are happy to support.

Ideally, the FGC would be held at the very early stages of involvement with the family, preferably before the child is accommodated. If not, it should be held at an appropriate stage during the proceedings unless there are reasons why this would not be in the child's interests. The following factors should always be taken into account:

- Consent: in most circumstances, FGCs should only take place with the consent of the parents and the child if old enough. The court, however, may decide that the child's interest overrules the parents' rights to refuse consent.
- Recommendations or requirements: the court cannot require relatives to attend, but it can recommend that such a conference is called; this may help encourage relatives to attend by giving it legitimacy.
- Timing: in determining the most appropriate timing for the FGC, consider:
  - Will the wider family have the information they require from any assessments to make an informed decision?
  - Do the parents agree to the conference?
  - Are the views of any of the wider family known?
- Disclosure of information: what information does the wider family require in order to make a decision? Has consent been obtained to disclose this information?
- Experience and knowledge: does the local authority have a family group conference service? If not, how do they propose to organise an FGC?

All such conferences should be run according to nationally accepted standards and the Family Rights Group's Guidance has been welcomed nationally; above all, the process must be child-centred.[18]

There is a preparatory phase, and three key stages to the FGC, with the possibility of follow-up meetings.

The preparatory phase, on average five to six weeks, starts with a referral to an independent coordinator who convenes the conference. She spends time identifying the family network, helping the child to express her views, where appropriate with the assistance of an advocate. She prepares the family and professionals for the meeting, and negotiates which family members can attend. The family will be consulted on arrangements for the meeting, including the time and venue.

Stage 1 involves the coordinator, as Chair, introducing everyone present, and facilitating professionals sharing concerns about the child with the family. The coordinator ensures that the language used is that chosen by the family, and the information is in an accessible form (e.g. through a signer). The family can ask questions. The professionals and coordinator then leave the meeting.

In Stage 2, the family meets on its own to draw up a plan, provided with culturally appropriate food and drink, and as much time as they need. No record is kept of the discussion, unless the family wishes to do this.

In Stage 3, after a plan is agreed, the family meets with the coordinator and professionals to present their plan. The only ground for refusing to accept it is if it places the child at risk of significant harm. If so, and it proves impossible to negotiate an agreement, the matter will have to go before a court.

The child who is the subject of the FGC should be involved if at all possible. At the early stages of preparation the coordinator should consider how this can be done, which could involve arranging an independent advocate to support the child.

The advantages of the FGC are:

- a plan agreed in this way may save time and a confrontational court hearing;
- it means that the child can be told her family had made the decision about her future, even if this means a move to a placement outside the family;
- a kinship placement is the more likely outcome;
- it ensures the extended family is involved in the process of planning, and the family members are considered as carers;
- it may provide an opportunity to help parents reach a decision about relinquishment of their child.

10.15 CARE PLANNING UNDER THE ADOPTION AND CHILDREN ACT 2002

New guidance is to be issued on the role of the care planning process in ensuring that children are securely attached to carers capable of providing safe and effective care for the duration of their childhood.[19] The emphasis is on seeing permanence in the context of the whole system of services for children.

An effective care plan will have a plan for permanence, setting out objectives for work with the child, birth family and carers in relation to her developmental needs. A clearly articulated plan to achieve permanence must be agreed by the second statutory review (four months after the child becomes looked after).

Once the plan has been decided and the arrangements for carrying it out have been agreed, it can only be altered by a statutory review. The review is a process of continuous monitoring and reassessment. All relevant placement options must be considered when planning for permanence for a looked after child.

Local authorities are required to make all reasonable efforts to reunite looked after children with their parents whenever possible. Circular LAC (98) 20 stressed the need to achieve the right balance between efforts to reunite the child with her family, and the importance of 'child time' in achieving permanence.

The draft guidance identifies the range of placements for a child, and states that local authorities should exercise their powers to ensure that options for the child are not inappropriately restricted solely because of considerations about access to support services, including financial support.

Living with parents: services for a child in need are available under Children Act 1989, s.17.

A home with family or friends: this needs to be approved as foster carers and fostering allowances and support are provided under Children Act 1989, s.23.

Fostering: this enables the child to maintain her attachments to parents and the wider family, particularly for the older child with strong links of that kind, who does not want or need the formality of adoption. Fostering allowances and support will be provided under s.23.

Residential care: this may be appropriate for certain children; where this is the care plan, it must address how the child's need for secure attachment to significant adults will be achieved and supported.

A residence order: this may be used to increase the degree of legal permanence in a placement. The Adoption and Children Act (ACA) 2002 allows the routine extension of orders to the age of 18. Parental responsibility will be shared, but the parent's ability to exercise it will be controlled by the person with whom the child lives. A local authority may contribute towards the cost of accommodation and maintenance of the child, where a residence order is made to a person other than a parent or step-parent of a child, under Children Act 1989, Sched.1 para.15.

Special guardianship order: this gives the holder parental responsibility without severing the legal ties to the child's parents. The order will cease to apply at age 18. Support services, including financial support, will be available in accordance with regulations to be made under Children Act 1989 s.14F (inserted by ACA 2002).

Adoption: this can offer the child a legally 'permanent new family. Adoption Support services, including financial support, are available (in accordance with the Adoption Support Services Regulations 2005, SI 2005/691).

Contingency planning: where birth parents have been assessed as unlikely to make and sustain the necessary changes in parenting abilities, this may be used to avoid delay in securing a permanent family for the child. Birth parents need to understand that the two plans, reunification and alternative permanence, are being pursued at the same time.

ACA 2002 introduces a new provision (Children Act 1989, s.31A) prohibiting a court from making a care order unless the local authority has prepared a care plan in the prescribed manner. There is no statutory requirement to file an interim care plan, but the Judicial Case Management Protocol requires this.

10.16   COSTS OF AN ASSESSMENT OF SUPERVISED CONTACT

The Legal Services Commission may exceptionally meet the costs of an assessment of supervised contact[20] (as opposed to supported contact) for an independent social worker's or other assessment of contact (but not contact centre fees for supported contact) provided that:

- CAFCASS cannot reasonably be expected to assist through a report or other support;
- contact sessions are reasonable in number and extent, and the court has ordered an assessment report of the contact to be submitted to assist in the final determination of an application pending before the court; and
- any charges for, or expenses in relation to, treatment, therapy or training are met elsewhere.

10.17   PLANS, RECORDS AND THE FUTURE

Looking After Children records are used by the majority of social services departments in England and Wales to provide a systematic approach to planning, but electronic records and the requirements of the new Common Assessment Framework may introduce new documentation.

The Integrated Children's System[21] provides a framework for assessment, planning, intervention and review building on the Framework for Assessment and the Looking After Children System. It brings together every process that may be needed in local authority work with a child, and provides exemplars designed to be used by an electronic information system, to record information on a single data entry basis as the care plan progresses.

This is part of the information-sharing strategy identified in the Every Child Matters change programme. Introduction of electronic records and plans for all social care, health and police services is planned for 2005.

NOTES

1   J. Timms and J. Thoburn, *Your Shout*, NSPCC (2003).
2   Bracewell J in *Re D and K (Care Plan: Twin Track Planning)* [1999] 2 FLR 872. See also Children Act Advisory Committee, *Best Practice in Children Act Cases* (June 1997); Wall J, 'Concurrent Planning – A Judicial Perspective' (1999) 11(2) *Child and Family Law Quarterly*.
3   E. Monck , J. Reynolds and V. Wigfall, *The Role of Concurrent Planning: Making Permanent Placements for Young Children*, BAAF (2003).
4   Children Act Guidance, vols. 3 and 4.
5   *Disabled Children: Directions for their Future Care*, DH (1998).
6   LAC (99)29.
7   LAC (98)20.
8   LAC (2000)13.
9   *Ibid.*, s.10.
10   Special Educational Needs Code of Practice 2001; and *Inclusive Schooling*, DfES, DfES/0774/2001 (November 2001).
11   LAC (2001)27.
12   See consultation paper *Me, Survive, Out There? New Arrangements for Young People Living in and Leaving Care*, LASSL (99)15 (July 1999).
13   LAC (99)29.
14   LAC (98)20, paras 11–18, and see research, including J. Butt and K. Mizra, *Social Care and Black Communities*, Race Equality Unit (1995).
15   J. Sudbery, S. Hicks, S. Thompson, H. McLaughlin and C. Bramley (eds) with K. Wilson, *A Bibliography of Family Placement Literature*, BAAF (2005).
16   As set out in Children Act Guidance, vols. 3 and 4.
17   See e.g. **www.frg.org.uk**.
18   By the Department of Health, Local Government Association, Association of Directors of Social Services, Barnardo's and National Children's Homes.
19   One of the Government's objectives for children's social services – see *Modernising Social Services*, DH (1998).
20   See DfES website and 'Every Child Matters' materials.
21   LSC *Focus* 48 (August 2005): amendment to Funding Code, para. 1.3.

CHAPTER 11

Looked after and leaving care

Key sources

- Children (Leaving Care) Act 2000 (amends Children Act 1989, ss.19, 22 to 24)
- Adoption and Children Act 2002, s.118
- Homelessness Act 2002
- Review of Children's Cases (England) Regulations 1991 and Review of Children's Cases (Amendment) (England) Regulations 2004
- CAFCASS (Reviewed Case Referral) Regulations 2004
- Children Act Guidance and Regulations (1991), vol. 3, ch. 9 and vol. 4, ch. 7
- National Standards for the Provision of Children's Advocacy Services 2002, DH
- *Getting It Right* resource pack, DH (2000); *Get It Sorted*, DfES (2004)
- *Independent Reviewing Officers Guidance*, DfES (2004) and Welsh Assembly (2004)

11.1 INTRODUCTION

A looked after child needs access to ongoing help during and after proceedings and care: this chapter provides an outline of the issues that may arise when she wants to express her views or make complaints, and in the monitoring of care plans and the duties owed to care leavers.

Accessible and useful advice is also available on the Resolution children's committee website at **www.care.org.uk**.

The child's health and education are particularly important. Abuse survivors may need ongoing counselling and support long after proceedings and post-care. For others, despite their experiences, support with education and training will be the overriding priority to overcome disadvantage. Once proceedings are over, the child's access to independent help and advice is limited: the role of the new 'independent reviewing officer' will therefore be extremely important in reassuring the child her care plan will be properly implemented, and challenged if not.

Other relevant chapters are Chapter 8 on assessments, Chapter 10 on care plans, Chapter 13 on education and Chapter 14 on housing.

11.2   HUMAN RIGHTS AND DIVERSITY

Enhanced help and support with physical and/or mental health needs may be needed. Article 39 of the UNCRC states that 'all appropriate measures should be taken to promote the physical and psychological recovery and social reintegration of a child victim of any form of neglect or abuse'.

It should be made clear to children that they have as much right to access complaints and representation procedures and appeals as adults. They should be given information to enable them to participate in decision-making and to mount challenges where and when they wish to do so.

All looked after children and care leavers should receive the same quality of service as their peers.[1] Particular consideration is needed for those from backgrounds where family and community ties are strong: all should be encouraged to explore issues of heritage and culture to prepare them for leaving care and supporting them thereafter.

Asylum seekers and refugees

Asylum seekers' children need enhanced support, especially for health, education and accommodation, and well-planned help with immigration issues: becoming 18 can place some in difficulties (see Chapter 17). Legal provisions on leaving care apply to those looked after and accommodated by the local authority in their entirety regardless of any other special status that unaccompanied children may have.

SEN and disability issues

Nearly 25 per cent of looked after children are disabled and remain in care longer. They need personalised services, good transitional arrangements to adult services and integrated multi-agency planning. Those whose impairment may affect their ability to express their wishes should be given particular consideration, especially over the timing of leaving care.

Many are in full-time residential school placements or in respite/health care. They will spend most, if not all, of their childhood living away from home, are unlikely to return and are as much estranged from their families as other looked after children, and just as much in need of plans and advice. Decisions are often based on sweeping assumptions about their abilities, rather than formal assessment of their aptitude or their wishes, and many are simply transferred from one environment to another and given no opportunity to consider independent living or access to mainstream education and employment services. Unlike parents, care workers rarely stay in post throughout the child's minority, so those looked after children often particularly suffer from the lack of continuity of care.

11.3   CARE OF THE LOOKED AFTER CHILD

Local authorities' safeguarding duty includes:

- collective responsibility (under Children Act 1989, s.22(3)) to act as the child's champion and advocate;[2]
- effective interagency consultation and cooperation;[3]
- good educational provision;
- a statutory duty on local education authorities (LEAs), schools and governors under Education Act 2002, s.175;[4]
- a duty to consult with all appropriate interested agencies and individuals in continuous planning and monitoring of plans via the Looked After Children Statutory Review.

The statutory review should be amalgamated with review of the Education and Pathway Plans in preparation for leaving care. Guidance strongly recommends adhering to any preference expressed by a young person for a trusted adult to attend reviews to express her wishes and views.

Education

School can be a source of stress for a child, but many looked after children say they like school, some see it as a lifeline and it can be the one source of stability in an otherwise difficult life.

Corporate parenting should continue beyond compulsory schooling and up to 21, and encourage transition to post-16 opportunities for learning and training available in colleges of further education or in some schools.

Effective education must be a central part of care planning and placement support, and requires corporate effort, which includes:

- a speedy and sensitive response by schools, LEAs and social services to help children catch up when education is disrupted;
- a wide range of resources to address stability, exclusion, attendance, behavioural management, special educational needs, literacy and bullying;
- no lesser obligations than those of a responsible parent, e.g. regular school attendance at a school suitable to the child's needs, and bringing appeals about exclusions, admissions and special educational needs.

When a child enters public care, social services must notify LEAs of a child's placement (Arrangements for Placement of Children (General) Regulations 1991, SI 1991/890) and inform the school. Information should be circulated to agreed contacts on a need-to-know basis[5] depending on the child's legal status.

The social worker must initiate a Personal Education Plan (PEP) in partnership with the child, designated teacher, parent and/or relevant family member, carer and any other relevant person, e.g. educational psychologist, learning support assistant or health professional. Agreement on the PEP should be reached as soon as possible and at maximum within 20 school days (in time for the first 28-day review) of joining a new school. An LEA officer should liaise with the social worker if a child has no school place.

Where a looked after child is to be educated in an independent school or a non-maintained special school, the placing authority should ensure through its agreement with the school that arrangements are satisfactory for dealing with her needs, and good liaison agreements are in place.

Important transitions should be well planned and resourced, especially those from nursery to school and from primary to secondary education. Secondary transfer transition plans are due in early February of the transfer year and children with special needs require good advance planning if they are not to miss out on choice of schools.

Where the local authority is applying to discharge a care order, those representing the child should be satisfied that all necessary support and services have been put in place and any transfers of responsibility have been negotiated and properly resourced. If not, then it may not be in the child's best interests to discharge the order at that stage.

Health

Attention to physical and emotional well-being and mental health is an essential part of good care. There must be holistic health assessment and plans throughout a child's time in local authority care.[6] Where a child has complex health needs, the division of roles and responsibilities between the parents and the various agencies should be clear and well understood.

Control and restraint

Various guidance is available (see Chapter 13), but professionals must be trained in appropriate techniques that maintain the child's physical dignity and safety as well as that of others.

Overnight stays

The freedom to stay overnight with friends is part of being treated 'normally', and statutory guidance has been issued to enable such visits without the need for CRB checks as a precondition: decisions are delegated to carers.[7]

11.4   COMPLAINTS, REPRESENTATIONS AND RIGHTS

Local authority duties

The local authority must make arrangements for advocacy services to children making or intending to make complaints/representations under Children Act 1989, s.26A (see Chapter 26 for further details). Statutory national standards apply and the *Get it Sorted* guidance gives relevant details.

The Children's Commissioner and Children's Rights Director

The Welsh Commissioner can investigate individual cases, unlike the English Commissioner. The role of the Children's Rights Director in the Commission for Social Care Inspection (CSCI) is therefore extremely important: CSCI has a statutory duty to safeguard and promote the child's welfare and her rights in inspections. A good deal of helpful information and advice is also available on a dedicated CSCI website (**www.Rights4me.org.uk**) designed for ease of access, which provides rights' guides on education, health, employment and relevant care standards.

Independent reviewing officers

Some local authorities will have children rights officers or even directors, but all must now have independent reviewing officers (IROs) (under Adoption and Children Act 2002, s.118 amending Children Act 1989, s.26). The judgment on care plans (House of Lords in *Re W and B, Re W (Care Plan)* [2001] 2 FLR 582) decided the courts have no general power to monitor discharge of a local authority's function post-care order, but that human rights challenges could be mounted against an authority which had failed in its duties. The new provisions are intended to offer a remedy for judicial concern that some children might have no effective means to do this.

The IRO may be a member of the local authority's staff, but must be independent of the management of the case and of the allocation of resources to it. The IRO's role is to:

- participate in and monitor reviews of all looked after children (including a child accommodated under Children Act 1989, s.20, a child placed for adoption, a young person in secure accommodation or young offenders institution, and a child on a care order);
- monitor the local authority's actions;
- chair review meetings;
- work with the child, social workers and management;
- negotiate with the local authority where poor practice is identified;
- refer suitable cases to CAFCASS where negotiation fails;

- ensure the child is aware of complaints procedures, and the right to an advocate.

A CAFCASS Practice Note emphasises that referrals should be made as a last resort. It sets out the documents to be sent, including the original care plan, guardian's report, all post-care order review documents and the IRO's report.

If further action is taken, CAFCASS may refer the case to the original children's guardian. Where the case is more suitable for the Official Solicitor, such as litigation against someone other than a local authority, or which does not arise out of treatment as a looked after child, it will be referred on.

CAFCASS action may include further family proceedings, a freestanding application under the Human Rights Act 1998 or an application for judicial review. However, where Children Act 1989 proceedings are pending, the case may be referred back to the relevant service manager in CAFCASS to consider whether an application should be made for a remedy in those proceedings (see Wilson J in *Re C (Adoption: Religious Observance)* [2002] 1 FLR 1119).

Cases should *not* be referred where a child is of sufficient age and understanding to bring proceedings herself, or an adult is willing to bring proceedings on behalf of a child.

11.5 CARE LEAVERS

Circumstances

Care experiences can be a positive or negative experience, impacting on attitudes, confidence and self-esteem, and relationships in adult life. Personal challenges include:

- making sense of the past and the reasons for being looked after;
- lack of family support and establishing/re-establishing contact;
- friendships, family relationships and support networks;
- education, training, finance, employment and accommodation;
- substance abuse, ill-health, bereavement and young parenthood.

Care orders end at age 18 and young people generally leave care post-16. Historically, support has been more akin to the sudden withdrawal of assistance by virtually every state agency[8] instead of the help a good parent would provide.[9] Outcomes have been well documented, with care backgrounds featuring in statistics on the young single homeless,[10] the unemployed and the prison population.

Young parenthood in itself, despite difficulties, can be a positive experience, increasing maturity and independence.[11] But success in obtaining, and remaining in, employment, training or education and housing is more likely if a young person has:

- a stable care history or stability in personal circumstances on leaving care;
- self-reliance and a positive attitude;
- professional and informal support;
- emotional encouragement, often from family/substitute family members;
- support with practical aspects of independent living.

Location can exacerbate problems, particularly in rural areas, with dispersion of support networks, barriers to travel and limited training and employment opportunities.

Education

Research shows clear links between poor educational attainment and unemployment, vulnerability to exploitation, high levels of homelessness and a greater susceptibility to social exclusion in later life.

Around 75 per cent of care leavers have basic skills needs, but nearly half are not in education, training or employment. Many leave with no qualifications and do not go on to further education, deterred by lack of funding, misunderstanding of entitlements, allowances that do not take account of independent living and complicated benefit rules.

Accommodation

Many leave residential care because it is assumed they will move on at 16: half move to semi-independent placements but two years later most have their own accommodation. But most care leavers cannot get housing benefit until they are 18, and housing are likely to refer them back to social services if under 18.

Some older care leavers can get accommodation from the housing department if they can show priority need, e.g. vulnerability because they:

- have not had a stable home since leaving;
- have previously slept on the streets;
- have children or are pregnant; or
- have physical/mental health problems.

The legislation

The Children (Leaving Care) Act 2000 and Children (Leaving Care) (England) Regulations 2001, SI 2001/2874 and (Wales) Regulations 2001, SI 2001/2189 (W.151)[12] amend and extend the duties in the Children Act 1989 to ensure young people are looked after until they are ready to leave care, properly prepared for independence and receive appropriate support thereafter: research findings show, e.g.:

- care leavers have to cope with adult responsibilities far earlier;
- moving should be 'needs' and not 'age' related – informal practices and formal policies which pressure young people to move on before they are ready to do so should be challenged;
- some may need somewhere to return to if they cannot cope;
- many are slow to catch up with peers because of the traumas they have suffered and the earlier disruptions to their development;
- those from foster care tend to be much better prepared than those leaving residential care.

Duties are now owed towards 'eligible' and 'relevant' care leavers until at least age 21. Statutory guidance (issued under Local Authority Social Services Act 1970, s.7), to be read in with 1989 Guidance and Regulations,[13] gives detailed advice on the specific duties owed by local authorities and clarifies agency responsibilities. Note that, although the Act is not retrospective, the government indicated its spirit should be administered for the benefit of *all* care leavers, regardless of when they left.

Key themes:

- involving the child in all arrangements for leaving care;
- multi-agency assessment, preparation and planning;
- access to a range of accommodation, support and skills;
- information on available services, including leaving care guides;
- contingency provision, including respite care;
- personal support after leaving care;
- improved financial arrangements: benefit entitlement was abolished to remove local authority incentives to 'encourage' leaving care at 16.

Responsible local authority

The responsible local authority is the authority where the child was looked after, regardless of where she lives after leaving care. It owes duties to 'eligible', 'relevant' and 'former relevant' children, wherever they live, to assess and meet their care and support needs; keep in touch with all of them and provide them with a Pathway Plan and a personal adviser.

It must also assist with provision of accommodation, costs of education and training and assistance in kind or in cash in certain qualifying circumstances.

Where under 18 and entitled to financial support under the 2000 Act, a young person may experience problems if living elsewhere. But a responsible authority can transfer funds to another authority, for which there is a good practice protocol[14] containing useful recommendations on rates, and the type of support that should be offered.

Those who qualify under the old rules remain entitled to benefits, and the local authority should provide assistance with any difficulties in claims.

Definitions

Whether a person is owed the wider duties will depend on age, the period looked after, legal status and the date she left care. But being looked after includes being accommodated under Children Act 1989, s.20, remanded to local authority accommodation (even if subsequently not given a custodial sentence, if the period of remand is for 13 weeks or more), and young people seeking asylum (if looked after for the qualifying 13 weeks).

Those who do not qualify under the 2000 Act may nevertheless still qualify under the 1989 Act as a 'qualifying person' (Children (Leaving Care) Act 2000, s.24(1)) entitled to aftercare support under the old 'advice and befriending' rules (see Children Act 1989, s.24, Sched. 2).

Preparation for leaving care

No later than her sixteenth birthday, the eligible child is entitled to be provided with a personal adviser, a Pathway Plan and a needs assessment to determine appropriate advice, assistance and support.

Both adviser and Pathway Plan are retained until at least age 21 and up to 24 if she is still being supported through higher education or training.

Personal adviser

The guidance sets out the role of the personal adviser in some detail: she does not have to be a social worker, but must be chosen with respect paid to the young person's wishes, bearing in mind ethnic origin, gender and race. The responsibilities include acting as mentor, providing support and guidance and the principal contact, negotiator and broker for anything relating to the Pathway Plan, taking over responsibility for the maintenance and review of this from the social worker post-care.

Pathway Plan[15]

This must cover statutory matters (see the Schedules to SI 2001/2874, SI 2001/2189), and be drawn up with the young person and her social worker, building on the care plan and PEP. It must be started well before leaving and be completed within three months of the child's sixteenth birthday *at the latest*.

Care leaving schemes

Most authorities now have leaving care teams or services, also known as Pathway teams, and some recruit older care leavers as mentors.

Schemes should include:

- flexible appropriate provision and clear informed guidance;
- early support for emotional and behavioural problems;
- consistent, readily available emotional, practical and financial assistance;
- 'befriending' professionals, rather than those with statutory duties;[16]
- mentoring/key worker systems;
- informal help from ex-foster carers, family and substitute family and other significant adults.

Formal agreements/protocols between departments and agencies, such as housing, education, youth work and mental health, are important and schemes should also address the mobility of care leavers and local authority placement practices and improved access to education, training and employment.

Accommodation strategies should involve the housing department and organisations providing accommodation and be based on assessment of need.

Homelessness legislation also imposes duties on local authorities (see Chapter 14).

As regards education and training, note that students with child care needs can apply directly for funding for child care of up to £4,000 per year per child.

11.6 PRACTICAL CONSIDERATIONS

The practitioner should ensure the child client is aware of her rights:

- to complain and to appeal, balancing the need to ensure relationships with professionals and carers are restored where necessary and maintained appropriately for the future;
- to a PEP and a Pathway Plan and adviser in preparation for leaving care, and that she knows she does not have to leave until she is ready to do so and has appropriate support.

Consider the issues likely to arise on leaving care, including the possibility of resumption of contact with family and former carers, and how this can best be dealt with if there are any ongoing proceedings, particularly if these involve younger siblings.

On application for discharge of a care order, consider whether the issue of the leaving care plan for eligible children has been adequately addressed, including referral to adult services.[17]

NOTES

1 Denise Platt, Chief Inspector of Social Services, 'Putting Young People at the Centre', speech to Leaving Care Conference, May 2003.

2 See Quality Protects guidance.

3 See Children Act 1989, ss,17 and 26 on 'Children and young people's plans' and Special Educational Needs Code of Practice, DfES (2001).

4 *Safeguarding Children in Education*, DfES (2004).

5 See *Working Together to Safeguard Children*, DH, Home Office, DfEE (1999), para. 7.27.

6 *Guidance on Promoting the Health of Looked After Children*, LAC (2002)16.

7 *Guidance on the Delegation of Decisions on Overnight Stays for Looked After Children*, LAC (2004)4.

8 Young care leaver to the House of Commons debate on Leaving Care Bill, and see Sir W. Utting, *People Like Us*, DH and Welsh Office (July 1997).

9 *Lost in Care*, report of the Tribunal of Inquiry into abuse of children in care in the former county council areas of Gwynedd and Clwyd since 1974, Welsh Assembly (June 2000).

10 Of those leaving care aged 16 or over in 1999/2000, 45% were from foster placements, 19% from children's homes and hostels, 50% had been looked after continuously for two or more years, 25% for less than six months. Children in care are three times more likely to be cautioned/convicted than their peers.

11 See M. Allen, *Factors that Influence Young People Leaving Care*, Joseph Rowntree Foundation (2003).

12 For Wales see also the Children (Leaving Care) (Wales) (Amendment) Regulations 2004, SI 2004/1732, and *Children Leaving Care Act Guidance*, Welsh Assembly (September 2001) at **www.wales.gov.uk/subichildren/toc-e.htm** under Guidance.

13 This replaces *An Introduction to the Children Act 1989: After-care – When a Child Ceases to be Looked After*, DH (1991), paras 5.33–5.37; see now Children Act Guidance, vol. 3, ch. 9, Family 'After-care: Advice and Assistance' and vol. 4, ch. 7.

14 *National Protocol: Inter-Authority Arrangements for Negotiating Support For Care Leavers Resident Outside of their Responsible Authority*, LASSL (2004)20 (9 August 2004).

15 For model plans see DfES website.

16 See M. Allen, *Factors that Influence Young People Leaving Care*, Joseph Rowntree Foundation (2003).

17 *Good Practice in Child Care Cases*, Law Society (2004).

CHAPTER 12

Adoption under the Adoption and Children Act 2002

Key sources

- Inter-country Adoption (Hague Convention) Regulations 2003
- Independent Review of Determinations (Adoption) Regulations 2004
- Adoption Agencies Regulations 2005
- Adoption Support Services Regulations 2005
- Disclosure of Adoption Information (Post-commencement Adoptions) Regulations 2005
- Special Guardianship (England) Regulations 2005
- National Adoption Standards (2001)
- LAC (2003)12 and *Intercountry Adoption Guide*, DH (2003)

12.1 INTRODUCTION

The aims of the Adoption and Children Act (ACA) 2002 are to:

- bring adoption law into line with the Children Act (CA) 1989;
- expedite the process of adoption within the court system;
- amend the CA 1989 with particular reference to parental responsibility;
- introduce a new 'special guardianship order' mainly to provide permanence for children looked after by local authorities, short of severing all ties with the birth family;
- replace freeing for adoption orders under the Adoption Act 1976 with placement orders;
- require that the court timetable the application and give directions to avoid delay.

Certain provisions are already in force (as at February 2005):

- fathers whose names are registered on the birth certificate acquire parental responsibility (with effect from 1 December 2003);
- provisions relating to adoption support (with effect from 31 October 2003);
- the provisions concerning intercountry adoptions (with effect from June 2003);

- the independent review mechanism (1 May 2004);
- the provisions for independent reviewing officers in connection with the review of cases of children who are being looked after, or for whom accommodation is being provided (with effect from September 2004; see Review of Children's Case (Amendment) (England) Regulations 2004, SI 2004/1419, and see Chapter 11).

This chapter is a guide to the main provisions of the new law, regulations, rules and guidance which are relevant to child care practitioners. The changes to placement for adoption which will be implemented in 2005 make it essential that practitioners are familiar with adoption practice, in order to provide adequate representation for their social work/lay client in care proceedings.

12.2   THE NEW APPROACH TO ADOPTION

The provisions of ACA 2002, s.1 apply whenever a court or an adoption agency is coming to any decision relating to the adoption of a child. This includes any decision by the court about whether or not to dispense with parental consent to adoption, or when considering making a contact order. The welfare test is brought into line with that in CA 1989, but in addition the court must consider the child's welfare throughout her life. Section 1 replicates many of the provisions of CA 1989 s.1, but extends the factors to be considered by the court and adoption agency to take account of relatives and friends with whom the child might cease to have a relationship after adoption; placing emphasis on the need for those people to be investigated before a placement outside the family is considered; and to look at alternatives to adoption, such as a special guardianship or residence order, before deciding upon adoption.

Whenever a court or adoption agency is coming to a decision relating to the adoption of a child (ACA 2002, s.1(1)) which includes (s.1(7)) the revocation of such an order, the making or revocation of a placement order, or the making or revocation or variation of a contact order, the paramount consideration must be the child's welfare throughout her life (s.1(2)). They must bear in mind that any delay is likely to prejudice the child's welfare (s.1(3)) and they must have regard to the following matters (among others) (s.1(4)):

- the child's ascertainable wishes and feelings regarding the decision (considered in the light of the child's age and understanding);
- the child's particular needs;
- the likely effect on the child (throughout her life) of having ceased to be a member of the original family and becoming an adopted person;
- the child's age, sex, background and any of the child's characteristics which the court or agency considers relevant;

- any harm (within the meaning of CA 1989) which the child has suffered or is at risk of suffering;
- the relationship which the child has with relatives, and with any other person in relation to whom the court or agency considers the relationship to be relevant, including:
  - the likelihood of any such relationship continuing and the value to the child of its doing so;
  - the ability and willingness of any of the child's relatives, or of any such person, to provide the child with a secure environment in which the child can develop, and otherwise to meet the child's needs;
  - the wishes and feelings of any of the child's relatives, or of any such person, regarding the child.

In placing a child for adoption, the agency must give due consideration to the child's religious persuasion, racial origin and cultural and linguistic background (s.1(5)).

The court or agency must always consider the range of powers available to it; and the court must not make any order under ACA 2002 unless it considers that making the order would be better for the child than not doing so (s.1(6)).

12.3 THE ADOPTION PANEL

The composition and role of the adoption panel will be very similar to that under the Adoption Act 1976. The significant changes proposed are that:

(a) the chairperson must be independent of the agency;
(b) membership of the panel is permitted for five years instead of the current three-year term;
(c) the quorum is reduced from six to five (and in the case of a joint adoption panel from seven to six);
(d) the regulations provide for the panel giving advice to the agency about contact arrangements;
(e) whereas under current regulations the panel 'shall' obtain legal advice, under the new regulations, the panel shall obtain legal advice in relation to a recommendation that a child is approved for adoption, and it is discretionary in relation to approval of a prospective adopter, and the matching of the child with that person.

A new requirement, followed in current practice, is that before making any recommendation the panel must invite the prospective adopters to meet the panel.

When considering matching a child with a prospective adopter, the panel 'may' obtain legal advice, make a recommendation about the need of the child or prospective adopter for adoption support services, or give advice to the agency about arrangements it proposes to make for allowing 'any person' contact with the child.

12.4 ADOPTION AGENCY

The duties of the adoption agency are extended. The requirement to provide counselling and information when it is considering adoption for a child is broadened, to require that the child's wishes and feelings are ascertained, not only in relation to adoption but also as to her contact with her parent, guardian or other relative or other person connected with her. Similarly, the agency must ascertain the wishes and feelings of the parent or guardian as to contact with the child if the agency is authorised to place the child for adoption.

Fathers without parental responsibility are to be provided with counselling, and their wishes as to placement and contact ascertained, if the agency is satisfied that 'it is appropriate to do so'. Previously, there was no requirement in relation to contact, and that in relation to counselling was phrased 'as far as practicable and in the interests of the child'. The agency must also ascertain whether he wishes to acquire parental responsibility, or intends to apply for a residence order. The agency also has a duty to inform a child's father without parental responsibility of its decision in relation to matching, if it considers that it is appropriate to do so.

The draft court rules include an express provision to enable an adoption agency or local authority to ask the High Court for guidance on the need to give a father without parental responsibility notice of the intention to place the child for adoption, placement proceedings or adoption proceedings. Where no proceedings have started, the procedure set out in Part 8 of the Civil Procedure Rules is to be used (Adoption Rules 1984, SI 1984/265, rule 59).

The report on the child to be prepared for the panel, which replaces form E, has a greater focus than previously on contact between the child and birth family, and requires that the views of the child's carer about adoption are included.

If the agency proposes not to approve a prospective adopter, and makes a 'qualifying determination' the provisions as to independent review apply.

After a decision to match has been made, detailed information must be provided to the prospective adopter. This is far more extensive than under previous regulations. It will include the assessment of the child's needs for adoption support services and the agency's proposals for meeting those needs.

12.5 PLACEMENT FOR ADOPTION

General

These provisions provide for the replacement of freeing for adoption, and restrict the right of the agency to place a child for adoption. An adoption agency will be able to place a child for adoption only if it has either the formal consent of the parents with parental responsibility, or if it obtains a placement order.

Placement order

A placement order is an order made by the court 'authorising a local authority to place a child for adoption with any prospective adopters who may be chosen by the agency' (ACA 2002, s.21(1)). It may only be granted if the child is subject to a care order, or the court is satisfied that the threshold criteria are met (CA 1989, s.31(2)) or the child has no parent or guardian (ACA 2002, s.21(2)).

A placement order can be made only with the consent of the parent or guardian or, without it, if the court is satisfied that the consent should be dispensed with (s.21(3)).

Once made, the order continues until an adoption order is made, or the child attains the age of 18 or marries or it is revoked (s.21(4)).

An application to revoke may be made by the child or local authority, or any other person if the court gives leave, and the child has not been placed for adoption (s.24).

The local authority must apply for this order where (s.22):

(a) it has placed the child for adoption or the child is being provided with accommodation (pursuant to CA 1989, s.20); and
(b) no adoption agency is authorised to place the child for adoption; and
(c) it considers the conditions in CA 1989, s.31(2) are met; and
(d) it is satisfied that the child ought to be placed for adoption; or
(e) if it considers that a child ought to be placed for adoption and it has a care order or is in the process of obtaining a care order.

It may apply for a placement order in respect of a child in care where each parent or guardian has consented.

Applications for the making or revocation of a placement order become specified proceedings, i.e. a children's guardian will be appointed and the child will be separately represented unless the court decides this is unnecessary (ACA 2002, s.122 amending CA 1989, s.41).

Consent to placement

Consent is given to a placement for adoption. The parent or guardian may at the same time, or subsequently, give consent to the making of an adoption order, either by the prospective adopters identified in the consent, or by any prospective adopters chosen by the agency.

Consent is only effective in respect of a mother if given six weeks or more after birth, and must be given unconditionally with full understanding of what is involved (under the 1976 Act the consent was required in addition to be 'freely' given). It must be given in accordance with the Rules.

The court can dispense with consent if 'the welfare of the child requires consent to be dispensed with' or the parent cannot be found or is incapable of giving consent.

The consent must be in a prescribed form and must be witnessed by a CAFCASS officer. Where the parent or guardian is prepared to consent to placement for adoption, and the making of an adoption order, the agency must request CAFCASS to appoint an officer to obtain the written consent and return it to the agency. The request must be accompanied by those documents specified in the Adoption Agencies Regulations 2005, SI 2005/389, reg.20 and Sched. 2.

If consent is not forthcoming, or the CAFCASS officer has any query about the consent, she will provide a short report to the agency.

Where the parent lives outside England and Wales, a consent form will be sent to them for signing. On an agency placement, the agency will have to provide all relevant information. In a non-agency case, the parent or guardian 'should be made fully aware of the impact of filing the consent form'.

Effect of consent to placement

Consent to placement has the following effects:

- the consent binds a parent who acquires parental responsibility after the consent is given (ACA 2002, s.52(10));
- parental responsibility is given to the adoption agency but shared with the parent/s (s.25);
- when a child is placed with prospective adopters they acquire parental responsibility (s.25).

The adoption agency may restrict the exercise of parental responsibility by either the parents or the prospective adopters. Where a child is placed by an adoption agency with consent, or within six weeks of birth, only the adoption agency can remove the child from the prospective adopters and an unauthorised removal is a criminal offence.

Where a child is not placed, and is accommodated, and the adoption agency has not applied for a placement order or has had a placement order application refused, a parent can demand the return of the child who must be returned within 14 days (unless the agency applies for a placement order).

A person who has given consent may notify the agency that they do not wish to be informed of any application for an adoption order.

Effect of a placement order

On the making of a placement order, the adoption agency acquires parental responsibility, which is shared with the parents (ACA 2002, s.25(2)). When a child is placed with prospective adopters they also acquire parental responsibility (s.25(3)). The adoption agency may restrict the exercise of parental responsibility by either the parents or the prospective adopters (s.25(4)).

Revocation of a placement order

The order may be revoked upon application to the court by (a) the local authority authorised to place the child, or (b) the child.

Any other person may apply to revoke the order provided that the court has given leave, which may only be given if it is satisfied that there has been a change of circumstances, and the child is not placed for adoption.

When the court determines an adoption application and decides not to make an order, it may revoke any placement order (s.24(4)). This means that a parent who successfully opposes an adoption application will not necessarily regain care of their child.

Where a child is not placed and a revocation application is pending a child cannot be placed without leave of the court (s.24(5)).

Contact under a placement order or a consent to place

There can be no application under CA 1989 for an order for contact, but there can be an application under ACA 2002, s.26 by:

- the adoption agency;
- the child;
- parent, guardian or relative;
- any person who had a contact order which ceased to have effect on the making of the placement order;
- any person who had a residence order before the authorisation to place for adoption;
- any other person with leave of the court.

The court may make a contact order on its own initiative. The court may impose any conditions it considers appropriate (s.27). Contact orders can be varied or revoked (s.26) on an application made by the child, agency or person named in the order.

The agency has power, notwithstanding a court order, to refuse contact in the event of an emergency, for not more than seven days.

When the court is considering the issue of a placement order, it has to consider the arrangements for contact, proposals for contact and invite all parties to the proceedings to give their views on contact (s.27(4)). Any conditions the court considers appropriate may be attached to a contact order (s.27(5)).

Miscellaneous consequences of a placement order

On the making of a placement order, any existing care order is suspended whilst the placement order is in force and any existing CA 1989, s.8 order or supervision order ceases to have effect. No s.8 orders may be made (save for a residence order in limited circumstances) (s.29(3),(4)) and no child assessment order or supervision order may be made (s.29(3)). No special guardianship order may be made (save in limited circumstances) (s.29(5)).

Neither a placement for adoption with consent nor a placement order authorises a change of name or the removal of the child from the UK for a period in excess of one month by the child's carer without leave of the court or with the written consent of each parent or guardian (s.28(2)–(4)).

12.6   ADOPTION APPLICATIONS

Residence qualifications

The period during which the child has to be resident with the applicant before an adoption application is made (ACA 2002, s.42) is 10 weeks prior to the application, in respect of agency placements or pursuant to an order of the High Court, or where a parent applies. For step-parent adoptions, the period is after six months' residence. If the applicants are local authority foster parents, it is a condition that the child must have resided with them at all times during the period of 12 months preceding the application.

In all other non-agency cases, the child must have her home with the applicant for a period of not less than three years whether continuous or not, during the period of five years preceding the application.

ACA 2002, s. 44 provides for notification to a local authority of an intention to apply to adopt where the child has not been placed by an adoption agency An adoption order may not be made unless the notice has been given not more than two years, or less than three months, before the date on which the application is made.

Applications for adoption

The significant differences between the Adoption Act 1976 and ACA 2002 are that a same-sex couple, or heterosexual couple who are not married, may apply to adopt; and that a child who reaches 18 years before the adoption order is made can be adopted. The requirement that the applicant(s) should be habitually resident here prevents applications from persons who are resident abroad, but claim that they are domiciled here.

The requirements to be satisfied are that:

(a) all previous orders under CA 1989 and orders for payment of maintenance are extinguished;

(b) adoption orders cannot be made without the parents' consent (ACA 2002, s.20) or the court dispensing with it (s.52);

(c) if a parent has consented to a placement order under CA 1989, s.9 she cannot oppose the making of an adoption order without the court's leave which cannot be given unless there has been a change in circumstances;

(d) an adoption order cannot be made in respect of a child who is or has been married;

(e) applications for adoption can be made by a couple (of the same or different genders), where both have attained the age of 21 (or if one is a parent, has reached 18) (ACA 2002, s.50);

(f) an application can be made by one person who has attained 21 and is not married; or where the applicant is married, but the spouse cannot be found, or they have separated and this is likely to be permanent, or where the spouse is by reason of ill-health, whether physical or mental, incapable of making an application to adopt;

(g) the applicant or one of a couple must be domiciled in the British Isles;

(h) the applicant or both applicants must have been habitually resident in a part of the British Isles for not less than one year ending with the date of the application;

(i) an application for an adoption order may only be made if the subject of the application has not attained 18 years at that date;

(j) an adoption order cannot be granted if the child has attained the age of 19;

(k) no application for an adoption order can be heard if a previous application was refused, unless there has been a change in circumstances, or for any other reason, it is proper to hear the application (s.48).

Dispensing with parental consent

The court cannot dispense with parental consent to the child being placed for adoption or to the making of an adoption order, unless the court is satisfied (s.52) that the parent cannot be found or is incapable of giving consent or the welfare of the child requires the consent to be dispensed with.

Contact

Before making an adoption order, the court must consider whether there should be arrangements for contact between the child and any other person, and must obtain the parties' views about this matter. The court may make a contact order on making the adoption order, and may hear an application under CA 1989, s.8 at the same time as the adoption application.

12.7 ADOPTIONS ABROAD

Where it is intended to adopt a child outside the British Isles, the court may grant parental responsibility to a person or persons where they are not domiciled or habitually resident in England and Wales, the child has lived with them for the preceding 10 weeks and the applicants have satisfied the requirements of any relevant regulations (s.84).

ACA 2002, s.84 (which replaces Adoption Act 1976, ss.55, 56) enables a child to be adopted in circumstances where the applicants are not domiciled or habitually resident in this jurisdiction, and where this would prevent the child from being adopted by them. The child might be placed with a relative who is domiciled abroad; or she may be placed by an adoption agency with a foreign national who does not acquire domicile or habitual residence here.

A child who is a Commonwealth citizen or habitually resident in the UK must not be removed for the purpose of adoption unless parental responsibility has been granted to the applicant under s.84 (s.85).

12.8 INTERCOUNTRY ADOPTIONS

There are two kinds of intercountry applications, those that are covered by the Hague Convention, and those that are not.

Hague Convention adoptions

On 1 June 2003, the UK ratified the Hague Convention on Protection of Children and Co-operation in Respect of Intercountry Adoption 1993 (Hague Convention). A list of those countries that have ratified the Convention appears in the *Intercountry Adoption Guide*[1].

This does not apply to a child brought into the UK for the purposes of adoption by a parent, legal guardian or relative, as defined.

In summary the procedure is as follows. The prospective adopters must have applied to an adoption agency in this country for assessment of their suitability to be adoptive parents and to follow the adoption agency procedures and provide all the information required for the adoption agency's assessment.

The applicants must be more than 21 years old, have been habitually resident in the British Isles for one year and, if they are a couple, they must be married.

The agency report must include police checks in respect of the whole household and eligibility and any additional requirements of the country of origin.

The report of the agency then goes before the adoption panel for approval in the usual way.

The decision of the agency is sent to the UK central authority, the Department of Health in England or National Assembly for Wales. If satisfied that the regulations have been complied with, it will send the adoption agency report and its certificate of eligibility to the central authority for the country of origin. After matching, that central authority sends the UK central authority information about the child, which is transmitted to the adoption agency.

The applicants travel to meet the child and confirm their intention to proceed.

If the child is not already adopted in the country of origin, the adopters may be allowed to bring the child to England and Wales. Within 14 days of arrival in the country, the prospective adopters must give written notice to the local authority of the area of residence. The child becomes a protected child.

If adoption proceedings are pending in the country of origin, the local authority has a duty to monitor the placement, and will usually be required to produce a report for the central authority of the country of origin. Pending the making of a Hague Convention adoption order, applicants may not change the child's name or remove her from the UK for more than one month without the agreement of the local authority or a court order (Adoption Rules 1984, SI 1984/265, rule 48(b), as amended by the Adoption (Amendment) Rules 2003) and Inter-country Adoption (Hague Convention) Regulations 2003, SI 2003/118, reg.16)

Where there is an adoption in the country of origin, the central authority must ensure that all necessary consents have been obtained, and that the relevant persons have been counselled as to the consequences. The central authorities will reach agreement to proceed and will then notify the agency of the adopters. If the child is adopted in the country of origin, that order will be recognised in the UK on the basis of a certificate from the central authority in the country of origin.

If the adoption breaks down or the adoption application does not proceed, the applicants must notify the local authority. It may start the process for finding an alternative placement in the UK or may arrange for the child's return to her country of origin.

It is not necessary for the court here to consider the matter of parental consent if the child arrives here following an agreement between central authorities. However, the appointment of a guardian is mandatory. The child acquires British nationality on the making of a Hague Convention adoption order in the country of origin if one of the adopters is a British citizen and both applicants are habitually resident here. If no order has been made there, entry clearance must be obtained, and an application for citizenship to be granted must be made to the Immigration and Nationality Directorate.

A criminal offence will be committed if the Inter-country Adoption (Hague Convention) Regulations 2003 are not followed. If a child is brought in to the UK without following the correct procedure, there may be an unlimited fine or 12 months' imprisonment. It is an offence to write an unauthorised home study report for the purposes of a foreign adoption (Adoption Act 1976, ss.57, 72(3A) and *Re M (Adoption: International Adoption Trade)* [2002] EWHC Fam 219, [2002] 1 FLR 1111).

Non-Convention adoptions

Judicial guidelines on the appropriate course of action in these cases has been given (by Bracewell J in *Re R (Inter-country Adoptions: Practice)* [1999] 1 FLR 1042).

If a foreign child arrives at a port of entry for the UK accompanied by a non-related adult, the written consent of the parent should be produced. The Home Office should give notice to the Department of Health and on to the relevant local authority. The local authority should attempt to contact the child's parents, and where parental consent has not been given, the local authority should notify the Home Office and the Department of Health.

The court will draw up a timetable to avoid delay. If the intention to adopt was not disclosed to the immigration officer, and the applicants were unable to produce parental consent or failed to comply with the guidelines on inter-country adoption, the application will be transferred to the High Court. CAFCASS will be invited to nominate a children's guardian to act and file an interim report and there must be a further directions hearing within six weeks.

If the birth parents oppose the application, the court should consider making orders within wardship for the immediate return of the child to them. The guardian must be proactive and seek directions from the court in order to prevent delay. Priority should be given to interviewing the parents, effecting personal service on them and advising them about legal representation and options available to them.

In June 2003 the President of the Family Division issued an Intercountry Adoption Supplement to her guidance *Adoption Proceedings: a New Approach*. The amendments to the guidance apply to all intercountry adoption applications issued on or after June 2003.

An intercountry application must be issued at one of the courts which have been designated as an 'intercountry adoption centre' (a list appears in the Supplement). If the application is issued elsewhere, it will be transferred to one of the convenient designated centres.

The proceedings will be listed before a High Court Judge or a circuit judge who is an adoption judge and is authorised by the Family Division Liaison Judge to hear intercountry cases. Directions may be listed before a district judge at an intercountry adoption centre.

Where the making of an adoption order would confer British citizenship on a child, the Home Office must be notified of the application, so that the Secretary of State can decide whether or not to intervene (and see *Re W (A Minor) (Adoption: Non-Patrial)* [1986] Fam. 54, [1986] 1 FLR 179; *Re K (Adoption and Wardship)* [1997] 2 FLR 221). Notification should be made through the office of the President of the Family Division (see Appendix 2).[2]

Although there were clear benefits arising from acquisition of citizenship and the right to live in the UK which could not be ignored in consideration of an intercountry adoption application, the child's welfare was still the first consideration and was not over-ridden by immigration policy (*Re B (A Minior) (Adoption Order: Nationality)* [1999] 1 FLR 907; *Re S and J (Adoption Non-Patrial)* [2004] 2 FLR 111).

12.9   CONTACT WITHIN ADOPTION

It remains to be seen whether practice in relation to contact post-adoption will change after implementation of ACA 2002. The following is a summary of current practice.

Indirect contact by way of progress reports, sending of cards and letters through postbox arrangements, is the norm. It is not uncommon for the adopters and birth parents to meet, usually before the adoption hearing. Direct, face-to-face contact between the child and birth family is becoming less uncommon. For information about research carried out into post-adoption contact, see Appendix 1. Practice around contact has differed vastly across voluntary and statutory agencies and across regions, and contact has been identified as 'one of the most contentious practice issues' encountered.[3] It has also been suggested that 'face-to-face contact did not interfere with the development of close relations between adopters and their adopted child and adopted children could enjoy a relationship with birth relatives, even though they did not yet understand about adoption'.[4]

Adoption with contact under a CA 1989, s.8 order or by way of formal or informal agreement or a recital attached to the order raises the potential for ongoing litigation.

Case law clearly indicates that courts are strongly governed by the wishes of the adopters and are exceedingly reluctant to impose conditions or orders upon them: 'the court would not, except in the most exceptional case, impose terms or conditions as to access to which the adopting parents did not agree' (*Re C (A Minor)(Adoption Order: Conditions)* [1988] 2 FLR 159).

Where agreement is reached between the prospective adopters and birth family as to post-adoption contact, a recital should be drawn up and attached to the adoption order. This will indicate the intentions of the parties as to contact, and should also include the support which will be offered by the local authority to all parties to ensure that the contact takes place, even though contact will be in the hands of the adopters once the order is made. The prospective adopters should have been supplied with details of the support services to be provided, which will include assistance in relation to contact.

The court will rarely entertain an application for contact post-adoption. If an application for leave is sought, the procedure is as follows (*Re C (A Minor)(Adoption Child: Contact)* [1993] 2 FLR 431). The persons to be notified of such an application are:

- the local authority which was a party to the adoption application;
- the Official Solicitor, not just as *amicus curiae* but as a respondent (from 1 April 2001 it is the Special Casework unit of CAFCASS which should be notified);
- the adoptive parents, only if the court is satisfied there is a *prima facie* case for leave, and then the notice should be communicated by the Official Solicitor and not by the court.

The court has further held that such applications for leave would only be granted rarely, the implication being that the proper course of action is for conditions, orders, agreements to be sought within adoption proceedings and not afterwards.

In a later case, it was held that a case need not be transferred automatically to the High Court and even when so transferred there is no general rule that the Official Solicitor should be brought in (Balcombe LJ (disagreeing with Thorpe LJ) in *Re T (Minors) (Adopted Children: Contact)* [1995] 2 FLR 792).

Where prospective adopters had agreed that they would provide annual reports which they subsequently stopped, a parent successfully applied for leave to issue a contact application. It was held that it was not acceptable for adopters to resile from an agreement without good explanation (*Re T* [1995] 2 FLR 792).

In a case where the social worker dealing with the case promised that photographs and news of schooling would be forwarded, no written agreement was entered into. The adopters did not comply, later denying any knowledge of the arrangement. The birth parents sought leave to apply for a contact order under CA 1989, s.8. Leave was granted but dismissed on appeal. The Court of Appeal held that the birth parents were the victims of unfairness which was real, but that did not mean leave should be granted. The proper approach was to apply in the county court for amendment of the adoption order or to appeal out of time and it was wholly inappropriate to have fresh proceedings under CA 1989 (*Re E (Adopted Child)(Contact: Leave)* [1995] 1 FLR 57).

Adoption Contact Register

Dating from 1991, the Adoption Contact Register (in force 1 May 1991: Adoption Act 1976, s.51A, by virtue of CA 1989, Sched. 10 para. 21 and SI 1991/828) provides a channel through which an adopted person and a birth relative may register their wish for contact with the other person.

A birth relative may register their wish for contact in Part 11 of the Register for a fee. They must provide evidence of their relationship to the adopted person. They will need to know:

- the name in which the adopted person was registered at birth;
- the date and place of birth;
- the birth mother's name;
- the birth mother's maiden name and birth father's name if these were included on the original birth certificate.

When registering, the relative may give his own name and address for transmission to the adopted person, or that of an intermediary. If the adopted person registers, they will be sent details of the relative who has registered and this action will be notified to the relative.

An adopted person can register in Part 1 of the Register for a fee. They need to complete an application form giving certain information which can be obtained from the adoptive parents, or by applying to the Registrar General for access under Adoption Act 1976, s.51. The information required is:

- the name in which the birth was registered;
- their birth mother's name and surname;
- the birth mother's maiden name and birth father's name if these were included on the original birth certificate.

The leaflet available from the General Register Office makes it clear that counselling is available both to adopted people and birth relatives, and provides the names and addresses of organisations which will provide inter- mediate and counselling services in relation to contact, which may be of great assistance at what can be a very emotional time.[5]

NOTES

1   *Intercountry Adoption Guide*, DH (2003) and LAC (2003)12.
2   President's Guidance (December 2002).
3   N. Lowe, M. Murch *et al.*, *Supporting Adoption: Reframing the Approach*, BAAF (1999).
4   E. Neil, *Contact with Birth Relatives after Adoption: A Study of Young, Recently Placed Children*, Norwich, UEA, unpublished PhD thesis (2000); E. Neil, 'Contact after Adoption; The Role of Agencies in Making and Supporting Plans' (2002) 26(1) *Adoption and Fostering* 25.
5   See Pam Hodkgin, *Birth Records Counselling: A Practical Guide*, BAAF (1991).

CHAPTER 13

Education, special educational needs and disability

Key sources

- Disability Discrimination Act 1995; Special Education Needs and Disability Act 2001
- Education Acts 1996 (as amended) and 2002
- Circulars CI (96)14, LAC (99)25, LAC (2000)13 and LAC (2001)27
- *Guidance on the Education of Children and Young People in Public Care*, DH, DfES (May 2000)
- SEN Code of Practice, DfES (England) (2001), Welsh Assembly (Wales) (2002)
- Code of Practice for Schools, Disability Rights Commission (2002)
- *Who Does What*, DfES (2004, revised 2005)
- *Safeguarding Children in Education*, DfES (2004)

13.1   INTRODUCTION

This chapter briefly sets out some issues in a crucial but complex area. Chapters 3 and 4 cover education and safeguarding, but Chapters 8, 10 and 11 are also relevant.

There are a wide range of abilities in children and adults, and/or difficulties arising from educational experience, special needs or disability, and some may have significant implications for communication, planning, support and outcomes. But education is often overlooked – it is important to every child, but more so to a looked after child, especially if she has special educational needs (SEN) or is disabled. For those unable to attend full-time education because of legal status, health or other reasons, it can be critical.

Education plays a crucial role in healthy development from the early years onwards, with a significant influence on placement stability, health, self-esteem and confidence. Changes of school and/or placement that result in loss of friends, familiar adults and environments can exacerbate the effects of other disruptions and undermine ability to make and sustain relationships. Problems often first emerge at school. Without careful planning, coordinated support and early intervention (especially for young children and those with special educational needs/disabilities), the likelihood of poor outcomes is increased.

Regular attendance, early literacy and support from carers and/or mentors,[1] all contribute to future success. However, looked after children:[2]

- are over-represented in exclusions (especially those with special educational needs);
- are more likely to experience delay in school placement, bullying and intrusive questioning;
- do not always have special educational needs identified/addressed or adequate consideration of diversity[3] (e.g. racism can seriously disrupt educational development);
- their educational outcomes on leaving care are poor;
- may require alternative educational provision because of health needs (e.g. a significant number have mental health problems).[4]

Education must therefore be an integral part of safeguarding and effective care planning and the same principles of partnership, interagency information-sharing and joint work apply to the education sector as for any other agency. But drift, delay, fragmented provision, negative professional attitudes and assumptions that traumatic experiences bar effective learning or create emotional/behavioural difficulties, all present obstacles.

Collaboration is not assisted by local management of schools, which gives schools autonomy in the deployment of resources, but funding models vary from central specialist support and resourcing, with budgets 'devolved' or 'delegated' to schools, and referral practices vary widely, as does coordination for those with multiple problems, often leaving social services to find, and fund, solutions.

It is intended that in future there will be integrated education and social care, with 'extended schools' in each area by 2006.[5]

Relevant issues are under topic headings, but the law on many of these is complex and extensive and only a limited number of education lawyers are available. Further specialist help can be sought from organisations, especially the Advisory Centre for Education, Children's Legal Centre and Who Cares Trust, listed in Appendix 2.

13.2 HUMAN RIGHTS AND DIVERSITY

Human rights

In ECHR terms, education is a negative right (ECHR Protocol 1 Article 2), i.e. a right *not to be denied* access to pre-existing educational facilities or an effective education. It encompasses the child's whole education and personal development, the entire process by which beliefs, culture and values are transmitted. Although not confined to school, it is not an absolute right to learn whatever/wherever desired.

Education is not a 'civil right or obligation', but ECHR Article 6 applies to exclusion procedures (*Re S, T and P* v. *Brent LBC and Others*; *Oxfordshire CC, Head Teacher of Elliott School and Others* v. *Secretary of State for Education and Skills* [2002] ELR 556) and may apply in future to appeal procedures (see *Simpson* v. *UK* (1989) 64 DR 188, EComHR).

Articles 3, 5, 6, 8, 9, 10 and 14 are relevant, for example:

- a right to be taught in the national language, but not necessarily in the family's own language (*Belgian Linguistic Case (No. 2)* (1968) 1 EHRR 252);
- no right to a particular chosen school, if an alternative is available (*Belgian Linguistic Case (No. 2)* (1968) 1 EHRR 252);
- parents can be required to cooperate in, e.g., assessments of attainment – sanctions for failure to comply are permissible (*Family H* v. *UK* (1984) 37 DR 105);
- failure to provide education in remand prison (*Bouamar* v. *Belgium* (1989) 11 EHRR 1; ECHR Article 5(1)(d)) or secure accommodation *may* be a breach (*Re K (Secure Accommodation Order: Right to Liberty)* [2001] 1 FLR 526);
- without discrimination, failure to provide a particular kind of teaching may not be a breach;
- fair and proper treatment of minority views, and a qualified right to respect for religious or philosophical beliefs (the qualified right to practise or demonstrate religion or beliefs in public and in private covers protected non-religious beliefs as well as religious ones: *Re Crawley Green Road Cemetery, Luton* [2001] Fam. 308);
- removal by parents from sex education classes is permitted (objectively-presented information is not a breach).

UK compliance is subject to compatibility with the provision of efficient education and training and the avoidance of unreasonable public expenditure (under the UK government's reservation). There is no right to the most expensive provision if cheaper suitable alternatives exist. Those in young offender institutions, secure accommodation or excluded from, or educated out of, school have no specific entitlement to full-time education.

Human rights issues may arise, e.g. in admissions and exclusions and SEN provision, including potential for discrimination. Education policies should be shown to exist to pursue a legitimate aim, to be proportionate to that aim and to integrate human rights principles throughout.

Discipline, if necessary and proportionate, is not incompatible with ECHR Articles 3 or 5. Fair and reasonable sanctions for unacceptable conduct/behaviour must be stated in school policy, must not constitute physical punishment (even if by parental demand) or ill-treatment within Article 3, and must not be onerous, nor conflict with parental religious/philosophical convictions or be discriminatory.

Exclusion is compliant, provided it does not breach a parent's Article 9 rights or amount to discrimination, prevent enrolment at another school or access to alternative educational facilities (School Standards and Framework Act 1998, s.64, otherwise there may be a breach of ECHR Article 3 or Protocol 1 Article 2), or amount to inappropriate punishment in the particular circumstances.

Most of the rights belong to adults (parents) and are exercised on behalf of children, who have few individual rights. Education law acknowledges the importance of the child's interests, but these are not *paramount*.

Diversity

Schools in particular need to be sensitive to religious, cultural and sex discrimination issues and aware of the protection afforded in relevant legislation, especially since the UK curriculum is largely eurocentric. Discrimination provisions only apply to racial groups, so particular care is needed to address ignorance and prejudice regarding dress codes and religious practices, e.g. for Muslims.

Poor proficiency in literacy/language can bar academic progress, and future employment success. Refugee and asylum-seeking children's rights are the same as others provided their UK education starts before 16 and they are not in a detention centre (Detention Centre Rules 2001, rule 11 refers to maintenance and care, but not education). But obstacles to admission are frequent, apparently from concern about the effects of trauma and language difficulties.[6]

A range of cases on disability issues and service provision provide a detailed analysis of disabled children's rights and positive obligations under ECHR Articles 3 and 8 (see *A* v. *East Sussex CC* [2003] EWHC Admin 167; [2003] All ER (D) 233 and *R (Howard League for Penal Reform)* v. *Secretary of State for the Home Department* [2002] EWHC Admin 2497, [2003] 1 FLR 484).

13.3   DUTY TO EDUCATE

A child of compulsory school age (the beginning of the term following fifth birthday, but most are accepted at start of term in which they reach five) must receive efficient full-time education suitable to her age, ability and aptitude and any SENs (Education Act 1996, s.7). This includes a child who will not receive education for any period due to illness, exclusion or 'otherwise' (Education Act 1996, s.19),[7] refugee and asylum-seeking children and those temporarily resident for long enough to attend school (e.g. children of travellers or armed forces personnel).

The duty is on the parent (which has the same meaning as in SEN jurisdiction, s.28Q(8)(a) 1995 Act; s.576 1996 Act), someone with parental responsibility (or her legal guardian), or the local education authority (LEA) if she is a looked after child.

Regular attendance may be affected by, e.g. illness, pregnancy, behaviour difficulties or exclusion. The LEA must make arrangements for alternative provision for these children (see below) (Education Act 1996, s.19).[8]

13.4 EDUCATIONAL PROVISION

Early years

Children may benefit from:

- nurseries: entitlement to free places (for every eligible four-year-old and some three-year-olds);
- Early Excellence Centres: education and extended care for three to four-year-olds;
- Early Years Development and Childcare Partnerships;
- childminders, playgroups, private day nurseries or independent schools;
- Sure Start and Home-Start programmes (see Chapter 4).

Schools

'Schools' (as defined by Education Act 1996, s.4 and see School Standards and Framework Act 1988, ss.20(7), 22(9) and Education Act 1996, ss.463, 342) includes maintained, independent/non-maintained, mainstream/special schools, voluntary/grant-aided or foundation schools, City Technology Colleges and Pupil Referral Units (PRUs) (Education Act 1996, s.19(2)) or DfES registered PRU units in schools.

Alternative provision

For children out of school LEAs may provide:

- education in PRUs, full or part-time;
- home teaching services;
- education in teaching centres;
- hospital schools or therapeutic/psychiatric units (see School Standards and Framework Act 1998, s.31, Sched. 6);
- education in secure units, young offender institutions or asylum centres;
- extended work experience or vocational placements;
- flexible programmes for 14 to 16-year-olds;
- education in teenage parents units;
- NVQs or further education;

- packages combining, e.g. a PRU and occasional attendance at a teaching centre, or work experience and home tuition;
- PRUs working jointly with mainstream schools for dual registered pupils (i.e. registered both at a school and in alternative provision).

Parents are entitled to educate a child at home (under Education Act 1996, s.7), but can be required to cooperate in attainment assessments (*Family H* v. *UK* (1984) 37 DR 105), and the LEA must ensure education is satisfactory.

Post-16

Careers guidance for Years 9 to 11 is compulsory under Education Act 1997, s.43. Care leavers must have personal advisers and Pathway Plans and Connexions has particular obligations to those with SENs and/or disability.[9] Further education provision and funding is the responsibility of the Learning and Skills Council (LSC) in England and the National Council for Education and Training in Wales (CETW). Fees may be charged if a student is part-time or over 19, but e.g. grants, allowances[10] and benefits are available.

13.5 PARTICIPATION AND PARTNERSHIP

Participation

Pupils' views are important, especially in tackling racism, bullying and violence, and they should have access to formal procedures on complaints, exclusions or admissions. Consultation with pupils on decisions affecting them is now required of LEAs, schools and governors (see Education Act 2002, s.176 and guidance on pupil participation).

Special educational needs: the pupil's participation in assessments and reviews is required,[11] with her views recorded, and exploration of reasons for any differences between her and professionals.

Partnership with parents

Unless particular circumstances dictate otherwise, parental involvement should be supported. This helps maintain relationships and continuing commitment can motivate a child. Parents have a right to clear, accurate reporting and safeguarding is the only justification for less information (see Chapters 5 and 24).

13.6   INSPECTION

Ofsted is responsible for regular inspections of *all* schools, maintained or independent and from September 2005 has the lead responsibility for joint inspections covering safeguarding and other services. Reports are publicly available, but care should be exercised in ensuring that any information used from them is up to date.

13.7   LOCAL AUTHORITIES, LEAs AND SCHOOLS[12]

Local authority duties

The LEA is part of the local authority, whether or not functions are contracted out. It must provide, e.g.

- full-time education for all children up to 16;
- alternative suitable educational provision for children up to 16 who would not otherwise receive it because of illness, exclusion from school or other reasons;
- full-time education to any 16 to 19-year-old who wants it;
- inclusion in mainstream schooling for pupils with SENs (but see below);
- educational support to looked after children;
- lists of schools and early years settings;
- free school meals for all those on means-tested benefits and refugee and asylum seekers supported by the National Asylum Support Service (Immigration and Asylum Act 1999, Sched. 14, para.117);
- transport for certain pupils (Education Act 1996, s.444(5)).

The LEA must make the above provision in such a way as to avoid unreasonable delay in securing school placement, to promote high standards (Education Act 1996, s.13A and School Standards and Framework Act 1998) and disseminate policies, practice and procedures and relevant guidance, and to comply with race relations law and promote good race relations.

Other duties include:

- safeguarding (Education Act 2002, s.175 with effect from 1 June 2004, s.157 for the independent sector and see Education (Independent Schools Standards) (England) Regulations 2003, SI 2003/1910 and Non-Maintained Special Schools (England) Regulations 1999, SI 1999/2257);
- corporate parenting of looked after children, including promoting educational achievement (CA 1989, s.17 as amended by Children Act 2004, s.53);
- a common law duty of care to all pupils;
- health and safety under the Health and Safety at Work etc. Act 1974;
- planning and support;
- addressing behavioural needs;

- children and young people's plans (a legal requirement under Children Act 2004, ss.17, 26, with effect from April 2006);
- policies and plans on placement and care planning, admissions and exclusions, SENs, early years and post-16 provision.

Policies and procedures

The LEA is responsible for formulating frameworks for, e.g. child protection, staff vetting, recruitment and allegations against them, behaviour and discipline, physical restraint of pupils, anti-bullying, racist behaviour, sexual harassment and complaints. Schools should have their own policies, using the LEA's as models.

Safeguarding

The education sector's role is set out in the Education Act 2002 and advisory guidance (see Chapters 4 and 5). There is also a DfES Education Protects website.[13]

The Children Act 2004 excludes the education sector (save for a general duty to cooperate in assessments under s.22) so its duty of cooperation is solely derived from CA 1989.

Guidance states that staff should ensure adequate assessment, early intervention and well-coordinated planned provision with other services. There should be clear LEA criteria for joint work on safeguarding and all staff must respond to concerns from children or adult observation.

The ethos of both schools and LEAs can significantly promote/inhibit safeguarding through quality of care, curriculum opportunities to explore issues safely and support, advice and guidance for staff.

All staff should:

- listen to children, encourage trust, and take them seriously;
- deal with them fairly and consistently;
- tackle bullying openly, firmly and fairly, using widely understood policies.

Vetting of staff

Appropriate procedures in schools on recruitment should include pre-appointment checks on:

- identity;
- academic qualifications (where relevant);
- professional and character references;
- previous employment history;
- Criminal Records Bureau and Protection of Children list;[14]
- health.

Recommendations from inquiries may lead to further requirements for interview processes, training and databases in both England and Wales.[15]

Designated teacher

Every school should appoint a 'designated teacher' to be the safeguarding focus for all pupils, a key resource for children, staff, families and carers and all children's services, especially in joint working and a supporter and advocate for those looked after.

Looked after children

The DfES 2000 guidance[16] emphasises the child's right to a Personal Education Plan; time limits for educational placements and suitable education; good information-sharing between professionals and carers and the appointment of designated teachers as advocates and for resources and liaison with other agencies.

Corporate parenting and joint services are covered elsewhere (see Chapters 4 and 11), but effective education, as a central part of care planning and placement support, includes:

- a legal duty on social services to notify LEAs of a child's placement (Arrangements for Placement of Children (General) Regulations 1991, SI 1991/890;[17]
- helping children catch up;
- resources for inclusion, attendance, behaviour, SENs, etc.;
- ensuring regular school attendance;
- continuing responsibilities beyond compulsory schooling.

Policies should set out:

- the child's entitlement to full-time education in mainstream schools;
- access to help for the child and her carers, including SEN support;
- the roles of social workers, carers, LEA and social services and designated teachers;
- arrangements for those placed outside the area and monitoring of educational progress;
- relevant national and local targets.[18]

Policies should also address children's circumstances without singling them out as 'different', encompass diversity, and unaccompanied asylum-seeking children, provide access to redress and complaints procedures and specify a lead person (usually the designated teacher).

13.8   PARTICULAR ISSUES

Admissions

The Codes of Practice on Admissions and Appeals are statutory guidance.[19] Statutory LEA Admission Forums[20] should agree a coordinated approach for vulnerable children, and schools' admissions policies should give children with special educational needs and looked after children 'top priority' in oversubscription criteria.[21]

Religious convictions must be recognised (*R (K) v. Newham LBC* [2002] ELR 390, a Sikh father's preference for single sex school for his daughter). Parents can express a preference, with which the LEA must comply (Education Act 1996, s.9 and see *R (K)* v. *Newham LBC* [2002] ELR 390), but subject to the school's admission policy (see below). Maintained schools must not give priority simply because a child lives in the LEA area. Schools can refuse to admit a child if to do so would mean that the efficient education of other pupils *with whom she would be educated* would be adversely affected or would entail an inefficient use of resources, or where the child has been excluded from two or more schools.

Schools cannot refuse to admit a child at the beginning of the school year if a place is available (although they have discretion at other times under Education Act 1996, s.344(1)) or solely because she is a looked after child.

Reasons for refusal must be given and there is a right of appeal, usually time limited – particularly important for asylum-seeking children.

Looked after children

LEAs are expected to secure school placement within 20 school days, to provide temporary alternative education if the time limit is exceeded, and to address any process delays.

The designated teacher should take responsibility for induction, addressing the risk of isolation/bullying and ensuring preservation of appropriate confidentiality.

Absence/out of school

LEAs must[22] assess the pupil's needs and arrange suitable placement at PRUs or other alternative education centres; check provision is of acceptable quality and monitor attendance and achievements.

DfES Good Practice Guidance is available on children missing, or at risk of going missing, from education and on protocols for hard to place children.

Attendance/truancy

See Education Act 1996, Part VI, Chapter II. Attendance registers must record absence with/without permission. Where a child fails to attend, the LEA must serve a school attendance order on the parent/carer (s.437), who can return the child to the school, make suitable alternative arrangements, or risk being prosecuted (with a fine and/or imprisonment under ss. 443, 444) or having an education supervision order (ESO) imposed (Children Act 1989, s.36, Sched. 3).

The LEA must consider whether an ESO is appropriate before instituting proceedings (Education Act 1996, s.447(1), although both criminal and civil routes can be used, see *Graves* v. *Islington LBC* [2003] EWHC Admin 2817, [2004] ELR 1).

The LEA must ensure a looked after child attends, by monitoring, coordinated records and liaison with school staff (assisted by the designated teacher), social workers and primary carers, and should consider home visits by the LEA education welfare officer (EWO).

Behaviour

Until April 2006, LEAs must have Behaviour Support Plans detailing arrangements for educating children with behavioural difficulties (Education Act 1996, s.572A).[23]

Unmet emotional needs or difficult home circumstances can lead to bad behaviour, truanting and exclusion. Behavioural sanctions should be ECHR compliant, with policies covering school premises and en route to/from them, on bullying, violence, racist/sexual harassment and homework (i.e. sanctions for failure to do it, although it is not legally compulsory).

Harassment by a pupil may be treated as bullying, but child protection issues should also be considered. Violence or sexual harassment by a teacher qualifies as gross misconduct leading to instant dismissal.

Detention after school hours without consent is allowed, provided prior notice is given, it is reasonable and meets safety requirements.

Physical intervention can be used by staff, and reasonable physical force (under Education Act 1996, s.550A) to break up a fight, to stop pupils endangering themselves, other pupils or school property or to prevent a pupil from committing a criminal offence.

Guidance is available for staff, LEAs and special schools: Circular (98) 10 on the use of force to control or restrain pupils[24] and Circulars LEA (2002) 242 and LEA (2003) 264 on the use of restrictive physical interventions with children who display extreme behaviour.[25]

However, intervention measures in public places are confined to the usual powers of any ordinary citizen at common law.

Bullying

All schools should have an anti-bullying policy. Lack of response may result in actions for, e.g. negligence against the school, and against the LEA for failure in their duty of care.

There is a national Anti-Bullying Alliance[26] and some useful websites listed in Appendix 2.

Carers

Carers can influence regular attendance and strong home-school links are vital. Information should be given to foster/kinship/residential carers as soon as possible about the designated teacher, liaison arrangements with the school, LEA and other children's services, and any home-school agreements (i.e. document drawn up by governors in consultation with parents, but not legally binding).

The respective roles of social worker and carer are set out in a DfES guide,[27] which states that the social worker should be actively involved in Personal Education Plans and any special educational needs or disability assessments, and the carer should provide a suitable environment for study and attend, e.g. parents' evenings (unless told otherwise).

Residential placements should not be made without a written statement specifying requirements for staff involvement in education.

Complaints

School policy and procedure (required under Education Act 2002) should include statutory guidance on what must be done if a complaint raises child protection issues.[28]

Curriculum

Looked after children should have equal access to the National Curriculum (which applies in all schools unless specifically disapplied), and to tests/examinations. They may require extra support to participate in extra-curricular activities and suitable work experience placements.

Disapplication from compulsory subjects is rare, but flexible learning packages[29] are available: policy on 14 to 19-year-olds encourages an alternative non-academic curriculum where appropriate.

Disability

Disability is broadly defined as a physical or mental[30] impairment, which has a substantial and long-term adverse effect on the ability to carry out normal day-to-day activities. It overlaps with, but is not the same as, SENs – a child with a disability will not necessarily have special educational needs. The legislation and Code of Practice for Schools contain further details.

The local authority or LEA can provide support following appropriate assessment under the Chronically Sick and Disabled Persons Act 1970, although there is no comprehensive right to resources (see Chapter 4 and *R (Spink)* v. *Wandsworth LBC* [2005] 1 FCR 608). But LEAs, schools and further education establishments must not discriminate[31] against pupils in admissions, provision of education or 'associated services' and temporary exclusions (for claims, see below).

Exclusions

Much DfES[32] and independent guidance is available. National guidance must be followed in exclusion decisions and procedures.[33] Proper procedures must *not* be avoided, even when well-motivated (e.g. to avoid a child getting a 'record'), since this may deny access to appropriate remedies and a fair hearing.

The head teacher should conduct a full investigation, and may exclude the pupil, if satisfied on the balance of probabilities, she did what was alleged. But the criminal standard of proof applies to any allegation amounting to a crime (*R (McCann)* v. *Crown Court at Manchester and another* [2002] UKHRR 1286 (a case concerning ASBOs); *Clingham* v. *Kensington and Chelsea RLBC* [2002] UKHL 39, [2003] 1 CA 787).

Exclusion is temporary or permanent, but only appropriate for serious breaches of behaviour policy; and where the education/welfare of the pupil or others in the school would otherwise be seriously harmed.

Temporary or 'fixed term' exclusions (or suspensions) (*A* v. *Head Teacher and Governors of the LG School*, 26 June 2003, QBD, per Burnton J) are usually for one to three days: more than 15 days should be rare. A maximum of 45 days is allowed in any one school year.

Permanent exclusion should be a last resort, unless there are immediate risks or threats to safety (but the safety of the pupil being sent away from school premises must also be considered). All other available strategies should be tried first.

Appeal procedures may not breach ECHR Article 6 (see *Simpson* v. *UK* (1989) 64 DR 188; *R (McCann)*), but the right not to be permanently excluded is a civil right (*Re S, T and P* v. *Brent and others*; *Oxfordshire CC Head Teacher of Elliot School and Others* v. *Secretary of State for Education and Skills* [2002] ELR 556 per Schiemann LJ). The right of appeal to governors on temporary exclusion may not be sufficiently independent and impartial to satisfy Article 6 and judicial review may be insufficient to cure this (see *R(S)* v. *Governing Body of YP School* [2003] EWCA Civ 1306, [2004] ELR 37).

The Governors' Discipline Committee must review each case and decide if reinstatement is appropriate. If permanently excluded, the LEA must arrange for an independent appeal panel hearing for the pupil, procedures for which are set out in statutory guidance.[34]

A child out of school for a long period may need a reintegration package, although separate tuition with access to facilities may be deemed sufficient (see *Re L (A Minor by his Next Friend and Litigation Friend)*, 27 February 2003, 3:2 majority).

Finance/funding

Difficult issues of interdepartmental, agency and authority funding responsibilities can arise for placement of looked after children, particularly in cases concerning SENs or disability (see conflicts in interpretation between Children Act 1989, s.108 and the Education (Areas to which Pupils and Students Belong) Regulations 1996, SI 1996/615). Protocols and multidisciplinary panels should exist: knowing how such decisions are taken and can be challenged, especially for out of authority placements, is crucial.

Health: education and medical needs

If sickness or injury prevent attendance, the LEA's named senior officer must arrange suitable alternative education (Education Act 1996, s.19) to minimise disruption to normal schooling and provide continuing access to as much education as the condition allows, and to maintain the momentum of education and progress and ensure future mental and physical development.

Medical diagnosis does not necessarily imply a special *educational* need exists, but proper assessment should be considered.[35] Circulars contain relevant standards, including:[36]

- minimum entitlement on hours;
- curriculum access;
- liaison arrangements;
- provision of work/home tuition;
- specialist services input;
- transfer of information and plans for reintegration to school.

Records

Information on educational progress must be kept (other personal information may be). Copies of records (excluding information about other pupils) must be supplied on written request from a pupil, parent or carer, unless the record holder believes disclosure would cause serious harm to the pupil or someone else, and the record is relevant to child abuse of a pupil.

Reviews

Schools should be consulted on, and participate in, statutory reviews on children looked after and those with SENs/disability. Where the child wants a particular person to attend, or to do so herself, this should normally be respected.

School phobia

Distinguished from pure truancy, school phobia is an anxiety-related condition characterised by intense fear of going to school, recognised by the DfES as a medical need,[37] increasingly regarded by educational psychologists as an SEN and, if a long-term mental impairment, may also qualify as a disability.

It can arise from transfer to another educational setting, from special educational needs (particularly if unmet), from an unsympathetic school environment or reaction by a vulnerable child to social and family pressures (e.g. substance misuse, mental health problems, marital conflict, bullying).

Further guidance on symptoms and treatment is available in LAC (2001) 17, including statutory assessment of special educational needs (and see Tribunal appeals below).

Transition/transfer

Transition must be well planned: support, especially for secondary transfer, is critical and must be in place early. LEAs are required to notify places by February of the year of transfer.

Transport

Children with special educational needs or disability are most likely to need transport and the LEA must take into account their age, medical or mobility needs. This may include a need for escorts.

Plans/records

All plans and records must be accurate, include positive information and provide continuity. Practitioners must ensure the child's care plan takes account of the following:

- Personal Education Plan (PEP): required for looked after children;
- Individual Education Plan (IEP): for a child with SENs;
- Statement of Special Educational Needs (see below);
- Pastoral Support Programme or Learning Mentor Action Plan;
- National Record of Achievement and/or child's progress file;

- careers action plan and Pathway Plans (see the Children (Leaving Care) Act 2002).

Personal education plans[38]

PEPs must be initiated by the social worker and involve the child, designated teacher, parent and/or relevant family member, carer and any relevant specialist professionals. If a child has no school place, an LEA officer should liaise with the social worker. The PEP should be agreed as soon as possible and at least within 20 school days of entering care (i.e. in time for the first 28-day review) or of joining a new school. The PEP should ensure full access to services and support, provide an accurate educational record and reflect all other existing relevant plans to avoid duplication.

An up-to-date copy should be kept with the care plan: in future there will be a single plan incorporating the PEP and Health Care Plan.[39] The PEP should focus on:

- placement stability;
- clear objectives, and any behavioural issues, with timescales for action and review;
- accurate, comprehensive recording of achievement and potential: negative/ambivalent/inaccurate information should be challenged;
- identifying developmental, educational and any particular or special needs.

It should be reviewed, at minimum, every six months, usually concurrently with the care plan. Significant decisions about education should not take place without this, which must involve the child.

13.9   SPECIAL EDUCATIONAL NEEDS AND DISABILITY

General

Children separated from their families need support and advocacy – their emotional and behavioural responses may give rise to special needs, albeit temporary. A disproportionate number are also disabled, face additional prejudice, isolation and low expectations. Many are not consulted or involved in decisions and are much more likely to have a Statement of SENs, the importance of which is not often fully understood.

Parental preference is recognised, but carries no right to an independent or a residential school unless, in the latter case, there is an educational need for such placement. There is a right of inclusion in mainstream education (Education Act 1996, s.316), subject to exceptions based on the efficient education of other children or the efficient use of resources by the LEA.[40] The relevant law is particularly complex and specialist advice is recommended.

Special educational needs

A child has SENs if she has:

- a significantly greater difficulty in learning than the majority of children of the same age;
- a disability that prevents/hinders access to educational facilities of a kind provided for children of the same age in schools within the LEA's area; or
- is under five years and falls within either of the above categories, or would do so if special educational provision were not made.

Further information can be obtained from the numerous organisations listed in Appendix 2.

Statutory duties under the Education Act 1996 (as amended) to identify, assess and provide may involve:

- a multidisciplinary assessment in consultation with parents;
- various professionals (e.g. educational psychology, mental health and other specialist disciplines) in advising, assessing or giving evidence;
- specialist services for the hearing/visually impaired, advisory teachers for particular areas of need (e.g. autistic spectrum disorder), or therapists, some employed by the LEA, others by the health service or voluntary bodies.

The statutory Code of Practice[41] contains detailed guidance, supported by the (advisory) Special Educational Needs Toolkit. Needs may be provided for at 'School Action' (action within school), 'School Action Plus' or in a Statement. Statements are legal documents, which must describe the child's needs (Part 2) and specify and quantify the appropriate provision to meet them (Part 3) (this is legally guaranteed by the LEA, regardless of which service actually provides it or budgetary constraints) (Education Act 1996, s.324(5)(a)(i)). Part 4 names the child's placement, but should not normally name a PRU.[42]

Although most children should be provided for in mainstream education, some may need placement (either part time or full time) in specialist settings such as units attached to mainstream schools or (more rarely) in specialist schools. Those with very severe needs may require residential placements.

Special Educational Needs and Disability Tribunal (SENDIST)

Parents and carers (including foster carers, see *Fairpo* v. *Humberside CC* [1997] 1 FLR 339) have a right of *appeal* against the LEA for:

- refusing a statutory assessment;
- deciding not to issue a Statement of SENs;
- changes to a Statement;
- refusing to reassess a child with a Statement;
- refusing to change the name of a school in a Statement;
- ceasing to maintain a Statement.

Disability discrimination is defined as either 'less favourable treatment' and/or 'failure to make reasonable adjustments' (Disability Discrimination Act 1995, ss.5 and 6; the alleged discrimination must have arisen since 1 September 2002). *Claims* can be made by parents and carers to SENDIST against 'responsible bodies' (school and/or LEA) in relation to school admissions, providing education or 'associated services', temporary exclusions, or victimisation of a child as the result of making allegations of discrimination. SENDIST powers include ordering apologies, and training of staff, but not financial compensation (s.28I(4)(b)).

The child/young person who is the subject of an appeal/claim is not a party, but Tribunal Regulations specifically provide that she is entitled to have her views sought and to attend the hearing (Special Educational Needs Tribunal Regulations 2001, SI 2001/600 and Special Educational Needs and Disability Tribunal (General Provisions and Disability Claims Procedure) Regulations 2002, SI 2002/1985). There is a SENDIST protocol for such attendance; each tribunal panel has power to determine the extent of attendance and participation.

NOTES

1   See National Children's Bureau at **www.ncb.org.uk**; National Foundation for Educational Research at **www.nfer.ac.uk** and National Learning Mentor Network at **www.nmn.org.uk**.
2   Of those continuously looked after for at least 12 months in 2002, 27% had SEN statements (cf. 3% of all pupils), 1% were permanently excluded (0.1%), 53% of Year 11 pupils had at least one exam qualification (95%), and about 25% were unemployed on leaving school (6%).
3   See Highlight no. 208 on **www.ncb.org.uk**.
4   Around 100,000 per annum; see Access to Education Circular DfES (2001)732, DH HSC Circular (2001)19 and LAC (2001)27 and *Mental Health of Children and Adolescents*, Office of National Statistics (March 2000): such problems occurred in 10% of 10,000 children aged 5–15.
5   A DfES checklist of 'core services' for extended schools, including study support, parenting support, child care and targeted provision for those with special needs is due.
6   See *Another Country*, Audit Commission Report (2000).
7   This could include voluntary withdrawal because of, e.g. bullying (unless persistent and school is unable to prevent), but might cover exceptions, e.g. sexual assault by another pupil, see *R (G by RG)* v. *Westminster City Council* [2004] EWCA Civ 45.

8   Behaviour Support Plans Circular DfEE (98)1; after April 2006 see LEA (2005) 24 *PRUs and Alternative Provision – Guidance for Local Authorities and Schools*.

9   Connexions is likely to be subsumed into Children's Services: see Green Paper, Youth Matters (2005).

10   See **www.dfes.gov.uk/ema**.

11   Special Educational Needs Code of Practice (2001).

12   See Code of Practice LEA–School Relations, DfES (1999).

13   See **www.dfes.gov.uk/educationprotects**.

14   Confidential list of those barred or restricted by the Secretary of State from employment in posts bringing, or likely to bring, them into contact with children, e.g. teachers cannot be registered with the General Teaching Council if they are so barred.

15   The Bichard Inquiry (2004) and, in Wales, the Clwych Report (2004) by the Welsh Children's Commissioner. See *Bichard Inquiry Recommendations Progress Report*, Home Office (December 2004).

16   *Guidance on the Education of Children in the Public Care*, DfES (2000) covers all maintained primary, secondary and special schools, and PRUs.

17   See *Working Together to Safeguard Children*, DH, Home Office, DfEE (1999), para. 7.27 onwards for full responsibilities.

18   LEAs must produce Education Development Plans (EDPs) with key targets, including National Priorities Guidance target for looked after children (School Standards and Framework Act 1998).

19   DfES (2003)31.

20   See **www.dfes.gov.uk/sacode**.

21   Codes of Practice on Admissions and Admission Appeals, DfES (2003), para. 7.22.

22   See LEA (2005)24.

23   LEA (Behaviour Support Plans) Regulations 1998, SI 1998/644 and see Circular (98)1. Repealed by Children Act 2004: behaviour to be covered in 'children and young people's plans'.

24   See **www.dfes.gov.uk/guidanceonthelaw/10_98/summary.htm**.

25   See **www.dfes.uk/sen**.

26   See **www.teachernet.gov.uk/antibully**.

27   See *Who Does What*, LACWDW (September 2004); *Who Cares*, DfES, ODPM, ACE at **www.dfes.gov.uk/educationprotects**.

28   *Clwych Inquiry Report* (2004), para. 19.45.

29   Involving temporary disapplication from or modification of the curriculum by a period of part-time attendance at a further education college or work-based programme. See *Social Inclusion: Pupil Support*, DfES Circular (99)10.

30   Mental impairment must be a clinically well-recognised condition by reference to authoritative sources such as the World Health Organisation's classification, see **www.who.int/classification/icf**.

31   See Disability Discrimination Act 1995, s.27 and DfES Guidance on Matters to be Taken into Account, available at **www.drc-gb.org/thelaw/ practice.asp**.

32   See **www.dfes.gov.uk/exclusions**.

33   *Improving Behaviour and Attendance: Guidance on Exclusion from Schools and Pupil Referral Units*, DfES (2003) 87.

34   Circular DfES (99)10: *Social Inclusion: Pupil Support* (as amended), DfES (2003)87: *Improving Behaviour and Attendance: Guidance on Exclusion from Schools and Pupil Referral Units*.

35   Under the Code of Practice on the Identification and Assessment of Pupils with Special Educational Needs, DfES (2001).

36 LAC (2001)17, para. 1.14.
37 See LAC (2001)17.
38 See Chapter 11 and for PEP model format see **www.dfee.gov.uk/incare/ pep.htm**.
39 See the Integrated Children's System for revised electronic Looking After Children records.
40 Note that LEAs were given time to put in place necessary arrangements, but the adequacy of these in some areas is debatable (see *Slough BC* v. *C* [2004] ELR 546).
41 DfES (2001).
42 *Social Inclusion: the LEA Role in Pupil Support*, DfEE (99)11; *Pupil Support and Social Inclusion*, Welsh Assembly (99)3.

CHAPTER 14

Housing issues

Key sources

- National Assistance Act 1948, s.21; Immigration and Asylum Act 1999, s.95; Asylum and Immigration (Treatment of Claimants, etc) Act 2004
- Protection from Eviction Act 1977; Landlord and Tenant Act 1985, s.11; Housing Acts 1988, 1985; 1996, Pts 6 and 7
- Homelessness (Suitability of Accommodation) Order 1996, Homelessness (England) Regulations 2000 and Homelessness (Priority Need for Accommodation) (England) Order 2002, and Wales regulations
- Circular LAC (2002)13
- Homelessness Code of Guidance for Local Authorities (July 2002, revised ch. 15 January 2005)
- *Anti-Social Behaviour: Policy and Procedure – Guidance for Housing Associations*, Housing Corporation (August 2004)

14.1 INTRODUCTION

This chapter provides an overview of the extensive and complicated law relating to homelessness and housing. Housing law is complex and extensive and is subject to constant legislative reform.[1] The chapter addresses the four main types of question that a client who has housing problems is likely to want answered:

- I have nowhere to live, what can I do?
- Can I stay in my home?
- How can I afford my home?
- My home is not suitable for my needs or is in disrepair – what can I do?

The answers focus on the legal position of a parent or carer with responsibilities for children, but also provide some information about the law relating to asylum seekers and their children and care leavers and other young people who need housing advice. The greatest amount of detail is provided in relation to the law on homelessness. The other areas are summaries only to raise issues and provide a basis for seeking further advice.

Practitioners should note that effective collaboration between social services, health authorities and housing departments is not widespread and, despite statutory duties in the Homelessness Act 2002, the needs of vulnerable children and young people are not well addressed.[2]

Practice issues

There are a decreasing number of solicitors who specialise in this area of law so it is wise to understand the basics and know what expertise is available in your local area. In addition, you should use the Codes of Guidance on Homelessness and Allocations, be familiar with your local housing authority's practices and procedures, including its homelessness strategy and allocations policy, and know the procedures of your local housing associations. Excellent further advice is available on the Shelter websites.[3]

14.2 HUMAN RIGHTS

The definition of 'priority need' should be considered carefully in regard to housing assistance for those with dependent children who are the subject of immigration control. The relevant part of the Housing Act 1996 may be incompatible with ECHR Article 14 (see Housing Act 1996, s.185(4), *R (Morris)* v. *Westminster City Council* [2005] 1 FLR 429 and the test in *Wandsworth LBC* v. *Michalak* [2002] EWCA Civ 271 and see *Ghaidan* v. *Godin Mendoza* [2004] UKHL 30).

14.3 HOMELESSNESS

I have nowhere to live – what can I do?

The starting point in answering this question is to consider the responsibilities of the local housing authority towards the client. If she is not owed any accommodation duties then social services may have some responsibility to provide or assist in the provision of accommodation. Otherwise she will have to seek accommodation within the private sector.

The statutory obligation placed upon local housing authorities by Part 7 of the Housing Act 1996 is to make available suitable accommodation for a person who must be eligible for assistance, homeless, in priority need of accommodation and not intentionally homeless.

The duty is subject to the local connection provisions of the 1996 Act. These responsibilities are amplified by the Homelessness Code of Guidance.[4] Decisions are subject to an internal review procedure and challenge in the county court.

The first step that must be taken is to apply to a housing authority for accommodation, or help in obtaining accommodation. Following an application, if the housing authority has reason to believe that the person may be homeless or threatened with homelessness, the housing authority must make inquiries under Housing Act 1996, s.184 to satisfy themselves whether the applicant is eligible for assistance and, if so, whether a duty is owed to that person under Part 7 of the 1996 Act.

Eligibility for housing assistance

No duty is owed by the housing department to anyone who is ineligible for assistance (Housing Act 1996, s.185 and Homelessness (England) Regulations 2000, SI 2000/701). The provisions that deny eligibility to certain groups of people from abroad are very technical. In brief, people are eligible for assistance if they are British citizens or EEA citizens habitually in the Common Travel Area (CTA), i.e. the UK, the Channel Islands, the Isle of Man and the Republic of Ireland. Most people subject to immigration control granted refugee status, given exceptional leave to remain or given indefinite leave to remain are also eligible for assistance.

Annexes 12 to 22 of the Code of Guidance[5] provide a great deal of further information.

Definition of homelessness

A person is homeless if she, together with any person she can reasonably be expected to live with, has no accommodation which they are entitled to occupy and which it would be reasonable for them to continue to occupy (Housing Act 1996, s.175). Accommodation includes accommodation overseas. A person does not have to be actually homeless to qualify under the Act, if he or she is likely to become homeless within the next 28 days.

Homelessness and violence

It is not reasonable to continue to occupy accommodation (s.177(1)) if 'if it is probable that this will lead to domestic violence or other violence against [the applicant] or against (a) a person who normally resides with him as a member of his family, or (b) any other person who might reasonably be expected to reside with him'.

Domestic violence is defined as violence or threats of violence from an 'associated person' with whom the applicant was living, such as a relative, a cohabitee or a member of the same household. It is not confined to violence within the home, but includes violence outside the home from an associated person.

Housing authorities should not insist on applicants seeking injunctions to prevent violence. The Code of Guidance (at para. 6.20) states: 'Housing authorities should recognise that injunctions ordering persons not to molest, or enter the home of, the applicant will not always be effective in deterring perpetrators from carrying out further violence or incursions. Applicants should not automatically be expected to return home on the strength of an injunction.'

Priority need

Only if an applicant, or someone who can be expected to live with the applicant, is in priority need (as set out in Housing Act 1996, s.189(1) and Homelessness (Priority Need for Accommodation) (England) Order 2002, SI 2002/2051)[6] will the main duty to secure accommodation be triggered. The priority needs categories are:

- pregnant women;
- people with dependent children, which can give rise to particular issues in private law (see *R (Bibi)* v. *Camden LBC* [2004] EWHC Admin 2527, [2005] 1 FLR 413);
- those vulnerable as a result of old age, mental illness or handicap or physical disability or some other special reason;
- an applicant homeless as a result of an emergency, flood, fire or other disaster;
- 16 and 17-year-olds;
- those over 21 having been looked after, accommodated or fostered by social services and vulnerable as a result;
- care leavers under 21 years;
- an applicant having been a member of the armed forces and vulnerable as a result;
- an applicant having been in custody and vulnerable as a result;
- an applicant fleeing violence or threats of violence and vulnerable as a result.

Vulnerability

Certain categories of applicants must be vulnerable before they are owed duties under the legislation. The vulnerability test has recently been clarified (by the Court of Appeal in *Griffin* v. *Westminster City Council* [2004] EWCA Civ 108): the local authority has to decide whether the applicant, when homeless, would be less likely to fend for him or herself than an ordinary homeless person so that injury or detriment would result when a less vulnerable person would be able to cope without harmful effect. The current Code of Guidance (at para. 8.13) misstates the test of vulnerability for applicants because it dilutes the statutory test through importing a notion of likelihood of injury or detriment.

If the applicant:

- is elderly, mentally ill, mentally or physically disabled;
- is over 21 and has been looked after, accommodated or fostered by social services;
- has been a member of the armed forces;
- has been in custody;
- is fleeing violence or threats of violence

then inquiries will be made into their specific vulnerability before a decision is made that they are in priority need. In most cases it should be straightforward to demonstrate the relevant vulnerability. The Code provides further information on the meaning of vulnerability in particular circumstances.

Intentionality

The housing authority has to decide if the applicant became homeless *intentionally* (Housing Act 1996, s.184). This is a crucial aspect of decision-making in homelessness and has led to a great deal of litigation. Before an applicant can be found intentionally homeless she has to have had accommodation which it would be reasonable to continue to occupy and by some deliberate act have lost it (s.191).

The same criteria apply to threatened homelessness (s.196). Someone who fails to pay their mortgage through careless financial management may be found to be intentionally homeless; someone who suffers genuine financial hardship will not be intentionally homeless. Each case is decided on its own facts, but yet again the Code is helpful in suggesting an appropriate decision-making process.

Local connection

If neither the applicant nor a person who would reasonably be expected to live with them has a local connection (i.e. normally resident in the area, or employed there, or having family ties (s.198)), but does have a local connection with another local authority's area, the local authority can transfer its responsibilities to the applicant by notifying the other authority.

The local connection proviso does not apply to an applicant who has a local connection, if return would be to the probability of violence, including domestic violence. Accommodation provided by NASS whilst an asylum claim is determined will in most circumstances create a local connection with that area.[7]

Duties owed by housing authorities to applicants once inquiries are complete

The Housing Act 1996 provides a range of duties dependent upon the decision reached by the housing authorities. They owe a duty to secure accommodation only to applicants who are found to be unintentionally homeless and in priority need. The full range of more limited duties owed to other applicants are set out in Chapter 9 of the Code. Remember, whatever the decision, the housing authority must inform the applicant in writing and with reasons of the decision and what help if any it will provide. It must give the details of the right to seek, within 21 days of notification, a review of its decision (s.184).

Securing suitable accommodation

Local housing authorities must provide permanent accommodation themselves, or ensure that some other person provides it, or give such advice and assistance as will enable the applicant to secure accommodation.

The accommodation offered must be suitable for the applicant and her household. Refusal of an offer of suitable accommodation will discharge the duty of the housing authority and may well lead to an 'intentionally' homeless decision if a further application is made. Applicants may have to spend some time in temporary accommodation before an offer of permanent accommodation is made.

'Suitable' means it 'must be suitable in relation to the applicant and to all members of his or her household who normally reside with him or her, or who might reasonably be expected to reside with him or her ... Housing authorities should therefore have regard to all the relevant circumstances of the applicant and his or her household. Account will need to be taken of any medical and/or physical needs, and any social considerations relating to the applicant and his or her household that might affect the suitability of accommodation. Any risk of violence or racial harassment must also be taken into account'.[8] Accommodation that is not affordable[9] or is located at a distance from essential facilities may be found to be unsuitable.

Challenging the local authority's decision

Internal review

There is a right to a review by the housing department of certain decisions on homelessness, followed by a right to appeal to the county court (Housing Act 1996, s.202). The procedure of the review is prescribed (by the Allocation of Housing and Homelessness (Review Procedures) Regulations 1999, SI 1999/71) and the review must be requested within 21 days of the authority's decision. Decisions that may be reviewed are:

- any decision about eligibility for assistance;
- any decision as to what duty, if any, is owed under ss.190–195;
- local connection decisions;
- suitability.

Housing authorities have the power to accommodate the applicant pending a review. Decisions whether to provide accommodation in these circumstances should be made reasonably.

Appeals to the county court

There is a right of appeal on a point of law to the county court where the applicant is dissatisfied with the decision on review or the applicant is not notified of the decision on the review within a prescribed time period (s.204). The appeal must be brought within 21 days of the decision. The court may give permission for an appeal to be brought after 21 days, but only where it is satisfied that there is good reason for the applicant's delay. The county court can also hear appeals from decisions of housing authorities not to accommodate the applicant pending the appeal.

Social services responsibilities

Social services may provide a final safety net for certain categories of vulnerable homeless people if they are not owed duties under Part 7 of the Housing Act 1996.

Homeless clients with children

In general lone children will, where appropriate, be accommodated under the Children Act 1989, s.20. Where, however, a child should be accommodated with their family or in exceptional cases, where a child does not need to be looked after but needs help with accommodation, then social services departments are able to provide accommodation (Children Act 1989, ss.17 and 22, as amended by the Adoption and Children Act 2002).

There is guidance for social services,[10] stating that the child should be assessed in accordance with the Framework for Assessment (see Chapter 8) and which points out that any accommodation provided must be suitable for the families and children for whom it is intended. It suggests that older asylum-seeking children who have no parent or guardian in the country but are competent and wish to look after themselves may be appropriately accommodated under Children Act 1989, s.17. However, this duty to an individual child is very limited (see House of Lords in *R (G)* v. *Barnet LBC; R (W)* v. *Lambeth LBC; R (A)* v. *Lambeth LBC* [2003] UKHL 57, [2004] 1 FLR 454) since it sets out duties of a general character intended for the benefit of all children in need in the local area in general. The assessment of a child's needs does not transform the general duty to a specific duty owed to the child as an individual. Whilst social services departments are able to provide accommodation, the provision of residential accommodation to rehouse a child so that she could live with her family is not the principal purpose of the legislation. Housing is the function of the local housing authority, governed by detailed statutory provisions of a kind which are entirely absent from the Children Act 1989. In other words, whilst a homeless child is very likely to be a child in need and should be accommodated by social services, this does not impose a duty upon the local authority to provide accommodation for the child's family as well, which is consistent with previous understanding of the law (see *R v. Northavon DC, ex p. Smith* [1994] 2 AC 402).

If social services place a child in temporary accommodation, an assessment must be made of its suitability and the results recorded on the child's case file. If it is unsuitable, this should be reported to a senior officer.

Disabled adults and children

Disabled adults are owed statutory duties under National Assistance Act 1948, s.21 and other disability legislation, and their needs should be assessed under the NHS and Community Care Act 1990 and if special or adapted accommodation is necessary, the social services department must provide it.

Accommodation should be suitable to the needs of disabled children, but the financial resources of parents can be taken into account when providing aids and adaptations (*R v. Gloucestershire CC, ex p. Barry* [1997] AC 584; *R (Spink) v. Wandsworth LBC* [2004] EWHC Admin 2314, [2005] 1 FLR 448).

Asylum seekers

Asylum seekers and their dependants who are ineligible under Part 7 of the 1996 Act will be accommodated by the National Asylum Support Service (NASS) if they are without adequate accommodation or any means of obtaining it (Immigration and Asylum Act 1999, s.95). However, asylum seekers who are disabled are still owed duties under National Assistance Act 1948, s.21. The exclusion of asylum seekers from s.21 is limited to destitute asylum seekers (s.21(1A)). Therefore asylum seekers can have their needs assessed and suitable accommodation provided by social services.

However, because the 1948 Act applies to adults and not children, the disabled children of asylum seekers have to be housed by NASS. The nature of this duty owed by NASS to disabled children has been held (in *R (A) v. NASS* [2003] EWCA Civ 1473, [2004] 1 All ER 15) to be limited to the provision of 'adequate' as opposed to suitable accommodation. There was said to be no significant difference between the meanings of the two words, although 'adequacy' had to be tested by reference to the needs of the persons to whom the duty was owed and the circumstances of each relevant individual had to be considered, including the locality of the accommodation. Because the duty was a continuing one, what might have been suitable at one moment might become unsuitable later. Where there were disabled children, a balancing exercise had to be carried out, with the question whether the accommodation was adequate for the needs of the disabled children in the circumstances persisting at that moment at the forefront of the decision-making process.

14.4 ACCESSING HOUSING

If an applicant does not qualify for housing under the homelessness provisions of the Housing Act 1996, she will have to consider the alternatives.

Allocating social housing

Not all social housing is allocated via the homelessness route. Some will be allocated via what is colloquially known as the 'waiting list'. The legal framework for allocation of local authority housing is set out in law and guidance.[11] People who are eligible should be allocated a tenancy on the basis of the local authority allocation scheme. Decisions on eligibility can be reviewed under Housing Act 1996, s.167(4A).

When local housing authorities decide who to house they must give 'reasonable preference' in allocating accommodation to those:

- who are homeless;
- who are owed duties under the homelessness provisions of the Housing Act 1996;
- with medical or other problems;
- who need to move to a particular locality in the district of the authority, where failure to meet that need would cause hardship to themselves or to others;
- who need help moving out of poor quality or insecure housing.

Housing authorities may decide to give additional preference to particular categories of people in urgent housing need. Other factors which may be taken into account when housing authorities are devising an allocation scheme include the financial resources available to a person to meet her housing costs, the behaviour of any person or a member of her household which affects suitability to be a tenant, and any local connection which exists between a person and the authority's district.

Recently, there has been a move away from bureaucratic allocation systems to choice-based lettings. In this system, vacant dwellings are advertised and the advertisements detail any qualifying conditions, such as household size.

Rules for applying and a reply coupon are included alongside the advertisements. Practitioners should find out details of any such schemes locally in order to advise clients properly.[12]

Local authority tenancy

Accommodation offered by local authority landlords will be either secure tenancies (under Housing Act 1985) or introductory tenancies (under the Housing Act 1996), as public bodies must be ECHR-compliant and are judicially reviewable. Local authority tenants can complain to the Local Government Ombudsman about maladministration of housing matters.

Housing association tenancy

Most housing associations are legally defined as registered social landlords (see the Housing Act 1996). Registered social landlords are registered with the Housing Corporation, which regulates the operation of registered social landlords. Housing association tenancies are generally obtained either through a waiting list run by the individual housing association, or via nominations from the local housing department.

Housing associations are not automatically public bodies for the purposes of the Human Rights Act 1998. Housing association tenants can complain to the Housing Ombudsman Service about their landlord.

Private sector tenancy

Some people may prefer to rent property in the private sector, or have no choice either because they are not owed housing duties under the Housing Act 1996 or because there is such a high demand for housing locally that there is no real prospect of them being rehoused by the local housing authority allocation scheme. Private accommodation is advertised in local papers and the local housing office may have a list of landlords. Accommodation agencies (which are regulated by the Accommodation Agencies Act 1953) may offer a service to people looking for private sector accommodation, but their services are often expensive and may not be relevant to people on benefits. Note that private sector landlords can select their tenants in any way they choose, and have no obligations over and above anti-discrimination legislation.

The most important advice for those seeking accommodation in the private rented sector is to check that it is affordable. Most private sector landlords require deposits and rent in advance, which are not automatically covered by income support or social fund payments. More importantly, housing benefit, which covers rent payments, is not only means-tested but also has limitations with regard to the level of payments which can be made on any particular property. Several local housing departments run schemes to help people rent in the private rented sector which aim to speed up housing benefit decisions and support tenants in their dealings with their landlord.

Private sector landlords are most likely to offer assured shorthold tenancies (under the Housing Act 1988).

14.5 EVICTION

Can my landlord evict me?

The answer to this depends on the client's legal status. Legal status depends on three issues:

- Does the client have a tenancy or a licence?
- If a tenancy exists, what kind of tenancy is it? (The answer largely depends on the date of commencement of the tenancy and who the landlord is.)
- Is the particular tenancy arrangement specifically excluded from statutory protection? The most significant exclusion is the tenant with a resident landlord.

Note that any eviction involving children should trigger an assessment of the child's needs under Children Act 1989, s.17.

Tenancy or licence?

To be a tenant, the person or persons renting must be entitled to three things: (a) to exclusive possession; (b) of identifiable premises; (c) for a known period (such as a weekly period) (*Street* v. *Mountford* [1985] AC 809).

Licensees are in the premises by permission of the occupier and their right to continue there can be withdrawn. Whilst there are continuing difficulties with shared accommodation and hostel accommodation, for the average person renting the property it is probably safe to assume a tenancy unless there are strong indications to the contrary.

Young people

There are two obstacles to young people becoming tenants:

- they have to be 18 or over to acquire such a 'legal interest in land';
- contracts with those under 18 are only enforceable if they are 'contracts for necessities'.

These hurdles can be overcome. In most circumstances, a contract to rent accommodation would be considered by the courts to be a contract for necessities. Even if landlords cannot grant legal leases, they can grant 'equitable leases'. In very simple terms, these are leases which do not comply with all the legal formalities but the courts consider should be treated as if they do. Such agreements would attract the normal provisions of security of tenure.

Types of tenancies and the relevant statutory framework

In simple terms, all private tenancies created on or after 15 January 1989 must be either *assured* tenancies or *assured shorthold* tenancies (governed by the Housing Act 1988) or if created before that time are *regulated* tenancies (governed by the Rent Act 1977). Where the local authority is the landlord then the Housing Act 1985 is the relevant statute, and local authority tenants have secure tenancies regardless of the commencement date.

Assured tenancies

The Housing Act 1988, as amended by the Housing Act 1996, governs private sector and housing association tenancy agreements commencing from 15 January 1989 to date. It creates two forms of tenancy: the assured tenancy and the assured shorthold tenancy. The key feature of the assured tenancy is that the tenant must occupy the property as her only or principal home.

In order to evict the tenant, the landlord must serve a notice seeking possession, which must specify grounds for possession and set out the period of time before which court proceedings cannot be issued. The grounds for possession are set on in Schedule 2 to the Housing Act 1988. Note that there is a particular ground for eviction, ground 8, which is available to the landlords of assured tenants where there are two months' arrears of rent outstanding at the date of the notice of seeking possession and at the date of the eviction. This ground is mandatory and therefore the reasons for the non-payment of rent are irrelevant. The court must order possession (see *North British Housing Association Ltd* v. *Matthews* [2004] EWCA Civ 1736).

Assured shorthold tenancies

Assured shorthold tenancies (ASTs) provide very limited security of tenure and are the most common form of tenure within the private rented sector. Tenants can be evicted from an AST with two months' notice once the first six months has expired. Previous notice requirements in the 1988 Act were abolished in the 1996 Act. All tenancy agreements created on or after 28 February 1997 are automatically ASTs unless the landlord serves notice otherwise. Housing association landlords usually serve a notice on the tenant saying that the tenancy is to be an assured tenancy. Private landlords do not serve such a notice, therefore all tenancies in the private sector which commenced after 27 February 1997 are likely to be ASTs.

During the initial six months of an AST the landlord can recover possession only by obtaining a possession order from the court based upon a limited range of grounds (which, however, includes all of the rent grounds). If a landlord wishes to evict an assured shorthold tenant, he or she can use a paper-only procedure: the 'accelerated possession' procedure. Note that the accelerated possession procedure is also available for some grounds which can be used to evict the assured tenant.

Secure tenancies

This term covers all local authority tenancy agreements whenever they were commenced, and housing association tenancies created before 15 January 1989. The key requirement of the secure tenancy is that the tenant occupies the property as her only or principal home. Subletting the whole of the property removes the tenant from protection. Secure tenancies come with a bundle of other important rights, which are summarised in the Tenant's Charter. These include the right to buy, the right to take in lodgers, the right to consultation and other significant rights.

Secure tenants have extensive security of tenure. Before a secure tenant can be evicted the landlord must serve a notice of seeking possession which must specify the grounds for possession. There are no mandatory grounds for possession. The court must be satisfied that a possession order is reasonable, or that there is suitable alternative accommodation for the tenant. Where the property is of a particular type (e.g. adapted for a disabled person, or adjacent to special facilities for the elderly), the court has to be satisfied both that there is suitable alternative accommodation and that possession is reasonable.

Introductory tenancies under the Housing Act 1996

A local authority or a housing action trust is entitled to grant new tenants a tenancy for a trial period of one year which can be extended by a further six months in particular circumstances. These tenancies are called 'introductory tenancies' (under Housing Act 1996, Pt V; the power to extend the period by six months was provided by the Housing Act 2004). Not all local authorities use introductory tenancies, although their use has grown recently. The landlord can obtain possession at any time during the introductory period by applying to the court, and the court must order possession if the correct procedure has been followed. There is no need to prove any grounds; all the tenant can do is to ask (within 14 days of the notice that the landlord intends to evict the tenant) for the landlord to review its decision to evict.

Following the introductory period, the tenancy becomes secure, and grounds are needed before a court can order eviction.

Demoted tenancies under the Anti-social Behaviour Act 2003

The Anti-social Behaviour Act 2003 provides for a form of less secure tenancy by amending the Housing Acts 1985 and 1988. The provisions are very complex. In brief, they allow local authorities and registered social landlords to apply to court to reduce the security of tenants. In essence the provisions make the concept of the introductory tenancy available to social landlords during the lifetime of the tenancy. The demoted tenancy lasts one year, during which time it can be terminated without grounds being proved. At the end of one year the tenancy is 'promoted' to its former levels of security. The relevant provisions were implemented on 1 July 2004. It is not clear if social landlords will make extensive use of demotion.

Illegal eviction

There are civil and criminal remedies for illegal eviction and harassment and procedures set out a minimum of protection for all residential occupiers – except those specifically excluded from the provisions (see the Protection from Eviction Act 1977). Injunctions are available to restrain a landlord from harassing his or her tenants and to order that the landlord re-admits the occupiers.

But not all residential occupiers are statutorily protected. Lettings made on or after 15 January 1989 that are holiday lets, temporary lettings to squatters, where the landlord is a resident landlord who shares living accommodation with the tenant, or is hostel accommodation provided by a social landlord, are excluded (s.3A of the 1977 Act). Therefore, the landlord can recover possession without court proceedings, so long as reasonable notice is given, which will usually be four weeks or contractual notice, which could be as short as a week.

If a client is excluded from her accommodation then it is necessary to take extremely speedy court action. However, if the landlord is making low level threats or suggesting that she has to leave at the end of the month, it can be very useful to contact the tenancy relation officers at your local council. They will visit the landlord and explain the law to him and the consequences of breach. This may make it possible to sustain the tenancy over a longer term.

14.6   RENT AND BENEFITS

Deposits and rent in advance

People seeking to rent accommodation are often asked for deposits and rent in advance. Housing benefit will not cover such payments which will also be given a very low priority by the Social Fund. The social services department has the power to pay deposits and rent in advance for families where children are in need under Children Act 1989, s.17. Local authorities may run a tenancy deposit scheme designed to support people seeking accommodation in the private rented sector.

One real difficulty with deposits is getting them back at the end of the tenancy. The Housing Act 2004 introduces compulsory statutory protection of tenancy deposits. It is expected that the provisions will be implemented in autumn 2005 making it much easier for tenants to recover their deposits.

Rent control

Housing Act 1988

The assured tenant is taken to have freely agreed the original rent with the landlord and therefore cannot legally challenge it. If she has agreed rent review clauses, then she is similarly bound. If there are no provisions for rent increases, the landlord may increase the rent annually via a notice procedure. The tenant can challenge the increase, but the Rent Assessment Committee will intervene only if the rent has been raised above the market rent level; and as the Committee can raise the rent as well as lower it, the tenant has to be very sure before challenging any increase. The rent control provisions for ASTs are notionally more rigorous. The tenant is allowed to challenge the initial rent during the first six months, but only if the rent is significantly higher than the market rent. However, it is extremely unlikely that any tenant with such limited security is going to risk her future in the property by commencing such a challenge.

Housing Act 1985

There are no rent control provisions in the Housing Act 1985 other than the right of the landlord to charge a reasonable rent for his property. Tenants must be given notice of rent increases. Reasonableness of rent rises can be challenged via judicial review. However, past challenges have had very little success.

Housing benefit

The principal way that unemployed tenants, or tenants on low or irregular wages, afford rent is through housing benefit. Housing benefit is an income-related benefit designed to assist people on income support and low income to pay their rent. It is paid by local authorities.

Someone may be entitled to housing benefit if:

- they are liable to pay rent;
- their capital (i.e. savings and investments) is less than £16,000;

- they receive income support or income-based jobseeker's allowance or are on a low income as prescribed by the Housing Benefit Regulations.[13]

Certain people are generally excluded from Housing benefit. These include:

- people who live in residential care homes;
- people subject to immigration control or defined as persons from abroad;
- full-time students (there are exceptions here, and further advice will be necessary);
- people who live with their landlord or they are a close relative;
- if the landlord is a former partner of the claimant;
- if the landlord is a parent of the claimant's child;
- if the tenancy is not made on a commercial basis.

Anyone excluded from housing benefit should seek specialist welfare rights advice.

Not all of the money which is payable to the landlord will be covered by housing benefit. Payments for charges such as water charges, fuel costs, meals and other services provided by the landlord are excluded.

There are other restrictions that may affect the amount of housing benefit that will be paid. These restrictions are most relevant where the claimant is renting in the private rented sector. No housing benefit will be paid above the maximum rent level. The maximum rent may be based on the reasonable market rent for the property. It may be based on the local reference rent which is based on the rent officer's valuation of the average of all rents for properties in the particular area which are in a reasonable state of repair and the same size as the claimant's. It may be based on a smaller home that the one the claimant is renting if the rent officer considers that the house is too large for the claimant's needs. In most cases, if the claimant is under 25 years of age, the rent officer will assess a single room rent which is based on the average costs for one room homes with shared use of toilet and kitchen. This is the case even if the claimant is living in a bigger property.

Certain groups of claimants are protected from rent restrictions. If a client's rent is restricted, seek specialist welfare rights advice.

It is possible to find out how much housing benefit will be paid prior to the client moving into the new accommodation by getting a pre-tenancy determination which will relate to the particular accommodation the client has been offered. Unfortunately, in areas where there is a restricted supply of affordable rented housing, landlords are unlikely to wait for confirmation that the rent is affordable.

14.7   REPAIR

Disrepair

The law on disrepair is complex and because many tenants lack security, often ineffective. However, tenants who do have security have a wide range of legal remedies available to them. The most important of these is Landlord and Tenant Act 1985, s.11, and many common problems of disrepair can be tackled using this provision. However, there are other legal remedies available. Clients with disrepair should seek advice from a specialist housing practitioner. Part 1 of the Housing Act 2004 provides for a Housing Health and Safety Rating System which, once implemented (expected in autumn 2005), will radically transform local authorities' powers and duties relating to disrepair.

Adaptations

The tenant may be entitled to a disabled facilities grant from the local authority. Disabled facilities grants are available under Part I of the Housing Grants, Construction and Regeneration Act 1996, which can help towards, e.g. installing an access ramp for wheelchairs, putting in a stair lift or lowering work tops to make it easier to prepare and cook food.

Application forms for disabled facilities grants can be obtained from the local authority. The council must give the applicant a decision in writing within six months of receipt of a completed valid application, together with any additional information it may require.

Unsafe/unsuitable accommodation

This takes us back to the beginning of this chapter. If a client's accommodation is so unsafe or unsuitable that it is not reasonable to remain there, then the client is homeless under Part 7 of the Housing Act 1996.

NOTES

1   The Anti-social Behaviour Act 2003 added new complexities. There will be further reform as a result of the Housing Act 2004. In addition the Civil Partnership Act 2004 reforms succession to tenancies and the rights of co-habiting same sex couples.
2   See **www.homelessnessact.org.uk**.
3   See **www.homelessnessact.org.uk** and **www.shelternet.org.uk**.
4   Published by ODPM and available at **www.odpm.gov.uk**.
5   Homelessness Code of Guidance for Local Authorities (July 2002).
6   And see Homeless Persons (Priority Need) (Wales) Order 2001.

7   The impact of *Al-Ameri* v. *Kensington and Chelsea LBC*; *Osmani* v. *Harrow LBC and Glasgow CC* [2004] UKHL 4, [2004] 2 AC 159 has been overturned from 4 January 2005 with the implementation of Asylum and Immigration (Treatment of Claimants, etc.) Act 2004, s.11 which amends the local connection provisions of the Housing Act 1996.

8   Code of Guidance, para. 12.1.

9   Code of Guidance, para. 12.7.

10 LAC (2002)13.

11 Housing Act 1996, Pt 6 as amended by the Homelessness Act 2002 and Code of Guidance on Allocations (November 2002).

12 For an example of the operation of a particular local system see **www.neath-port talbot.gov.uk/homesbychoice/**.

13 See **www.dwp.gov.uk/housingbenefit/regulations/legislation.asp**.

CHAPTER 15

Mental health

Key sources

- Mental Health Act 1983
- Mental Health (Hospital, Guardianship and Consent to Treatment) Regulations 1983
- DH and Welsh Office, 'Mental Health Act 1983: Memorandum on Parts I to VI, VIII and X' (1998) and 'Mental Health Act 1983: Code of Practice' (1999)
- Circulars LAC (2000)3, LAC 99(11) and LAC (86)15
- *Practice Notes* (Official Solicitor: Appointment in Family Proceedings) [2001] 2 FLR 155, (CAFCASS: Appointment in Family Proceedings) [2001] 2 FLR 151, (Medical and Welfare Proceedings for Adults who Lack Capacity) [2001] 2 FLR 158, (Incapacitated Adults) [2002] 1 WLR 325
- Royal College of Psychiatrists Council Reports, *Child Abuse and Neglect: The Role of Mental Health Services* (April 2004), *Patients as Parents* (June 2002)

15.1   INTRODUCTION

This is an overview of a complicated and specialist area of law and practice, currently undergoing major change.[1] Adult and children's mental health are demarcated where relevant, although the two areas overlap.

Misunderstandings and stigma are common, but mental illness is as common as asthma: one in four experience problems in any one year,[2] and one in six have a recognised mental illness including anxiety, depression and psychosis (such as schizophrenia). The mentally ill are ordinary people who have, for whatever reason, more severe emotional difficulties to cope with, but stereotypes of them as violent and dangerous fuel stigma and may prevent an individual seeking help.

A complex interaction of biological, environmental, social and personal factors underlie mental health, including factors commonly arising in care cases such as low self-esteem, social isolation, abuse, trauma, poor and inconsistent parenting, poverty and substance misuse (which in itself can exacerbate mental health problems). Higher rates of illness occur in refugees and asylum seekers, pregnant teenagers, victims of severe abuse or domestic violence, prisoners, and those with physical/life-threatening illnesses.

'Dual diagnosis' is not uncommon, e.g. mental illness with a personality disorder and/or substance misuse; autism with obsessive compulsive disorder, or emotional /behavioural difficulties, or conduct disorder, with depression.

Mental health issues may impact on:

- parenting capacity and risks to children's health and development, including the relationship of mental illness to abuse, neglect and fabricated illness;
- effective assessments, which must include comprehensive family and health histories;
- legal representation, capacity to give instructions and ability to participate in decision-making and proceedings;
- case management, court jurisdiction and transfer of proceedings;
- consent to treatment and to tests;
- the right of access to records and to disclosure of information;
- the exercise of parental responsibility by a parent and a local authority respectively;
- private law;
- detention and treatment of children and young people;
- placement decisions, reviews and adoption;
- special educational needs and disability;
- the health needs of care leavers and their rights to support (see the Children (Leaving Care) Act 2000 which amends the after-care provisions of the Children Act 1989).

Further help, particularly in complex cases, is crucial and information on policy, good practice and services is available from the Department of Health and the Royal Colleges of Psychiatry, and Paediatrics and Child Health respectively. Non-governmental organisations (NGOs) such as the Mental Health Foundation, Mind and Young Minds, all produce excellent information leaflets on particular types of illness. The National Institute for Mental Health publishes a free Directory of mental health problems and relevant treatment, sources of help and a list of organisations by topic.

Specific professional guidance is also available for particular situations, such as substance misuse[3] and domestic violence[4] (and see Chapter 16 on criminal issues).

Access to specialist legal advice is available from the above NGOs, and there are firms specialising in mental health law. The Official Solicitor acts for those under a disability and should be consulted in appropriate situations.

15.2   HUMAN RIGHTS AND DIVERSITY

Human rights

In addition to ECHR Articles 8 and 6 (see Chapter 1), other relevant Articles are Article 3 (torture, inhuman or degrading treatment), Article 5 (right to liberty and security of person) and Article 2 (right to a full life).

Children and young people have a right to the 'highest attainable standard of health' (UNCRC Article 24(1)), protection from all forms of physical violence (ECHR Articles 3 and 8, UNCRC Articles 19(a) and 37) and freedom from arbitrary deprivation of liberty (UNCRC Article 24(1); ECHR Article 5).

Detailed guidance is in the Code of Practice,[5] but note people to whom the Mental Health (MHA) Act 1983 applies should:

- receive recognition for their basic human rights;
- be respected as individuals and full account taken of their age, gender, sexual orientation, social, ethnic, cultural and religious background, without generalised assumptions;
- have their needs taken fully into account within available resources;
- be given necessary treatment or care in the least controlled and segregated facilities compatible with their own health or safety or that of others;
- have their self-determination and personal responsibility promoted in treatment and care, consistent with their own needs and wishes;
- be discharged from detention or other legal powers as soon as it is clear that justification for these no longer exists.

There is an obligation to protect the health of those deprived of liberty. A lack of appropriate medical treatment may be a breach of ECHR Article 3. In particular, compatibility with Article 3 must be assessed by also taking into account the vulnerability of the mentally ill and their inability, in some cases, to complain coherently or at all about how they are being affected by any particular treatment (*Keenan* v. *UK* (Application No. 27229/95) (2001) 33 EHRR 28, ECtHR).

Protective measures for children and young people undergoing involuntary placement and treatment should be more stringent than for adult mental health patients.[6] ECHR Articles 5 and 8 are relevant to children detained/treated against their will, but these are subject to a parent's Article 8 rights (see, e.g. *Nielsen* v. *Denmark* (1998) 11 EHRR 175), and parental authority over competent children is increasingly a contentious issue.

Diversity

Members of minority ethnic cultures may have specific, and very different, mental health needs and problems, often compounded by higher levels of poverty and unemployment; refugee children's experience of violence, abuse, torture and killing, and the lack of translation/interpreting services, making the diagnosis or assessment procedure unreliable and highly stressful.

They are over-represented in compulsory detention and assessments under MHA 1983 and in child protection assessments and referrals, and may experience a severe lack of social support, poorer access to health services (particularly primary care) and a greater likelihood of referral to specialist services through the criminal justice system.[7] They may experience cultural/racial stereotyping and discrimination in assessment, treatment and provision[8] and are less likely to make, or accept, a strict distinction between mental and physical health problems: conflict can arise between the explanations relied on by different cultural groups and Western psychiatric models.

Assessments must take account of ethnicity, culture, language and religion and care plans and services offered should accommodate individual religious, cultural and spiritual beliefs and be equally accessible by all.[9]

15.3   GENERAL INCIDENCE AND OUTCOMES

Defining mental illness is not easy and subject to controversy about terminology. Factsheets, lists of disorders and definitions are on several websites listed in the notes to this chapter. The ICD-10 classification of mental and behavioural disorders[10] lists all recognised mental and behavioural disorders including, e.g. eating disorders, dyslexia, attention deficit (hyperactivity) disorder and conduct disorders.

Early help is more likely to result in coping strategies and reasonable outcomes. The relative effectiveness of methods of treatment and approaches has been evaluated for adults, but is lacking for physically and emotionally abused children, although descriptions of the practical use of therapies for sexually abused children are available.

A coexisting personality disorder (indicated by forensic history, severe relationship difficulties and recurrent complex problems) may make treatment of most disorders more difficult and possibly less effective.

Those with severe and enduring mental illness are likely to require specialist services working with other agencies, particularly those providing social care, housing and employment.

15.4   SERVICE DELIVERY[11]

The division of social care into adult and children's services, unfortunately for all concerned, has been reinforced by the Children Act 2004. This can increase difficulty and lack of provision.

Changes to the health service place a greater emphasis on 24-hour primary care and integrated community mental health teams, closer working between primary care and specialist mental health services and access to independent specialist advocacy services, commissioned by Primary Care Trusts and subject to standards and a Code of Practice.

The National Service Framework for Mental Health contains standards relevant to five areas of services for those with severe mental illness. These cover prevention, crises, help and timely access to appropriate and safe mental health placements.

Essential elements of good health practice include professional competence, good relationships with patients and colleagues, observance of professional ethical obligations[12] and observance of legal requirements.

Knowledge of the law and good practice is especially important for psychiatrists, who, uniquely within medical practice, have statutory power to override fundamental rights of personal decision-making.

The Care Programme Approach[13] is the current model of good practice, based on assessment, care planning, key working and the involvement of patient and carers in decision-making. Community-based treatment is the preference of most service users and carers.

Contact is usually with primary care services, particularly GPs, but there should be a continuum of services through to highly specialised services. However, crisis intervention, assessment and treatment, out-of-hours service, support including accommodation, and assertive outreach services, identification and management of children's needs and arrangements with children's services are still poor in many areas. Staff may lack specialised training needed to assess and treat complex cases and waiting lists for specialised services can be long.

A new focus on community services is central to the NHS changes, based on GPs and pharmacists, NHS nurse-led walk-in centres and Community Mental Health/Primary Care Liaison Teams, as well as:

- Crisis Resolution/Home Treatment Teams (rapid response, assessment, treatment and referral service for acute psychiatric disorder);
- Assertive Outreach Teams/programme of assertive community treatment (PACT) (for adults with severe and persistent mental disorder and other complex needs, e.g. dual diagnosis of substance misuse, high level of disability, history of violence or persistent offending, homelessness, significant risk of persistent self-harm or neglect, poor response to previous treatment and at high risk of losing contact with services);
- diversion at point of arrest (DAPA) schemes or court diversion schemes;
- Early Intervention Teams (specialist service for untreated psychosis in young people).

Some very limited services exist to rehabilitate young abusers and youth offending teams also include representatives from services such as health, education and substance misuse.

Treatment in education settings is also relevant, and guidance is available to the education sector and child and adolescent mental health services (CAMHS) on joint working to promote children's mental health and emotional well-being and to intervene effectively with those children experiencing problems.

Some parenting programmes exist, usually run by voluntary organisations. Some CAMHS provide these where families are having specific difficulties.

15.5   SAFEGUARDING

All mental health professionals in the statutory, voluntary and independent sectors should 'bear in mind the welfare of children, irrespective of whether they are primarily working with adults or with children and young people'.[14] The Children Act 2004 imposes a statutory safeguarding duty, which covers *all* health services including primary care staff, hospital and community services, adult mental health services, forensic, psychotherapy, substance misuse and learning disability services.

All should therefore be aware of the safeguarding principles, familiar with local ACPC/LSCB and health-specific child protection procedures and be prepared to make referrals where concerned about a child's welfare.

Each ACPC usually has a health service representative (required for LSCBs), but adult mental health, CAMHS and substance misuse services should also be represented.[15]

Conflicts of interest between child and parent can arise, particularly if the mentally ill parent denies abuse, or cannot provide safe and adequate care. The crucial issue is often not the adult's prospects for recovery, but potential harm to the child through delay. Professionals must therefore distinguish between their respective welfare roles: those who see their primary responsibility as promoting the interests and needs of the adult are not safeguarding the interests of either child or their patient.

Principles on consent to treatment, patient confidentiality and the maintenance of privacy and dignity in assessment and treatment apply to both adult and children's services. But the paramountcy principle is still not consistently understood or accepted. Professionals may be involved in cases for different purposes, but all should be aware of their legal duties to cooperate and to share information and liaise closely on safeguarding issues (Children Act 1989, ss.27, 47, Children Act 2004, s.10 (England) and s.25 (Wales),[16] and should understand they may have to override their duty of patient confidentiality in order to do this, even where they do not have the patient's consent.

Information should be shared on a 'need to know' basis, with patients, families and carers kept informed. Participation in decision-making should be encouraged, subject to the paramountcy principle, which requires:[17]

- constant awareness of the possibility, or risk, of abuse or neglect of children;
- participation in, and commitment to, multidisciplinary and multi-agency approaches to risk assessment, and safeguarding interventions;
- a clear understanding that the duty to patients is overridden by the safeguarding duty.

Each health authority/trust must have designated senior staff responsible for leading on safeguarding. The 'named doctor' should consult and advise in cases of suspected or actual child abuse or neglect and be contacted by staff if there is any doubt about the seriousness of the situation and/or referral to social services.

15.6   ADULT MENTAL HEALTH

Services and safeguarding

Professionals have a safeguarding duty in primary care, community or hospital based services, which include forensic, psychotherapy, substance misuse, learning disability and psychiatry. Guidance is available on their contribution, which emphasises that good practice includes finding out whether a patient is also a parent, and ensuring that services support the task of parenting whilst also meeting the child's needs.[18]

Risks and outcomes

Emotional well-being can affect the physical health of both adults and children and healthy development in childhood. Personal or parental mental health problems can lead to neglect, abuse or even death,[19] and trauma during childhood can affect all functions of the developing brain.

Children most at risk feature in parental delusion, become the target of parental aggression or rejection, or are neglected. But the consequences of parental mental health may include:

- impeded access to social activities;
- inappropriate caring roles;
- depression or anxiety;
- neglect of physical and emotional needs, or behavioural and physiological problems in the children of mothers with post-natal depression;[20]
- direct/indirect abuse resulting from bizarre/violent parental behaviour;
- emotional, cognitive, behavioural and psychological difficulties including self-harm, insecure attachments, dysfunctional relationships, drug abuse and aggression.

Outcomes of sexual abuse include depression and anxiety and the dysfunction it causes tends to persist. Childhood sexual and other abuse features more frequently in mental health histories, and the consequences of domestic violence for children are beginning to be understood.

Children who adapt well to a parent's mental illness usually:

- are older when the parent becomes ill, and develop a greater range of coping resources;
- are more sociable and able to form positive relationships;
- have greater intelligence;
- have support from alternative adults who provide a positive, trusting relationship;
- are successful outside the home; or
- are those whose parent has mild, short or discrete episodes interspersed with good periods.

Parents

Where mental health problems impact on children's well-being, there should be a proper assessment of needs and access to appropriate services. Both adults and carers now have extended legal rights (see Carers and Disabled Children Act 2000).

15.7   CHILDREN AND YOUNG PEOPLE'S MENTAL HEALTH

Incidence and outcomes

Mental health problems in young people are a clear predictor of problems in adulthood. Early assessment and intervention pre-school and in school can reduce later problems, even where disorders are more serious and enduring. Increasing numbers are experiencing mental health problems and incidence tends to increase with age, when problems become more complex and more serious.[21]

High risk groups include:

- young people with physical and learning disabilities;
- looked after children or care leavers;
- those excluded from school or in the criminal justice system;
- the young homeless;
- young carers, especially of a parent with mental illness;
- the chronically ill.

As many as 50 per cent of looked after children have mental health problems, affected by exposure to risk factors arising from experience of problems in early childhood, or dislocation to lives on coming into care.

Children and young people's plans (required under Children Act 2004, s.17 (England), s.26 (Wales)), local authority responsibility to promote the well-being of communities (under the Local Government Act 2000), and corporate responsibility to children in need or looked after should result in appropriate services such as education for children with mental health needs.[22]

Specialist services[23]

GP recognition of psychiatric disorder in children tends to be better where disturbance is more severe or the family situation stressful. Child and Adolescent Mental Health Services (CAMHS) exist in a wide range of hospital, community and educational settings, but often in different trusts from other health services.

Clinical or therapeutic services are limited particularly for young children displaying behaviours associated with clinical depression, for young people with learning disabilities and mental health problems, for adolescents generally, and especially emergency, and appropriate non-psychiatric, provision and for dual diagnosis, substance misuse cases or older children.

RCPCH guidance to primary care professionals on commissioning specialist services[24] stresses:

- early intervention;
- close working relationships between CAMHS and other children's services;
- resources for the management of behavioural disorders in childhood;
- primary child mental health workers involved in service delivery;
- psychological assessment, support and care of children, especially those with specific disorders, or depression, self-harm, eating disorders or substance abusing;
- liaison with parenting schemes and Sure Start;
- protocols in line with national guidance;
- multi-agency plans for those at risk of harming themselves or others;
- dedicated facilities for adolescents.

15.8   DIAGNOSIS AND ASSESSMENT

Extent

Difficulties are generally seen as serious when sufficient to interfere substantially with day-to-day functioning or when behaviour becomes a concern. Mental health factors impacting on parenting capacity are often identified in initial assessments by social services, which should recognise children's developmental needs and the need for a core assessment, especially where families are experiencing difficulties in all three Framework for Assessment domains.

Mental health professionals

These can provide expertise or specific skills likely to prove evidentially significant, e.g. in substance misuse and learning disability, and the assessment of risks posed by parental mental disorder or cognitive disabilities, and/or abusive, violent or offending behaviours. They can also provide expertise in assessment, especially of disorders, disabilities or special educational needs and the very young or those with communication difficulties, and in prognosis and treatment, with relevant timescales.

They should:

- see mental health problems within a social and family context;
- be aware of the interrelationship and interaction between mental health of both parent and child and the impact on child health and development;
- address the impact on children of complex comorbid factors, such as substance misuse;
- be aware of the impact of such issues as chronic physical illness, eating disorders, maternal depression and anxiety and learning disabilities;
- maintain close links with other agencies, including specialist services, to provide specific support to enable a parent to meet a child's needs and ensure her safety;
- see cases as an opportunity for preventive intervention and facilitate earlier intervention.

Patients as parents

Working Together stresses that, regardless of the threshold criteria or the presence or absence of 'classic' symptoms, there should always be an assessment of parental mental illness and its implications for any child involved in the family.[25] Comprehensive Royal Colleges guidance on the relationship between mental health and child protection and factors affecting parenting capacity, contain principles generally applicable to mental health professionals and to issues in proceedings.

Further details are in Chapter 8, but note it is not usually within the remit of an adult psychiatrist to assess parenting, and it may be preferable for a forensic psychiatrist or psychotherapist to assess personality disorder.[26]

Risk assessment is also covered in Chapter 8, but this should be done routinely, since a patient may be more of a risk to themselves than to others, or at risk from the attitudes of others, vulnerable due to self-harm or neglect or at risk of physical, psychological or sexual abuse or of financial exploitation.

15.9 CARERS

Assessments

Assessments of needs and sustainability of role must be done where carers provide (or intend to provide) regular substantial care for people with severe mental illness. Carers need consistent information, help, support and advice at all stages, and in appropriate languages, supported by advocates or other agencies.

Children

Many children provide varying levels of unpaid care,[27] which sometimes subjects them to enormous pressure. Risk factors increase for children who care for parents with a mental health problem, and significant harm may be caused through neglect, or risks to the child's future mental health. They can experience inconsistent parental attention and behaviour and take on a protective and domestic role. Age, and whether a supportive adult is present in the household, are relevant to coping ability.

15.10 CONFIDENTIALITY, DISCLOSURE AND RECORD-KEEPING

General

Mental health professionals differ in their approach, but many professional obligations are contained in advice from professional bodies and government departments (but see changes due 2005 in new guidance).[28]

Accurate record-keeping is essential: making and keeping full notes and writing reports properly describing a patient's difficulties and recording any serious concerns is critical to evidence-based decisions and to the ability to protect children's interests and rights.

Some Trusts have single records for each patient/client containing information on both medical and social care, and accessible to their staff. Paper records may exist alongside an electronic clinical register system accessible to mental health, primary care and social care teams, including staff at A and E departments. The NHS number is used for all patients but this can be complicated where aliases are commonly used.

Recording or disclosure decisions that raise difficulties should be discussed with a senior colleague or a designated professional. There is a Caldicott guardian in each health service, responsible for confidentiality and issues on access requests, who should have knowledge and understanding of safeguarding law, guidance, practice and principles.[29]

Disclosure

General principles (subject to the public interest test and new guidance due December 2005) are:

- patient confidentiality is central to the relationship with the treating professional: information is only disclosed with patient consent unless there are exceptional circumstances, i.e. 'necessary for the purpose';
- no one can consent on behalf of another adult, so if the patient cannot consent, sharing of information must be in her best interests and the patient informed;
- where a patient is believed to be a victim of neglect or abuse, information should usually be disclosed in order to prevent further harm, but applying the same principles;[30]
- children should have the same degree of confidentiality as adults, subject to any factors such as age, developmental maturity and their capacity to understand;
- disclosure without consent is legally permitted for the sake of the safety and welfare of children.

However, the public interest overrides the duty of confidentiality and disclosure may be necessary if failure to disclose would result in exposure to risk, e.g. of death or serious harm to the patient or others. This is supported in other guidance, e.g. to psychiatrists: where risk is so serious it outweighs the normal right to privacy, the patient's consent should be sought if practicable;[31] a referral should be made where a patient discloses they have been, or are, perpetrating abuse, even if risk is believed to be low or non-existent.[32]

Advice on safeguarding issues is available[33] pending anticipated government guidance under the Children Act 2004.

Account must be taken of a patient's right of access to their clinical notes under the Access to Health Records Act 1990.

Particular issues

Guardianship

ECHR Articles 6 and 8 entitle a parent to disclosure of local authority files including the recommendations and reports leading to an application for guardianship of a child as mental patient under MHA 1983 (Court of Appeal in *R (S)* v. *Plymouth City Council, ex p. C* [2002] EWCA Civ 388).

Correspondence

Correspondence of detained patients can be inspected or withheld in certain circumstances, subject to specified exceptions, which include correspondence from the patient's legal adviser. There are no restrictions on informal patients' correspondence (MHA 1983, s.134).

Videotape recording

Guidance[34] outlines the procedures on confidentiality, prior negotiation with the patient or a responsible adult, including verbal or written explanations and obtaining formal consent. All recordings are important evidence and must be kept safely, particularly if they contain disclosures or references to abuse. *Achieving Best Evidence*[35] gives statutory guidance on videotaping for legal purposes and must be followed by specialist health professionals in interviews for investigative purposes.

15.11   OTHER RELEVANT ISSUES

Domestic violence/abuse

This issue, discussed in more detail in other chapters, is linked to poor mental health, psychiatric illness, depressive disorder, suicide, anxiety, alcohol and drug misuse and post-traumatic stress disorder (PTSD). Questions about past and present domestic abuse should be a routine part of the clinical assessment of all patients and their families.[36]

Counselling and therapy

Psychological therapies are provided by a range of mental health professionals, including clinical and counselling psychologists, psychiatrists, psychotherapists, art and drama therapists, and counsellors and treatment can take a variety of different forms, with different cost consequences, including individual or group therapy, day hospital programmes, therapeutic communities, etc.

Guidelines[37] on treatment choices in psychological therapies and counselling suggest that cognitive behavioural therapy is most likely to work with abusing families.

Witnesses who may need therapy prior to a criminal trial are the subject of Practice Guidance.[38]

15.12   MENTAL HEALTH ACT 1983

Compulsory treatment and admission

Extensive law and practice relating to adults is set out in readily accessible codes and guidance material – but change is imminent. The position on children and young people is less clear: they have significantly less protection than adults. A wide range of overlapping, and sometimes conflicting, methods are used, most of which do not carry a right to independent representation for the child.

The legal principles governing the treatment of adolescents are very confusing, exacerbated by the fact that compulsory admission does not carry the legal power to treat a young patient against their wishes. Medical practitioners can get round the problems by obtaining parental authority for an informal admission and then to treatment, with complex cases being referred to the High Court under the inherent jurisdiction to authorise compulsory steps.

There have been cases where the local authority, having gained parental responsibility through a care order, has given consent on a young person's behalf, ignoring the spirit of the Children Act 1989 guidance indicating that a secure accommodation order should be applied for in such circumstances (see *R* v. *Kirklees MBC, ex p. C* [1993] 2 FLR 187). But the use of secure accommodation does not authorise treatment and permission must therefore be obtained from the young person, the parent or the court.

Most young people, despite their objection to compulsory assessment and treatment, comply with parental wishes and enter units voluntarily, often with little other proper supervision. Many are on 'open' wards but often feel unable to leave, perhaps due to prescribed medication.[39] A parent's decision to place a child in a closed psychiatric ward for a long period against his wishes, despite his lack of a defined mental illness, has been deemed reasonable and not yet overturned (*Nielsen* v. *Denmark* (1988) 11 EHRR 175).

It is therefore arguable that it is better practice to use MHA 1983 procedures, which at least involve a careful regulation of processes and strict legislative safeguards, including a right of appeal to the Mental Health Review Tribunal (MHRT). Certainly, in cases of anorexia nervosa and other eating disorders, this has become much more common. However, professionals are generally reluctant because of perceived stigma. In the absence of parental consent, the preference is for court applications, in which the child is normally independently represented (in contrast to mental health legislation).

For formal detention of young people, psychiatrists almost exclusively use MHA 1983 rather than Children Act 1989, s.25.[40]

The prospect of successful human rights challenges to the use of compulsory powers have led to proposals to strike a balance between ECHR Articles 5 and 8 by reforming MHA 1983 to include the safeguards to protect children and young people likely to be subject to compulsory treatment with parental consent; and by treating 16 and 17-year-olds as adults, with a greater say in decision-making.

However, until these are implemented, practitioners should be aware that there is no minimum age limit for admission to hospital under MHA 1983.

The legal framework governing admission and treatment of children is complex and specialist legal advice may be required. The revised Code of Practice 1999 applies to all voluntary and compulsorily-detained patients under 18: the guidance includes issues of particular importance to children including entitlement to information, consideration of views and wishes, confidentiality, educational provision,[41] capacity to consent to treatment and consideration of all possible alternatives for suitable placements.

Where detention is formal rather than informal, psychiatrists almost exclusively use MHA 1983 measures rather than secure accommodation under the Children Act 1989, but their knowledge of the 1989 Act and consent issues is lower than for MHA 1983.

There is little evidence of a challenge by families to the confusion and lack of services for children.

Local authorities have specific duties to safeguard the welfare of hospital patients. Treatment should be designed to avoid compulsion or the use of physical restraint wherever possible. Children should be accommodated with peers in children's wards or adolescent units, separate from adults. Where accommodation has to be used in an adult ward, discrete facilities, security and staffing appropriate to the child's needs should be provided.

Contact

Directions and guidance on visits by children and young people to named patients in secure hospitals[42] and to psychiatric patients,[43] emphasise the importance of facilitating contact with a parent or other key family members wherever possible, but making decisions based on the child's best interests, not the patient's.

There should be designated 'safe areas' for such visits, and it should be borne in mind that conditions in the elderly, such as dementia, might give rise to sexually inappropriate behaviour towards children.

Mental Health Review Tribunals

Advocacy services are an increasing feature of MHRT work. Legal represen-tation is available for MHRT appeals. Public funding is available on a non means- and effectively non merit-tested basis but the financial limits are stricter and public funding will only be granted to firms who hold a franchise. These are far fewer in number than firms with family franchises.

Advice should be sought from a mental health law specialist. The Law Society maintains a register of those accredited and should be able to indicate those who are members of both the Children Panel and the Mental Health Panel. The Mental Health Lawyers Association address is listed in Appendix 2.

Welfare considerations are much less significant than in child law: the MHRT is a statutory body that must consider whether the grounds for detention are made out under MHA 1983, and whether discharge would be in the patient's best interests.

The child applicant instructs the lawyer directly – there is no provision for a tribunal-appointed 'guardian'.

15.13   CONSENT AND CAPACITY ISSUES

Consent to treatment

General professional guidance is contained in comprehensive Department of Health documentation, covering adults, children and those with learning difficulties or in prison.[44]

Capacity to instruct a solicitor

Assessment of capacity is crucial: practitioners cannot be retained by clients incapable of giving instructions. Particular care should be taken in relation to children and young people and those, e.g. with learning disabilities, mental health problems, brain damage, or any combination of these characteristics. It is all too often assumed that the presence of one or more of these factors inevitably gives rise to incapacity, but this is not the case, nor should it be assumed that a client under a legal disability is incapable of giving instructions.

Where a client lacks capacity, a willing and suitable next friend or guardian *ad litem* must be found to conduct any litigation on their behalf (Family Proceedings Rules 1991, SI 1991/1247, rule 9.2). A CAFCASS officer cannot fulfil this role on behalf of an adult party. The Official Solicitor will act in the absence of anyone else willing and suitable and his office should be contacted without delay.[45]

Where there is any doubt about whether a client (or another party) is a patient (rule 9.1), the Official Solicitor can provide a standard medical certificate to be completed by the person's medical attendant.

NOTES

1   See NHS Plan 2000; *National Service Framework for Mental Health* (1999); and draft Mental Health Bill (2004), at **www.dh.gov.uk**.
2   Survey by Office of National Statistics, *Social Trends* (2001); National Service Framework 1999.
3   See, e.g. London Child Protection Committee Guidelines 2003.
4   *Domestic Violence*, Council Report CR102, Royal College of Psychiatrists (2002); *Domestic Violence: Recognition and Management in Accident and Emergency*, London British Association for Accident and Emergency Medicine (1993); *Domestic Abuse in Pregnancy*, paper 19, London, Royal College of Midwives (1997); *Position Paper on Domestic Violence*, London, Royal College of

Nursing (2000); *Domestic Violence: A Resource Manual for Healthcare Professionals*, DH (2000).

5   *Mental Health Act Code of Practice*, DH, Welsh Office (1999).

6   See Council of Europe, *White Paper on the Protection of the Human Rights and Dignity of People Suffering from Mental Disorder*, SM(2000)23 Addendum, para. 8.1.

7   See, e.g. National Centre for Social Research, *Ethnic Minority Psychiatric Illness Rates in the Community*, DH (2000).

8   Audit Commission, *Finding a Place: A Review of Mental Health Services for Adults* (1994).

9   *Modernising Mental Health Services: Inspection*, CI (2002)7 (June 2002).

10 See *International Classification of Diseases*, World Health Organisation, **www.mentalhealth.org.uk**.

11 A guide to entitlement to health services is at **www.nhs.uk/nhsguide**.

12 See, e.g. guidance from General Medical Council including *Seeking Patients' Consent: The Ethical Considerations* (November 1998); *Confidentiality: Protecting and Providing Information* (September 2000) and *Handbook of Ethics and the Law* (2004).

13 For principles see *Building Bridges*, DH (1995).

14 *Working Together to Safeguard Children*, DH, Home Office, DfEE (1999), para. 3.39.

15 *Ibid.*, paras 3.20, 3.21, 4.11 and 4.12 .

16 *Ibid.*, para. 3.46.

17 See *Child Abuse and Neglect: The Role of Mental Health Services*, Council Report CR120, Royal College of Psychiatrists (April 2004).

18 See *Patients as Parents*, Council Report CR105, Royal College of Psychiatrists (2002).

19 See A. Falkov, *Study of Working Together 'Part 8' Reports: Fatal Child Abuse and Parental Psychiatric Disorder*, DH (1995).

20 This affects 10–15% of mothers, with greatly increased likelihood of severe mental illness in the first month after childbirth.

21 15% of pre-school children and 8% of primary children have mild mental health problems, 10% aged 5–15 and 11.2% of 11–15 year-olds experience clinically defined mental health problems, 6% of boys and 16% of girls aged 16–19 have some form of mental health problem, 7% of them severe. Adolescents are particularly vulnerable: rates of self-harm and suicide significantly increase, and mid to late adolescence are peak ages for onset of depression and schizophrenia.

22 *Access to Education for Children and Young People with Medical Needs*, DH, HSC (2001)19; DfES (2001)732; LAC (2001)17.

23 *Mental Health Policy Implementation Guide: National Minimum Standards*, DH (2002).

24 *Specialist Health Services for Children and Young People: A Guide for Primary Care Organisations*, Royal College of Paediatrics and Child Health (January 2003).

25 *Working Together*, para. 2.22.

26 *Child Abuse and Neglect: The Role of Mental Health Services*, Council Report CR120, Royal College of Psychiatrists (April 2004).

27 Office of National Statistics, Census (2001); J. Morris, *The Right Support: Report of the Task Force on Supporting Disabled Adults in their Parenting Role*, Joseph Rowntree Foundation (2003).

28 *Good Psychiatric Practice: Confidentiality*, Royal College of Psychiatrists (2001); *Confidentiality*, General Medical Council (2000); *What to Do If You are Worried a Child is Being Abused*, DH (2003), App. 3 (subject to change in new *Cross-Government Guidance – Sharing Information on Children and Young People*, in draft 2005).

29 *What to Do If You are Worried a Child is Being Abused*, App. 3.

30 *Working Together*, paras 7.41 and 7.42.

31 *Good Psychiatric Practice: Confidentiality*, Royal College of Psychiatrists (2001).

32 *Child Abuse and Neglect: The Role of Mental Health Services*, Council Report CR120, Royal College of Psychiatrists (April 2004).

33 See *What to Do If You are Worried a Child is Being Abused*, App. 3 and *Public Sector Data Sharing: Guidance on the Law*, DCA (2003).

34 See the Royal College of Psychiatrists guidance for all child and adolescent psychiatrists: *Guidance for the Use of Video Recording in Child Psychiatric Practice*, CR79 (2000).

35 *Achieving Best Evidence in Criminal Proceedings*, Home Office, LCD, CPS, DH, Welsh Assembly (2002).

36 RCP, *Domestic Violence*, CR102 (2002) and *Child Abuse and Neglect: The Role of Mental Health Services*, CR120 (2004), but see also *Domestic Violence: A Resource Manual for Health Care Professionals*, DH (2000).

37 *Treatment Choice in Psychological Therapies and Counselling, Evidence Based Clinical Practice Guideline*, DH (2001).

38 *Provision of Therapy for Child Witnesses Prior to a Criminal Trial*, and *Provision of Pre-trial Therapy for Adults, Practice Guidance*, Home Office, CPS, DH (2001): both documents available at **www.cps.gov.uk** and **www.homeoffice.gov.uk**.

39 For further discussion, see J. Fortin, *Children's Rights and the Developing Law*, 2nd edn, Butterworths (2003).

40 Attempts have been made to clarify these questions and to provide guidance for practitioners, see R. White, A. Harbour and R. Williams, *Safeguarding for Young Minds*, 2nd edn, Gaskell (2004).

41 See also LAC (2001)17.

42 Health Service Circular (1999)160.

43 *Guidance on the Visiting of Psychiatric Patients by Children*, HSC (1999)222; LAC (99)32 and Mental Health Code of Practice, para. 26.3.

44 See **www.doh.gov.uk/consent**.

45 *Official Solicitor: Practice Note (Appointment in Family Proceedings)* [2001] 2 FLR 155. See also *Practice Note (Officers of CAFCASS legal services and special casework: appointment in family proceedings)* [2001] 2 FLR 151.

CHAPTER 16

Criminal issues

Key sources

- Children and Young Persons Acts 1933, 1963 and 1969, s.23(5) and (5AA) (as amended)
- Bail Act 1976 (as amended)
- Crime and Disorder Act 1998
- Youth Justice and Criminal Evidence Act 1999
- Domestic Violence, Crime and Victims Act 2004
- Home Office Circular 2003(20)
- *Provision of Therapy for Child Witnesses Prior to a Criminal Trial*, Home Office, CPS, DH (2001)
- *Achieving Best Evidence in Criminal Proceedings*, Home Office, LCD, CPS, DH and Welsh Assembly (2002)
- ACPO Pilots: Police/Family Disclosure Protocol (2004)
- *Guidance on Investigating Child Abuse and Safeguarding Children*, ACPO and Centrex (2005)

16.1   INTRODUCTION

Criminal matters that can affect the conduct of civil child law cases are not simply confined to those arising out of child protection investigations. Practitioners are advised to keep a close eye on developments in any concurrent criminal setting, wherever these concern the arrest, trial and detention of adults, or children and young people, who may be directly concerned in care cases.

This chapter covers criminal issues that may impact on care proceedings generally, including youth justice. Matters specific to the role of police in child protection investigations are in Chapter 5, but Chapter 24 on disclosure, and Chapter 6 on emergency powers are also relevant. Further useful information is available on websites such as Home Office Crime Reduction,[1] Crown Prosecution Service (CPS) and the Association of Chief Police Officers.[2]

16.2   HUMAN RIGHTS AND DIVERSITY

UNCRC Article 40 protects the rights of the child alleged/accused or recognised as having broken criminal law 'to be treated in a manner consistent with the promotion of the child's sense of dignity and worth'. In England and Wales, although the Children Act 1989 does not apply directly to prisons and young offender institutions in the sense of imposing any functions, powers, duties and responsibilities on them, the functions, powers, duties and responsibilities of local authorities (especially Children Act 1989, ss.17, 47) take effect and operate subject to the necessary requirements of imprisonment. In other words, the Children Act 1989 applies to children in young offender institutions (*R (Howard League for Penal Reform)* v. *Secretary of State for the Home Department* [2002] EWHC Admin 2497, [2003] 1 FLR 484). Note that:

- there is a right to representation in order to challenge the reasons for being placed in segregation (*R (SP)* v. *Secretary of State for the Home Department* [2004] EWHC Admin 1418);
- the local authority for the area owes duties to those in custody under 18 and there is relevant safeguarding guidance requiring agreed local protocols for referral, assessment and services, e.g. in line with local ACPC/LCSB procedures;[3]
- a child on remand in a young offender institution must be subject to Young Offenders' Institution rules.

The right of young offenders to bring an action under Human Rights Act 1998, s.7 is important given the conditions in which most of them are detained. The possibility of evidence, including cross-examination of witnesses from the Home Office, may be a 'powerful incentive' for compliance with obligations to young detainees (Moses J in *R (BP)* v. *Secretary of State for the Home Department* [2003] EWHC Admin 1963) but given the particular difficulties in finding appropriate placement for girls, legislation to give them preference for local authority secure accommodation pursued a legitimate aim and was a proportionate response to the problem and the provisions in the Children and Young Persons Act 1969, s.23 regarding the remand of young males were not discriminatory (see ECHR Article 14 and *R (SR)* v. *Nottingham Magistrates' Court* [2001] EWHC Admin 802, (2001) 166 JP 132).

The failure of local authorities to provide suitable care and accommodation upon release may also be challenged (see *R (J)* v. *Caerphilly CC* [2005] EWHC Admin 586 and there are pending cases against Tower Hamlets, Surrey County Council and Birmingham City Council).

The police and youth justice system are affected by the race relations legislation and have guidance on diversity issues and good practice.[4] But there are serious concerns about higher levels of prosecution, conviction and sentences for certain categories of young black and minority ethnic males.[5] Young offenders in prison or on remand, particularly black and ethnic minority boys are subject to racism and victimisation and many say they are not safe.

16.3   CRIMINAL JUSTICE SYSTEM

Prevention and investigation

The police have a duty to investigate all serious, violent and sexual offences. But there has been a flood of procedures, protocols and initiatives, particularly in the wake of the Climbié and Bichard Inquiries, and police are expected to give child protection prominence in clear strategies, adequate resources and proper training, and to improve their response to domestic abuse, information-sharing and victim and witness support.

All local and police authorities have a duty to exercise their functions with regard to the effect on crime and disorder in their area, and to do all that they reasonably can to prevent it (Crime and Disorder Act 1998, s.17). Greater pressure for policing to be improved in child protection and domestic abuse has led to the development of minimum standards of best practice. The 2005 guidance on the safeguarding role of police is comprehensive, providing a list of priorities, definitions, evidential considerations and checklists, and covers:

- a wide range of investigations associated with child abuse, including domestic abuse, paedophilia (including Internet offences), sudden infant death, fabricated illness, trafficking, prostitution and institutional abuse;
- organised, complex or multiple abuse;[6]
- post-arrest and suspect management;
- Child Abuse Investigation Units and multi-agency working;
- vetting, information-sharing, etc.

Anyone involved in a Crime and Disorder strategy under the Crime and Disorder Act 1998, s.115[7] has power to disclose information to a 'relevant authority' (police, probation, health or local authority), but this does not override other legal obligations.

Criminal justice reform programme

Case management has been introduced for the criminal justice system to address its shortcomings[8] (delays in trials, many witnesses failing to give evidence, and poor case preparation). The Criminal Case Management Programme (CCMP) and the Criminal Case Management Framework (CCMF) (issued July 2004) are concerned with three important elements of criminal justice reform: charging, effective trial management programme

(ETMP) and 'No Witness, No Justice'.[9] The CCMF is closely aligned with the Criminal Procedure Rules 2005, SI 2005/384, that came into force in April 2005. They were made to bring about a culture change in the management of criminal cases coming before the courts. Under the new Rules, everyone involved is made responsible for helping to enable the case to go ahead effectively and efficiently under the supervision of the court. Part I of the Rules states the overriding objective and the Rules themselves apply to all participants in the case.

The Rules cover 10 main areas and are meant to be 'evolutionary' in the sense that they can be added to by the Criminal Procedure Rule Committee once agreed by the Secretary of State for Constitutional Affairs and the Home Secretary. The 10 main areas are: general matters, preliminary proceedings, custody and bail, disclosure, evidence, trial, sentencing, confiscation orders, appeals and costs.

The Charging Initiative means that the Crown Prosecution Service (CPS) is responsible for taking the decision to charge in all but routine or minor cases. This should ensure that the initial charge is the correct one thus leading to considerable savings in time and cost. A system called CPS Direct is being rolled out nationally to allow the police to have out-of-hours contact with CPS lawyers. The expectation is that, given a more definite hearing date, both defence and prosecution will be fully prepared.

Witness protection

New dedicated Witness Care Units,[10] are to ensure police and CPS work together to provide victims and witnesses with help and support, including:

- a single point of contact;
- initial needs assessment (child care, transport, language difficulties, medical issues, and concerns including intimidation);
- witness care officers to coordinate services and steer witnesses through the criminal justice process;
- continuous review of victims' and witnesses' needs by CPS and police;
- greater communication with witnesses about cases including the outcome of cases/trials.

Crimes against children

The 2005 guidance and Chapter 5 should be referred to for further details, but the police are the lead agency in criminal investigations: '"Child protection policing" is no more or less than the investigation of crime. To treat it otherwise or to remove it from mainstream policing in either philosophy or operational practice is to do a grave disservice to the victims of such crime'.[11]

New offences

Domestic abuse

Under the Domestic Violence, Crimes and Victims Act 2004, even if a survivor withdraws support for the prosecution, or does not wish to give evidence, the case may continue on the strength of other evidence gathered at the scene by the police. In some cases the violence is so serious, or the previous history shows such a real and continuing danger to the survivor or the children or other people, that the public interest in proceeding with the prosecution outweighs the survivor's wishes.

Internet grooming

Following concern about sex offenders' access to children over the Internet, a new offence, triable either way, of using the Internet for the purposes of 'grooming' was introduced, punishable by a maximum of 10 years' imprisonment (Sexual Offences Act 2003, s.15). The offender must either have met or communicated with the child on two previous occasions, and either meet him or her, or travel with the intention of so doing and of committing a relevant sexual offence.

Causing or allowing the death of a child or vulnerable adult

Under the Domestic Violence, Crime and Victims Act 2004[12] this applies where the death:

- is as a result of unlawful conduct;
- was caused by a member of the household;
- occurred in anticipated circumstances; and
- the defendant was, or should have been, aware that the victim was at risk, but either caused the death or did not take all reasonable steps to prevent the death.

It is not necessary to show which member of the household caused the death and which failed to prevent the death.

Police surgeons

The work of police surgeons is often critical in cases involving allegations of child abuse, rape and assault: professional conduct and procedures are governed by guidance on, e.g. consent and confidentiality and forensic examinations, especially in child sexual abuse. Some of these may be revised in the light of recent court cases involving allegations of fabricated illness.[13]

Prosecution

Crown Prosecution Service (CPS)

After the police have charged a defendant, the file is referred to the CPS, who must decide whether to proceed with the case, using the appropriate tests set out in the Code for Crown Prosecutors, including:

- *The evidential test:* is there sufficient evidence to provide a reasonable prospect of conviction?
- *The public interest test:* (only considered if the case passes the evidential test) is a prosecution in the public interest, taking account of such factors as the consequences for, and views of, the victim?

Further information on the way in which particular cases are dealt with is available on the CPS website.[14] But note that, although the CPS recognises that the use of previous civil proceedings as evidence in criminal proceedings is problematic, if it learns of any breaches of civil injunctions or occupation orders in family proceedings, it will usually consider this relevant in providing extra weight in prosecutions.

Its general rule is that all cases are prosecuted where there is enough evidence and no other factors to prevent this. Each region should have specialist staff, including coordinators for specific areas such as domestic abuse, with experience in prosecuting particular cases.

Burden of proof

The evidential burden is proof beyond reasonable doubt that the defendant committed the offence and rests with the prosecution. Decisions about whether proceedings should be initiated are principally based on whether there is sufficient evidence to prosecute, the proceedings are in the public interest and whether a prosecution is in the child's best interests.

The child and other vulnerable witnesses

Children, rape victims and those with learning difficulties and mental disorder find the criminal justice process especially stressful and sometimes traumatic. This reduces their ability to participate, respond or recall events. In addition, those coming to terms with severe personal difficulties and trauma may have the process of recovery delayed or set back by being involved in a court case.

The key document is *Achieving Best Evidence*.[15] Practitioners should have access to a copy: those directly concerned in criminal investigations should have been trained in this very detailed guidance, which covers:

- categories of vulnerable witnesses, which includes those who have disabilities or have been victimised or intimidated;
- planning and conducting interviews, including pace, duration, questioning techniques and diversity issues;
- witnesses: support, preparation and at court, including pre-trial preparation and special measures available at trial, protection from cross-examination by defendants in person and admissibility of videorecordings.

The Appendices contain the Framework for Assessment guidance on interviewing disabled children, identification parades, and various issues relating to videos and specimen forms.

Preparation for court

Advance preparation for trial with any witness is important, but especially so with child or other vulnerable witnesses, in order to provide information about the legal process, address concerns and reduce anxiety. The timing of this must be balanced between doing it too soon and increasing anxiety and doing it at the last minute, making assimilation of the information difficult.

Special measures in relation to 'vulnerable' witnesses

Under the Youth Justice and Criminal Evidence Act (YJCEA) 1999 a court can, for certain categories of witnesses, make special measures directions for the purpose of improving the quality of a witness's evidence. Such special measures can include videorecorded evidence-in-chief, giving evidence via live link and the use of screens.

A witness under 17 is always eligible for assistance in this regard. However, in proceedings concerning offences of a sexual nature, kidnapping, false imprisonment or which involve an assault or injury or threat of injury, a child witness is deemed to be in need of special protection and it is conclusively presumed that the use of videorecorded evidence-in-chief and evidence given by live link will maximise the quality of the witness's evidence (YJCEA 1999, s.22(5)). In other words, special measures are mandatory in such cases. It should be noted that the special measures do not apply to defendants under 17.

Disclosure

Requests for information to be obtained from third parties may be made at various stages in a criminal case by the police, the prosecutor, the defence, or the court. The purpose of these should be to elicit a genuine and focused search for relevant information, so they should explain the issues in the case, be reasonably precise and avoid speculative inquiries or 'fishing expeditions'.

There are now two Protocols applicable.[16] The one on exchange of information with family proceedings is currently being piloted.

Therapy before trial

All pre-trial discussions, including therapy, may raise the possibility of undermining the reliability of evidence at trial. Children usually determine when they are ready to talk about their experiences, but possible consequences may include allegations of coaching, therapists and others having to give evidence, and, at worst, the failure of the criminal case.

The decision about whether a child receives such therapy must be based on the child's best interests, so it can therefore only be taken by all the agency professionals responsible for her welfare, in consultation with carers and the child herself, if of sufficient age and understanding.

The following must be considered:

- the child's identified needs and what therapeutic services are needed, as described in the child protection plan;[17]
- the possible impact of therapy on the criminal trial;
- the consequences for the child of either having therapy or not;
- the guidelines on the use of pre-trial therapy.

The decision in respect of therapy for any witness, child or adult is *not* one for the police or the CPS, but both agencies must try to:

- identify cases in which therapy before trial might have some material impact on the evidence and assess the likely consequences;
- ensure these cases are dealt with as quickly as possible;
- safeguard the confidentiality of therapy sessions wherever possible, but also ensure the defence and the court are aware of the existence of information relevant to either the prosecution or the defence.

Confidentiality cannot be guaranteed in advance, so it must be made clear to those involved, from the outset, in what circumstances material obtained during treatment may have to be disclosed.

But therapists should take legal advice from appropriate professional sources about requests for disclosure, who should be careful to liaise with the local authority legal department. Patient confidentiality principles and the importance of maintaining trust as central to therapy mean that therapists are usually advised it is only appropriate to breach confidentiality in compliance with a court order, and should not have to disclose those aspects of the therapy that have no material relevance to criminal proceedings.

Two broad categories of therapeutic work are usually undertaken:

- counselling, which addresses the impact of the abuse, provides information on dealing with abusive relationships for future protection, and aims to improve self-esteem and confidence;
- psychotherapy, which seeks to treat, e.g. emotional and behavioural disturbance, post-traumatic stress disorder, and trauma that may affect mental health.

Both may require long-term involvement, depending upon the degree of the trauma suffered and cognitive ability.

Offences and types of trial

This section applies mainly to adult courts: Youth Courts have a different approach regarding either way and indictable offences, known as the 'grave crime procedure' (see below).

'Either way'

This term refers to a case that is 'triable either way' or an 'either way offence', to be heard either in the magistrates' court or the Crown Court. These include theft, deception, criminal damage where the value is more than £5,000, assault occasioning actual bodily harm and possession or supply of certain prescribed drugs.

Summary offence

This can only be tried before magistrates and without a jury, and includes most relatively minor offences (e.g. common assault and battery).

Indictable offence

This is an offence triable on indictment, i.e. the case starts in the magistrates' court and once the magistrates have deemed that the offence is indictable the case will be referred to the Crown Court. It includes most serious offences such as murder and rape.

Practical issues

Bail

Bail is granted to release someone held in custody awaiting trial or appealing against conviction. Conditions may be imposed and the needs of children and families should be given full consideration. There are two types of bail as outlined below.

POLICE BAIL

The police can release a defendant before charge, while they make further enquiries, or after charge, pending a court hearing. Defendants on police bail are listed to appear in court on the first available date, usually within two or three days of conditions being imposed. Alternatively, the police may keep the defendant in custody to appear before the magistrates' court the next day.

COURT BAIL

There is a presumption in favour of bail. At the hearing, the court will decide whether the defendant should be bailed or kept in custody until the full hearing. If the court is asked to remand the defendant in custody, the prosecution must show that bail conditions would not be enough to prevent the defendant from committing further offences or interfering with witnesses, or ensure attendance at the full hearing.

The decision and any conditions are recorded on a standard form: breaches of the latter will lead to arrest, with a court power to remand in custody.

Conditions include:

- not to contact, either directly or indirectly, a named person; and/or
- not to go to a named place; and/or
- to reside at a named place; and/or
- to report to a named police station on a given day or days at a given time.

These cease to have effect once the criminal case is concluded, so any restrictions on contact or from visiting/entering the family home also end, unless restraining orders/injunctions are granted in other proceedings.

Bail applications

Practitioners involved in care cases need to keep an eye on criminal cases, not least because an unanticipated successful application for bail can throw the best laid care plans astray and undermine effective case management. It is the role of the police officer responsible for child protection to keep parties informed, but asking without waiting to be told is the better practice.

Concurrent proceedings

The question of which comes first has long exercised the courts. In some areas there has been joint case management by a single judge, but these schemes have thrown up some difficult issues.

16.4   YOUTH JUSTICE SYSTEM

Introduction

Children and young people involved in crime also have safeguarding needs, but the tensions between these issues continue, despite the clear need for a flexible, holistic approach to family problems.[18] This can be most acutely seen in the increasing use of anti-social behaviour orders (ASBOs), and the provisions of the Crime and Disorder Act 1998 reviving a direct criminal route into care (against the spirit of the Children Act 1989).

The High Court has highlighted the obvious potential for a conflict of interest to arise between a local authority's application for an ASBO and its safeguarding duty, and set out guidance on the proper approach to be used (e.g. in *R(M)* v. *Sheffield Magistrates' Court* [2004] EWHC Admin 1830, [2004] 3 FCR 281). In making a decision as whether or not to apply for an ASBO the authority must ascertain the wishes and feelings of the child. This should be done by a social worker who should then report to the court and be available as a witness in the proceedings. In the event of a breach of a child safety order (see below), a court can make a care order without the threshold criteria being satisfied. Although the paramountcy and no order principles apply, the welfare checklist is not applicable, and the child is not a separate party, even though her parents and the local authority can be represented.

The system

The youth justice system is concerned with children and young persons (aged 10 to 17 inclusive) who have been accused or charged with committing criminal offences. It is made up of different agencies, professions, bodies and individuals all with a statutory duty to have regard to its principal aim to prevent offending (Crime and Disorder Act 1998, s.37).[19] Courts must also have regard to issues of both welfare and just punishment.

The main bodies are local authorities, police and the courts and their roles provide the main focus of this chapter. Health authorities and education authorities are also placed under certain statutory duties.

Powers of local authorities

Local authorities have duties and responsibilities (under the Crime and Disorder Act 1998 and Children Act 1989) to establish a Youth Offending Team (YOT) comprising probation officer, social worker, police officer and representatives from health and education authorities; and to produce an annual Youth Justice Plan for the provision and funding of local youth justice services and YOTs.

There are a range of interventions and punishments designed to help local communities and youth justice agencies take effective action to tackle youth crime, including the following (Crime and Disorder Act 1998).

Local child curfew schemes are designed to restrict young people to particular places within certain hours, but have been successfully challenged.

Child safety orders (CSO) are designed to intervene with children under 10 at risk of getting into trouble and divert them from crime and are made by a Family Proceedings Court if one or more of the following conditions are satisfied:

(a) the child has committed an act that would have been an offence if she had been 10 or over; or
(b) a CSO is necessary to prevent the commission of such an act; or
(c) the child has contravened a ban imposed by a curfew notice; or
(d) the child has acted in a manner that caused or was likely to cause harassment, alarm or distress to one or more persons of a different household.

ASBOs are designed to deal with serious, but not necessarily criminal, anti-social behaviour by those aged 10 and above.

Police powers to remove truants to designated premises are designed to allow the police, in conjunction with local authorities, to tackle one of the main factors seen as putting young people at risk of offending.

Police

On arrest, a young person has rights under the Police and Criminal Evidence Act (PACE) 1984 additional to those given to other police station detainees:[20]

- legal representation;
- the presence of an 'appropriate adult';
- no detention in a police cell without good reason;
- frequent visiting;
- if charged, and bail is not appropriate, transfer to local authority accommodation unless the custody officer certifies this is impracticable. If aged 12 or over, this must be to secure accommodation, unless none is available and any other local authority accommodation would not be adequate to protect the public from serious harm.

The appropriate adult can be a parent, guardian, social worker (as long as they are not a witness, victim or suspect) or any other responsible person at least 18 years old, not a police officer or employed by the police. She supports the young person and gives advice, and is present throughout the police interview to ensure undue distress is not caused to the young person, she understands what is happening and is able to get her views across.

Avoiding court

Even if arrested and interviewed, a young person may still avoid going to court. There is a reprimand and warning scheme (under Crime and Disorder Act 1998, ss. 65, 66), which provides that where a young offender has not previously been convicted/reprimanded/warned for an offence, a police officer may reprimand if there is sufficient evidence of commission of the offence and if prosecuted, a realistic prospect of conviction, the offence is admitted, and he is satisfied prosecution is not in the public interest.

A warning can be given if the same criteria apply but not if one was given previously in the last two years. A referral must be made to a YOT which must assess the young person and, if appropriate, arrange for participation in a rehabilitation programme.

Both reprimands and warnings can be cited in criminal proceedings in the same circumstances as a conviction.

Youth courts

Procedure

The basic rule is that a charge against a child or young person must be heard by a Youth Court. If facing an indictable or either way offence (in the case of an adult) she has no right to elect to be tried in the Crown Court. But in certain circumstances, the proceedings must be committed for trial to the Crown Court, for example:

- where the youth is charged with homicide;
- under the 'grave crime procedure';
- where the youth is jointly charged with an adult and the court considers it necessary in the interests of justice.

The 'grave crime procedure' applies where the youth is facing a charge that, in the case of an adult, carries 14 years' or more imprisonment. It also applies for certain prescribed offences. In essence, before plea, the court must ask itself whether it would be proper for the Crown Court dealing with the defendant for the offence of which he is charged to sentence him to a period greater than two years (the maximum in the Youth Court; the minimum period of detention is four months). The court is entitled to have regard to any antecedents to assist in its decision. If it considers this would be appropriate, then jurisdiction is declined and the youth is committed for trial. If jurisdiction is retained, there is no subsequent power to commit for sentence following a conviction.

There are automatic restrictions on publicity and proceedings are held more or less in camera. The usual requirement is for magistrates of both genders to sit.

Maximum time limits are prescribed for certain stages of proceedings (Prosecution of Offences (Youth Courts Time Limits) Regulations 1999, SI 1999/2743), but disposal is rare at first hearing. Cases have to be adjourned and the position regarding bail considered: magistrates may remand on bail, into local authority accommodation or custody. They also have power to impose electronic monitoring requirements on 12 to 16-year-olds and in some metropolitan areas Intensive Supervision and Surveillance bail packages are being piloted.

However, 17-year-olds are adults for this purpose, and can be remanded to an adult prison if bail is refused (Bail Act 1976); conditions can be attached as with any grant of bail.

Otherwise, where bail is refused, remand will normally be to local authority accommodation, with power to impose conditions (e.g. residence and reporting).

The court can also impose a 'security requirement' on 12 to 14-year-olds and females aged 15 or 16 remanded to local authority accommodation on condition that the child or young person is charged with or has been convicted of a violent or sexual offence or an offence punishable for an adult with imprisonment for 14 years or more, or one or more imprisonable offences which, taken together with any other convictions for imprisonable offences, amount to a recent repeated history of such offences and, in the court's opinion, only a security requirement would be adequate to protect the public from serious harm from her or to prevent her committing imprisonable offences. It must consider all other options and consult the local authority (under Children and Young Persons Act 1969, s.23(5), (5AA) before imposing such a requirement.

For 15 and 16-year-old males, the position is slightly different. The 1969 Act provisions still apply but the court must remand to a remand centre, or a prison if none is available. However, if it declares such a remand would be undesirable by reason of physical/emotional immaturity or a propensity to harm himself, it must remand him into secure accommodation if available.

Where a child or young person under 17 is remanded to local authority accommodation, the authority can apply under Criminal Justice Act 1991, s.60(3) for her to be placed into secure accommodation, on the criteria set out in Chapter 7, which relate to convictions for serious/violent/sexual offences or a recent history of absconding combined with charges or convictions for an imprisonable offence.

Conviction and sentence

The Youth Court's range of powers include:

- referral order;
- absolute discharge and conditional discharge;

- compensation;
- fine;
- binding over parents;
- reparation, action plan or attendance centre orders;
- supervision;
- probation, community service, combination order or curfews (if 16 or over);
- detention and training order;
- ASBOs (under Crime and Disorder Act 1998, s.1C).

Referral order

A referral order lasts between three and 12 months, is compulsory on certain conditions and referral is to a Youth Offending Panel, which must arrange meetings with the offender to agree a Youth Offender Contract – a programme of behaviour aimed at preventing re-offending. This can include financial or other reparation, mediation with the victim, unpaid work in the community, curfew, school attendance and specified activities, but not tagging or physical restriction of movement.

Anti-social behaviour order

The Youth Court can also make this order ancillary to any other sentence imposed, if satisfied that the offender has acted in a manner that caused, or was likely to cause, harassment, alarm or distress to one or more persons in a different household and that it is necessary to protect persons in any place from further anti-social behaviour by her. The minimum period is two years and the subject cannot apply to have it discharged before then.

Parenting order

This can include requirements which the court considers necessary in the interests of preventing any repetition/commission of any further offence. Parents may also be required to attend such counselling and guidance sessions as may be specified. Such an order is made where:

- a child safety order is made in respect of the child;
- an ASBO is made (or sex offender order);
- a child or young person is convicted of an offence; or
- there is a conviction for failing to comply with a school attendance order or failing to secure regular attendance at school as a registered pupil.

Where a person under 16 is convicted of an offence, the court is obliged to make an order unless it believes it is unnecessary.

Reparation order

The child or young person is required to make reparation to a person identified by the court as a victim or a person otherwise affected by the offence, whose consent is required. The court must be sure that the order does not conflict with the offender's religious beliefs, interfere with school timetables or any current community order.

It cannot be made where the court proposes to pass a custodial sentence, a community or combination order or an action plan order.

After considering a written report and being satisfied that arrangements for implementing them are in place, the approach of the court should be in favour of making it – if it does not, it must give reasons.

Action plan order

An action plan order may be made where the court wants to secure the rehabilitation of the offender or prevent her commission of further offences. Potentially wide-reaching, it can place the offender under the supervision of a responsible officer, and impose requirements on her for compliance with an action plan/directions, arrangements for education and/or participation in activities, attendance at specified places or before specified persons, exclusion from specified places, reparation or to attend a court hearing. The same religious, educational and reporting considerations apply as above.

It cannot be made if the offender is already subject to such an order, or in conjunction with a custodial sentence, community/supervision/attendance centre order.

Curfew order

This requires the young offender to remain at a specified place for a specified period (between two and 12 hours) for the duration of the order (maximum six months for 16-year-olds or over, three months otherwise). The offender's whereabouts are monitored by a specified person and electronic monitoring arrangements are available for 10 to 17-year-olds.

Once again, the court has to have regard to the young offender's religious beliefs and educational requirements.

Drug treatment and testing order

This order is only available where the young offender is 16 or over and the court is satisfied as to dependence on, or propensity to misuse, drugs which requires, and may be susceptible to, treatment.

'Treatment' can be as a resident at a relevant institution or non-resident, and 'testing' requires provision of urine/blood samples.

Most of these sentences are also available for adults convicted of criminal offences. Supervision orders can also be made by the Youth Court and include requirements.

Custodial sentences

Convictions for serious offences may leave the court no option but to impose such a sentence. The Youth Court has power to impose a detention and training order (DTO) in certain cases for a maximum of two years. For 12 to 15-year-olds, the Youth Court must be satisfied that the young offender is a persistent offender (there is no statutory definition).

More occasionally, young offenders are charged with offences that, in the case of adults, attract custodial sentences of 14 years or more (e.g. robbery). The law recognises that a two-year DTO may be insufficient punishment/ deterrence if a young person is convicted of a 'grave crime'. In such cases, jurisdiction must be considered (see above). If a younger person committed to the Crown Court is then convicted and sentenced, she will be detained in such place and on such conditions as the Secretary of State may direct.

'Dangerousness'

This is a new concept introduced by the Criminal Justice Act 2003. For specified offences (sexual/violent) the court now has to assess whether or not a youth is to be regarded as 'dangerous'. The test is whether there is a significant risk to members of the public of serious harm occasioned by his commission of further such offences. 'Serious harm' means death or serious personal injury, whether physical or psychological.

This assessment takes place before plea and in addition to the 'grave crime procedure' (see above). If assessed as 'dangerous' then he is sent to the Crown Court to be dealt with. The Crown Court is then able to pass:

- an 'extended sentence' adding up to five years' imprisonment for a violent offence and up to eight years' imprisonment for a sexual offence; or
- a 'sentence for public protection', which is indeterminate.

Note that, if the Youth Court does not assess a youth as 'dangerous' before a plea is taken, the assessment is done again if the youth is convicted of the specified offence.

The future

The Youth Court's powers of sentencing are wide-ranging and it is arguable that this is necessary to achieve the government's principal aim of preventing offending by children and young persons. However, many of the orders available overlap and there is a risk that the wrong, as opposed to appropriate, sentence is imposed. To some extent, this has been recognised in the government's 2003 Green Paper on children,[21] which included a section on youth justice.

Timescales for new legislation are uncertain, but a single main sentencing purpose of preventing offending is being proposed, supported by requirements for sentences to take into account the extent to which punishment is needed, the need to protect the public from persistent offending, the individual's age and vulnerability, whether there should be a restorative approach, parental obligations and previous interventions. The range of sentences would be simplified to include:

- the nine non-custodial sentences being called an action plan order (with built-in elements from the existing range of orders);
- increased emphasis on parenting orders and ASBOs;
- a new intensive supervision and detention order.

Whether a new streamlined approach will achieve the stated aim to prevent offending remains to be seen, however, it would allow interventions to be tailored specifically to individual circumstances and to be more effective.

The Criminal Justice Act 2003 has brought, and will continue to bring, wholesale changes to the criminal justice system. Early in 2005, for example, changes were brought into force affecting the admissibility of bad character and hearsay evidence, such that the courts' approach is now an inclusionary one as opposed to an exclusionary one.

In the adult jurisdiction sweeping changes were made in relation to the types of sentences that a court can give (there are more changes to come, such as the introduction of a sentence known as 'intermittent custody'). These changes have not affected the criminal youth jurisdiction as yet, but the legislation is in place and is likely to be brought into force by 2007 (for 16 and 17-year-olds). There have also been changes in the legislation in respect of ASBOs: in effect, courts can make them of their own volition in criminal proceedings.

The recommendations of the Bichard Inquiry will result in new guidance on handling sexual allegations and a registration scheme for those seeking work with children or vulnerable adults. Consultation was due to be completed by June 2005.

NOTES

1   See **www.crimereduction.gov.uk** or **www.homeoffice.gov.uk**.
2   See **www.cps.gov.uk** and **www.acpo.police.uk**.
3   *Safeguarding and Promoting the Welfare of Children and Young People in Custody*, LAC (2004)26.
4   See Home Office Research Development Statistics, **www.homeoffice.gov.uk/rds**.

5   *Minority Ethnic Young People in the Youth Justice System: Differences or Discrimination?*, Youth Justice Board (2004) (see **www.youth-justice-board.gov.uk**).
6   Also the subject of other practice guides and protocols.
7   See *Crime Reduction Toolkit: Information-Sharing* (2003) for details, available at **www.crimereduction.gov.uk/toolkits**.
8   See the Effective Trial Management Programme, Charging Initiative and Victim and Witness Care Scheme, which is part of the government's overall Criminal Case Management Programme (**www.homeoffice.gov.uk**).
9   'No Witness, No Justice' Project 2004.
10 *Ibid.*
11 Lord Laming, *Climbié Inquiry Report* (2003).
12 See Home Office Circular (2005)9 and *Protecting Children and Vulnerable Adults: The New Law on Familial Homicide*, Home Office (February 2005).
13 Available from the General Medical Council, the Department of Health, the Association of Police Surgeons and the Royal College of Paediatrics and Child Health. See *Guidance on Paediatric Forensic Examinations in relation tto Possible Child Sexual Abuse*, RCPCH and Association of Police Surgeons (April 2002).
14 See **www.cps.gov.uk**.
15 *Achieving Best Evidence in Criminal Proceedings*, Home Office, LCD, CPS, DH, Welsh Assembly (2002) replaces the Memorandum of Good Practice, no longer applicable. See **www.cps.gov.uk/publications**.
16 Protocol between CPS, Police and Local Authorities in the Exchange of Information in the Investigation and Prosecution of Child Abuse Cases, CPS, Home Office, ADSS, DfES (2003) and Information Sharing Pilot between Police and Family Courts, ACPO, CS, DCA (2004).
17 *Working Together to Safeguard Children*, DH, Home Office, DfEE (1999), para. 5.82.
18 Dame Elizabeth Butler-Sloss, Paul Sieghart Memorial Lecture, British Institute of Human Rights, King's College London, April 2003.
19 There are also targets for reducing the levels of offending in the looked after population – see LAC (2001) 28.
20 See PACE Code, paras C:1.5 to C:1.7.
21 Green Paper, *Every Child Matters* (2003).

CHAPTER 17

Immigration, asylum and nationality

Key sources

- Immigration Acts 1971 and 1988; Asylum and Immigration Appeals Act 1993; Asylum and Immigration Act 1996; Immigration and Asylum Act 1999; Nationality, Immigration and Asylum Act 2002; Asylum and Immigration (Treatment of Claimants etc) Act 2004
- Children Acts 1989 and 2004
- Human Rights Act 1998
- Asylum and Immigration Tribunal (Procedure) Rules 2005
- UN Convention relating to the Status of Refugees 1951 and Protocol 1967
- UNCRC 1990 and ECHR 1950
- Home Office IND Immigration Rules (HC 395), Asylum Policy Instructions (APIs) and NASS Policy Bulletins
- *Handbook on Procedures and Criteria for Determining Refugee Status*, UNHCR (1972, revised 1992)

17.1 INTRODUCTION

Immigration and asylum law, practice and procedure is a field subject to seemingly constant change and revision. Since 1993 there has been a major new Act at least every three years, the latest being the Immigration and Asylum (Treatment of Claimants etc.) Act 2004 which introduces new criminal offences of arrival without documentation and restructures the current appeals system. This chapter cannot provide practitioners with anything more than an outline of some of the key issues in this field of law and is restricted to children and young people claiming asylum. The material referred to includes the principal texts and a by no means exhaustive selection of current resources.

At the time of publication, the government's five-year strategy has been published announcing the intention to replace Indefinite Leave to Remain for refugees with temporary protection status and to enforce the removal of unaccompanied children.

Immigration and asylum

Refugee law should be seen as distinct from immigration law. Refugee status determination law is based upon the international obligations the UK committed to in ratifying the UN Convention relating to the Status of Refugees 1951 (the 'Refugee Convention'). These obligations are incorporated into domestic law by statute, by the Immigration Rules[1] and by case precedent.

The Immigration Rules set out the criteria for applicants and decision-makers to follow across a wide range of entry and stay categories, e.g. visitor and student applications, family settlement, access to children, work permits, etc.

The rules also lay down the practice for the determination of refugee claims, refusals and rights of appeal, deportation and administrative removal.

17.2 PRINCIPLES

Concessions and policies generally

Outside the main immigration rules there exists a body of extra-statutory concessions and policies. Some are formal, in the form of Ministerial statements and Home Office published guidance, such as the policies concerning long residence and deportation/removal of children[2] and where a child is in the care of a local authority. Others are less obviously accessible, in Home Office letters sent directly to solicitors or replies to parliamentary questions found in *Hansard*. They may, for example, set out a specific current Home Office practice on regularisation of overstayers or 'amnesty', make provision for the temporary suspension of removals to a particular country or enlighten an interpretation of the rules in a particular way. Concessions and policies apply to immigration and asylum cases but these cannot be more restrictive than the Immigration Rules and are open to judicial challenge if misapplied.

Welfare and paramountcy

The UN Convention on the Rights of the Child (UNCRC) ratified in 1989 by the UK requires that in all actions concerning children undertaken by public and private institutions and courts of law, the best interests of the child shall be a primary consideration (UNCRC Article 3).

The Children Act 1989, s.1(1) brought this obligation into UK domestic law in a limited way stating that the welfare of the child shall be the court's paramount consideration when determining any matter with respect to the upbringing of that child.

Crucially, the UK entered a reservation when ratifying the UNCRC, which maintains the primacy of immigration control over child welfare.

It has been held that, other than in adoption cases, a decision in the family courts cannot deprive the Home Secretary of the power to remove a child and that the Home Secretary does not have to apply the paramountcy principle but instead performs a balancing exercise between the child's welfare and the need to maintain effective immigration controls (Munby J in *Re A* [2003] 2 FLR 92, see also (2004) 4 *Legal Action* 31).

Delay

The Children Act 1989, s.1(2) sets out the principle that delay is likely to prejudice the welfare of the child.

The Immigration and Nationality Directorate (IND) recognises this in its own guidance: 'Attempts should be made to deal with cases swiftly and efficiently, as the longer a child remains the more upsetting it is likely to be if he is required to leave'[3] but cases may still be subject to lengthy delay.

If this happens a written complaint to the IND Complaints Unit (see Appendix 2) followed by a letter before action in judicial review proceedings should be considered.

Consideration should be given to asking the child's constituency MP to write to the Minister to seek to expedite the decision. The MP can also be asked to involve the Parliamentary Ombudsman.[4]

17.3   LEGAL AND PRACTICE ISSUES

Asylum

It is not possible to apply for asylum in the UK before arrival and consequently lawful entry as a person seeking recognition as a refugee is not possible. Asylum seekers are protected against penalty for illegal entry or presence in the UK by Article 31(1) of the Refugee Convention which prohibits the imposition of penalties on refugees. This prohibition has been incorporated into domestic law in a narrowly construed way by providing statutory defences against prosecution in the Immigration and Asylum Act 1999, s.31 (*R (Pepushi)* v. *Crown Prosecution Service* [2004] EWHC Admin 798).

A child's right to be recognised as a refugee is no different from that of any other person. The Refugee Convention (Article 1(A)) states that a refugee is a person who:

(a) owing to a well founded fear of being persecuted
(b) for reasons of race, religion, nationality, membership of a social group or political opinion

(c) is outside her country of origin and

(d) is unable or, owing to such fear is unwilling to avail herself of the protection of that country, or who, not having a nationality and being outside
the country of her former habitual residence as a result of such events is
unable or, owing to such fear, is unwilling to return to it.

In order to succeed, a claim must satisfy all the elements of the Refugee
Convention.

The burden of proof is upon the claimant to establish to a lower standard
of proof than the civil balance of probabilities that on 'a reasonable degree
of likelihood' she would be at real risk of serious harm if returned (*R* v.
SSHD, ex p. Sivakumaran [1988] Imm AR 147 at 150).

A child may have claimed asylum in her own right either because she is an
unaccompanied child or as a named dependant of a family member's claim.
In unaccompanied children cases, the child will need to give an account of
her case as best as she is able given her age and understanding.

In cases where a child is a named dependant, care should be taken to
assess whether she should be asked about her own account of events. If a
child is a dependant of a family member's claim she does not have to give a
statement as she will be ordinarily granted or refused status in line with the
principal applicant. If there is evidence particular to the child which supports
the main claim or justifies making her own separate but related claim then
this should be put forward at the initial stage to the Home Office and if
refused, on appeal.

The approach to the consideration of asylum claims made by children is
and should be different from that of an adult to reflect age and understanding.

The UNHCR Handbook[5] calls for a 'liberal application of the principle of
the benefit of the doubt'.

One-stop procedures and human rights

Under a simplified 'one-stop procedure' (Nationality, Immigration and
Asylum Act 2002, s.120), asylum applicants are required to provide a statement of all additional grounds they seek to rely upon, which should include all
compassionate grounds, relevant concessions and policies and human rights-
based arguments against removal, supported by evidence where available.

Human rights arguments must be made relevant to the facts of the client's
case and not simply asserted in the statement of additional grounds. The
main rights relied upon under the European Convention on Human Rights
(ECHR) in immigration and asylum claims are Article 3 (an absolute right),
prohibiting cruel, inhuman or degrading treatment, Article 8 (a qualified
right), the right to respect for family and private life and Article 2 (a qualified
right), the right to life. All articles of the ECHR should always be considered
and cited where relevant but individually these must now amount to a

flagrant violation and are unlikely to succeed in persuading the Home Office or the appellate courts to allow the claim unless the harm crosses a very high threshold (*R* v. *Special Adjudicator (Respondent), ex p. Ullah (FC) (Appellant)* [2004] UKHL 26 and *R (Razgar)* v. *Secretary of State for the Home Department* [2004] UKHL 27).

Nonetheless, children's cases should always be treated as special cases and the assessment of proportionality/lawful interference should be differentiated from adult cases.

Age

A child is a person who is under 18 years of age or who, in the absence of documentary evidence establishing age, appears to be under that age.[6]

An unaccompanied child is 'a person below the age of 18 who arrives in the UK unaccompanied by an adult responsible for them, whether by law or custom and for as long as they are not effectively taken into the care of such a person; it shall include minors who are left unaccompanied after they entered the UK'.[7]

The United Nations High Commissioner for Refugees (UNHCR) definition includes:

- children who have become separated from their parents and have arrived in the UK by themselves;
- children who are being cared for by older siblings, distant relatives and family friends – therefore, not their usual carers;
- children who arrived in the UK with family, other relatives or family friends but whose care arrangements break down after arrival.[8]

Where age is disputed either by the Home Office or the local authority this can have a damaging effect on both the way in which the claim is considered and on access to appropriate support and accommodation.

The burden is on the applicant to show that she is a child. However, recently, the High Court has laid down guidance (see *R (B)* v. *Merton LBC* [2003] 2 FLR 888) on the steps a local authority must take to carry out its own assessment independent from the Home Office's view. Age assessment is an inexact science and the British Medical Association states that it is 'extremely difficult to accurately assess the age of a child and almost impossible when the child is between the ages of 15 to 18'.[9]

Guidance[10] from the Royal College of Paediatrics and Child Health urges caution in giving an opinion on whether a refugee child is under or over 18, whether requested by the child's legal representative or by a government agency, advising in June 2003 that:

- the determination of age is a complex and often inexact set of skills, where various types of physical, social and cultural factors all play their part, although none provide a wholly exact or reliable indication of age, especially for older children;

- assessments of age should only be made in the context of the overall assessment of the child;
- as there can be a wide margin of error in assessing age it may be best to word a clinical judgment in terms of whether a child is probably, likely, possibly or unlikely to be under the age of 18;
- it is inappropriate for x-rays to be used merely to assist in age determination for immigration purposes.

Where a child reaches the age of 18 before her application has been decided or before appeal then the applicant will continue to be treated as if she is a child.[11] If her claim is refused and a decision is made to remove her from the UK then there is no requirement to ensure that satisfactory reception arrangements are in place in the home country, unlike when considering the return of children.[12] However, the Children Leaving Care Act 2000 may, for qualifying young people, now arguably require a local authority to consider the suitability of return arrangements as part of its duty to prepare pathway plans.[13]

Making an asylum application

A child arriving in the UK often comes to the attention of the authorities in several ways:

- by presenting to or being stopped by an immigration officer at the port of entry;
- being taken to an immigration adviser by a friend, contact or the facilitating agent;
- being left at a social services asylum seekers team office.

Where a child comes to the attention of immigration services at port, formal arrangements are in place with local social services authorities to register their claim and take responsibility for their welfare.

In situations where a child either presents at a social services office or is left with an immigration adviser, the priority should always be to ensure that she is provided with support and accommodation before any other steps are taken. This will involve requesting the local authority to carry out a child in need assessment.

An in-country claimant must attend the Immigration and Nationality Directorate in Croydon or Liverpool in person to make their asylum application. This applies equally to child claimants.

A child should not attend the Home Office to register their claim without the presence of a responsible adult. This should be a person independent from the Home Office, i.e not an immigration or police officer.

The Refugee Council Panel of Advisers for Unaccompanied Refugee Children should be contacted and a panel member allocated to act as a non-legal advocate for that child. The Panel is funded by the Home Office, however, resource issues may in reality restrict the service to taking a child to their initial screening interview and drop-in advice/assistance and liaison with local agencies.

All unaccompanied asylum-seeking children will meet the definition of a child 'in need'. Unaccompanied children are *always* the responsibility of social services and not the National Asylum Support Service (NASS). Local authority support and accommodation is *not* conditional upon first making an asylum claim.

The asylum claim should be made as soon as possible after arrival in the UK. Welfare support and accommodation is provided for adults and families by NASS but not unaccompanied children. It is now contingent upon claims being made as soon as reasonably practicable under the Nationality, Immigration and Asylum Act 2002, s.55 (see 'Support' at p.306).

The initial screening interview should not touch on the substantive reasons for claiming asylum. It serves to gather the basic details of the claimant including identity, date, means of arrival into the UK and any countries travelled through. Fingerprints and photographs are taken at the initial screening interview and an asylum registration card (ARC) and Statement of Evidence Form (SEF) are issued. An SEF (with a strict return deadline) is used for the child to complete with their lawyer. Failure to return the completed SEF within the deadline can result in the application being refused on non-compliance grounds.[14] Children are not usually interviewed, although this practice is currently under review.

At this point an asylum claimant may be detained and transferred to an immigration reception/detention centre for fast tracking of their claim or given temporary admission into the UK pending consideration of their claim. Unaccompanied children should not be detained.[15] However, age disputed children are increasingly being discovered in immigration detention. This has recently been accepted by the Secretary of State for the Home Department to be unlawful (*R(A)* v. *Secretary of State for the Home Department*, CO 12858/2004). Since October 2001, children as part of a family unit can be detained under adult detention policy provisions.

Taking instructions from child clients

The principles for interviewing child asylum and immigration clients are exactly the same as for all other child clients. Extra consideration needs to be taken of the trauma of the journey to the UK, separation from other family members and of the physical and mental harm suffered and feared by the child. Language is a significant barrier to a child being able to give their account of what has happened to them. An interpreter experienced with working with children is essential. Considerable time is required to enable a child to develop confidence and trust in those responsible for presenting their claim. This conflicts directly with the fast asylum claim timetable and appeal procedures and is now further affected by new LSC immigration contract conditions.

In all cases the practitioner should make an assessment of the extent to which a child is capable of expressing a reasoned view and is able to understand the situation she finds herself in.

Putting Children First[16] contains a very detailed chapter on taking instructions from a child immigration client.

Consideration should be given early on to referring the child for specialist counselling, e.g. to the Medical Foundation for the Care of Victims of Torture.[17]

The Children Panel of the Law Society sets best practice standards for the conduct of cases involving child clients and it is a mandatory requirement for practitioners to hold a specialist child care LSC contract. Panel membership is not a requirement for immigration practitioners working under LSC contracts but the same standards and principles should be applied.

Particular care and priority should always be given by the Home Office to consideration of applications from unaccompanied children on account of their vulnerability.[18] In practice this may not happen.

A child will not be interviewed by the Home Office about the substance of her claim if it is possible to obtain by written enquiries or from other sources sufficient information properly to determine the claim[19] but where an interview is necessary it should be in the presence of a parent, guardian, representative or another adult taking responsibility for the child but not an immigration officer, an officer of the Secretary of State or a police officer.

Assessing evidence of children

When assessing the evidence of a child, it should not be assumed that she does not have a well-founded fear of persecution simply because she does not have sufficient maturity to have formed a well-founded fear.[20]

The younger the child, the less likely they are to have full information about the reasons for leaving their country of origin or the arrangements made for their travel. Depending on the maturity of a child the emphasis might need to be upon documentary and expert evidence rather than oral evidence or the child's statement.[21]

The assessment of the well-foundedness of her fear 'may call for a liberal application of the benefit of the doubt' (*Jakitay* (12658) 15 November 1995, IAT).

Where a child turns 18 before her claim is decided, her evidence should be considered as if she were still a child.

Trafficked children

There is growing concern at the numbers of children who appear to be brought to the UK to be exploited by traffickers, either sexually or for domestic or other forced labour. A child may present as an unaccompanied child or say that they are being looked after by a friend or family relative when in reality they are being controlled by that person or other unidentified adult in what they say to their legal advisers and what they do. The Home Office anti-trafficking toolkit[22] and a recent in-depth report on child trafficking in London[23] are essential reading in understanding the factors that may identify whether a child has been trafficked.

Care should be taken always to consider the possibility that a child is a trafficking victim. Subject always to the duty of client confidentiality, where this is identified the adviser should ensure that the child is protected by the appropriate agencies, i.e area child protection team and specialist police departments.

The trafficking abuse itself should also form the basis of an additional claim for protection either on Refugee Convention grounds and/or human rights grounds.

Leave to remain

A child's claim should be decided without delay. Where a decision is made to recognise the child as a refugee, Indefinite Leave to Remain (ILR) will be granted together with confirmation of recognition as a 1951 Convention refugee (but see comments under 'Immigration and asylum' above).

Humanitarian protection leave and discretionary leave

A child who is not recognised as a refugee has the right of appeal (Nationality, Immigration and Asylum Act 2002, ss.82–83). She may in addition be granted temporary protective leave to remain for a number of reasons.

According to published Home Office policy[24], Humanitarian Protection (HP) will be granted to anyone who is unable to demonstrate a claim for asylum but who would face a serious risk to life or person arising from the death penalty, unlawful killing, torture, inhuman or degrading treatment or punishment.

HP should be granted for up to three years. If at the end of three years, following an active review, it is decided that further protection is needed, a claimant will usually receive ILR. If protection is no longer needed and a person has no other basis of stay in the UK, they will be expected to leave.

The same policy notice states that Discretionary Leave (DL) may be granted to an applicant who:

- has an ECHR Article 8 claim;
- has an ECHR Article 3 claim only on medical grounds or severe humanitarian cases;
- is an unaccompanied asylum-seeking child for whom adequate reception arrangements in their country are not available;
- would qualify for asylum or HP but has been excluded or is able to demonstrate particularly compelling reasons why removal would not be appropriate.

The notice states that unaccompanied children should normally be granted DL for three years or until their eighteenth birthday, whichever is earlier. After the DL period has expired the claimants' situation will be actively reviewed with further leave granted only if appropriate.

Grant of DL to unaccompanied children to age of 18 and not refugee status and ILR is the most common form of leave currently granted to unaccompanied children.

Despite the policy notice guidance on DL, unless an application to extend leave to remain is made by the legal representative *before* the child's eighteenth birthday, then leave to remain ends and the child is left without a lawful right to remain in the UK. She also loses the right to benefits and may lose appeal rights. This may leave a young person destitute and treated as an illegal entrant.

Where an application to extend leave has been made within the period of existing leave then that leave to remain automatically extends until a decision on the new application is finally determined (including on appeal under the Immigration and Asylum 1999 s.3). This has the effect of preserving appeal rights and entitlement to accommodation and welfare benefits.

If a child has not yet had a decision on their asylum application and has not been granted exceptional (now discretionary) leave to remain they will become the responsibility of NASS to support not the local authority.

NASS have issued a Policy Bulletin[25] on transition at age 18 which sets out guidance to its caseworkers and local authority social services departments on handling claims for support from former unaccompanied asylum-seeking children who have been looked after by local authorities.

Since October 2001 the Home Office has agreed not to disperse children previously accommodated by a local authority under Children Act 1989, s.20. Responsibility for providing suitable accommodation for these young people will remain with the local authority.[26]

Support

The Immigration and Asylum Act 1999 sets out the legal framework for the responsibility for support for asylum seekers. Unaccompanied children are, for the purposes of support, excluded from the definition of 'asylum seeker' in that Act (s.94(1)) and in consequence are outside the remit of NASS. Instead they come within the Children Act 1989 duties of a local authority in the same manner as any other child in need (Children Act 1989, s.17).

Support for families with children under 18 continues throughout the child's minority irrespective of the outcome of their asylum application and any subsequent appeals, unless leave is granted in which case entitlement to mainstream benefits will succeed NASS or local authority support. However, since the coming into force of the Asylum and Immigration (Treatment of Claimants etc.) Act 2004, s.9, support may be withdrawn from families who fail to cooperate in procedures to redocument them for removal. This is still in a test phase restricted to three pilot areas in London, Greater Manchester and West Yorkshire. Children of these families are still owed Children Act 1989 duties. For unaccompanied children, the duty to support is determined by age not the outcome of an asylum application. The local authority retains a duty to ensure that the needs of a child (and a young person leaving care) are met even if they become eligible for mainstream benefits following a grant of leave to remain.

Support responsibility will fall to the local authority in whose area the child presents in need. The Refugee Council has operated a rota system in London which has shared the duties across authorities by consent. However, where there is a dispute between authorities a child should not be adversely affected whilst the local authorities reach a decision. Guidance has been issued on how to make such decisions and resolve disputes.[27]

The judgment in *R (Berhe) and Others* v. *Hillingdon LBC* [2003] EWHC Admin 2075, helpfully clarified that an unaccompanied child (whether or not she is an asylum seeker, whether with leave to remain or not) who has been looked after for a total of at least 13 weeks prior to her eighteenth birthday since the age of 14 will be eligible for leaving care services under the Children (Leaving Care) Act 2000, ss.1 and 2.

Whilst Children Act 1989, s.17 establishes the general duty to safeguard the welfare of a child in need, an unaccompanied child should be accommodated by the local authority under Children Act 1989, s.20.[28] Despite the Hillingdon judgment, this is now especially important as a failure to define a child as looked after (under s.20) will now exclude her from looked after services and subsequent leaving care duties following amendment to Children Act 1989, s.22 by Adoption and Children Act 2002, s.116 (with effect from 7 November 2002).

Complaints about inadequate service provision by local authority asylum services can be pursued under Children Act 1989, s.26 procedures and involve the independent reviewing officer. In urgent cases, High Court remedies may be more effective.

Refusal of leave and appeals

The Nationality, Immigration and Asylum Act (NIAA) 2002 sets out the current provisions regarding rights of appeal (see Part 5). A new and more limited appeals process under the Asylum and Immigration (Treatment of Claimants etc.) Act 2004 came into force in April 2005 when the first and second tiers of the appellate body[29] were merged and leave to appeal further highly restricted. The vast majority of immigration decisions attract a right of appeal (NIAA 2002, s.82) and in particular the refusal of an asylum claim (s.83). The excluded categories are currently set out in Part 5 of the NIAA 2002 but are too detailed for commentary here. Asylum and human rights claims from certain prescribed countries are now also subject to a non-suspensive appeal procedure which precludes an appeal until after removal from the UK (NIAA 2002, ss.92–94 and under Asylum and Immigration (Treatment of Claimants etc.) Act 2004, Sched. 3 Pts 1 – 6). Children's claims are also to be subject to the non-suspensive appeals process and this adversely affects the children from such countries by limiting discretionary leave to 12 months or shorter.[30]

A notice of decision and appeal forms together with a grant letter and/or reasons for refusal will be served on the client and their immigration representative.

The appeal forms *must* be completed within 10 working days of receipt and the grounds should address the reasons for refusal. Specialist advice is essential. Following a refusal, decision work on the notice and grounds of appeal will not be funded by the LSC under Legal Help. Instead, an application has to be made to the LSC for Controlled Legal Representation before continuing out of public funds. This is subject to a strict merits test.

Failure to appeal the refusal will prevent challenging the decision at a later stage.

A child should be carefully prepared for the hearing of her appeal at court by her representative and an appropriate adult, e.g. social worker or relative, including explaining the purpose of the hearing and what will happen, what is expected of her and the role of all the parties involved. If possible, a child should be taken to visit the court before the hearing by a responsible adult to allow her to familiarise herself.

Whilst not always possible, the child should meet the advocate representing her at court before the hearing. The child should always be accompanied by a responsible adult at the hearing.

A child can be required to give oral evidence but the adjudicator should consider whether cross-examination is permitted. This should be kept to a minimum and dealt with as much as possible on the written statements, submissions and evidence[31].

A child's appeal should not go ahead in the absence of a legal representative or an appropriate adult without the adjudicator carefully considering how to proceed, including adjourning to allow representation to be obtained or involving the Refugee Council children's panel[32].

Public funding and the Legal Services Commission

Public funding is available for asylum and immigration advice and assistance through the LSC Legal Help scheme and is subject to strict time thresholds, means and sufficient benefit tests. Appeals preparation and representation before the AIT is funded through the Controlled Legal Representation scheme subject to means and merits tests. However, a new retrospective funding arrangement for reviews by the AIT now requires an application to be made to the AIT for a funding order for the appellant's legal costs only after the review has been considered: see Asylum and Immigration Tribunal (Procedure) Rules 2005, SI 2005/230, r.33. Emergency and full public funding certificates are available for applications to the higher and appellate courts.

In April 2004 new contract conditions were issued for all LSC specialist help level immigration contract holders[33] removing devolved powers from many legal advisers. The new specification introduced restricted time and costs thresholds for the amount of preparation time at the initial advice and application stage and limiting advocacy time/costs at first appeal stage. Disbursement costs are subject to prior authority requests including to pay for expert reports, interpreters and counsel's fees.

Particularly for cases involving children, unless the prospects of success on appeal are poor, i.e. below borderline/unclear, the representative completing the merits test should justify continuing with funding to appeal on the basis that the case is of overwhelming importance to the client, i.e. it concerns the life, liberty or physical safety of the client or her family, or the roof over her head, or the case raises significant issues of human rights.[34]

All immigration practitioners, both solicitor or non-solicitor advisers, must hold an LSC contract at Specialist Help level to carry out publicly funded casework and also meet the criteria for case management and supervision set out in the Quality Mark guidance.

With effect from April 2005, all immigration practitioners must have passed the Law Society Accreditation Scheme to continue to offer immigration advice, though there will be phased implementation.[35]

Under the Immigration and Asylum Act 1999, all immigration advisers are regulated by the Office of the Immigration Services Commissioner (OISC). Solicitors are exempt as Law Society members but are still subject to OISC powers of investigation as well as their own professional complaints procedures.

It is a criminal offence to give immigration advice whilst not registered or exempted.

A list of specialist help level contract holders can be searched on the LSC website[35] and the Immigration Law Practitioners Association (ILPA) can provide a list of their own members on request.[37]

Education[38]

Asylum-seeking children are entitled to attend a state school until they are 16 and the local education authority should be requested to place a child in their local school as soon as they arrive.

Provided that she started before the age of 16,[39] a child can continue in school until 18, otherwise provision of a place is the decision of the head-teacher. Children aged 16 to 19 can study at sixth form or further education colleges but may be charged fees. If fees are charged then the local authority should be asked to cover these costs as part of its support responsibilities, including those owed to care leavers.

Fees for higher education courses are dependent on immigration status. A young person without status pending an asylum claim is not 'settled' and must therefore pay the overseas student rate unless the college operates special provisions for asylum seekers. They are ineligible for student support for help with fees or loans.

For further education courses an asylum-seeking child or young person may be treated as a home student and also eligible for remission or nil fee provisions.

If refugee status is recognised and ILR granted or if Exceptional Leave to Remain (ELR), HP or DL is granted, then colleges and universities must charge the home fees rate for courses.

Eligibility for student support grants and loans is amongst other criteria dependent upon meeting an 'ordinarily resident in the UK for three years' provision. For recognised refugees there is no requirement to show this, unlike persons granted ELR/HP and DL.

NOTES

1   House of Commons Cmd HC395 (as amended).
2   DP 4/95, 3/96, 4/96 and 069/99.
3   Immigration Directorate Instructions, ch. 8, Annex M, section 2, para. 7.1.
4   See Law Society information note 'Helping Your MP to Help Your Client' (2004), available from the Law Society Parliamentary Unit.
5   At para. 219. See also the UNHCR's *Refugee Children, Guidelines for Protection and Care*, HCR/IP/4/ENG (1979).
6   Immigration Rules, para. 349 (HC 395).
7   EU Council Directive 2003/9/EC of 27 January 2003: minimum standards for the reception of asylum seekers, preamble to para. 15, in force from 6 February 2005.

8   Jill Rutter, *Working with Refugee Children*, Joseph Rowntree Foundation (2003), p.41 (available at **www.jrf.org.uk**).

9   Letter from BMA to Association of Visitors to Immigration Detainees (AVID) of May 1998 as referenced at J. Coker, N. Finch and A. Stanley, *Putting Children First: A Guide for Immigration Practitioners*, LAG (2002), p.85.

10 Issues covered in detail in *The Health of Refugee Children: Guidelines for Paediatricians*, available on RCPCH website at **www.rcph.ac.uk. publications/past-publications/refugee.pdf**.

11 Immigration Rules, paras. 349–352 and also see 'Evidence' below for differences in assessment of adult and child claims.

12 IND, *Asylum Process Manual*, section 5, 'Processing Applications from Children', para. 13.3.2. See **www.ind.homeoffice.gov.uk** under Laws and Policy/Operational Processes.

13 See note 23 below.

14 Immigration Rules, para. 340, but even if late the Secretary of State for the Home Department still has a duty to consider the application substantively.

15 *Immigration Service Operational Enforcement Manual*, para. 38.7.

16 J. Coker, N. Finch and A. Stanley, *Putting Children First: A Guide for Immigration Practitioners*, LAG (2002), pp.147–59.

17 See **www.torturecare.org.uk/about/aboutReferring.htm**.

18 Immigration Rules, para. 350.

19 See M. Symes and P. Jorro, *Asylum Law and Practice*, Butterworths, p.462 with regard to Immigration Rules, para. 351 and UK Immigration Service, *Best Practice Guide* (30 June 2003).

20 *UNHCR Handbook on Procedures for Determining Refugee Status*, Geneva (1992), paras. 213–219.

21 Adjudicator Guidance Note No.8 (April 2004), s.5 'Assessment of Evidence', paras. 5.3 and 5.4.

22 See **www.crimereduction.gov.uk/toolkits/tp01.htm**.

23 ECPAT report, C. Somerset, *Cause for Concern* (March 2004) available at **www.antislavery.org/homepage/antislavery/Cause for Concern.pdf**.

24 IND Asylum Policy Unit Notice 01.2003, see **www.ind.homeoffice.gov.uk.**

25 NASS Policy Bulletin 29, issued 25 February 2004.

26 *Ibid.*, para. 5.3.

27 Social Services Inspectorate letter ref. CI (91)2 of 23 January 1991 updated 9 November 1999.

28 LAC (2002)13, *Guidance on Accommodating Children in Need.*

29 The IAA and IAT became the Asylum and Immigration Tribunal (AIT) under Asylum and Immigration (Treatment of Claimants etc.) Act 2004, s.26 on 4 April 2005.

30 IND, Application of Non Suspensive Appeal (NSA) Process to Asylum Seeking Children, APU Notice 5/2004 at **www.ind.homeoffice.gov.uk** under Laws and Policy/Policy Instructions/APIs.

31 Adjudicator Guidance Note No. 8, para. 4, now incorporated into Asylum and Immigration Tribunal Practice Directions, Annex C (available at **www.ait.gov.uk** under 'Practice Directions'.

32 *Ibid.*

33 See **www.legalservices.gov.uk/civil/how/asylum.asp** for funding criteria/ guidance.

34 See note above in particular guidance on criteria 13.4 and 13.5 of the Funding Code.

35   See **www.legalservices.gov.uk/civil/immigration/accreditation.asp**.
36   See **www.clsdirect.org.uk**.
37   At info@ilpa.org.uk.
38   For a more detailed overview of education and asylum see the Council for
     International   Education   (UKCOSA)   student   guidance   at
     www.ukcosa.org.uk/images/asylum.pdf.
39   Since February 2005, Article 10 of Council Directive 2003/9/EC of 27 January
     2003 laying down minimum standards for the reception of asylum seekers help-
     fully sets out minimum rights to education for child asylum seekers.

CHAPTER 18

Children in private law proceedings

Key sources

- Children Act 1989
- Family Law Act 1996
- Family Proceedings Rules 1991, rule 4.11 (as amended 2003–2005)
- Family Proceedings Courts (Children Act 1989) Rules 1991, rules 11 and 12
- *Family Law Protocol*, Law Society (2002)
- *Practice Direction* (Family Proceedings: Representation of Children) [2004] 1 FLR 1188
- President's Guidance (The private law programme) (9 November 2005)

18.1   INTRODUCTION

Private law proceedings in themselves are outside the scope of this book, but best practice will be greatly assisted by membership of one or both of the specialist panels established by the Law Society and the Solicitors Family Law Association (now known as Resolution).

All solicitors practising family law in England and Wales are expected to comply with the Law Society's Family Law Protocol: compliance will become a requirement of membership of the specialist family Panels.[1] The Family Law Protocol contains important emphasis upon mediation, family dispute resolution and the interests of children in the family.

Resolution's Codes of Practice are designed to achieve an approach that is 'sensitive, constructive, cost-effective and most likely to result in an agreement'. There is specific practice guidance in areas such as service, correspondence, disclosure, acting for children, working with the Bar, and cases with an international element. Resolution also provides courses on the psychology and dynamics of family law.

The law relating to divorce and separation is wide-ranging and complex. Private law affects a far greater proportion of children than public law,[2] but issues such as the exercise of parental responsibility, contact, residence and specific issues orders, abduction, domestic abuse, exclusion and ouster orders, can all have relevance to the conduct of public law cases, with direct or indirect impact.

The context in which private law disputes take place is fraught with difficulties, to which individuals will react very differently: 'any litigation is stressful but all family practitioners recognise that family disputes are the most stressful of all . . . . The breakdown of marriage or other partnership and the issues that have to be resolved in the heat of the emotional turmoil of the failed relationship require the most careful and sensitive handling' (President of the Family Division, introduction to the Family Law Protocol 2002).

Disputes over a child's upbringing may arise at any time, but are most likely when the parents' own relationship is breaking up. The polarisation of adult hostilities can lead to parents and other family members fighting over children as if they were items of property, with obvious consequences. Children have few, if any, direct rights in such situations and consideration of their interests often has little influence over parents' plans for the future.[3]

However, most disputes are also settled without recourse to court proceedings, with the help of family practitioners and other professionals, through conciliation and mediation processes, negotiated settlements or simply by agreement between the parties themselves. The vast majority of separating couples reach their own agreements, although there is little research on how they do this, what outcomes are achieved, or how child centred these arrangements are. New government proposals on relationship breakdown are likely to lead to further changes in the way in which such disputes are dealt with in and outside court (see Green Paper, *Parental Separation: Children's Needs and Parents' Responsibilities* (July 2004).

Only the court and the CAFCASS officer have statutory duties. So negotiations, settlements and arrangements may be conducted and/or achieved without proper reference to children's wishes, feelings or interests, exclude them entirely, or mask situations of abuse.[4]

The status of children in these proceedings continues to be the subject of debate: they are not always sufficiently seen or heard by the use of the Children and Family Reporter (CFR) and human rights 'may require an increased use of guardians' (Court of Appeal in *Re A (Contact: Separate Representation)* [2001] 1 FLR 715). Representation under Family Proceedings Rules 1991, rule 9.5 has increased, but growing numbers may have both legal and welfare representation from 2006 (Adoption and Children Act 2002, s.122(1) amends Children Act 1989, s.41 to permit applications for s.8 orders to be added to the list of specified proceedings by Rules of Court). This requires knowledge of a growing number of protocols and practice notes and an understanding of the issues that arise.

18.2 PRINCIPLES

Children in England and Wales have no legal right to be consulted over the arrangements to be made for their future (contrast the requirement in

Children (Scotland) Act 1995, s.6(1)). Often they are not adequately prepared for separation or given proper explanations and have no one to turn to for independent advice. All children should have access to such advice,[5] and there are some children caught up in extremely acrimonious circumstances who need separate representation.

Clients should be told of the child's right to apply to be joined as a party to the proceedings in the event that the CAFCASS CFR is unable or declines to represent the child's wishes in a way the child deems appropriate.[6]

In the fraught circumstances of relationship breakdown, it is important for all practitioners to emphasise the principles of the child's welfare being paramount, the avoidance of delay and findings in European Court case law (*Yousef* v. *The Netherlands* [2003] 1 FLR 210 and see Chapter 1).

18.3   PRIVATE LAW AND PARAMOUNTCY

When dealing with questions about a child's upbringing, her welfare is the court's paramount consideration (Children Act 1989, s.1(1)). When acting for parents, practitioners must be prepared to advise their clients accordingly, pointing out this overrides the wishes of the parents, children or both. Practitioners should dissuade clients from making/opposing applications where motivated by contrary intentions, such as seeking contact or residence in order to 'teach the other party a lesson' or from a perception that this would improve financial claims.

They should encourage clients to consider what, when and how they intend to tell their children about a parental separation, and encourage them to consider doing so with the other parent, giving them details of mediation or counselling.

They should discuss with unmarried parents legal arrangements for parental responsibility and arrangements on death, and discuss parenting plans.

Practitioners should be sensitive to suggestions from clients that a child is showing any signs of serious emotional disturbance, with referrals to other agencies where appropriate. Wherever possible in cases concerning allegations of child abuse, whether physical, sexual or emotional, they should encourage clients to inform the appropriate authority.

When appropriate, practitioners should tell clients there are exceptional circumstances involving children where a practitioner may reveal confidential information to an appropriate authority,[7] including abuse, or may disclose the whereabouts of a child who is the subject of a seek and find order: the rules of client confidentiality are overridden by the need to protect the child's welfare.

18.4   INVOLVEMENT OF CHILDREN IN PROCEEDINGS

It is not the usual practice in private law family proceedings for children to give evidence (*Re M (Family Proceedings: Affidavits*) [1995] 2 FLR 100) and the general view has been that, except by direction of the court, children should not attend any hearing.[8] The President's 2005 Private Law Programme sets out a model scheme for in-court dispute resolution, requiring an early first hearing dispute resolution appointment attended by the parents, a CAFCASS officer and children aged nine or over, who will not be represented, but will have an opportunity to talk to the CAFCASS officer on their own.

Consistent application of the overriding principles of the Children Act 1989 and better outcomes require much greater consideration of the child's perspective and critical and creative thought about the challenges involved in ensuring children's voices are facilitated, heard and listened to.

Competence of the child

Unlike public law, the child is not automatically either a party to the proceedings or represented. But in the county court and the High Court (but not the Family Proceedings Court), a child may apply to be made a party to the proceedings and be represented, apply to act with a solicitor alone, without a guardian ad litem (*Re N (Residence Order: Procedural Mismanagement)* [2001] 1 FLR 1028) or commence proceedings. Where representation is thought appropriate, for practical reasons the child should be joined as a party (*L* v. *L (Minors) (Separate Representation)* [1994] 1 FLR 156).

Where a child wishes to start proceedings, or be a party to them, without a next friend or guardian, the court must give leave, but on the basis that she is able to give instructions.

She may instruct a solicitor to commence proceedings or represent her if that solicitor considers she is able, having regard to her understanding, to give instructions in relation to the proceedings; and has accepted instructions to act for her (Family Proceedings Rules 1991, SI 1991/1247, rule 9.2A(1)(b)).

The decision as to competency to give instructions is not exclusively a matter for that solicitor: the court has the ultimate right to decide whether the child has the necessary capacity (Court of Appeal in *Re CT (A Minor) (Wardship: Representation)* [1993] 3 WLR 602, [1993] 2 FLR 278). If an investigation is considered necessary before a decision can be made, it should be a swift pragmatic enquiry involving minimum delay and least distress to the child. Where the court decides that she lacks such competence, it can in any event appoint a next friend or guardian ad litem (under Family Proceedings Rules 1991, rule 9.5 and see the Court of Appeal in *Re S (A Minor) (Independent Representation)* [1994] 1 FLR 96). There would be no objection in principle to the solicitor continuing to act.

The child's ability to take advantage of rule 9.2A to instruct a solicitor may be curtailed by the court if it does not regard it as appropriate for the child to be a party. The court will consider (*Re H (Residence Order: Child's Application for Leave*) [2000] 1 FLR 780):

- determination of competency;
- whether there are conflicting statements;
- whether there is any advantage in the child being legally represented: the child's wishes will be considered but are not determinative;
- disadvantage in the child seeing all the evidence.

The essential question for testing competence has been described as 'not whether the child was capable of articulating instructions, but whether the child was of sufficient understanding to participate as a party in the sense of being able to cope with all the ramifications of the proceedings and giving considered instructions of sufficient objectivity', the court having regard to the nature of the proceedings, their length to date and likely future conduct, and the likely applications needed (High Court in *Re N (Contact: Minor Seeking Leave to Defend and Removal of Guardian*) [2003] 1 FLR 652).

There is a growing acknowledgement of the autonomy and consequential rights of children and young people, however, and it has been accepted by the Court of Appeal that courts must, in the case of articulate adolescents, accept that the rights to freedom of expression and participation in family life outweigh the paternalistic judgment of welfare (*Mabon* v. *Mabon and Others* [2005] EWCA Civ 634; [2005] 2 FCR 354.

Joinder of the child as a party

Practice Direction (Family Proceedings: Representation of Children) [2004] 1 FLR 1188 confirms that the child should only be made a party in the minority of cases where there is an issue of 'significant difficulty', e.g. where:

- a CAFCASS officer notifies the court of his opinion the child should be made a party;
- the child has a standpoint or interest inconsistent with or incapable of being represented by any of the adult parties;
- contact has ceased or there is implacable hostility and the child is suffering harm;
- the child's views and wishes cannot adequately be met by court report;
- an older child is opposing a proposed course of action;
- there are international complications (outside child abduction) and possibly discussions with overseas authorities or a foreign court;
- the proceedings concern more than one child and the welfare of children in conflict or one child's position is particularly disadvantaged;
- there is a contested issue about blood testing.

The direction also encourages the court to consider alternative ways of progressing the case, e.g. requesting a CAFCASS officer to do further work, making a referral to social services or obtaining expert evidence.

From 1 April 2005, such appointments will normally only be made by a Circuit Judge (unless exceptional circumstances require it to be made by a District Judge), who must consider whether to retain the case.[10]

Who should represent the child?

Practice Direction (CAFCASS: Representation of Children in Family Proceedings) [2004] 1 FLR 1190 deals with the procedure to be adopted if the court takes the view that a child ought to be separately represented and appoints a CAFCASS officer. An existing CFR should continue as guardian. High Court cases will be handled by CAFCASS Legal; in the county court, a local CAFCASS officer will be allocated and will appoint a local solicitor.

Family Proceedings Rules 1991, rule 9.5 leaves it open to the court to appoint 'some other proper person' to be the guardian ad litem (if he consents), possibly a Children Panel solicitor (*Re K (Replacement of Guardian Ad Litem)* [2001] 1 FLR 663) or the National Youth Advocacy Service (under rule 9.5(1)). Such a guardian may be appointed in non-specified proceedings in the county court/High Court, but not in the Family Proceedings Court (FPCt) (see *Essex CC* v. *B* [1993] 1 FLR 866 at 872). This leaves open the possibility that a child can be joined as a party in the FPCt, and instruct her solicitor, who may choose to obtain welfare advice through the use of an expert witness (whether social worker or other expert).

18.5   CONTACT DISPUTES

Mothers and fathers have equal rights before the court, and though in practice the majority of children remain with their mother after separation, the importance of the child's relationship with the absent parent is recognised by the court (as the President stressed in *Re S (Contact: Promoting Relationship with Absent Parent)* [2004] EWCA Civ 18). But proportionality is important: the length to which a court should go to enforce contact on an unwilling child and on an apprehensive carer has to be weighed in the balance: there is 'a limit beyond which the court should not strive to promote contact ... the overriding obligation [is] to put the welfare of the child at the forefront and above the rights of either parent'.

Four judgments given in 2004 highlighted the issues in contact disputes, especially the complex and protracted cases heard (*Re D (Intractable Contact Dispute: Publicity)* [2004] 1 FLR 1226; *Re S (Contact: Promoting Relationship with Absent Parent)* [2002] EWCA Civ 18, [2004] 1 FLR 1279; *Re O (Contact: Withdrawal of Application)* [2003] EWHC Fam 3031; *V* v. *V*

(Contact: Implacable Hostility), *The Times* 28 May 2004, per Bracewell J). The strength of feelings engendered and sometimes their intractable nature makes these amongst the most difficult and sensitive cases. Courts are not anti-father and pro-mother, but rather children of separated parents are entitled to the love and society of both of their parents. The court system presents serious faults in the slowness of procedures, the detrimental delays and the counter-productive adversarial nature of the litigation. Joint residence orders are not the answer – they are not a panacea.

Intractable disputes could be partly remedied by, e.g. judicial continuity, case management, timetabling and pro-active orders, with early effective intervention by officers of CAFCASS. Nonetheless, legislation is needed giving the judiciary powers to:

- enforce orders for contact through referral to mediation or a psychiatrist at any stage;
- place a parent on probation with a condition of treatment;
- impose community service orders;
- award financial compensation.

Arguably, it can no longer be complacently assumed that the conventional approach to such cases 'meets the standards required by Articles 6 and 8' (Munby J in *Re D (Intractable Contact Dispute: Publicity)* [2004] 1 FLR 1226). Therefore, the simplest cases should be 'fast tracked', using lay justices and district judges, and the timetable measured in weeks not months. The more serious and complex cases should be allocated to the multi-track, and the overall timetable measured in months not years. Principles comparable to those in the public law protocol should be applied to all but the most straightforward cases.

A consistent judicial approach is needed in relation to:

- separate representation of children;
- independent social workers, who can remain with children long enough to form a long-term relationship;
- experts and other outside agencies, who can help facilitate contact rather than writing reports;
- allegations of misconduct, which should be speedily investigated and resolved;
- timetabling, which needs a clear and hard-headed approach.

The Draft Children (Contact) and Adoption Bill published in February 2005 proposes provision of a wider range of court powers, including;

- directions to the parties to attend information meetings, meetings with a counsellor, or parenting programmes/classes and other activities designed to deal with contact disputes (defined as 'contact activities' in Children Act 1989, s.11E);

- power to attach conditions to contact orders which may require attendance at such a meeting, class or programme (contact activity conditions, s.11B);
- where a contact order has been breached, power to impose 'enforcement orders' for unpaid work or curfew, and to award financial compensation from one parent to another (e.g. where the cost of a holiday has been lost).

18.6   CONTACT IN DOMESTIC ABUSE CASES

In its judgement given in four cases heard in 2000 (Court of Appeal in *Re L; Re V; Re M; Re H (Contact: Domestic Violence)* [2000] 2 FLR 334), the Court of Appeal issued guidance about how contact decisions in cases involving domestic abuse should be decided.[11]

Family courts need heightened awareness of the existence and consequences on children of exposure to interparental violence. Allegations of violence made in the course of applications must be adjudicated upon and determined before a final order.

Proven domestic violence is not of itself a bar to contact, but one factor in a complex equation (*Re H (Contact: Domestic Violence)* [1998] 2 FLR 42). Important considerations in assessing the impact of past violence are the ability of the violent party to recognise past conduct, to be aware of the need to change, and to make genuine effort to do so.

When making an interim order, before adjudication on factual allegations, the court should ensure the safety of the child and residential parent are secured before and after any contact. Every application must be determined in accordance with the paramountcy principle (Children Act 1989, s.1).

Other principles established through case law are that past domestic violence can provide a necessary cogent reason for refusing contact (*Re A (Contact: Domestic Violence)* [1998] 2 FLR 171). The weight to be attached to past domestic violence should not be minimised by the court (*Re M (Contact: Violent Parent)* [1999 2 FLR 321). Where the effect of past domestic violence on a mother would in turn harm the child if contact occurred, indirect contact only may be ordered (*Re K Contact: Mother's Anxiety)* [1999] 2 FLR 703).

18.7   PARTICULAR ISSUES

Implacable hostility or parental alienation syndrome

Parental alienation syndrome (PAS) is 'a condition through which one parent will, by any means available, inappropriately seek to subvert other parent's power and consequent ability to care for, or even to continue to have any relationship with, their child . . . at immense cost to the child'.[12] PAS is now recognised by UK courts (Court of Appeal in *Re C (Prohibition on Further Applications)* [2002] EWCA Civ 292; *White v. White* [2001] SLT 485).

A denial of direct contact can be justified where a child has a genuine fear of the father, and it is found that the consequent distress to the mother of contact taking place would transfer to the child (see, e.g *Re H (Contact Order) (No. 2)* [2002] 1 FLR 22). The court draws a distinction between an implacably hostile mother and cases where the mother's unwillingness is regarded as well-founded and in the best interests of the child (*Re D (Contact: Reasons for Refusal)* [1997] 2 FLR 48 and *Re K (Contact: Mother's Anxiety)* [1999] 2 FLR 703).[13]

Children should be separately represented where all contact has ceased and the issue of contact has become intractable (*Re M (Intractable Contact Dispute: Interim Care Order)* [2003] EWHC Fam. 1024, [2003] 2 FLR 636).

Indirect contact orders

Indirect contact orders (contact, e.g. via letters), may be appropriate to re-establish some contact after a lengthy non-contact period, perhaps where there has been past violence (*Re S (Violent Parent: Indirect Contact)* [2000] 1 FLR 481 and *Re P (Contact: Indirect Contact)* [1999] 2 FLR 893).

If it is not possible to access an appropriate contact service then the issue of face-to-face contact should be carefully reviewed. Other forms of contact might be suggested such as telephone calls, audio/videotapes and cards.

Use of section 91(14) orders

Where repeated applications, or the fear of them, cause the custodial parent distress, they can be prohibited for a period of time (*Re M and B (Children) (Contact: Domestic Violence)* [2001] 1 FCR 116). However, such an order represents a substantial interference with a citizen's right of access to the courts and it must be shown to be an exceptional case before it will be made (*Re C (Contact)* [2000] 2 FLR 723). The court must apply the paramountcy principle (*Re P (A Minor) (Residence Order: Child's Welfare)* [2000] Fam. 15).

Historically, they have been used where there has been a range of frequent, vexatious or frivolous applications and where the child would suffer if this were allowed to continue. However, an order was made for two years where the father had never abused the family justice system, had never attempted to disturb the mother's primary care, and had always used the intervention of the court in a responsible manner (*Re B (Section 91(14) Order: Duration)* [2003] EWCA Civ 1966).

Gradually increasing contact

The courts have attempted to overcome resistance by a programme of gradually extended contact, building up from indirect contact. Sometimes it is regarded as necessary to involve a CAFCASS CFR, where the custodial parent is not sufficiently to be trusted, e.g. to read out correspondence from the absent parent (*Re S (Violent Parent: Indirect Contact)* [2000] 1 FLR 481).

Use of child contact centres

Child contact centres are a valuable, but limited, resource for which there is a set of national standards and a judicially endorsed Protocol for Referrals.

The majority provide *supported* contact which can facilitate, where appropriate, handover of a child via a third party, avoiding face-to-face parental contact, or contact in the centre itself.

Practitioners should explain to clients the difference between supported and supervised contact beforehand, make it clear on referral forms if other family members can be present and discuss with the resident parent the need to prepare the child for the visit. They should encourage clients to visit the centre beforehand.

Their use should be considered where violence is an issue. Especially in cases involving criminal proceedings or injunctions, initially *supervised* contact will generally be necessary. A small number of centres undertake high vigilance supervision – the National Association of Child Contact Centres have details (see Appendix 2).

The centre coordinator must be given the full background (orally, if necessary) about details of violent or abusive behaviour. Centres are not equipped to deal with abusers who pose a serious threat and must be allowed to decide whether or not the centre can accommodate the family. Referral forms must be completed as fully and accurately as possible: if clients refuse to consent to revealing the information required, a referral should not be made.

Centres must be warned if there is a fear of, or threats of, abduction, although none can give guarantees a child will not be removed. Practitioners should consider the resident parent giving the centre recent photographs of the children and of the contact parent and retaining the passports of parents having contact and/or those of the children if there is a possibility of abduction abroad.

Clients should be advised to inform centres when they are no longer needed – they are regarded by the court only as a temporary solution. Generally, volunteers and staff do not provide reports or statements for any type of court proceedings unless a child is believed to be at risk of harm.

See LSC *Focus* 48 for position on funding for supervised contact.

The local authority

The local authority should not be joined as a party to private law proceedings (*F* v. *Cambridgeshire CC* [1995] 1 FLR 516; *Re K (Contact: Psychiatric Report)* [1995] 2 FLR 432) but may be ordered to provide a report or conduct an investigation, or required to give evidence, attend court and produce documents (RSC Order 38, rule 13 (High Court) or CCR Order 20, rule 12 (county court) and see *Re A and B (Minors) (No. 2)* [1995] 1 FLR 351 at 364). The local authority should normally make the author of a Children Act 1989, s.7 report available to give evidence at any important hearing where oral evidence is required.

NOTES

1　Law Society Family Law Panel; Resolution Specialist Accreditation Panel.
2　108,000 s.8 orders were made in 2002 compared to 6,300 care orders and 1,500 supervision orders: *Judicial Statistics* DCA (2002).
3　See, e.g,. J. Flowerdew and B. Neale, *Looking Back at our Parents' Divorce*, University of Leeds, Young Voice (2004).
4　For further discussion and research references, see Part 2 of J. Fortin, *Children's Rights and the Developing Law*, Butterworths (2003).
5　See Green Paper, *Parental Separation* (2004).
6　*Family Law Protocol*, Law Society (2002).
7　Law Society, *The Guide to the Professional Conduct of Solicitors 1999*, Principle 16.02 (note 4).
8　The Children Act Advisory Committee, *Handbook of Best Practice in Children Act Cases*, CAAC (1997), para. 58, and see *Practical Steps to Co-Parenting*, Resolution (2004).
9　For further consideration, see Justice Thorpe and Justine Cadbury, *Hearing the Children*, Jordans (2004).
10　Guidance from the President's Office, 25 February 2005.
11　See C. Sturge and D. Glaser, 'Contact and Domestic Violence, Experts' Court Report' [2000] Fam Law 615, and Report to the Lord Chancellor by the Advisory Board on Family Law, *Children Act Sub-Committee on the question of parental contact in cases where there is domestic violence* (April 2000).
12　T. Hobbs, 'Parental Alienation Syndrome and the UK Family Courts' [2002] Fam Law 182.
13　C. Humphreys, 'Judicial Alienation Syndrome, Failures to Respond to Post Separation Violence' [1999] Fam Law 313; T. Hobbs, 'Parental Alienation Syndrome and UK Family Courts' [2002] Fam Law 182.

CHAPTER 19

Acting for the child or young person

Key sources

- Family Proceedings Rules 1991, rule 4.11 and Family Proceedings (Magistrates' Courts) Rules, rules 11 and 12
- Review of Children's Cases (Amendment) (England) Regulations 2004 and Review of Children's Cases (Amendment) (Wales) Regulations 2004
- *The Guide to the Professional Conduct of Solicitors 1999,* Law Society
- National Standards for the Provision of Advocacy Services 2002, DH
- *Guide to Good Practice for Solicitors Acting for Children*, Resolution (2002)
- Law Society Guidance on Acting in the absence of a Children's Guardian (2003)
- LAC (2004)11

We don't want you to be: disrespectful, ignorant, insensitive, judgmental, lazy, patronising or prejudiced. We also don't want you to be: unbelieving, uncaring, uninterested or to always put winning before the client. In short, we believe that lawyers sometimes act like children, and think young people from the care system are different from their own or other people's children . . .

We want you to listen to us, not put words into our mouths, let us do the talking. Be prepared to talk to us at our level, ask what will make us comfortable, show us that you care and be on our side, not on the side of the system. Be interested in us, speak up and speak out about the many injustices there are (especially when it comes to children) in the judicial system.[1]

19.1 INTRODUCTION

Practitioners will differ in their personal views and experiences of children, and may decide that the task of representing some of the most vulnerable members of society is not for them. It should be noted that just because a practitioner is also a parent does not necessarily make her suitable to work with children: indeed, some choose not to do so precisely because they are unable to maintain the right emotional distance. The decision not to act should not be criticised: the task of representing children and young people, and the standards of good practice required, present particular challenges, not least of which is the extent to which children and young people can, and should, be involved in the decisions which affect their lives.

There are a range of views and attitudes towards representation, from those who seek to protect children from the consequences of adult decisions wherever possible and would regard their welfare as taking precedence over their rights, through to those who actively seek to promote the child's right to be heard and to participate in decision-making. The extent to which a child participates in the process of child protection and family proceedings, and the manner in which she is able, or enabled, to do so, depends on a variety of considerations. The child's age and understanding, cognitive development, cultural and ethnic background, personality, physical and mental character-istics, and personal preference must all be taken into account. What is essen-tial is that the most appropriate balance is found between enabling a child to be involved, whilst at the same time protecting her from exposure to stresses and conflicts that are inconsistent with her health, welfare and safety.

19.2 PRINCIPLES

The following are directly relevant to standards of representation.

The UN Convention on the Rights of the Child (UNCRC) entitles chil-dren to laws and measures that protect them from all forms of harm and ensure they develop to their full potential. In particular, Article 12 states 'State parties should assure to the child who is capable of forming his or her own views the right to express those views freely in all matters affecting the child, the views of the child being given due weight in accordance with the age and maturity of the child'.

The Human Rights Act (HRA) 1998. came into force on 2 October 2000 and the expectation is that this 'encourages a human rights culture and this will have important benefits for all issues concerning children ... [and] will assist the general direction of children's participation and children's rights'.[2]

The Challenge of Partnership in Child Protection (1995) sets out principles for supporting, involving and empowering the child in child protection work:

Deciding upon the level and nature of their involvement and participation ... provides one of the most demanding challenges for professionals. Decisions have to be made about each individual in relation to his or her own needs and abilities, and each child's wish to be involved in decision-making ... work of this nature needs careful preparation and planning by all those undertaking it ... Applied in practice, the [key] principles [in the Children Act 1989] represent a significant opportunity for professionals to involve children in decisions which affect their lives. The involvement of children as contributors in the child protection process which is primarily concerned with communication between adults and in which there is a diverse range of players, many of whom have different and conflicting objectives, raises particularly complex issues.[3]

Working Together to Safeguard Children[4] makes clear from the outset that all children deserve the opportunity to achieve their full potential.

Children Act 1989 s.22(5)(a) provides that 'Before making any decision with respect to a child . . . a local authority shall, so far as is reasonably practicable, ascertain the wishes and feelings of the child'.

The Children Act 2004 amends the Children Act 1989 to provide that the child's wishes and feelings must be ascertained and given due consideration by the local authority in the provision of services (Children Act 1989, s.17A(4)) and in child protection investigations (s.47A(5)).

There is an increasing awareness that children and young people have views about issues affecting them and are entitled to have them heard.[5] Looked after children now have access to an independent reviewing officer and entitlement to advocacy services (under Adoption and Children Act 2002, ss.118, 119 and see Chapter 11).

In the majority of care cases, the child's welfare will be represented by the children's guardian, working with the child's solicitor. A good working relationship is crucial, most importantly for the child, but also in the interests of progressing the case towards the best outcome for her (see Chapter 20). Neither has a monopoly of knowledge nor understanding about how a child should be represented. The tandem model of representation requires a sharing of information, appreciation of each other's role and respect for each other's views.

Both under domestic legislation and the ECHR, if the rights of a parent and child conflict, then domestic law requires the conflict to be resolved by reference to the child's best interests (*Yousef* v. *The Netherlands* (Application No. 33711/96 [2003] 1 FLR 210, and see Chapter 1). But there may be a breach of the child's right under Article 8 if a parent is compelled to represent herself during care and subsequent freeing proceedings (*Re P, C and S* v. *UK* (2002) 35 EHRR 31).

19.3 INITIAL INSTRUCTION

A practitioner may be instructed to act for a child who is the subject of the proceedings by a children's guardian, the court or the child. Different provisions apply to public law and private law proceedings.

Family Proceedings Rules 1991, rule 4.12

This requires the appointed solicitor (under s.41(3) or in accordance with rule 4.11A(1)(a), (2)) to represent the child in accordance with instructions received from the guardian, *unless* the solicitor considers, having taken into account the views of the guardian and any direction of the court (under rule 4.11A(3)) that the child wishes to give instructions which conflict with those of the guardian and that she is able, having regard to her understanding, to give such instructions on her own behalf, in which case he must conduct the proceedings in accordance with the child's instructions.

Where no guardian has been appointed for the child and the condition in s.41(4)(b) is satisfied, the appointed solicitor must represent the child in accordance with the child's instructions, or in default of such instructions, in furtherance of the best interests of the child.

The appointed solicitor must serve and accept service of documents on behalf of the child (in accordance with rule 4.8(3)(a) and (4)(a)) and, where the child has not been served and has sufficient understanding, advise her of the contents of any such document.

A child can apply to the court for an order terminating the appointment of her appointed solicitor, who must be given, as must the guardian, an opportunity to make representations. The court must give written reasons for terminating the appointment.

19.4   KEY FACTORS IN THE CLIENT RELATIONSHIP

The child is your client and should always be afforded the same respect as an adult client. The central task for the child's lawyer is to ensure that the child participates in the proceedings to the fullest extent that she is able, by providing information, consultation, attending meetings and ensuring that the child receives a record of decisions.

The child's age and understanding will determine the extent to which her participation can be ensured.

The relationship between children and young people and their legal representatives is quite separate from other relationships they may have with adults, including their relationship with the guardian. Acting for a child involves a high degree of personal commitment, expertise, knowledge and training, which is reflected in the requirement to sign, and abide by, the Children Panel undertaking.

You should not work in isolation in this area of law, whatever your level of experience and expertise. Seek the advice of the guardian or other appropriate person whenever you require it, and ensure that you have someone you trust to whom you can turn when you are in professional difficulties.

The relationship with your child client and the way in which you carry out any instructions from the child must be characterised by a particular regard to her need to maintain continuing relationships. Crucially, remember that you are not dealing with the child client in isolation from her family: regardless of the possible outcome of the case, you must ensure you personally try to avoid any adverse effects on any of the child's relationships with family or professionals likely to remain involved with the child. Even if children are separated from their birth families, they need to retain whatever positive links and memories they can, however tenuous, in maintaining their sense of identity. Your work will end with the case; their relationships with others will continue.

The solicitor is the independent voice of the child or young person and should ensure that wherever possible their views and wishes are listened to and recorded in all decision-making that affects them.

The quality of the relationship with a child is likely to have an impact on what the child tells you. Usually children need to trust the adult they are talking to before they will communicate relevant personal information and such trust can take time to develop. Many children involved in family proceedings will have been badly let down by adults. The following are some of the key ingredients in developing a trusting and effective relationship.

First of all, *being focused on the child*.

Honesty: telling the truth and providing information. Basic information is particularly important. Even though decisions may be made for a child, proposed decisions should be checked out with the children themselves to ascertain their views.

Genuineness, warmth and empathy: research shows these are the key ingredients in helping relationships,[6] and the same is true of advocating for children. Empathy requires finding out how a child feels about an issue rather than assuming it. 'All I ever got was a pat on the head. Nobody ever spoke to me about it – and I'm not one to go to somebody and talk about it. Professionals need to emphasise they're willing to listen and try to understand. If they're willing to listen, I'm willing to tell.'[7]

Sensitivity to, and respect for, the child: ensure you have sufficient time to see and speak to the child and that she can tell you things, or give you instructions, in a relaxed and unhurried manner. This is important not only in personal interviews but also at court hearings. Be on time and do not make promises you cannot keep: many children are adept at spotting 'bullshit and false promises'.[8] Develop and cultivate an approach that is age appropriate but neither patronising, controlling nor overly familiar.

Knowledge, skills and resources: the process of representing children properly is a never-ending exercise in learning. You should have a basic knowledge of child development (see Chapter 3) and an understanding of how children function, particularly when distressed. In facilitating effective communication, you should know, e.g. where to access appropriate services for children with different intellectual abilities, language or special needs.

Professional objectivity: cases involving children give rise to some difficult emotions to deal with, but it is important that you retain a professional and objective relationship with your child client. Do not allow your own emotional response to the child or to any issue in the case to interfere with your relationship with the child: vulnerable children and young people need you to be level-headed and clear. Recognise the extent and the limitations of your professional duty towards her and how your relationship differs from those with the other professionals involved (see Chapters 18, 20, 22).

Getting the balance right: there is a risk the solicitor will take over the litigation. Employ extra awareness and sensitivity in conducting a case: a child may wish to please, or be pressured into agreement that she may later regret. Have regard to the child's pace and allow the child to change course, participate in the process when they feel capable of so doing, or ultimately to withdraw from the process: 'the most effective ways of involving children can only be discovered when each individual child's needs, wishes and feelings are identified and then analysed . . . with the child as partner'.[9]

Gender, sexuality, and age: resources do not always allow a suitable matching of a solicitor to a child, but you should be aware that your personal characteristics may well, on occasion, render you unsuitable to represent a child client, or to see them on your own. You should consider whether your gender or age or sexual orientation give rise to factors that might affect how and where you see and interview children or whether you continue to act for them, e.g.

- caution is needed in cases involving sexual abuse: a male solicitor will not always be the most appropriate person to represent an abused female and, should, in any event, ensure that interviews are conducted in such a way and in such locations that he does not invite criticism;
- it will rarely, if ever, be appropriate for a male solicitor to represent a female Muslim, or for a female to do so on behalf of a male Muslim.

If there are factors that affect, or prevent, representation, you should seek professional advice and, if necessary, withdraw from the case in favour of a more suitable alternative solicitor.

Race, culture and religion: a solicitor must be sensitive to issues of race, culture and religion in the conduct of a case, and particularly so where she is not from the same background as the child client or their family. To make sensitive and informed professional judgments, you must be aware of, and sensitive to, differing family patterns and lifestyles, varying child-rearing patterns in different racial, ethnic and cultural groups, and of the broader social factors that serve to discriminate against black and minority ethnic people.

Commitment to equality and anti-oppressive practice is essential, as is an understanding of the effects of racial harassment, racial discrimination and institutional racism, as well as cultural misunderstanding or misinterpretation. Be aware that, e.g. in some cultures the idea of a child having rights separate from their family is not readily comprehensible, and the concept of a child having a lawyer to represent them would pose a challenge to the family's thinking. For some cultures, lawyers represent authority figures that are neither welcome nor trusted.

Sensitivity to religious practices is also required in the arranging of appointments and in communication with children and young people.

The shortage of sufficient research and statistical information in family proceedings on diversity does not help the average white European practitioner, but some evidence suggests cases involving black and ethnic minority children are perceived as, or actually treated as, more complex and challenging,[10] and cases concerning black children and children of mixed parentage are significantly more likely to be transferred to the High Court.

To what extent racism may have been a contributory factor in what happened to Victoria Climbie is 'a centrally important question ... the Inquiry [found] ... staff making assumptions that because people originated from a particular culture that behaviour could be described as being culturally determined, when in fact they knew nothing about that culture and had never visited the country: for example the way in which Victoria "jumped to attention" when Kouao was present was assumed by some to be a reflection of her upbringing on the Ivory Coast. In fact, the reality was quite different.'[11]

The lack of cases in which diverse cultural contexts are central to the issues in dispute is of concern because it might indicate acquiescence in the face of a lack of culturally informed evidence. Recent research[12] found substantive treatment of issues of diversity was less well documented at almost all stages of the proceedings: 'the court has no independent way of knowing if it has been considered or disregarded as irrelevant unless this appears in statements and reports'. For example, emotional abuse may have considerable cultural overtones and thus may be differently experienced by a child from a diverse cultural and ethnic group.

19.5 SEEING THE CHILD

You should always see the child for whom you are acting unless there is a very exceptional reason: do not assume that you do not have to do so just because they are very young, have a disability, or the guardian tells you there is no need to. You have an independent professional responsibility to ensure that the child receives appropriate legal advice and support where necessary, and is able to give you instructions if able to do so. Even where the child is too young or has such a profound disability that they cannot understand or take part in the process, it is important to realise that 'Once seen, the child will remain "live" as an individual client ... throughout the proceedings'.[13] 'In all cases the solicitor should see the child for whom s/he is acting and the solicitor should discuss with the guardian ... when and how it would be appropriate to see the child. This reinforces the point made in the Report of the Inquiry into Child Abuse in Cleveland 1987 that "the child is a person, not an object of concern"'.[14]

Young children and babies are affected significantly by their environment and research by child psychologists suggests that even the very young and babies are able to express some kind of feelings or basic desires that could be of significant relevance to the court.

This does not mean that you should act totally independently of the guardian, whose advice will be invaluable in planning when and how to see the child, and in providing any professional help and support in any problems of communication or perception. If the child is pre-verbal, it may be appropriate for the solicitor's first visit to take place with the children's guardian.

Consider carefully the timing and conduct of your first visit, including the most appropriate setting and style for meeting the child. Try to find out as much in advance as possible about the child's habits, likes and dislikes: the guardian may have already been able to establish much of this information from the carer. Where no guardian has yet been appointed, you should try and do this yourself from whatever sources may be helpful and readily accessible within the time constraints: e.g., ask for relevant information from a child's teacher or carer, taking the opportunity to do so when you make the initial telephone call to say that you intend visiting the child.

Your chance of making a good impression, or being able to communicate successfully with the child, is likely to be somewhat undermined if, e.g. you arrive in the middle of the child's favourite television programme. Ideally, the more information you acquire about a child's habits and history the better you can build a good relationship with them and represent them effectively.

It is important to decide where meetings should take place, and to take into consideration the child's age and background; some children do not want to be seen in particular settings such as their school, others will welcome the opportunity to do so, seeing such places as a neutral venue. Others may associate particular places with good, or bad, experiences: going to McDonalds or to a local park may not always be ideal if the child is used to having contact with a non-resident parent there, or may be associated with events that prevent the child from communicating with you properly. If the child is living in accommodation that means the only private place is in her bedroom, think carefully before suggesting that you talk there. Invasion of her private space may bring back difficult memories; there are also issues of personal safety for the solicitor to consider.

A child's age and familiarity with meeting professionals is an important factor in how to approach a first meeting. Depending on the age, experience and interests of the child, you may find it helpful to take a bag of toys, drawing pens and paper, books or material relevant to the child's interests as useful tools to break the ice.

You must, however, exercise caution: do not run the risk of overinterpreting a child's play and if you have any concerns about their behaviour or their play, be mindful of the Law Society's guidance on confidentiality.

There are a limited number of cases where it may be suggested that you should not see the child:

- where she does not want to see you, but take care to ensure that this is her own view;
- where you are advised that it may damage the child, e.g. on an application to discharge an order where the child is in a therapeutic residential unit, and where the professional advice is that visiting to discuss the application could be damaging to the child;
- where the guardian indicates that you should not see the child, but you should very rarely accept this unless one of the factors above applies.

If this situation arises, it would be advisable to notify the court, and seek the judge's guidance.

19.6   COMMUNICATION

Good, effective communication with children is a skill that requires awareness, understanding and regular practice, not attributes that all solicitors necessarily automatically have. A detailed description of good practice in understanding and communicating with children is not possible here, but you must at least have some understanding of the basics, including child development and in particular what is understood by cognitive development, i.e. the ability of children to think and conceptualise, in order to represent them effectively. Chapter 3 has a useful summary guide to these areas and to the factors to take into account in communication.

Your language and approach to the child client are particularly important since there is an enormous capacity for misunderstanding, even where the child apparently speaks good English. In many cases, engaging with a child may simply mean making sure they are given, and understand, all appropriate information. This can be done verbally, in writing or in other easily comprehensible forms. Giving information should not be a professional monologue, but rather a dialogue with the child using words and phrases appropriate to their understanding, and encouraging the child to ask questions, express fears and contribute ideas and wishes. As involvement becomes consultation, so are trust and understanding established to provide a firmer basis for further communication.

The purpose of talking to the child is to ensure that she understands as much of the situation as is possible and relevant to them. Children's perception of the legal process can be greatly coloured by information from the media, peers and family. Do not underestimate the capacity for misunderstandings: e.g. there is evidence from research[15] that many children believe, even at the end of a care case, that they have somehow been involved in criminal proceedings. All verbal children will require information about why they are being interviewed and about the legal proceeding in which they are involved if they are to participate appropriately.

The guardian's skills in understanding and listening to children are invaluable, but you will need to talk to the child at times, and especially where no guardian has been appointed. In order to communicate effectively, you will first need to obtain the child's trust and cooperation: the younger the child, the more you will need to enter into the child's world.

Ongoing communication with a child does not necessarily require face-to-face meetings. Remember the telephone, letters, text messages, but always ensure that you have checked out with the client how she wants communication to take place!

Interviewing

To be able to interview a child successfully, or to take their instructions in a way that is ultimately effective and meaningful to the child and to the process of successful representation, you must first have a basic understanding of how a child thinks and communicates in a given situation.

There is now a wealth of advice on good practice in interview techniques and it is not sufficient to rely on the necessarily limited training provided on the Children Panel Qualifying course.

The essentials are contained in the guides on communication and interviews recommended in Chapter 3, as well as *Achieving Best Evidence* (2002). The latter provides comprehensive guidance for those involved in interviewing child witnesses in criminal proceedings, but is also a useful guide to interviewing children in other circumstances, including family proceedings under the Children Act 1989. It follows the four stages of (a) establishing rapport; (b) asking for free narrative recall; (c) asking questions and (d) closure.

Interviews should be short and be taken at the child's pace. The first interview is particularly important in establishing a rapport with your child client, but is unlikely to provide sufficient time in which to communicate in a style meaningful to the child, and to interpret her responses, which takes time and effort.

As with any other client, do not assume that the child knows or understands what is going on, what is likely to happen, what courts are or how the court process works. One of the key initial tasks is to clarify any confusion she may have about the respective roles of solicitor, guardian, social worker and judge, etc. Carefully explain things in terms the child will be able to understand, including your own role and function and how it differs from the plethora of other adults the child is likely to encounter.[16]

Make clear to the child how you are going to represent them, how their views will be communicated and who will make decisions about their lives: children need to know in what way they have influenced decisions and they should always be kept fully informed about decisions about their lives and their future.

19.7 CONFLICTS OF INTEREST

Conflicts can arise between the child and other parties to the proceedings, between two or more children and between the child and the guardian.

The solicitor should not act for the child if he has been approached by a parent or any other party to the proceedings with whom the child's interests may or do conflict, or has acted previously for another party to the proceedings, e.g. in the context of separation or divorce proceedings, and in so doing has acquired relevant knowledge.

Where representing more than one child in the proceedings, the solicitor must be aware of the possibility of a conflict arising. This is most likely to happen when receiving instructions directly from one or more of the children. You must first determine whether or not one or more of them is of sufficient understanding to give direct instructions.

If you have instructions from the guardian and/or one or more children, you must consider whether there is a conflict of views and if there is, carefully consider whether you can continue to act for any of the children involved in the light of the information you have received up to that point.

If you conclude you must cease acting for all or some of the children, tell the guardian and the court so that the child or children can be separately represented. In this situation, you should not allow yourself to be influenced by the possibility that a child might lose confidence in any future arrangements for legal representation or might be disadvantaged by the involvement of a fresh solicitor.

Practice has long been characterised by widely diverse views on the competency of children to give instructions, some of which have been based on misconceptions about age and stages of child development, as well as confusion about the concept of 'Gillick competence' (*Gillick* v. *West Norfolk and Wisbech Area Health Authority and DHSS* [1986] AC 112) and its relationship to the Children Act 1989.

19.8 ASSESSING COMPETENCE TO GIVE INSTRUCTIONS

'In considering the duty to act in the client's best interests, the solicitor will need to draw a distinction between those children who are competent to give instructions and those who are not.'[17]

Principles

Assessment of capacity is an ongoing process, not merely a judgment to be made at first interview. Once made, the competent child should be represented in accordance with those instructions. If the child is not competent, the solicitor should act in the child's best interests.[18]

Assessment of competence is crucial in compliance with the best interests principle and the welfare checklist, reinforced by the requirement to consider wishes and feelings in direct relationship to age and understanding (Children Act 1989, s.1(3), reinforced by s.22(5)).

The level of competence required for consent to medical treatment is higher than that required to give separate instructions in care proceedings (Thorpe J in *Re H (A Minor)* [1992] 2 FCR 330 and FPCR r.12(1).

Gillick competence

The *Gillick* case concerned competence linked to a child's capacity to consent or refuse medical examination/assessment/treatment (see Children Act 1989, ss.38(6), 43(8), 44(7) and Sch.3, paras. 4(4)(a) and 5(5)(a)). It was an important watershed in recognising that a child's autonomy grows incrementally with increasing maturity; according to Lord Scarman: 'If the law should impose on the process of "growing up" fixed limits where nature knows only a continuous process, the price would be artificiality and a lack of realism in an area where the law must be sensitive to human development and social change'.

The philosophy is that, as children approach the age of majority, they are increasingly able to take their own decisions. The courts have long recognised that the child's integrity as a human being should be respected and her decision not lightly overridden on such a personal matter as medical treatment. The older the child, the greater the weight the court should give to her wishes, subject to welfare considerations that may outweigh these.

Gillick competence is confined to medical examination and treatment of children and their right to self–determination on these issues: there is no authority for extending this competence test beyond medical examination and treatment of children – the test is very different from that for a child to instruct her solicitor directly:

> there is an important distinction between the question posed by r.12(1)(a) and the question which the justices had considered under s.38(6). The level of understanding that enables a child to make an informed decision whether to refuse to submit to a psychiatric examination is in all practical senses a much higher level of understanding than is required to enable him to give instructions to a solicitor on his own behalf . . . if a child is only suffering from some emotional disturbance . . . there is little room to question his or her ability to instruct a solicitor . . . a child must have sufficient rationality within the understanding to instruct a solicitor. It may well be that the level of emotional disturbance is such as to remove the necessary degree of rationality that leads to coherent and consistent instructions . . . in these cases involving intelligent, articulate but disturbed children it is necessary for the court to apply Rules 11 and 12 realistically to ensure that not only is the professional voice of the guardian . . . heard through an advocate's presentation but that also the wishes and feelings of the child, however

limited the horizon, should be similarly presented. If there is any real question as to whether the child's emotional disturbance is so intense as to destroy the capacity to give coherent and consistent instructions, ... that question should be the subject of specific expert opinion from the expert or experts who are already involved in the case.

(Thorpe J in *Re H (A Minor) (Care Proceedings: Child's Wishes)*
[1993] 1 FLR 440)

It was held, e.g. that a 15-year-old boy suffering from obsessive-compulsive disorder did not have sufficient understanding to make an informed decision to refuse consent to a residential psychiatric assessment (Thorpe J in *Re H (A Minor) (Care Proceedings)* [1992] 2 FCR 330). An intelligent, articulate 15-year-old girl refused to consent to a life-saving heart transplant on medical grounds – but had a 'limited experience of life', was 'overwhelmed' by what was happening to her and lacked competence 'in the context of all the necessary details [about] which it would be appropriate for her to be able to form a view' (Re L *(Medical Treatment: Gillick Competency)* [1998] 2 FLR 810 at 813).

However, had the question arisen in public Children Act 1989 proceedings whether she was capable of instructing her solicitor directly, she might well have been considered competent.

Solicitor's assessment in care proceedings

Where you are instructed to represent a child, and a guardian is appointed, you must take your instructions from the guardian. However, if, having taken account of the guardian's views and any direction of the court (under Family Proceedings Courts (Children Act 1989) Rules 1991, SI 1991/1395, rule 11A(2)(b) and Family Proceedings Rules 1991, SI 1991/1247, rule 4.11A(3)(b)(1)), you consider that the child wishes to give instructions which conflict with those of the guardian and that the child is able, having regard to her understanding, to give instructions on her own behalf, you must conduct the proceedings in accordance with the child's instructions (SI 1991/1395, rule 12(1)(a) and Family Proceedings Rules 1991, rule 4.12(1)(a)).

To be competent, the child will need to understand what parents and other parties want for the child, what the children's guardian and other experts recommend for the child and the outline of essential law relevant to the proceedings.

There is no definitive methodology to assess this but the following guidance[19] may be useful:

- although understanding ordinarily increases with time, there is no absolute demarcation based on age (*Re S (A Minor) (Independent Representation)* [1993] 2 FLR 437, CA);

- understanding is not absolute but has to be assessed relative to the issues in the case (*Re S (A Minor) (Independent Representation)* [1993] 2 FLR 437, CA);
- if the child's instructions run counter to what the court would clearly consider to be in their best interests, then they are unlikely to be held competent (*Re CT* [1993] 2 FLR 278);
- there is a balance between the right of children to participate in their proceedings and the need to protect them from exposure to materials that may be damaging to them (*Re A (Care: Discharge Application by Child)* [1995] 1 FLR, CA);
- the child needs to demonstrate independent thought and maturity, together with clarity and consistency in their instructions (*Re SC (A Minor) (Leave to Seek a Residence Order)* [1994] 1 FLR 96);
- a child must demonstrate rationality as well as understanding, and this may not be the case where a child is seriously emotionally disturbed (*Re H (A Minor) (Care Proceedings: Child's Wishes)* [1993] 1 FLR 440); however, the fact that a child's instructions may be contradictory or influenced by emotional disturbance may not bar them (*Re CT* [1993] 2 FLR 278).

The assessment may involve knowledge and/or skills that lawyers do not have without adequate, and ongoing, training. It will also involve taking steps to plan carefully for, and make appropriate judgments, taking account of the following factors.

Race, ethnicity and culture: you should be aware of the possible need for, or the child's preference for, someone of the same or a different cultural group to be present at the initial interview if you are not from the same background or are not familiar with the child's culture.

The child's gender: practitioners need to be particularly sensitive and careful and take steps to avoid allegations that they have behaved inappropriately towards a child.

Health and physical status: including any special needs, whether special educational needs or otherwise, e.g. is the child in receipt of any medication that might affect her ability to communicate?

Educational and intellectual ability: a child's level of cognitive functioning may well affect the way in which she understands the world and communicates. In some instances, this can be a relatively straightforward matter, requiring only an assessment to establish it, in other cases it may need a specialist in conditions such as autistic spectrum disorder to determine the level and type of functioning of which a child is capable.

Family background and parental relations: what does the child think about lawyers? What is the level of understanding in the family about the role of lawyers and how have these influenced the child's perceptions?

Siblings and significant adults: what is their influence on the child's knowledge, language and perceptions?

Psychological status, personality and temperament: establishing the child's possible level of stress in being interviewed, their coping skills, and style of responding to questions.

Maturity can be assessed on the child's ability to understand the nature of the proceedings and to have an appreciation of the possible consequences of the applications before the court both in the long and short term, but legally speaking judgment of capacity is governed by the principle that the child must have 'sufficient rationality within understanding' (Family Proceedings Rules 1991, rule 12(1)).

Where no children's guardian has been appointed, unless the issue of competency is clear cut, it would be advisable to consider seeking leave of the court to instruct a social worker or psychologist, or other suitable expert, to assist in assessing this.

Changing competency

The solicitor's duty to assess competence arises at the outset of the case and continues throughout it. Assessment is an ongoing process, not merely the making of a judgment at the first interview (see *Re M (Minors) (Care: Child's Wishes)* [1994] 1 FLR 749).

If it appears that the child's competency has changed, the advice is to 're-assess the child's capacity and consult with the Children's Guardian, ... being careful not to breach the child's confidentiality or prejudice his case'.[20]

If you are in any doubt about a child's capacity to give you instructions and what the child is saying is in conflict with the guardian, you should seek the expert advice of the guardian or other expert professional advice and assessment from a child psychologist or child psychiatrist.

In seeking expert professional advice, including from social worker or teacher or other independent expert, you must remain sensitive to your duty of confidentiality to the child. Ultimately, if you cannot decide on the child's level of understanding, you can seek the assistance of the court by making an application, which should usually be done on notice (*Re J (A Minor)*, *The Times*, 15 July 1992).

The reality of direct instructions

Even if a child is competent to give instructions, consideration of when to take instructions directly can give rise to professional difficulties, since a real problem may arise when the guardian has taken a final view that is contrary to the child's.

The child has a right to a fair hearing (Family Proceedings Rules 1991, rule 12(1)), even if dissatisfied with the outcome. In many cases, she will realise she had little chance of success but will have had the opportunity to put up something of a fight. The child's right to tell the court what she wants directly rather than speaking through the guardian is reinforced by ECHR Article 6 and HRA 1998, s.6.

The mature child and direct instructions

Acting for the mature child can pose several challenges even to experienced practitioners.

As a vulnerable client, a child may be just as anxious to please you (and perhaps even more so in some cases) as she may be to please any other adult in a position of authority. You must be careful to ensure that the child understands the issues in the case and gives instructions freely. When the child follows your advice, make sure the child's instructions accurately reflect her wishes and feelings.

Consider how you are to elicit full and informed instructions. Even with an apparently clued-up client, there may be a risk of overwhelming her by the sheer quantity of documentation, which she may not fully understand and which may lead to her taking a simplistic view of the case and her involvement.

There may be difficulties in communicating with adolescents who may be monosyllabic if not openly hostile to your contact, but their wishes are likely to be given more weight by the court as they near maturity: it is as important that they are given proper legal advice and support as may be appropriate for young adults.

19.9 CONFIDENTIALITY

Chapter 2 sets out the Law Society's guidance on when it may be necessary to breach the duty of confidentiality.[21] The child must be made aware of that duty and the circumstances in which it may be breached. It is for the solicitor to judge whether to breach confidentiality, and consider:

- Does the information indicate that abuse is taking place, or is likely to?
- What is the child's capacity to give instructions and understand the consequences of non-disclosure?

The public interest in the protection of children is an important factor in making judgments. There may be exceptional circumstances where a solicitor should consider revealing confidential information to an appropriate authority. If information indicates that there is continuing sexual or other physical abuse, but the child refuses to allow disclosure, the solicitor must consider whether the threat to a child's life or their mental and physical health is sufficiently serious to justify a breach in the child's best interests. In judging this ' the solicitor will need to draw a distinction between those children who are competent to give instructions and those who are not'.[22]

If the abuse is of a mature child, the duty of absolute confidentiality applies, except where there is information that younger siblings (or others) are also subject to the abuse or the child client is in fear of her life or of serious injury.

You must try to persuade the child to report the abuse. If she is unwilling to do so, a decision must be made as to whether this indicates that she is not able to give direct instructions, or whether she is mature enough to be treated as any competent client.

19.10   ACCESS TO INFORMATION

The child has a right of access to personal information held by the local authority, and to education or health records, subject to exceptions set out in the appropriate Regulations.

Whilst the young person has the same right as any other client to see the full documentation in the case, you will need to consider when and how this may be done and whether all or only part of the documentation should be shared with the client. You should consider whether simply to produce a general summary of the case initially or to rely on this throughout the proceedings and what impact your decisions have on your ability to obtain appropriate, informed instructions.

The same rules on disclosure apply to an older child who commissions an adverse report as to an adult client, and where you receive material from a mature child, it must be disclosed even if this is contrary to the child's express instructions.

19.11   DUTY TO THE LEGAL SERVICES COMMISSION

Where wholly unreasonable instructions are being given by a child or young person, the duty to report this to the LSC is the same as it is for an adult client. However, it may be due to the child not fully understanding the implications of her instructions or the proceedings, and it may be that in those circumstances, you should cease to take direct instructions from the child.

19.12   ATTENDANCE AT CHILD PROTECTION CONFERENCES

Details of the principles and the Law Society guidance on the conduct of solicitors at child protection conferences is in Chapter 5 and should be followed 'unless very good reasons exist for not doing so'.[23]

Working Together emphasises the importance of full participation of children and parents at all stages of the child protection process, particularly in attending and contributing to child protection conferences.[24] Before a conference is held, its purpose, who will attend and the way in which it will operate, should always be explained to a child of sufficient age and understanding, who should be given the opportunity to attend if she wishes and to bring an advocate, friend or supporter. Where she does not wish to, or her attendance is not appropriate, the social services professional who is working most closely with her should ascertain what her wishes and feelings are, and make these known to the conference.

The child's solicitor should consider whether it would be appropriate for the child to attend, and discuss this with the children's guardian. In the event that the child is not to attend, the solicitor should endeavour to secure advance copies of the reports to be discussed at the conference so that the child's wishes can be ascertained. Although the social worker has this duty, the child who is represented should have the opportunity to discuss the subject matter of the conference with her lawyer and children's guardian, if appointed.

The children's guardian may attend, but if the solicitor alone attends she should take detailed instructions on the most appropriate arrangements for the child's future in order to put these forward.

The discussions should be reported to the child after the conference, using sensitivity about the extent of the information provided, and depending on the child's age and understanding. If the child is directly instructing the solicitor, and for an exceptional reason does not attend, the solicitor should assume that all the relevant information will be given to the child client.

19.13   RIGHTS AND ADVOCACY SERVICES FOR CHILDREN

If the solicitor approached by a child is unable to act in relation to a particular issue, she should consider whether another agency is available that could advise the child, such as the Voice for the Child in Care, National Youth Advocacy Service or the Children's Legal Centre.

With the increasing stress on the importance of the participation of children and young people in decision-making and statutory requirements for the provision of independent advocacy for them in formal complaints procedures, child protection procedures and for care leavers (see the Children (Leaving Care) Act 2000 and Children Act 1989, s.26A as inserted by the Adoption and Children Act 2002), these services have grown considerably. They are subject to statutory national standards and guidance.[25]

Children may be supported through child protection processes by advice and advocacy services, and should 'always be informed of those services which exist locally and nationally (such as those provided by the Family

Rights Group)'.[26] Local authorities must not treat participation as an optional extra, but ensure children and young people who wish to take part in individual decisions about their own care, and in service development and planning, do so.

Such services are generally focused on looked after children and young people, children in need and disabled children. However, some can also assist and support children and young people in claiming their rights under national and international law, including sex, race and disability equality.

The national standards state that they should:

- always have the opportunity to have their views considered when decisions about them are being made;
- have access to information about themselves or affecting decisions about their lives;
- in all settings be able to access easy-to-use procedures which can respond effectively to their complaints and concerns;
- have access to independent advocates who can advise, support and represent them.

Advocacy is about speaking up for children and young people, especially, and whenever possible, enabling them to speak up for themselves. It is also about helping them to achieve understanding, to participate in and influence decisions that affect their lives, particularly about representing their views, wishes and needs to decision-makers and seeking remedies for breaches of their human rights.

Advocacy services offer independent and confidential information, advice, advocacy, representation and support.

The standards and services are based on principles of:

- independence;
- respect;
- empowerment;
- choice;
- equal access;
- anti-discriminatory practice; and
- confidentiality.

The Appendices to the Standards specify that the usual vetting policies and procedures should be in place[27] and that advocates should understand clearly the principles of confidentiality and information-sharing and their importance.[28]

Services that do not demonstrate these standards and particularly those that do not accept the last two points should not be used.

It is important that children and young people have an advocate of their choice. Parents, carers or friends may provide informal advocacy and may look to formal services for advice and support in this role.

There are Regulations and guidance[29] on local authorities' duty to make arrangements for the provision of advocacy to children. The guidance contains information on the complaints procedure, on ways to maintain the independence of the advocate and on how to monitor the advocacy system.

The 2002 national standards set out details for the commissioning and delivery of advocacy services.

The role of the independent reviewing officer is set out in Chapter 11.

NOTES

1 Maggie Lane, 'Voice for the Child in Care', ALC conference, Durham 1996.
2 *National Advocacy Standards for Agencies Providing Advocacy for Children and Young People*, DH (November 2002).
3 *Challenge of Partnership in Child Protection*, DH, SSI (1995).
4 *Working Together to Safeguard Children*, DH, Home Office, DfEE (1999).
5 See *Learning to Listen*, Children and Young People's Unit, DfES (November 2000).
6 C. Truax, and R. Carkhuff, *Towards Effective Counselling and Psychotherapy*, Chicago, Aldine (1967).
7 I. Butler and H. Williamson, *Children Speak: Children, Trauma and Social Work*, London, NSPCC/Longman (1994), p.187.
8 D. Shemmings and D. Platt, *Making Enquiries into Alleged Child Abuse and Neglect: Partnership with Families*, Pennant Professional Books (1996); D. Shemmings, *Involving Children in Child Protection Conferences*, Social Work Monographs (March 1996).
9 *Ibid.*
10 J. Brophy, C.J. Wale and P. Bates, *Myths and Practices: A National Survey of the Use of Experts in Child Care Proceedings*, BAAF (1999), and see J. Brophy *et al.*, *Significant Harm: Child Protection Litigation in a Multi-Cultural Setting*, Lord Chancellor's Department (2003).
11 Extract from House of Commons Health Committee Report on the *Climbié Inquiry Report* (2003).
12 J. Brophy *et al.*, *Significant Harm.*
13 *Guide to Good Practice for Solicitors Acting for Children*, 6th edn, Resolution (2002).
14 D. Hershman and A. McFarlane, *Children Law and Practice*, Jordans (2002).
15 J. Masson and M. Winn Oakley, *Out of Hearing: Representing Children in Court*, Wiley (1999).
16 See, e.g. for young children, M. Bray, *Susie and the Wise Hedgehog Go to Court*, Hawksmere (1989).
17 *The Guide to the Professional Conduct of Solicitors 1996*, 7th edn, Law Society, Annex 16A on Confidentiality and Privilege: Child Abuse and Abduction (omitted from current 8th edition).
18 *Ibid.*
19 S. Stevens, 'Assessing the Competence of the Child to Give Instructions: The Solicitor's Role' in M. Ruegger (ed.) *Hearing the Voice of the Child*, Lyme Regis, Russell House Publishing (2001).
20 *Guide to Good Practice for Solicitors Acting for Children*, 6th edn, Resolution (2002), p.10.

21 *The Guide to the Professional Conduct of Solicitors 1999*, Law Society.
22 *Ibid.*, Annex 16.
23 Law Society Family Law Committee guidance, *Attendance of Solicitors at Child Protection Conferences* (June 1997).
24 *Working Together*, paras 5.57–5.58, and see *Challenge of Partnership*, ch. 2.
25 National Standards for the Provision of Children's Advocacy Services, DH (November 2002).
26 See *Working Together*.
27 National Advocacy Standards 2002, App. B.
28 *Ibid.*, App. A.
29 *Get it Sorted*, DfES (2004).

CHAPTER 20

Role of the children's guardian

Key sources

- Children Act 1989, ss.41 and 42
- *Practice Note* [2001] 2 FLR 151 and *Practice Direction* [2004] 1 FLR 1188
- LCD Statement of Good Practice in the Appointment of Solicitors Where It Falls to the Court to Do So In Specified Proceedings (2003)
- Law Society Guidance on Acting in the absence of a Children's Guardian (2003)
- Law Society and CAFCASS Guidance on Working Relationship between Children Panel Solicitors and Children's Guardians (March 2004)
- *Good Practice in Child Care Cases*, Law Society (2004)

For the purpose of any specified proceedings, the court shall appoint a guardian ad litem for the child concerned unless satisfied that it is not necessary to do so to safeguard his interests (Children Act 1989, s.41(1)).

The guardian ad litem shall be under a duty to safeguard the interests of the child (Children Act 1989, s.41(2)(b)).

20.1 BACKGROUND HISTORY OF THE GUARDIAN SERVICE

Maria Colwell died in 1973. She was a child in care, and went home to her mother and step-father after the care order was discharged. The only professional evidence heard by the court was that of the local authority social workers who supported the application. Maria subsequently died. The Report of the committee of enquiry into her death was published in 1974, and led to the creation of the guardian service.[1]

The Children Act 1975, s.20 created the role of guardian ad litem and reporting officer. Initially, guardians were only appointed in uncontested discharge applications (and adoption applications under the Adoption Act 1976). The Children Act 1975, s.103 also made provision for Panels of guardians ad litem and reporting officers, under the auspices of local authorities; this section was not implemented until 1983, and in the interim period, local authorities made use of senior staff to prepare the reports.

Under the Children Act 1989, ss.41 and 42, the role of the guardian was enlarged. The Guardians Ad Litem and Reporting Officers (Panels) Regulations, SI 1991/2051 left Panels under the umbrella of local authorities, although at arm's length. The Family Proceedings Courts (Children Act 1989) Rules 1991, SI 1991/1395 required that the guardian 'shall make such investigations as may be necessary for him to carry out his duties and shall, in particular: contact or seek to interview such persons as he thinks appropriate' (rule 11.9).

Following a judicial review of an attempt by one local authority to restrict the number of hours a guardian worked on a case, the then President of the Family Division stated 'I wish to emphasise how vital it is for Guardians not only to be seen to be independent, but also to be able to be assured themselves of their independence in the carrying out of their duties'.

Following a government consultation paper,[2] the Criminal Justice and Court Services Act 2000, s.12 established the Children and Family Court Advisory and Support Service (CAFCASS), and defined and limited its functions. It brought together court welfare officers, the children's section of the Official Solicitor and guardians (as from 1 April 2001). Guardians ad litem became children's guardians under the Court Amendment Rules, March 2001. CAFCASS formally transferred from the Department of Constitutional Affairs to the Department for Education and Skills in January 2004. This is a non-departmental public body attached to the DfES, under the Children's Minister. It is divided into nine regions plus Wales.

20.2 WHO ARE CHILDREN'S GUARDIANS?

They must be qualified social workers, who historically often used to have had a full social work career, including significant management responsibilities, before becoming a children's guardian; under the former Panel system, guardians tended to have 12 years' or more experience as social workers, but new recruits need only three years' post-qualification.

Former court welfare officers are being 'converged' into children's guardians, and may have had no child protection or public law experience.

There is no longer a bar on guardians working in an area covered by a recent previous social services employer.

A children's guardian may be a managed employed guardian or a self-employed guardian contracted to CAFCASS. Self-employed children's guardians take on a wide range of other professional activities, including training, chairing looked after children reviews, child protection conferences and family meetings, doing a range of assessments for social service departments, taking instructions as social work experts in court proceedings and teaching.

20.3   RESPONSIBILITIES OF THE CHILDREN'S GUARDIAN

The responsibilities of the children's guardian are wide-ranging, and under-pinning these, and uniquely in social work, they have personal professional responsibility for their advice.

> The Guardian is not a welfare officer; s/he is the independent voice of the child and the child's protection against bad social work practice and legal delays. Cases in which the local authority and the guardian end up supporting the same outcome for the child are commonplace; but it does not follow that the interest of the child would have been as well or better served without the guardian being separately represented. In my opinion, it is vital that a guardian should have access, throughout an enquiry, to his or her own legal advice. Furthermore, s/he needs access to the court at all times, and plays a pivotal role in case management and timetabling. It is the Guardian who will often be asked to instruct the important expert witness, whose instructions need to be drafted by a solicitor.[3]

Children's guardian are the child's protection against poor social work practice, procedural delay and collusive agreements. Their independence is fiercely guarded and recognised as valuable by the court (per Connell J in *Re G*, High Court, 12 May 1999).

Their responsibilities can be summarised as follows:

- safeguarding the child's interests in the immediate and long term, in the context of the welfare checklist (Children Act 1989, s.1(3));
- ensuring the child is legally represented;
- making an independent investigation of what is going on for the child in her world;
- ensuring that an accurate history for the child is known to all those involved in the case, and that the court has the best possible information on which to base any short-term or long-term decision;
- finding a way through the professional adult world for the child, helping the child understand who is who, what they do and trying to ensure that the child understands different issues of confidentiality;
- enabling the child to express her wishes and representation of those wishes to the court and others;
- corroborating or challenging evidence;
- making an informed analysis of all information;
- writing a stand-alone report in the recommended CAFCASS format, which is sufficiently detailed without duplicating other documents;
- presenting the case for the child's best interests;
- acting as a negotiator and mediator with and between parties, within families, within agencies and with the court;
- acting as a resource broker, identifying possible alternative ways forward;
- acting as a case manager / monitor on behalf of the court; being pro-active to avoid unnecessary delay and acting on the court's directions;

- collaborating with all involved in the current care of the child, without collusion;
- advising the family and professionals before criticising them publicly.

20.4   PRIVILEGED POSITION OF CHILDREN'S GUARDIAN

The children's guardian has a unique position in the case: she is often seen as neutral, but is highly partial on behalf of the child. She has personal professional responsibility for the child's interests and can focus exclusively on the child – she should not have to take account of organisational priorities. She is the person to whom everyone wants to talk, has the benefit of hindsight and is identified with the court. The children's guardian is the last to file evidence, to give evidence and to cross-examine others, and intervenes at a time when the stakes are particularly high, but has a limited and finite role.

20.5   TASKS OF CHILDREN'S GUARDIAN

The Rules of Court specify the role of the children's guardian in relation to the proceedings. Good practice will mean that she will cover the following areas:

- read, among other things:

    - current and past social services records (including) fostering and adoption records);
    - education records (e.g. EWO, school, SEN, etc.);
    - health records (GP, health visitor, school nurse, red book, percentile charts, ward notes, etc.);
    - ACPC/LSCB serious incident reports concerning other children of the family;

- appoint and instruct a solicitor for the child and advise on separate representation;
- make an initial investigation prior to first hearing;
- ensure in an age-appropriate manner that the child understands the process;
- if appropriate, take the child to see or attend court;
- see everyone necessary, and some more than once, including:

    - the child;
    - siblings;
    - parents;
    - wider family members;
    - informal networks, including those the child identifies;

- – past and present carers (night and day);
- – education professionals, including lay assistants;
- – health professionals;
- – social services staff, including decision-makers;
- – the police;

- see the child in various settings, including contact;
- see Police National Computer records (if accessible);
- consider the need for expert advice, e.g. paediatric, psychological, psychiatric;
- draft or approve position statements as necessary;
- attend meetings arranged by others, e.g. child protection conferences, LAC reviews;
- arrange meetings between some or all parties, with or without lawyers;
- negotiate, advocate, mediate – repeatedly;
- advise the court at hearings on the timetable, necessary directions and evidence;
- ensure that the child's immediate wishes are known to social services and carers;
- test the evidence through investigation (not only that which is before the court);
- convene and attend/chair experts' meetings, as directed;
- evaluate care plans throughout the proceedings;
- write a report, covering and containing:

  – the background to proceedings;
  – family structure;
  – children's guardian's investigation;
  – child's history, if not given in full elsewhere;
  – family history, if not given in full elsewhere;
  – child's wishes and feelings;
  – parents' views (which may be different from their statements);
  – actions of social services and other agencies;
  – children's guardian's assessment;
  – welfare checklist in respect of each child;
  – recommendations;
  – photographs of each child;

- instruct the solicitor on case presentation
- give evidence
- effect closure on the case, particularly with the child.

The children's guardian has the right to examine and take copies of records held by the NSPCC or local authority compiled in making, or proposing to make, any application concerning a child; and is entitled to use information from the case record in the preparation of her report or in giving evidence. Case law which established that documents covered by public interest immunity could not be disclosed has been superseded by *Re J (Care Proceedings: Disclosure)* [2003] 2 FLR 522, in which Wall J stated that public interest immunity does not arise where the children's guardian is entitled to see documents by virtue of Children Act 1989, s.42, as this has effect 'regardless of an enactment or rule of law which would otherwise prevent the record in question being admitted in evidence'.

The right to see documents extends to an ACPC Part 8 report, but care should be taken as to how the information is disseminated (*Re R (Care Proceedings: Disclosure)* [2000] 2 FLR 751, CA).

20.6   WORKING WITH THE CHILD'S SOLICITOR

The tandem model of representation in public law proceedings, to which CAFCASS has repeatedly confirmed its commitment, provides for both rights and welfare representation of the child. A good working relationship with the child's solicitor can make for the smooth running of the case. A poor relationship can make a difficult task even harder. It is essential that the solicitor and children's guardian discuss and agree at the beginning of their working relationship how this is to be managed; form an agreement covering issues such as what correspondence is to be copied to the guardian, through to whether or not they will communicate out of reasonable working hours, and how and when the solicitor will visit the child.

Issues which need consideration are as follows:

- the appointment of the solicitor, if she has not already been appointed by the court or where this has taken place, consideration as to whether or not to instruct that solicitor, or to appoint someone else; account must be taken of the child's age, ethnicity and the solicitor's length of time on the Panel;
- the need to confirm the personal representation undertaking with the solicitor;
- check if there is any conflict because of previous knowledge of the child/ family;
- negotiating teamwork;
- logistics:
  - methods of maintaining contact;
  - meeting;
  - office arrangements;
  - working hours;
  - holidays;
- what the solicitor will do between hearings;

- drafting of correspondence and instructions;
- contact between children's guardian and other lawyers;
- chasing late or missing evidence;
- limiting expert appointments;
- seeking directions, including avoidance of delay;
- sharing of information – nature and frequency;
- solicitor seeing child: when, where, how, with whom, how often;
- separate representation considerations;
- negotiations with other parties – influencing outcomes;
- maintaining involvement in court negotiations;
- where the children's guardian finds herself unable to work with the child's solicitor, e.g. if the solicitor refuses to act on instructions from the guardian, an application can be made for an order terminating the solicitor's appointment (Family Proceedings Courts (Children Act) Rules 1991, SI 1991/1395, rule 12(4),(5); Family Proceedings Rules 1991, rule 4.12(4),(5));
- the court can terminate the appointment of the children's guardian, e.g. on an application by the child's solicitor if instructions given by the children's guardian are unreasonable or unprofessional, but must allow the children's guardian to make representations before so doing (*Re M (Terminating Appointment of Guardian ad Litem)* [1999] 2 FLR 717).

20.7 GUARDIAN'S REASONABLE EXPECTATION OF REPRESENTATIVES OF OTHER PARTIES

At the same time as the children's guardian endeavours to meet the expectations of the court and parties, she will have certain expectations of them. These will include:

- continuity of representation and clarity about who actually has conduct of the case;
- lay clients being provided with an explanation of the role, particularly away from the court setting;
- both lay clients and professionals being encouraged to be open with the children's guardian;
- ensuring that the client understands the whole process;
- ensuring that clients are kept appropriately informed, and receive written evidence promptly;
- that evidence is filed in a timely manner as directed;
- that there will be discussions and meetings between hearings;
- that, when needed, e.g. where there are potential issues of personal safety, interview space will be provided to the children's guardian to facilitate the investigation;

- constructive discussions at court about the progress of proceedings;
- that suggestions will be passed to the children's guardian about possible lines of enquiry.

20.8 RETENTION OF RECORDS

At the conclusion of a case, the records will be kept in their entirety for 12 months and then stored or destroyed in accordance with CAFCASS procedures. The following items will be retained until the youngest child in the family reaches 18, after which they must be destroyed according to CAFCASS policy:

- the index of all documents filed at court;
- all reports prepared by the children's guardian that were filed at court;
- all expert reports filed with the court;
- the care plan agreed at the final hearing and any addenda;
- the final order.

In exceptional circumstances, the practitioner should retain any other key documents should the case be reopened; this might include children's notes and drawings and contemporaneous notes. This issue must be addressed immediately following the final hearing in discussion between the guardian and child's solicitor.

NOTES

1   *Report of the Committee of Enquiry into the Care and Supervision provided by Local Authorities and Other Agencies in relation to Maria Colwell and the Co-ordination between Them* (1974).
2   *Support Services in Family Proceedings* (1998).
3   Wall J in (1997) 9(4) CFLQ 345.

CHAPTER 21

Acting for parents

Key sources

- Family Proceedings Rules (FPR) 1991
- *Challenge of Partnership in Child Protection*, DH, SSI (1995)
- *The Guide to the Professional Conduct of Solicitors 1999,* Law Society
- *Practice Note* [2001] 2 FLR 155
- *Guide to Good Practice for Solicitors Acting for Children*, Resolution (2002)
- Law Society Guidance on Acting in the absence of a Children's Guardian (2003)
- *Good Practice in Child Care Cases*, Law Society (2004), Part 5

21.1   INTRODUCTION

Acting for parents is a highly skilled, often underrated, task. Solicitors acting for the local authority or child have professionals on hand to instruct and advise them at every stage. The parents' solicitor is acting for clients who are usually vulnerable, anxious, often angry and lacking in power. 'Parents who find themselves involved in cases such as this are often themselves vulnerable, sometimes very vulnerable; they may suffer from physical or mental disabilities or be educationally, economically or socially disadvantaged. They are often ill-equipped to cope with those whom they understandably see as "them"' (*Re G (Care: Challenge to Local Authority's Decision)* [2003] 2 FLR 42).

The task requires continual monitoring of the local authority work and that of the children's guardian, who should be taking a pro-active role, not merely reacting to events as they happen, being quick off the mark in questioning alterations in contact plans, and unsatisfactory arrangements for contact. It also requires the solicitor to be clear with her clients about what is expected of them by the court, the local authority, and how best they can assist the preparation of their case.

This chapter highlights some of the issues likely to arise in the course of acting for parents. It should be read in conjunction with *Good Practice in Child Care Cases.*[1]

21.2 HUMAN RIGHTS

'There is an implicit requirement in Article 8 that parents should be involved in the decision-making process when crucial decisions about the child's future are made, otherwise the decisions may be quashed' (*Re M (Care: Challenging Local Authority Decisions)* [2001] 2 FLR 1300).

The right to a fair trial in ECHR Article 6 is not confined to the 'purely judicial part of the proceedings' but applies to the administrative processes of the case as well: unfairness at any stage of the litigation might involve not merely a breach of Article 8 but also of Article 6 (*Re L (Care: Assessment: Fair Trial)* [2002] 2 FLR 730).

The rights afforded by Articles 6 and 8 can be protected by parents being notified of material criticisms of, and deficit in, their parenting or behaviour, and being advised on how they may improve this. In addition, a parent or other party who wishes should have the right to attend and/or be represented at professionals' meetings (*Re L (Care: Assessment: Fair Trial)* [2002] 2 FLR 730).

'The 1998 Act is of fundamental, indeed almost revolutionary importance. For the first time it confers upon the citizen and the denizen legally enforceable constitutional and human rights.'[2]

Some of the principles underlying state intervention in the family have been detailed in *Haase* v. *Germany* [2004] 2 FLR 39 (and see Chapter 1) in a decision of the European Court of Human Rights:

- the mutual enjoyment by parent and child of each other's company constitutes a fundamental element of family life: measures that hinder such enjoyment amount to an interference with Article 8 rights;
- although such measures may be in accordance with law and pursue a legitimate aim, they must be 'necessary in a democratic society';
- a failure to allow parents to participate in the decision-making process, and the methods used to remove a new-born child from her mother shortly after birth, must be supported by relevant and sufficient reasons;
- imminent danger must be established before public authorities resort to emergency measures;
- extraordinarily compelling reasons are necessary before a baby could be removed from the care of its mother immediately after the birth;
- in addition to the essential object of Article 8, there may be positive obligations inherent in an effective 'respect' for family life; where a family tie was established, the state must act in a manner that enables that tie to be developed and take measures that would enable parent and child to be reunited.

The need to involve parents in the decision-making process has been emphasised in pre-Human Rights Act decisions, and by the High Court:

Article 8 imposes positive obligations on a local authority to ensure that parents are properly involved in the decision-making process. Part of that obligation . . . is the obligation to ensure that the local authority's decision making process is properly documented and that there is proper and timely disclosure to parents of relevant documents. But in appropriate cases . . . the local authority's obligations will go further. Where for whatever reason – whether physical or mental disability, illiteracy or the fact that English is not their mother tongue – parents cannot readily understand the written word, the local authority must take whatever ameliorative steps are necessary to ensure that the parents are not for that reason prevented from playing a full and informed part in the decision-making process (*Re G (Care: Challenge to Local Authority's Decision)* [2003] 2 FLR 42 at para. 49).

Whilst Article 8 contains no explicit procedural requirements, the decision-making process leading to measures of interference must be fair and such as to afford due respects to the interests safeguarded by Article 8 (*McMichael* v. *UK* (1995) 20 EHRR 205 at para. 87).

The decision-making process must therefore be such as to secure that the parents' views and interests are made known to and duly taken into account by the local authority and that they are able to exercise in due time any remedies available to them . . . what therefore has to be determined is whether, having regard to the particular circumstances of the case and notably the serious nature of the decisions to be taken, the parents have been involved in the decision-making process, seen as a whole, to a degree sufficient to provide them with the requisite protection of their interests. If they have not, there will have been a failure to respect their family life and the interference resulting from the decision will not be capable of being regarded as 'necessary' within the remainder of Article 8 (*W* v. *UK* (1988) 10 EHRR 29).

Parents must have the opportunity to be legally represented (*P, C and S* v. *UK* (2002) 35 EHRR 31). Article 6 'may sometimes compel the State to provide for the assistance of a lawyer when such assistance proves indispensable for an effective access to court . . . by reason of the complexity of the procedure or of the case' (*Airey* v. *Ireland (No. 1)* (1979) 2 EHRR 305; *Munro* v. *UK* (1987) 10 EHRR 516).

However, the child's rights must prevail over those of the parents: 'In judicial decisions where the rights under Article 8 of parents and those of a child are at stake, the child's rights must be the paramount consideration. If any balancing of interest is necessary, the interests of the child must prevail' (*Yousef* v. *The Netherlands* (Application No. 33711/96 [2003] 1 FLR 210).

21.3   CONFIDENTIALITY

A solicitor is obliged to breach the duty of confidentiality owed to the client in the following circumstances.

As outlined in Note 4 of *The Guide to the Professional Conduct of Solicitors 1999*, 'there may be situations where an adult discloses abuse either by himself or herself or by another adult against a child but refuses to allow any disclosure. The solicitor must consider whether the threat to the child's life or health, both mental and physical, is sufficiently serious to justify a breach of the duty of confidentiality'.

A solicitor must breach confidentiality where directed by the court to do so, e.g. as regards the whereabouts of a child subject to a court order or who has been abducted (see Chapter 2).[3]

When the court has granted leave to disclose papers filed in the proceedings for a report to be obtained, there is a duty to disclose that report, even when it is adverse.[4]

Where information which is adverse to the client, but which has not been obtained in the course of the proceedings, comes to the attention of the parents' solicitor, there is a duty, in exceptional cases, to disclose it.[5] The solicitor has a duty not to mislead the court,[6] and a failure to disclose might be a breach of this duty.

'[I]f an advocate has certain knowledge which he or she realises is adverse to the client's case, the solicitor may be extremely limited in what can be stated in the client's favour.' In this situation, the solicitor should seek the client's agreement for full voluntary disclosure for three reasons:

- the matters the client wants to hide will probably emerge in any event;
- the solicitor will be able to do a better job for the client if all the relevant information is presented to the court;
- if the information is not voluntarily disclosed, the solicitor may be severely criticised by the court.

'If the client refuses to give the solicitor authority to disclose the relevant information, the solicitor is entitled to refuse to continue to act for the client if to do so will place the solicitor in breach of his or her obligations to the court.' Where the client refuses to disclose in the above circumstances, the solicitor will have to consider reporting this to the Legal Services Commission, on the basis that the client is requiring the case to be conducted unreasonably, and/or that the solicitor is uncertain whether it would be reasonable to continue acting: a failure to report in these circumstances may lead to costs being disallowed (Legal Services Commission (Disclosure of Information) Regulations 2000, SI 2000/442, reg. 4).

It is essential that the client understands the circumstances in which the solicitor may have to breach the duty of confidentiality. This should be committed to writing at the start of the solicitor/client relationship, to avoid misunderstandings and to avoid any suggestion that the solicitor has obtained information knowing that it may have to be disclosed, without giving the client the opportunity to decide not to disclose it.

When a situation arises which may require the solicitor to breach the confidentiality rule it would be advisable to seek advice from the Law Society's Professional Ethics Section, colleagues and professional insurers.

21.4   CLIENTS UNDER A MENTAL OR LEARNING DISABILITY

A solicitor cannot act for a client who is incapable of giving instructions.[7] This may include clients with a learning disability, mental health difficulties or brain damage. If the solicitor is uncertain about a client's capacity, contact should be made with the Official Solicitor, who will act in the absence of anyone else suitable and willing to act.[8]

In care proceedings it would be unlikely that any other individual would be suitable to act because of the confidential nature and complexity of the proceedings, despite provision in the rules for this appointment (Family Proceedings Rules 1991, SI 1991/1247, rule 9.2). The Official Solicitor will usually be unwilling to consent to act without having seen a certificate from a treating physician or psychiatrist giving an opinion as to the capacity of the client. His office can provide a standard medical certificate for completion by the doctor concerned.

There will be cases where the client is placed under a mental health section and deemed incapable of giving instructions, and will then have a guardian ad litem appointed. The order may be lifted, and she is then deemed to be capable of giving instructions. This may happen on a number of occasions during the proceedings, and delays may be caused by the need to apply for the appointment or termination of the appointment of the guardian. The court should be notified of these potential difficulties at the earliest possible stage of the proceedings.

See also Chapter 5.

21.5   ISSUES OF DIVERSITY

Following research findings in 2003 on child protection litigation in multi-faith, multicultural settings,[9] the Protocol Case Management Checklist[10] requires consideration to be given to the ethnicity, language, religion and culture of the child and other significant persons. The Protocol Code of Guidance for Experts[11] states that an expert must: 'in expressing an opinion take into consideration all the material facts including any relevant factors arising from diverse cultural or religious contexts at the time the opinion is expressed, indicating the facts, literature and any other material that the expert has relied upon informing an opinion'. These issues will be considered at the case management conference and the pre-hearing review, and should be at the forefront of the practitioner's mind throughout the case.

These factors will be relevant in relation to a variety of issues, e.g.

- dates and times of interviews with clients, and court hearings;
- the place of the interview, gender of the person who conducts it and those who are present;

- who is appropriate to act as interpreter or translator (see below);
- the level of and manner of engagement of the client with the solicitor, social workers and experts;
- the level of the client's understanding of actions by social workers;
- the family's approach to medical treatment;
- the requirement for religious observation centring on the organisation of the day around prayer;
- child care beliefs and practices;
- the instruction of an expert.

If the child is placed with foster carers, the parents' solicitor should assist her clients to provide as much information as possible about the child's lifestyle, her language, diet, practice of her religion, skin and hair care, and contact with other family members or family friends. The parents are likely to experience a variety of emotions when their child is removed, and their first reaction may be one of lack of cooperation. Their solicitor can greatly assist the family by encouraging them to cooperate for the sake of their child, particularly when she may be placed in an environment which is not only unfamiliar, but in a placement with a different culture, religion, language and ethnicity.

It is essential that, where relevant, statements from parents should deal with culturally specific information about the family lifestyle, circumstances in their country of origin which caused them to move to the UK (which might include details about the impact of civil war), and the reason for misunderstandings arising between the family and professionals which may arise from cultural, religious and ethnic differences.

Many solicitors will have had little or no training in issues of diversity, and may lack crucial knowledge relating to the client's ethnicity, culture, religion or language. Information about these issues should be obtained at an early stage of the proceedings in order for their significance in the context of the particular facts and allegations being made to be assessed.

21.6 USE OF INTERPRETERS

For the client who does not have English as their first language, both the contact with a lawyer and the proceedings are likely to be overwhelming and bewildering. Contact with authority, such as the courts, judges and social services, may cause fear and apprehension to clients who have fled to the UK from a country where their contact with authority has been negative.

Where English is not the client's first language, immediate consideration must be given to the use of an interpreter. Some clients may speak limited English, or indicate that they can understand sufficiently not to require an interpreter. Great caution should be exercised in making a decision not to use an interpreter. The subtleties of language and shades of meaning are difficult enough to understand for those clients who are fluent in the language. For those who are not, much of what is being detailed in statements or interviews will be incomprehensible.

Interpretation may be required for:

- meetings with the client;
- telephone calls to the client;
- the translation of letters and documents filed in the proceedings;
- court hearings.

Care should be taken to obtain interpretation in the correct language and dialect, and sensitivity must be used in choosing the ethnicity and nationality of the person concerned. The client may be anxious about members of her community coming to hear about her personal problems, or if she is a refugee or asylum seeker, she may be concerned about information passing back to her country of origin. A relative or friend should never be used to provide interpretation facilities, save in an emergency, when care should be taken not to compromise the client. A reputable interpretation agency should be approached for their services. The local authority service may be able to assist with a referral, or the service used by the courts.

It is essential to ascertain who is being used by the local authority to interpret, and to notify them immediately if the client has experienced problems understanding them.

The local authority has the responsibility of providing an interpreter for the court hearings, but the client will require their own interpreter to sit beside them when they are not giving evidence.

It does not come naturally to lawyers to speak slowly, and despite the move to the use of plain English in court, sometimes questions are put in a way that witnesses find confusing or incomprehensible. The solicitor must not hesitate to draw the judge's attention to potential or actual difficulties being experienced by the client and should ask for time to speak with the client outside court whenever the client appears to be experiencing difficulties.

The cost of a language interpreter is a disbursement recoverable from the Legal Services Commission.

21.7 CLIENTS WITH A HEARING IMPAIRMENT

Assistance with communication may be required from a British Sign Language interpreter (including Makaton), and with language.

It is unlawful for a service provider to discriminate against a disabled person by refusing to provide any service that it provides to members of the public (under Part III of the Disability Discrimination Act 1995). Where a sign language interpreter would enable a hearing impaired person to make better use of the service, it is the provider's duty to take such steps as are necessary to provide the service.

The Legal Services Commission apparently takes the view that the cost of a sign language interpreter should be borne by a solicitor's firm as part of the general overheads, despite anecdotal evidence that such fees have been paid in the past, both for legal help work and for certificated work. This is potentially an enormous burden on the solicitor's firm, and could lead to firms being unwilling to act for hearing impaired parents. The LSC should be approached for a definitive answer on whether or not it will allow the costs as a disbursement. The local authority should be approached for assistance. If all else fails, this issue should be raised with the court.

21.8   CONTACT WITH A CLIENT'S CHILD

Solicitors acting for parents should exercise great caution before agreeing to speak with their clients' child. It may be appropriate solely for the purpose of explaining that they are not permitted to speak with the child, and that they have their own legal advice. If the child is saying that she wants to change her solicitor or children's guardian, she could be given details of agencies who could advise her,[12] and/or the Law Society's Children Panel details. It may then be wise for the solicitor to notify solicitors acting for the other parties that they have done this.

21.9   ATTENDANCE AT CHILD PROTECTION CONFERENCES

Details of the purpose of the child protection conference, together with guidance on policy, procedure, participation, exclusion and the role of lawyers are set out in Chapter 5. Note, however, that *Working Together*[13] emphasises the importance of full participation of children and parents at all stages of the child protection process, particularly in attending and contributing to child protection conferences.[14]

There is a strong presumption that parents have a right to involve an advocate on their behalf at a conference: 'it seems to me that in general solicitors ought to be allowed to attend and participate unless and until it is felt that they will undermine the purpose of the conference by making it unnecessarily confrontational' (*R* v. *Cornwall CC, ex p. LH* [2000] 1 FLR 236).

The Law Society's 2004 guidance on the conduct of solicitors at child protection conferences[15] 'does not have the status of the rules of professional conduct, but it should be followed unless very good reasons exist for not doing so'.[16]

The parent's lawyer may accompany her client. Her role will be clarified by the Chair; this will vary from area to area. She should be able to assist her client to express her views and participate, either orally or by preparing a written statement in advance. She should be able to speak on her client's behalf, but should not be able to address substantive questions to the social worker.

Practice issues

Adults and any children who wish to make representations to the conference may not wish to speak in front of one another. Adequate arrangements should be made to deal with this situation.

The Chair should ensure that the conference proceeds at a pace that enables the parents to follow what is being said, and that they are given sufficient opportunity to consider what they wish to say without feeling pressurised: the solicitor should ensure that this is the case.

Where care and/or criminal proceedings are ongoing, or may take place, the solicitor will want to consider with her client whether it is appropriate for any comment to be made by the client during the course of the conference – nothing the client says will be confidential.

Where an interpreter or signer is used they must be seated suitably and given sufficient breaks to enable them to perform their task adequately. Sufficient time must be given in the course of discussion to ensure that the client understands what is being said.

Where a client has learning difficulties, the solicitor should ascertain whether an advocate will attend the conference to assist the client.

The conference should be timed to allow the attendance of parents who work, and/or who have to collect children from, or take them to, school; and so that the child who is at school can attend.

It is poor practice for reports to be produced at the last minute. Although the Chair will summarise them for the parent or child, it is usually impossible for them to take on board and reflect on the information in the short period available, or to be able to respond adequately.

21.10   IMPACT OF DOMESTIC VIOLENCE/ABUSE

Chapter 6 deals with this topic in greater detail, but note that the definition of 'harm' now includes 'impairment suffered from seeing or hearing the ill-treatment of another' (Children Act 1989, s.1(1) as amended by Adoption and Children Act 2002, s.120), so children who have lived in a domestic abuse situation may become the subject of care proceedings, in addition to being caught up in the conflict between their parents. A finding of fact made in the care court, or in family proceedings, will be relied on in proceedings in the other court.

In the conduct of the case where there is or has been domestic violence, reference should be made to the Law Society's Family Law Protocol Part VI for guidance on safety issues during the course of the case in relation to contact, attendance at court and at meetings.

More effective protection for victims of domestic violence has been provided by the Domestic Violence, Crime and Victims Act 2004.

The 2004 Act, which joins up the criminal and civil jurisdictions, will mean increasing numbers of parents will become liable to prosecution and to becoming Schedule 1 offenders, which will impact on their future contact with and care of their own and other people's children.

The 2004 Act also creates a new offence of causing or allowing the death of a child or vulnerable adult (see Chapter 16 for details).

Where one of two adults living in a household is alleged to have abused the child, the local authority should be invited to assist the alleged abuser to obtain alternative accommodation, to enable the child to remain at home (Children Act 1989, Sched. 2, para. 5(1)–(3)). Where it is not accepted that the alleged abuser would remain away, or that the carer would protect the child, then the local authority may apply for an exclusion order (see Chapter 6).

21.11   THE EXTENDED FAMILY

Where a child may not be able to remain with, or return to, her parents, the local authority must consider placement with a member of the extended family (Children Act 1989, s.23). Kinship care arrangements now account for 17 to 30 per cent of all placements in such circumstances.[17] Department of Health statistics estimate that relatives provided care for 14.15 per cent of children in need in 1996 and 16.6 per cent in 2000.

Where a local authority is not prepared to consider a family member as a carer, or to allow contact, they will have to consider whether to apply to be joined as a party and seek leave to apply for contact/residence in the proceedings. The court is required under the Children Act 1989, s.10(9) to consider:

- the nature of the proposed application;
- the applicant's connection with the child;
- any risk of that proposed application disrupting the child's life to such an extent that she would be harmed by it;
- where the child is being looked after, the local authority's plans for the child's future;
- the wishes and feelings of the child's parents.

The test that was applied (see Court of Appeal in *Re M (Care: Contact: Grandmother's Application for Leave)* [1995] 2 FLR 86) was whether the application had a reasonable prospect of success, that the client must have a 'serious issue to try and present with a good arguable case'. If the application was frivolous, vexatious or an abuse of process it must fail.

However, a number of decisions have now emphasised that the court should consider the statutory criteria (*Re J (Leave to Issue Application for a Residence Order)* [2003] 1 FLR 114; *Re P (A Child)* [2002] EWCA Civ 846, 31 July 2002 (unreported); *Re H (A Child)*, 20 February 2003 (unreported)):

> in my experience, trial judges have interpreted the decision in Re M as requiring in the determination of applications under s.10(9) the application of the threefold test formulated by Ward J to exclude applications . . . I am particularly anxious at the development of a practice that seems to substitute the test . . . for the criteria that Parliament applied in s.10(9). That anxiety is heightened [now] where applicants under s.10(9) manifestly enjoy Article 6 rights to a fair trial . . . Judges should be careful not to dismiss such a potential contribution without full inquiry. That seems to me to be the minimum essential protection of the Article 6 and Article 8 rights that grandparents enjoy.
>
> (per Thorpe LJ in *Re J* [2003] 1 FLR 114)

Public funding for a relative who wishes to apply for contact or care of a child during care proceedings is subject to means testing. So, in many cases it is left to those parties who may support kinship care/contact to pursue the case, and to call the family member as a witness as necessary.

The financial assistance that would be made available to the relative may be the deciding factor for them. In the past, local authorities discriminated between family members and non-family members when providing financial assistance. Paying relatives at a lower rate than other foster carers has now been held unlawful (Munby J in *R (L and Others)*; *R and Another v. Manchester City Council* [2002] 1 FLR 43) enabling relatives to come forward to offer care when they might have been unable to do so previously.

However, payment of allowances under a residence order may be substantially lower than that payable to a foster carer. Written confirmation of the financial assistance that would be available should be obtained from a local authority, as in some cases it may be advisable for the child to be placed with the relative in foster care rather than under a s.8 order.

21.12 PREPARATION OF THE CASE

Assessments

Assessments generally are considered in detail in Chapter 8. Where care proceedings are taking place, and one or more of the parties is considering an assessment, factors to consider will include the following:

- What is the type of assessment proposed?
- Who is to carry out the assessment? Is the person concerned sufficiently qualified for the task? What is the timescale and will the family see the completed assessment?

- Is there a need for a residential assessment? What if the parent has a treatable illness/addiction? The type of assessment must be identified at an early stage in the proceedings, especially where there is some sign of commitment and/or parenting skills.
- Is the assessment proposed appropriate? Are all the relevant family members to be included?
- It may be appropriate to reach a written agreement about the assessment before it commences, so that each party involved has a full understanding of the reason for it, and expectations after its completion.
- When a multidisciplinary assessment is to take place, check who will be carrying out which parts of the assessment, and that all those people will be available to give evidence.
- What criteria are being used to assess the parenting?[18]
- Is the proposal for assessment or treatment? Making the distinction can be difficult, but is essential, both in relation to the court's power to make a direction and in relation to funding issues.

In relation to funding issues and the power of the court to order an assessment (under Children Act 1989, s.38(6)), the essential question to be addressed by the court when an application is made is can what is sought be broadly classified as an assessment to enable the court to obtain the information necessary for its own decision? Applications will fail if what is proposed is not reasonable to enable the court to obtain the information necessary for its decision: if the child is peripherally involved; if what is proposed is a bare treatment programme for one or both parents, or if the cost of what is proposed has been established to be prohibitive (Court of Appeal in *Re G (Interim Care Order: Residential Assessment)* [2004] 1 FLR 876).

The local authority must produce evidence to support its contention that the cost is prohibitive and witnesses for cross-examination on the point. The court may be faced with a choice between directing a local authority to pay for a costly assessment, refusing it and moving inevitably towards permanent removal of the child and a potential breach of the Human Rights Act 1998. 'For the parents the only realistic prospect of averting a care order and a freeing order is the completion of a referral, directed under s.38(6). In the present case, if the order . . . were to stand, the child's prospect of upbringing by her parents would be, if not eliminated, much diminished' (Thorpe LJ in *Re G* [2004] 1 FLR 876).

Applications must be made as early as possible in the proceedings, in order to avoid presenting the court with this choice at such a late stage that the chances of success are diminished.

Use of professional/independent witnesses

The use of expert witnesses is discussed in Chapter 25. This section raises issues that are pertinent to the preparation of the case for the parents.

The instruction of experts in care cases is controlled by the court, and since the implementation of the Judicial Case Management Protocol, the court is likely to scrutinise even more carefully requests for leave to use experts. There is considerable pressure from the courts and from the Legal Services Commission to restrict the instruction of experts to one, jointly instructed, and usually with the child's solicitor as the lead solicitor. This should not prevent the parents' solicitor from considering whether there are aspects of the case that may require advice from, or the instruction of, another professional witness, one who is independent of the other parties. This may be:

- a GP to disclose, or comment on records;
- the treating psychiatrist to report on mental health, give a prognosis and detail support services which may be available to the parent in the future;
- a social worker to assess a member of the extended family where neither the children's guardian nor the local authority social worker proposes to do this;
- advice from an expert witness as to whether or not the instruction of an expert is necessary;
- advice from an expert about the relevant areas for cross-examination of an expert who is already instructed.

Where no children's guardian has been appointed, the parents' solicitor should urge the child's solicitor to seek leave to instruct an expert witness to provide advice on the child's welfare. Law Society guidance[19] addresses the task of the child's solicitor in this situation, including consideration of such an application. Where leave is granted, the instruction should follow the requirements of Appendix 3 to the Protocol in relation to the instruction of experts. If the parents' solicitor considers that the instructions are not wide enough to include investigation into certain aspects of the client's case, she should consider making her own application for leave to instruct a suitable expert pending the appointment of a children's guardian. For example, it may adversely affect the parents' case if the local authority refuses to arrange contact, or what the parents regard as sufficient contact, and there is no one independent of the authority to assess whether this is in the child's interests.

Making the best use of the Protocol

The Judicial Case Management Protocol is clear about the expectations the court has in relation to each party. The parents' representative must monitor adherence to it by the other parties, and ensure that the parents understand the requirement to comply with directions of the court, e.g.

- Has the local authority evidence been filed on time?
- Are the allegations of a shortfall in parenting supported by hard evidence?
- Is the source of the information stated?
- Does the evidence cover all the areas required by the Protocol?
- Is the decision-making process set out clearly?
- Has the expert been properly briefed, and received a copy of Appendix 3?
- Are the expectations of the client set out in writing?
- Are issues of ethnicity, culture, religion and language, and vulnerability of the parents and their witnesses being addressed by the local authority, the children's guardian and the court? If not, this must be raised at the case management conference.

Relationship with other parties

In the majority of child care cases, where the outcome is removal of the child from her family, this is unlikely to be the end of her relationship with them. She may continue having contact with them, whether direct or indirect, and they will remain her family. Experience shows that young people removed from their birth families often return to them in their adolescence. This has to be remembered by everyone involved in the case, including the lawyers.

An approach to the case which attacks the parents as people, rather than concentrating on their behaviour as parents, will do nothing to assist a working relationship between the social workers and parents and extended family after the case has concluded.

Similarly, adopting a partisan approach, attempting to score points in the course of the case by endeavouring to demonstrate how incompetent and negligent the social workers have been, and adopting an aggressive and hostile approach in court, will do little to encourage a positive attitude between those people who have to continue working together in the future. The social worker and foster carer will remain involved with the family. The lawyers leave at the end of the proceedings.

The way in which the child experiences the whole process will influence her relationship not just with the adults with whom she is involved at the time, but may also affect her own development towards adulthood. The child needs to see the adults around her working constructively towards a positive outcome, despite the trauma of the proceedings.

There is a fine balance to be struck between being assertive and promoting the client's case, and being aggressive and negative towards the other parties and their lawyers. The client may be pleased with, and indeed instruct the solicitor to send overly critical letters to the local authority, and to attack the social worker in cross-examination in court, but the solicitor must always ask herself what this will achieve. Placing on record dissatisfaction with the progress of the case and putting criticisms forward in cross-examination is appropriate. The other approach is short-sighted, verging towards the unprofessional, and is unlikely to achieve anything in the long run for either the child or parent.

Where there are current proceedings with the local authority on the record, solicitors for non-local authority parties should not contact members of social services departments directly, without the consent of the relevant local authority legal department,[20] or in accordance with any relevant local authority policy. If this is not the case, it is good practice to attempt to notify the legal department before contacting the social services department and to copy to both departments any written queries or correspondence directed to the social services department. It will usually be of assistance initially to contact the legal department, if only as a matter of professional courtesy.

Using other agencies

There may be particular aspects of the case which, at a particular time, would benefit from the involvement of another agency. For example, a grandparent may be considering putting themselves forward as a carer for the child, or seeking contact. It may not be appropriate for them to apply to be joined as a party to the proceedings. They could be referred, e.g. to the Grandparents Association.

The Family Rights Group has established an Advice and Advocacy Service. Any family member involved with social services in England and Wales (or their supporters) can access free advice through this organisation. The advocates work with families primarily in the area of child protection and a key part of their role will be to broker between the local authority and parent, with a view to promoting positive partnership and achieving an agreed child protection plan, especially as 85 per cent of children on the register live at home.

21.13 CLAIMS FOR COMPENSATION UNDER THE HUMAN RIGHTS ACT 1998

Any claim for compensation under ECHR Articles 3, 5 and 8 under the Human Rights Act 1998 should adopt the following procedure. An attempt to recover damages for maladministration by any procedure other than judicial review in the Administrative Court should be looked at critically. Since a claim for damages on its own, independent of an application for another order, may not be brought by way of judicial review, any such proceedings should be brought in the Administrative Court by way of an ordinary claim. In this kind of case, the Administrative Court will give permission to apply for judicial review, only after it has been explained why a complaint procedure, such as those operated by the Parliamentary or Local Government Ombudsman, is not more appropriate (*Anufrijeva* v. *Southwark LBC* [2003] EWCA Civ 1406 per Lord Woolf CJ).

This follows the general principle that the courts should not permit judicial review to go ahead if the parties can resolve a significant number of the issues between them outside the litigation process (*Frank Cowl* v. *Plymouth City Council* [2001] EWCA Civ 1935).

The Legal Services Commission has stated[21] that it will not grant certificates for representation in proceedings for compensation unless the above procedure is followed. In particular, the client must be able to demonstrate that only the court, not an Ombudsman, internal complaints procedure or other alternative means of dispute resolution, can adequately deal with the claim. The LSC requires to be satisfied that, following the principles set out in the *Anufrijeva* judgment and the tests in the Funding Code, the compensation that would be recovered would justify the expense of the proceedings.

21.14 THE PROTOCOL ON ADVICE AND ADVOCACY FOR PARENTS

Advocacy for parents will range from legal advocacy in court, to citizen or peer advocacy in other forums, where the advocate will assist the parent to express their views to someone who will make a decision affecting their life. The 2002 Protocol on Advice and Advocacy for Parents in Child Protection[22] was funded by the Department of Health.

Parents who are involved in child protection enquiries may not have instructed a solicitor; however, there is an expectation in *Working Together* that parents should be given information about how they can access advice and advocacy services from the commencement of the enquiries, and enabled to involve an advocate to support them throughout the process.[23]

An advocate's goal is defined as 'to empower parents to participate in the child protection process from an informed position, speaking for themselves wherever possible, and to promote good communication, and a positive working relationship, between the parents and the local authority'.[24]

If the parents' solicitor wishes to involve an advocate, details of advocacy services can be found through:

- the Area Child Protection Committee (or Local Safeguarding Children Board in future);
- the Citizen's Advice Bureau;
- local black and ethnic minority groups;
- national advice and advocacy services;
- Family Rights Group;
- social services.

The advocacy may be provided by an informal supporter, rather than a formal advocate. A supporter can be identified through local self-help groups, from the parents' family, local community groups and local voluntary agencies.

NOTES

1   *Good Practice in Child Care Cases*, Law Society (2004).
2   Munby J addressing NYAS in February 2004.
3   The court has the power under Family Law Act, s.33 to direct that persons who are not parties to the proceedings must disclose the whereabouts of a child.
4   *The Guide to the Professional Conduct of Solicitors 1999*, Law Society.
5   *Ibid.*, Principle 16.02, Note 5.
6   *Ibid.*, Principle 21.01.
7   *Ibid.*, Principle 24.04.
8   Official Solicitor, *Practice Note: (Appointment in Family Proceedings)* [2001] 2 FLR 155.
9   J. Brophy *et al.*, *Significant Harm: Child Protection Litigation in a Multi-Cultural Setting*, Lord Chancellor's Department (2003).
10 Protocol for Judicial Case Management in Public Law Children Act Cases [2003] 2 FLR 719, App. A.3.
11 *Ibid.*, App. C.
12 Voice for the Child in Care, the Children's Legal Centre, etc.
13 *Working Together to Safeguard Children*, DH, Home Office, DfEE (1999).
14 *Working Together*, paras 5.57–5.58 and see *Challenge of Partnership in Child Protection*, DH, SSI (1995), ch.2.
15 Law Society Family Law Committee guidance, *Attendance of Solicitors at Child Protection Conferences* (June 1997, under revision in 2005).
16 *Ibid.*, para. 1.4.
17 *Kinship Care: The Placement Choice for Children and Young People*, Russell House (2001); R. Greeff (ed.) *Fostering Kinship: An International Perspective of Kinship Foster Care*, Ashgate (1999).
18 Wall J (ed.), *Rooted Sorrows*, Family Law (1997); R. Kennedy, *Child Abuse, Psychotherapy and the Law*, Free Association Press (1997); R. Kennedy 'Assessment of Families' [2002] Fam Law 843.
19 Law Society, 'Guidance on Acting in the Absence of a Children's Guardian – Notice to Children Panel Members: Representation of Children in Public Law Proceedings' (October 2003).
20 *The Guide to the Professional Conduct of Solicitors 1999*, Principle 19.02.
21 LSC *Focus* 43 (December 2003).
22 Bridget Lindley and Martin Richards, Centre for Family Research, University of Cambridge (2002).
23 *Working Together*, paras 5.43, 5.57 and 7.19–7.21.
24 B. Lindley, M. Richards and M. Freeman, 'Advice and Advocacy for Parents in Child Protection Cases: What's Happening in Current Practice?' (2001) 13(2) *Child and Family Quarterly* 167.

CHAPTER 22

Representing the local authority

Key sources

- Children Act Guidance and Regulations (1991), vol.1
- *Reporting to Court under the Children Act, A Handbook for Social Services*, DH (1996)
- *Good Practice in Child Care Cases*, Law Society (2004), Part 3
- *Arrangements for Handling Child Care Cases*, Child Care Law Joint Liaison Group (2004)

22.1 INTRODUCTION

Local authority legal services are under pressure and have been for some time, and understanding how they are organised and the relationship between their staff and clients, is likely to assist all practitioners to conduct cases more effectively. The way in which formal professional links with other departments and agencies are created and maintained, and queries or referrals received, logged, cross-referenced and allocated may differ greatly between authorities.

22.2 HUMAN RIGHTS AND DIVERSITY

The general principles governing local authorities apply equally to their legal practitioners, whether directly employed or operating from an external source. They need to:

- give pro-active advice about, and ensure compliance with, human rights principles (particularly those set out in Chapter 1);
- ensure a child centred approach to practice and procedures;
- be aware of information and services that may facilitate participation and representation for both families and children;
- be aware of the implications of corporate parenting for their own work (see Chapters 5 and 6).

Both the Judicial Case Management Protocol and the Law Society's *Good Practice in Childcare Cases* (2004)[1] stress the importance of giving sufficient attention to diversity. Sufficient information should be made available by, or to, professionals, parties and the courts on these issues,[2] particularly for disabled children and adults and those whose first language is not English. The following questions need to be addressed as early as possible for both child and adults involved:

- Are venues and services suitable and accessible?
- Can sufficient access and support be provided for therapy? For contact?
- How is participation in decision-making to be encouraged and facilitated?
- Is there a need for an interpreter?[3]
- Is access to court facilities and proceedings readily available?
- Has the court been notified of any safety issues, or any special facilities required?

22.3 STRUCTURE OF LOCAL AUTHORITY SERVICES

The quality, consistency and structural integrity of many local authority legal services have been subjected to enormous pressures. Like the local authorities they serve, a 'typical' legal department may be wholly corporate or wholly outsourced to the private sector, or a mixture. Legal advice on safe-guarding is not immune from outsourcing, either generally through 'Best Value', or by assignment of individual cases to external solicitors/counsel. This can result in fragmented relationships between departments and with external agencies.

However, the usual model for children's services is an in-house, separate department of employed lawyers. The client departments will be social services, and increasingly, education, through its Directors (see Children Act 2004 and changes to children's services in England and Wales discussed in Chapter 4), generally acting through staff located in area offices, hospitals or joint teams. Direct instructions normally come through an individual officer, and attendance at strategy meetings and child protection conferences. The legal team will normally be headed by a senior lawyer (a principal or senior solicitor/lawyer), who is usually responsible for advising the ACPC/LSCB and answerable to an overall head of legal services (Head of Legal Services /Borough Solicitor) who is in turn answerable to the Chief Executive and Monitoring Officer.

Staff are usually specialist child care lawyers, legal assistants and unqualified staff, often required to work to quality standards such as Lexcel. They may also service other areas of policy and practice such as asylum and immigration, care standards and community care, crime and disorder, education (including work for the local education authority (LEA)), adult services and mental health. Many will also be involved in financial and other advice to councillors.

Internal and external competitive pressures on standards of good practice and conflicting demands inevitably arise. Balancing the requirements of court work in an environment of service level agreements, outsourcing, competitive tendering and restructuring is one problem. Efficient internal systems and good pro-active advice, as well as the integrity and stamina of even the most experienced practitioner, can be taxed by particular local authority 'cultures', inability to turn down work, difficulties in recruiting and keeping experienced, high quality staff, departmental budgets and financial cost centre management regimes (e.g. 'frontline first' approaches to saving money can have a disproportionate effect on legal services) and inadequate administrative and supervisory support, which may be shared with other teams doing very different work, with competing pressures and deadlines.

Procedures/protocols may exist for child protection conferences invitations/attendance, dissemination of conference minutes and liaison with other colleagues responsible for advising on education, housing, health (including separate external legal advice to hospitals and the medical profession), etc., an increasingly important requirement in the wake of the Children Act 2004.

No emergency action should be taken by a local authority on a case concerning an allegation of deliberate harm to a child without first obtaining legal advice.[4] In some areas this may mean there will now be a 24-hour duty service.

22.4 ROLE OF THE LOCAL AUTHORITY LAWYER

The way an authority chooses to present its case can have a profound effect on the outcome of the proceedings. The primary role of local authority practitioners is to advise the client with independence and impartiality, and to maintain the integrity of the local authority's case before the court by:

- giving clear, timely and pro-active advice on responsibilities, including any human rights consequences;
- ensuring all relevant information is given to the court and other parties;
- scrutinising the local authority's case at an early stage, testing the evidence for initiating proceedings;
- attending conferences and formal planning meetings whenever possible;
- ensuring cases are properly conducted;
- ensuring scrutiny of the local authority's case continues throughout the life of a case;
- observing the strictures on delay and meeting strict timetable requirements;
- assisting the court in its investigation, undertaking all necessary steps to arrive at an appropriate result in the paramount interests of the child's welfare and as an officer of the court.

371

22.5 PROPRIETY AND CLIENT RELATIONSHIP

The Law Society and Child Care Joint Liaison Group (CCJLG) publications contain essential guidance on handling child care cases. *Reporting to Court* is also an easy reference guide to the basic requirements.

Being an employed lawyer acting for a local authority, whether internal or external, is very different from private practice. Maintaining independence and impartiality in a corporate environment can be subject to enormous internal pressures from political and managerial imperatives. Empathy with the dilemmas of social work can turn into sympathy and overidentification, compounded by regular contact with other professionals tackling difficult issues, and by external pressures from the court process, media, society and politicians. This is overlaid with the high profile risk of getting things wrong.

Providers of outsourced services can encounter difficulties in adequately influencing the client, unless there are arrangements based on quality standards, a clear understanding of separate roles and professional responsibilities, Children Panel membership, and clear communication links for referrals, instructions and the resolution of disputes.

The legal duty to the court and the paramount interests of the child transcend all duties to the client and certain key issues are particularly important: the general duty of confidentiality to the client; not using professional position to take unfair advantage of anyone;[5] not communicating with another solicitor's client;[6] guarding against any conflict of interest, whether actual, potential or perceived (see below).

Recognition and maintenance of quality standards and good practice should mean:

- pro-active, consistent, appropriate advice on individual cases, and on policy, law, procedures and practice;
- legal advice before initiation of proceedings;[7]
- allocation of cases according to experience, expertise and knowledge;
- representation in contested proceedings by a lawyer with up-to-date knowledge of the law, appropriate training and recent significant practical experience;[8]
- Children Panel accreditation;
- maintaining control by keeping conduct of at least 75 per cent of cases in-house;[9]
- where work is outsourced being clear about who is ultimately accountable to the client (i.e. legal department or external provider);
- avoiding arrangements whereby staff can choose where and how to obtain legal advice/representation, or where practitioners are based in client departments.
- appropriate supervision and support from those who understand the specialist nature of the work;

- resolution of disputes between client department and legal practitioner at senior management level;
- taking account of the lawyer's overriding duty to assist the court to arrive at an appropriate result in the child's paramount interests;
- providing a designated child care lawyer for each case and consistency of representation and advice;
- specialist, interdisciplinary and skills training, professional development, mentoring and supervision;
- sufficient resources to enable proper management information, including a computerised system complying with Law Society Practice Management standards.

Practitioners should be aware of the role and responsibility of the local ACPC/LSCB, the different services and professional groups cooperating to safeguard the welfare of children and of any protocols and procedures between these agencies and social services.

Practitioners should also have regard to the importance of encouraging interdepartmental cooperation between social services, education and housing and be familiar with the Judicial Case Management Protocol, especially Appendix F.[10]

Contact between practitioners

Where there are current proceedings with the local authority on record, 'solicitors for non-local authority parties should not contact members of social services departments direct, without the consent of the relevant Local Authority Legal Department'.[11]

Practitioners should adhere to any local policies and there should be a clear protocol for communication between children's services and practitioners for other parties. If not, other lawyers should attempt to notify the legal department before contacting children's services and copy to both departments any written queries or correspondence.

This demonstrates professional courtesy and good faith, which, in return, may result in helpful information and a referral to the right department/individual.

Conflicts of interest and refusal of instructions

The general rule is that a practitioner should no longer continue to act if 'responsible for deciding on a course of action, the legality of which is in dispute in the proceedings': this would include a local authority decision to remove a child that is subsequently challenged.[12] However, local authority practitioners should rarely, if ever, be in this position: their functions are solely or primarily to provide legal advice and legal services, with policy decisions a matter for the managers they are advising.

Each practitioner should be able to give their professional opinion and advice freely, and evidence where necessary, without fear of recrimination. If problems prove intractable, advice should be sought from senior managers, who should support the principle of independent, impartial advice without fear or favour. The Monitoring Officer must ensure that the authority acts at all times within the law and observes due process and has statutory powers that can be exercised if she considers any proposed action of the authority to be unlawful.

Problems are more likely where the formal decision about initiation or pursuit of proceedings is delegated to the practitioner, unless she has other managerial or executive responsibilities for the issues;[13] or where correct advice to individual professionals and senior management is unwelcome and ignored, for reasons likely to impact on the conduct or outcome of proceedings, or seriously prejudice the rights and interests of others.

Social work resources and/or managerial pressures provide clear examples. Giving unwelcome advice requires clear communication and careful recording: where there is any reason to doubt the propriety of any action, the practitioner should ensure the client and, if necessary, any other relevant officers or members have received and understood any appropriate warnings or advice, and consequent instructions have their approval.[14]

The authority has the right to a legal representative of choice, but avoiding actual or perceived conflicts of interest needs care. Equality of arms, the authority's power and the sensitivity of care cases make it critical for an authority to be seen to be acting impartially. The court has power to refuse to hear a particular advocate: Courts and Legal Services Act 1990, s.27(4) and see *Re L (Care Proceedings: Cohabiting Solicitors)* [2000] 2 FLR 887), but this may cause some practical difficulties in areas where legal teams are small and the number of local franchised firms limited.

Advice and advocacy

Advice and advocacy is crucial for parents and carers in child protection enquiries. Creating and maintaining positive partnerships between families and the authority should be encouraged and supported because such access to legal advice and representation as early as possible is in the authority's interests[15] and specialist, experienced legal advice is essential to facilitate parental participation. It is also a clear expectation in government guidance.[16]

Parents/carers should routinely be given information about how to access advice and advocacy services from the outset and be encouraged and enabled to involve a legal adviser/other specialist advocate to provide independent support, information and advice throughout to ensure effective participation.

The practitioner should ensure general and case-specific advice to the client emphasises such access, advise the client to inform family members about it, providing the list of local Children Panel representatives[17] and explain the role of legal representatives to other professionals.

Lay supporter/specialist advocate

The early stages of a case may involve such support, but be followed by representation from a specialist legal practitioner. This raises the potential for confusion and conflict unless care is taken in communicating information and ensuring consistency. Local authority practitioners, from their position of familiarity with the principles of good legal practice, should assist in resolving these issues.

Their role is not covered in statutory guidance and comprehensive services subject to consistent standards do not yet exist. But lawyers providing them must comply with professional guidance and rules, which take precedence.[18]

22.6   GENERAL ADVICE TO THE CLIENT

Advice on assessment and services for a child in need and her family is increasingly important. This should be given well in advance of proceedings being contemplated or instigated wherever possible, given the importance of:

* early intervention;
* multidisciplinary decision-making and financial commitments;
* sound, comprehensive and culturally competent assessments and plans;
* the expectations of the Judicial Case Management Protocol;
* participation rights in decision-making processes (bearing in mind the principles set out in *Re L (Care: Assessment: Fair Trial)* [2002] EWHC (Fam) 1379, [2002] 2 FLR 730; *Re G (Care: Challenge to Local Authority's Decision)* [2003] EWHC (Fam) 551, [2003] 2 FLR 42);
* access to complaints procedures.

Given the overriding duty to the court and the child's interests, the advice should be independent, impartial and pro-active, based on up-to-date, high quality research and good evidence-based practice, accurate information and recent case law and guidance (especially in sexual abuse cases where poor practice in interview techniques is still being criticised for failure to follow appropriate guidelines) (*Re M (Minors)* [1993] 1 FLR 822).

22.7   ADVICE IN INVESTIGATIONS AND CONFERENCES

Well planned and effective action requires good liaison between the police, social services and practitioners based on trust and sound advice and a clear focus on good practice. Cultivating and maintaining good professional relationships is important, but the practitioner is charged with the ultimate responsibility for the conduct of proceedings, so objectivity in examining all material and decision-making is vital. This means:

- maintaining professional boundaries;
- testing evidence thoroughly and assessing witness reliability and competence;
- relationships which preserve fully independent judgment;
- seeing the files to prepare the case;
- not making assumptions;
- asking awkward questions and challenging the assumptions of others;
- ensuring everyone keeps on track: proceedings should be part of overall planning (above all for the child) and decision-making.

Concurrent proceedings

Particular care is needed with concurrent proceedings. The practitioner should work to agreed investigation and prosecution standards and ensure clearly understood information-sharing procedures exist, that take account of disclosure principles and current protocols (see Chapter 24 and 2005 pilot schemes).

Child protection conferences

Legal advice is important in the early stages of investigation and particularly at initial child protection conferences: lack of it may contribute to 'the failure of those most closely involved with the children to appreciate that the medical opinions they acted upon might not provide a satisfactory basis for applications in care proceedings . . . [and deprive] them of a useful check in consideration of the advisability of the removal of the children from home'.[19]

The relationship between the local authority practitioner and the conference Chair is pivotal: the Chair must be able to call on legal advice, particularly when court action is under consideration[20] and proceedings should not be initiated without legal advice.[21]

Attendance at, and an active role in, child protection conferences varies from authority to authority, but up to early 1994, legal practitioners advised on registration criteria as a judicially reviewable decision, directly questioned professional participants to explore evidence and advised on grounds for legal proceedings.

This role has changed as a result of the increased emphasis on partnership and conference participation. But resources, workloads and internal structures have also taken their toll. It is still desirable to have a lawyer present at all initial conferences and essential if legal proceedings are likely to be considered, although this decision is often taken in a separate meeting. Previous concern that prior knowledge of other proceedings or information on the child or family may have been limited to the practitioner has been considerably lessened by the use of independent Chairs.

The 1997 Law Society guidance (Attendance of Solicitors at Case Conferences) is not a specific practice rule but has some force as Code of Conduct guidance and should be followed unless very good reasons exist for not doing so. This is under revision, based on the presumption of participation by parents, significant others and children of sufficient age and understanding.

The attendance of practitioners can be valuable in advising the Chair, but the role must be clear: they attend as legal expert, not full participant (*Working Together*, para. 5.55 is not clear on this point but the professional conduct position is clear), and should not take part in the decision, the recommendations or the child protection plan. They may advise the conference to keep within its remit, but it is the Chair's responsibility to ensure it does so.

The practitioner's client is the local authority, not the individual agencies in attendance. Necessary legal advice to the local authority on their role in care planning and proceedings should be given *outside* the conference. But she may also need to consider advising the conference on whether its recommendation for court proceedings can be sustained by the available information, and assisting in the registration decision by advising whether the criteria are fulfilled, (because this is a decision open to legal challenge), but *not* voting on the issue, (because this amounts to participation in decision-making).

Direct questions of other participants may also be needed in order to widen the information being considered or to expand upon or clarify information already given.

Conferences differ substantially in context and purpose from proceedings and the evidence required. There is a distinction in evidential value between the information given in each (for further discussion see Chapters 4 and 5) and the conference should not be used as a pre-trial review of a case.[22]

Role in relation to parents

Where other parties' lawyers cannot attend, parties cannot object to the presence of the local authority practitioner, who should remind social workers about recognising the role of other practitioners for parents and other family members. She should make sure information is given about access to legal advice and assistance where parents are not represented and ensure they do not use their position to unfair advantage.[23]

For professional conduct reasons, the practitioner should not attempt to cross-examine or address parents on substantive questions. Situations that may lead to later conflict should be avoided, e.g. listening to the discussion and using that knowledge later in cross-examination. It was precisely this sort of problem that led to the current Law Society guidance.[24]

Withdrawals and exclusion issues

Where information needs to be discussed that may conflict with the interests of a parent or child present, the local authority practitioner should consider withdrawing. This should not be routine, but be considered in cases where prior warning of potentially damaging admissions is given and in order to prevent criticism at a later stage. Local criteria in ACPC/LCSB procedures should be based on national guidance on exclusions.[25]

See also Chapter 5.

Advising on initiation of proceedings

The client should be advised about the legal strengths, weaknesses and complexities of the case before proceedings are commenced,[26] including:

- Does the evidence satisfy the initial threshold?
- Will it satisfy the no order principle and the threshold criteria for a full order?
- Are there alternative orders available in other jurisdictions?
- What are the implications of any concurrent proceedings (crime, private law, housing, education, etc.)?
- What evidence and documentation is required by the Judicial Case Management Protocol, including the form and content of the initial social work statement and other local authority documents under Step 1?
- What is needed to address the case management issues and directions likely to be considered at first or allocation hearing?
- What orders should be sought and are they proportionate to the circumstances?
- Who are the parties to the proceedings and who should be given notice?
- What arrangements should be made for contacting, and disclosure to, the child's solicitor where there is no guardian?

The application should be scrutinised, the evidential weight of the support work and assessments carried out to date assessed (including whether further assessments are required), and the following considered:

- Has the client fully reviewed the case history and therefore all the files?
- Is there a complete set of all previous family assessments, minutes of statutory reviews and child protection conferences?

- Has written information been obtained from all other sources on whom the local authority wishes to rely?
- Has permission to disclose been obtained where the local authority is relying on evidence provided by others (i.e. doctors)?
- Has a running chronology been kept at the top of the social work file and updated (*Re E (Care Proceedings; Social Work Practice*) [2000] 2 FLR 254)?
- Does the interim care plan take into account the outcome of the child protection conferences and plans and does it deal properly with the child's contact needs?
- Have the child's and the family's race, language, culture and religion been addressed?

Before the issue of proceedings, the practitioner should also pursue the following issues.[27] Is there complete information on the wider family and friendship networks for interim and permanency care planning? Have reasonable but robust efforts been made at an early stage to locate both parents, notably non-resident parents, and to identify members of the extended family? Has the primary carer been the sole source of information on who is significant to the child, and if so, who/what else should be explored? Has parallel (or twin-track) planning been considered and is it appropriate in order to avoid delay?

Where proceedings are commenced in an emergency (e.g. emergency protection order), it is especially important that the legal adviser ensures that the limited information to be supplied to the court is as complete and balanced as possible.

22.8 CONDUCT, REPRESENTATION AND ADVOCACY

All cases should be based on good advice and thorough preparation and presentation. This should ensure:

- paramountcy of the child's best interests;
- sufficient consideration given to, and evidence obtained, of ethnicity, language, religion, culture, gender and vulnerability;
- a non-adversarial and cooperative approach;
- a constructive solution with the minimum of acrimony;
- respect and courtesy for all parties;
- information-sharing with all those with a 'need to know';
- compliance with the Judicial Case Management Protocol and all relevant judicial and other guidance;[28]
- compliance with the Code for Experts and Legal Services Commission guidance;

- scrutiny of the local authority's case;
- all relevant information is before the court and other parties, including the substantive significance of any cultural context and the seeking of any necessary directions for relevant evidence;
- early transfer of proceedings where appropriate;
- all timetable requirements are met;
- proper monitoring and supervision of cases and caseload;
- production of properly prepared bundles and other documentation required to be disclosed and/or filed with the court;
- full and frank disclosure.

The client and all relevant professionals must be kept informed about the progress of proceedings, with reasons for and implications of any changes in plan or delays. They must understand what is expected of them when they attend court, be reminded to bring relevant files with them to meetings and hearings and have the roles and responsibilities of respective people in the case explained to them.

The practitioner should[29] advise no significant change in the child's circumstances without prior consultation with her guardian and taking into account the wishes and feelings of the parents and any other relevant person. S/he should bring to the court's attention any significant changes to the final care plan in time for the pre-hearing review and be aware of the local authority's procedures for making decisions about issues such as placement with parents and funding for assessments, especially residential assessments.

Regard should be had to other plans that may overlap with the care plan e.g. personal education or Pathway plans (see Chapters 11 and 13), to special educational needs statements and assessments, and any other assessments on disability, mental health, housing, etc., and to the liaison and monitoring necessary for other processes and proceedings.

Controlling and monitoring the use of specialist advocates/counsel should be normal practice, but if used the practitioner should ensure s/he:

- retains full responsibility for the case;
- gives adequate instructions in sufficient time for counsel to prepare the case properly, including all material information;
- instructs those with adequate experience and accreditation in child law;
- retains the same advocate throughout the case; and
- adheres to Principle 20.04 on attendance at court.[30]

Some authorities have protocols for the instruction of external advocates, with requirements and principles similar to the Children Panel undertaking and other guidance and will only instruct a member of the Bar on an approved supplier list.

Full and frank disclosure

Whatever general rules and principles apply to access to information and information-sharing,[31] total equality of arms is unlikely to exist between a public body and an individual. Frankness in most civil proceedings is now encouraged, but the local authority's duty in care proceedings of full and frank disclosure of all relevant information, both positive and negative,[32] has long been clear (*Vernon* v. *Bosley (No. 2)* [1997] 2 FLR 304; *Re R (Care: Disclosure: Nature of Proceedings)* [2002] 1 FLR 755).[33]

This means ensuring that the legal adviser is proactive in considering disclosure and does not simply wait for requests from the other parties. Where there is objection to disclosure, the existence of the material should be disclosed. Full cooperation should be given to the guardian, including full access to the case files, and that evidence is balanced, i.e. true to the facts, fair, complete, full and frank.

The practitioner must also observe the *Reporting to Court* guidance (see Chapter 4), and the need to challenge any instructions that relevant documentation should not be disclosed: 'advocates must cease to act ... if the client refuses to authorise them to make some disclosure to the court which their duty to the court requires them to make'.[34] In practice such disputes will need to be resolved at senior management level, since the practitioner's only other recourse is to resign.

Copies of all papers relating to the child protection process should be sent to parents and their legal representatives at the earliest opportunity.[35]

Preparation of evidence, statements and witnesses

The practitioner must ensure that a statement represents the witness's evidence as accurately as possible, e.g. their manager should not control its contents unless there are justifiable reasons. The practitioner must ensure that the witness understands and signs every page[36] and that the witness is kept informed appropriately of case progress and hearing dates that require her attendance. Witness availability dates must be obtained and provided to the court and to other parties.

However, the practitioner must not[37] 'when interviewing a witness out of court place [them] ... under any pressure to provide other than a truthful account of their evidence; rehearse, practise or coach ... devise facts which will assist in advancing their client's case ... draft any [court document] ... containing any statement of fact or contention ... which is not supported by the client or by their ... instructions; any contention which they do not consider to be properly arguable'.

Agencies may present some resistance where concerned about their professional relationships with clients and families. The practitioner should make every effort to ensure the evidence is accurate, pointing out that omissions and alterations of emphasis that result in an incomplete, unbalanced or misleading account can lead to later difficulties in giving evidence.

Practitioners should check to see whether relevant information has been obtained from as wide a range of sources as possible, e.g.

- probation: useful for risk assessment, conditions of licence and the whereabouts of offenders on release;
- prison service: they can also provide risk assessment and notification of actual release date, likely to differ from the original date given;
- housing: reports on possession proceedings, environmental health issues, neighbour complaints, tenancy details and transfers or moves;
- ambulance or fire services: records of callouts, 999 calls, etc.

The preparation of the local authority's care plan should comply with the requirements of the 1999 circular on care plans. The care plan must be endorsed by a relevant senior officer. Evidence should be provided to demonstrate that the plan is achievable, e.g. evidence from the child placement team that it is likely that suitable carers will be found.

Other practical issues

The lawyer should also:

- ensure the child's placement is lawful by checking the social worker really understands the Fostering Services Regulations 2002, SI 2002/57, which require Panel approval of any placement with relatives/friends;
- obtain a birth certificate at the outset (needed in any event for babies born since December 2003 to establish parental responsibility);
- ensure all those involved understand the legal duties on safeguarding and information-sharing, especially health professionals;
- alert social workers to the need to apply for an adoption medical in good time.

NOTES

1   *Good Practice in Child Care Cases*, Law Society (2004), para. 2.2.
2   See e.g J. Brophy *et al.*, *Significant Harm: Child Protection Litigation in a Multi-Cultural Setting*, Lord Chancellor's Department (2003).
3   See *Guidance: Arranging Interpreters for People with a Hearing Impairment and for Foreign Languages*, Court Service, Civil Business Branch (September 2003).
4   *Climbié Inquiry Report* (2003), Recommendation 36.
5   See Protocol for Judicial Case Management in Public Law Children Act Cases [2003] 2 FLR 719, App. F 'Social Services Assessment and Care Planning Aide-Memoire'.
6   *The Guide to the Professional Conduct of Solicitors 1999*, Principle 20.02.
7   Children Act Guidance, vol. 1, Court Orders.

8   *Arrangements for Handling Child Care Cases*, Association of Council Secretaries and Solicitors and Solicitors in Local Government: Child Care Law Joint Liaison Group (2004); and *Good Practice in Child Care Cases*, para. 3.1.3.

9   *Arrangements for Handling Child Care Cases.*

10 Protocol for Judicial Case Management in Public Law Children Act Cases, App. F.

11 *The Guide to the Professional Conduct of Solicitors 1999*, Principle 19.02.

12 Law Society's Code for Advocacy 1993, para 4.1(e).

13 *Ibid.*

14 *Ibid.*, para. 8.2.

15 *Arrangements for Handling Child Care Cases*, para 3.3.1.

16 *Working Together to Safeguard Children*, DH, Home Office, DfEE (1999), paras 5.43 and 5.57, and paras 7.19–7.21.

17 *Good Practice in Child Care Cases*, para. 3.3.1 and App. 3.

18 See, e.g. *National Advocacy Standards for Agencies Providing Advocacy for Children and Young People in England*, DH (2002) and B. Lindley and R.M. Richards, *Protocol on Advice and Advocacy for Parents (Child Protection)*, DH (2002).

19 *Report of the Inquiry into Child Abuse in Cleveland* (1987), para. 11.

20 This appeared in the 1991 version of *Working Together*, para. 6.27 and is still good practice.

21 *Arrangements for Handling Child Care Cases*, para. 2.7.

22 *Good Practice in Child Care Cases*, para. 2.5.6.

23 *Arrangements for Handling Child Care Cases.*

24 Law Society Family Law Committee guidance, *Attendance of Solicitors at Child Protection Conferences* (June 1997).

25 *Working Together* and *Challenge of Partnership in Child Protection: A Practice Guide*, DH, SSI (1995).

26 *Good Practice in Child Care Cases*, para. 3.2.4.

27 *Ibid.*, para. 3.3, and as expected by the Protocol for Judicial Case Management in Public Law Children Act Cases.

28 'Each case should be conducted in compliance with guidance offered by the High Court and the Department of Health': *Arrangements for Handling Child Care Cases*, para. 4.13.

29 *Good Practice in Child Care Cases*, para. 3.5.

30 Replaces principle in print edition of *The Guide to the Professional Conduct of Solicitors 1999* and available online at **www.guide-on-line.lawsociety.org.uk**.

31 For further information see *Data Sharing Guide*, DCA (2003), Freedom of Information Act 2000 and other relevant legislation.

32 *Good Practice in Child Care Cases*, para. 3.4.4.

33 See *Arrangements for Handling Child Care Cases*, para. 4.5.

34 Law Society's Code for Advocacy 1993, para. 5.1(e),(f).

35 *Good Practice in Child Care Cases,* para. 3.4.7.

36 Children Act Advisory Committee, *Annual Report 1993/4*, p.23.

37 Law Society's Code for Advocacy 1993.

CHAPTER 23

Effective case management

Key sources

- Protocol for Judicial Case Management in Public Law Children Act Cases (2003)
- *Practice Direction (Care Cases: Judicial Continuity and Judicial Case Management)* [2003] 2 FLR 719
- Annex to the Practice Direction (Principles of Application) (2003)

23.1   INTRODUCTION

As from November 2003, case management has been in the hands of the judiciary. The court was always under a duty to set a timetable for cases, but the Protocol for Judicial Case Management in Public Law Children Act Cases ('the Protocol') has made it clear that lawyers involved in proceedings can no longer influence the process and management of them in the way they once did.

23.2   THE PRACTICE DIRECTION, PRINCIPLES AND PROTOCOL

Purpose and overriding objective

In August 2003 the President of the Family Division issued a Practice Direction, 'Care Cases: Judicial Continuity and Judicial Case Management', which annexed the Protocol and the Principles of Application.

The purpose of the Practice Direction, Principles and Protocol is to ensure consistency in the application of best practice by all courts dealing with care cases and, in particular, to ensure that care cases are dealt with in accordance with the overriding objective; that there are no unacceptable delays in the hearing and determination of care cases; and that except in unforeseen circumstances, every care case is finally determined within 40 weeks of the application being issued.

The overriding objective of the Practice Direction is to enable the court to deal with every care case:

- justly, expeditiously, fairly and with the minimum of delay;
- in ways which ensure, so far as is practicable, that the parties are on an equal footing, that the welfare of the children involved is safeguarded; and that distress to all parties is minimised;
- so far as is practicable, in ways which are proportionate to the gravity and complexity of the issues; and to the nature and extent of the intervention proposed in the private and family life of the children and adults involved.

The parties are required to help the court fulfil the overriding objective. It will further this by actively managing cases as required by Children Act 1989, ss. 11 and 32 (the timetabling provisions), and acting in accordance with the Practice Direction, Principles and Protocol.

The Practice Direction on court bundles[1] remains in force and is to be complied with, subject to the Protocol and any directions given by the case management judge.

The President's Direction on Judicial Continuity[2] ceases to have any effect in a case to which this new Practice Direction applies.

Every court in approaching the application of the Protocol has to keep its terms and its purpose in mind as explained in the Practice Direction and Annex (*Re G (Protocol for Judicial Case Management)* [2004] EWHC Fam 116.

The six steps

The Protocol is constructed around six steps, commencing with the application for a care/supervision order and ending with the final hearing. The route map at the beginning of the Protocol details the steps and action required at each stage of the proceedings. The objective of each step and the timescale within which the step is to take place is specified. The steps are:

- Step 1: The Application (day 1 to day 3)
- Step 2: The First Hearing in the Family Proceedings Court (on or before day 6)
- Step 3: Allocation Hearing and Directions (by day 11 (county court) or day 15 (High Court))
- Step 4: The Case Management Conference (between day 15 and 60)
- Step 5: The Pre-Hearing Review (by week 37)
- Step 6: The Final Hearing (by week 40)

Forms and checklists

The Appendices to the Protocol are:

- A/1: Standard Directions Form
- A/2: Case Management Questionnaire

- A/3: Case Management Checklist
- A/4: Witness Non-Availability
- A/5: Pre-Hearing Review Checklist
- B: details what should be contained in the case synopsis; social work chronology; initial social work statement and schedule of issues
- C: Code of Guidance for Expert Witnesses in Family Proceedings
- D: *Practice Direction (Family Proceedings: Court Bundles)* [2000] 1 FLR 536
- E: sets out what is required of the care centre and Family Proceedings Court Plan
- F: Social Services Assessment and Care Planning Aide-Memoire: a summary of existing guidance relating to assessment and care planning
- G: a summary of best practice guidance relating to requests made under Children Act 1989, s.37

The case management judge and parties must use the forms and standard documents referred to in Appendix A; prepare or require the parties to prepare the documents referred to in Appendix B; and comply with or require the parties and every expert to comply with the Code of Guidance in Appendix C.

The application of checklists forms a significant part of the Protocol. Both the case management checklist and the pre-hearing review checklist should be considered by the parties prior to each of those hearings.

The case management checklist consists of 63 issues for consideration, at the first hearing in the Family Proceedings Court, the allocation hearing in the care centre, allocation directions in the High Court and for the case management conference. The issues to be considered are grouped in 11 sections, headed: Representation of the child; Parties; Interim care order; Urgency, transfer and retransfer; Protocol documents; Preliminary directions; Listing; Evidence; Ethnicity, language, religion and culture; Care plans and final evidence; Other case management steps.

The issues to be considered include:

- representation of the child, including whether or not the child and children's guardian should be separately represented;
- whether all the significant persons involved in the child's care have been identified and, where necessary, served with notice of the proceedings;
- whether a father without parental responsibility has been or should be notified; and similarly in relation to members of the extended family;
- whether any other person should be joined as a party, or served with documents;
- what directions are required to ensure that the Protocol documents are/will be prepared;
- what directions are required in relation to the filing of evidence by parties other than the local authority, and in relation to disclosure of documents by the local authority within 20 days of the first hearing;

- listing the case management conference, the pre-hearing review, if necessary, the final hearing, and considering the venue and means of communication with the court, by videolink, electronic communication or telephone conferencing;
- a general review of the evidence which has been filed, will be filed, or ought to be obtained, including expert evidence and assessments;
- whether consideration has been given to the ethnicity, language, religion and culture of the child and other significant persons, and whether directions are necessary to ensure that evidence about these matters is placed before the court;
- whether a date has been set for filing the local authority care plan and final statements, and for responses to those proposals by other parties, and for the report of the children's guardian to be filed;
- whether a family group conference has been/is to be held;
- whether directions are required in relation to twin track planning and placement options;
- whether a finding of fact hearing is necessary, and if so, what directions should be made in order to effect such a hearing;
- directions for the final hearing.

The Pre-Hearing Review Checklist consists of 22 issues for consideration, which include:

- clarification of the issues to be determined at trial, and how much, if any, of the evidence is agreed;
- clarification of the witnesses to be called;
- time estimates for examination, cross-examination, submissions and judgment/reasons;
- whether the child will give evidence/see the judge, and if so, what arrangements need to be made;
- what arrangements are required for vulnerable/intimidated witnesses and/or parties, and for those with a hearing impairment or disability;
- whether or not interpretation facilities are required.

23.3 EVIDENCE

The evidence to be put before the court will fall into four categories: first, primary evidence, first hand evidence in the form of statements or affidavits, disclosed to the parties, and supported by oral evidence; then secondary evidence, which is opinion evidence, adduced by agreement of the parties or with leave of the court, and hearsay evidence, which is admissible in children's cases (see the Children (Admissibility of Hearsay Evidence) Order 1993, SI 1993/621; Civil Evidence Act 1995, s.1(1)); or tertiary evidence, which is textbook material on which expert evidence is based (see Douglas Brown J in

Rochdale BC v. *A* [1991] 2 FLR 191); finally, facts not needing proof: issue estoppel following res judicata, where there has been a previous decision by a court of competent jurisdiction, where the parties and the issues in both cases are the same (*K* v. *P* (*Children Act Proceedings: Estoppel*) [1995] 1 FLR 904).

Where there is an application for an issue of fact to be tried again, the court must consider on balance (*Re B* (*Children Act Proceedings: Issue Estoppel*) [1997] 1 FLR 283):

- whether public interest requires an end to litigation, and the delay factor, as against the prejudice to the child's welfare;
- whether there was a full hearing in the previous proceedings, and the testing of evidence;
- whether the accuracy of previous findings could have been attacked and, if so, why there was no appeal;
- whether there is any new evidence or information which may throw doubt on the original findings;
- whether a rehearing would result in a different finding of fact.

When considering what evidence should be filed, the following factors are relevant: whether the evidence is relevant to the issue to be tried and whether the evidence is cogent (*Re N* (*Child Abuse: Evidence*) [1996] 2 FLR 214, CA).

When deciding by whom evidence should be filed, factors to consider are:

- the source of the information and basis for any views;
- what the evidence will add to the case;
- if there is a proliferation of evidence on one point, who will be the most suitable witness;
- who is available to fill gaps in the evidence;
- the witness's likely performance under cross-examination.

23.4 EXPERTS

The instruction of experts is dealt with in the Code of Guidance in Appendix C; the objective of the Code is to provide the court with early information to enable it to determine whether it is necessary and/or practicable:

- to ask an expert to assist the court to identify, narrow and where possible agree the issues between the parties;
- to ask an expert to provide an opinion about a question that is not within the skill and experience of the court;
- to encourage early identification of questions that need to be answered by an expert;
- to encourage disclosure of full and frank information between the parties, the court and any expert instructed.

In the Annex to the Practice Direction, it is stated that 'expert evidence should be proportionate to the issues in question and should relate to questions that are outside the skill and experience of the Court . . . the Code is to be followed by the parties when it is proposed that the court gives permission for the use of an expert. It should form part of every letter of instruction so that experts can adopt best practice guidance on the formulation of their reports and advice to the court'.

23.5 SPLIT HEARINGS

The Children Act 1989 does not provide for split hearings, which are in fact part heard cases. 'An application for a care or supervision order . . . is a single application encompassing: first, the finding of the necessary facts; secondly, applying judgment as to whether the court is satisfied that the threshold criteria in s.31(2) of the Children Act 1989 are made out; and thirdly the exercise of discretion as to what will be in the best interests of the child' (*Re Y and K (Split Hearing: Evidence)* [2003] 2 FLR 273).

Care proceedings are suitable for a split hearing usually where the establishment of the threshold criteria under Children Act 1989, s.31 depends upon a discrete factual issue, e.g. whether or not injuries to a child are non-accidental, or whether or not injuries to a child were inflicted by one or both of her parents (*Re S (Care Proceedings: Split Hearing)* [1996] 2 FLR 773 per Bracewell J).

The essence of a split hearing is the clear identification of the issue to be tried first.

Evidence which is relevant to the assessment of the parents or other family members, if and when the threshold criteria are established, should not be permitted unless for some reason it is of direct relevance to the factual issue being tried. Assessments of the parties and their capacity to parent their children need to be carried out on the basis of the facts found by the court.

When timetabling a split hearing, it may be appropriate to timetable the second stage of the hearing which will take place if the threshold criteria are established. It would be appropriate to give a party leave prior to the hearing of the first stage to show the papers to the psychiatrist or psychologist if the threshold criteria are established, in order to save time, and a timetable for such an assessment to be drafted.

Split hearings can create delays: waiting for the court to list the preliminary hearing and because some expert reports, such as psychiatric assessments, cannot be commenced until after that hearing and findings have been made. Despite the point made by Hale LJ (in *Re G (Care Proceedings: Split Trials)* [2001] 1 FLR 872) that a timetable should be set which includes both hearings, and before the same judge, anecdotal evidence suggests that many cases are heard by different judges for the findings of fact and the disposal hearing, and that sometimes the same advocate is not available for both hearings.

The advantage of a split hearing is that it can enable assessments to proceed on a firm foundation of fact.

The disadvantages include that the initial delay in waiting for court time to make findings of fact will be compounded by the further delay in waiting for a disposal hearing. Many experts will not make a report when no findings of fact have been made (*Re D (Child: Threshold Criteria)* [2001] 1 FLR 274). The anxiety caused to the family by the very existence of proceedings is likely to be increased by the additional delay and the delay may result in a child who would not have been difficult to place becoming of an age where she falls into that category.

Any appeal against findings on factual matters should be made without waiting for the disposal hearing (*Re B (Split Hearing: Jurisdiction)* [2000] 1 FLR 334).

A local authority may reopen the issue of the threshold criteria even where these were determined by agreement at a split hearing, and there is no new evidence for the court to consider (*Re D (Child: Threshold Criteria)* [2001] 1 FLR 274).

Are split hearings compatible with the overriding objectives of the Protocol? Consideration of the necessity for a split hearing is to be given at the first hearing/allocation stage, or at the case management conference. The Protocol does not make it clear when this hearing should take place, or how it fits into the timetable. The local authority must file its schedule of findings sought by five days before the conference, and by that date the parties must file their case management questionnaires, in which they may request a preliminary hearing. If the conference does not take place until eight weeks after the application is made, there are then 32 weeks remaining to fit in both fact-finding and disposal hearings. The amount of work required after findings are made is considerable, e.g. assessments, drafting of the final care plan, presentation of the case to the Permanency Panel, and responses by other parties.

It is difficult to see how the expectation of the Protocol that there should be no more than four intermediate hearings save in unforeseen or exceptional circumstances can easily accommodate requests for split hearings, without creating the very delay which the Protocol has been designed to avoid.

23.6 TIME ESTIMATES

An accurate estimate of the time required for the final hearing is crucial to the efficient operation of the Protocol. Time estimates should be part of a cooperative planning process between the lawyers for the respective parties, which is designed to see that a case is properly prepared for trial (*Re M (Minors)*, 2 December 1993 (unreported)).

The following matters must be considered. Advocates should think realistically about their cross-examination of witnesses and include a realistic calculation of the likely length of each witness's evidence in the overall estimate of time given. Where medical experts are involved, there should be careful cooperative planning to ensure that sufficient time is set aside for their evidence. No estimate can be accurate unless time limits are obeyed and evidence produced on time. Late evidence distorts the timescale.

Advocates must also consider:

- the documents which the court will have to read and the time likely to be taken in reading;
- the likely length of the opening;
- the witnesses whose oral evidence will be required and the length in each case of the likely examination in chief, cross-examination and re-examination;
- the points of law or procedure which are likely to arise in the case and the length they will take to argue;
- the number and likely length of closing speeches;
- the time likely to be needed for an extempore judgment.

If a case seriously overruns due to negligent or incompetent estimation of time, the court may make an order for wasted costs against an advocate held responsible.[3]

23.7 PARALLEL/TWIN TRACK PLANNING

Timescales

It is necessary to consider how the timescales imposed on social services departments for plans, decisions and placement of a child tie in with the Protocol, bearing in mind the requirements of the Adoption Agencies Regulations 1983, SI 1983/1964, and the need to prepare documents for the Panel and lodge them well in advance of the Panel meeting.

If the case is transferred to the care centre, the allocation hearing will take place by Day 11; if not transferred, the court will have the first hearing by Day 6. At this hearing, the case management checklist will be considered (A/3). Paragraphs 57 and 58 require consideration of directions to ensure that, in the appropriate case, twin track planning has been considered, and whether dates have been fixed for the filing of the parallel plan, and in respect of the Panel timetable; also whether the Adoption Practice Direction has been complied with, i.e. have any proposed freeing proceedings been commenced?

The case management checklist will also be considered at the case management conference, which must take place between 15 and 60 days after commencement of the proceedings.

The national standards require:

- a plan to be made about the child's future by the date of the second review after she becomes a looked after child, i.e. after four months;
- a Panel recommendation to be made two months after that date, which must be communicated within 24 hours;
- the agency decision within seven days and communicated orally within 24 hours, and in writing within seven days;
- a match within six months of the decision for adoption, or six months from the court decision;
- placement within 12 months of becoming a looked after child.

It can be seen that the two sets of timescales do not match up. However, those imposed by the Protocol are not set in stone. What the court will require is an explanation as to how planning for the child is progressing, and when a definitive care plan can be prepared. Until the agency has taken a decision that adoption is in the best interests of the child, this is not the local authority plan, no matter what social worker statements it may contain.

Relevance of the Panel to the care plan

A decision that adoption is the care plan for a child can be made by the local authority, acting as an adoption agency, after a recommendation from the Adoption/Permanency Panel. The following matters must be taken into account.

Papers for the Panel usually have to be submitted to the Panel clerk four weeks before the Panel meeting.

The Adoption Agency Regulations 1983 require the agency to provide counselling to the parents, and child if she is of sufficient understanding. This does not have to be given by an employee of the agency, and in many cases it may be preferable for a counsellor to be used who is independent of the authority. Written information about adoption must be supplied to them, and good practice requires that the documents are in the language spoken by the family. Form E will contain information about the proposals for the type of placement, whether or not siblings are to be split, and in relation to contact post-placement.

If the agency decision-maker did not make a decision that was in line with the Panel recommendation, the reason for this must be given.

The children's guardian should ensure that she communicates her views about outcome of the proceedings, placement and contact in writing to the Panel Chair in advance of the Panel meeting.

Issues for solicitors

Solicitors will need to consider whether the adoption support package is adequate given the circumstances of the child. Does it include provision for therapeutic support?

Guardians will need to be aware of the range of possible adoption support services, which could be available to children and their birth relatives and adoptive families. Guardians will want to make sure that an adequate assessment of the need for adoption support services is made at the point of the best interests decision and matching decision for the child for whom the care plan is adoption.

Decisions reached by a local authority about financial support and contact arrangements before an adoption order is made will commit the placing local authority to be responsible for these services throughout the child's childhood, as long as they remain appropriate. Guardians will probably want to ensure that these decisions are put in place while they are involved so that they can check that an accurate assessment of need has been carried out, and that the child's entitlement to services is established. Financial support can begin at any point during childhood. The Regulations apply to existing and new placements for children.

Birth relatives are only included in, and can only request assessment for, adoption support services in relation to contact arrangements. The local authority still has duties to birth family members: to provide counselling, explain the legal implications of adoption and provide written information about this under the previous legislation and regulations, and this has not changed.[4]

23.8 POSSIBLE JUDICIAL BIAS

A judge should not hear the case when there is a real danger or possibility of bias. The Court of Appeal has set out the principles to be applied (*Locabail (UK) Ltd* v. *Bayfield Properties (and Others)* [2000] UKHRR 300). A judge is automatically disqualified from hearing a case where the outcome of the case could realistically affect the judge's interest. A party may waive their right to object, but such a waiver must be clear and unequivocal. The rule should be that the judge will be disqualified if, on examination of all the relevant circumstances, the court concludes that there is a real danger (or possibility) of bias. Where the judge is unaware of the allegedly disqualifying interest there would be no real danger of bias.

Objections based on religion, gender, ethnic origin, age, class, means or sexual orientation are most unlikely to be sustained; nor ordinarily could objections be soundly based on social or educational, service or employment history; membership of sporting or charitable bodies; or Masonic associations; or previous judicial decisions; or extracurricular utterances; or previous receipt of instructions to act for or against a party; or membership of the same Inn, Chambers or law society.

In a later case (*Re Medicaments and Related Classes of Goods (No. 2)* [2001] 1 WLR 700), Lord Phillips MR stated that the court must first ascertain all the circumstances which have a bearing on the suggestion that the judge was biased, then ask whether those circumstances would lead a fair-minded and informed observer to conclude that there was a real possibility, or a real danger (the two being the same), that the tribunal was biased.

Applying this test to judicial involvement in interdisciplinary activities, the appearance of bias arises where that involvement concerns individual cases, or the formulation of policies that could be brought to bear on individual cases, coming before the judge's court. Such involvement was recently considered by the President of the Family Division in a case involving a district judge who was a member of a legal sub group set up to discuss legal issues relating to a pilot project in concurrent planning (*M* v. *Islington LBC* [2002] 1 FLR 95).

23.9   ROLE OF THE CHILD'S SOLICITOR WITHOUT A GUARDIAN

The Department for Constitutional Affairs has requested that the Statement of Good Practice prepared by a sub-committee of the Lord Chancellor's Advisory Committee on Judicial Case Management should be treated by the courts as an Annex of the Protocol and an integral part of applying the Protocol. The Statement has been put into practice since 8 December 2003. Where a guardian has not been appointed as required by the Protocol, the court is reminded of its responsibility to consider appointing a solicitor to represent the child under Children Act 1989, s.41(3) to (5) and paragraph 1.4 of the Protocol.

The Law Society issued guidance[5] in October 2003, agreed by the SFLA (Resolution) and the ALC. This recommends that the solicitor should, where 'urgent welfare expertise is required' apply to the court for leave to instruct an expert social worker or other appropriate expert to provide the necessary report.

Given the overriding objective of the Protocol, solicitors without a guardian should make an application at the earliest possible stage for leave to instruct an expert, on a piecework basis, to advise on welfare issues, until such time as a children's guardian is appointed. Given the view of the Legal Services Commission as to rates to be paid to such experts, it would be advisable to seek court approval for the specific expenditure, or hourly rates, given that few social work experts would be prepared to work for the CAFCASS hourly rate.

23.10 PRACTICAL CONSIDERATIONS FOR THE CHILD'S SOLICITOR

- Ensure that the social work files have been searched for details of all relevant relatives.
- Obtain a birth certificate for the child or ensure that the local authority does so.
- Ensure that family abroad are located and notified at an early stage about proceedings.
- Ensure the children's guardian's views are communicated in writing to the relevant local authority Panel.
- Consider what documents in the proceedings should be disclosed to other family members; make the necessary application for disclosure.
- Consider requesting a family group conference at an early stage in the proceedings.
- Ensure that minutes are taken of all relevant meetings during the proceedings.
- Consider the attendance of parents and other relatives at such meetings.
- Do not accept the parent's view of other family members without investigation.
- Be cautious about the guardian having informal discussions with experts and social workers.
- Keep careful and contemporaneous notes of the investigation.
- Be prepared to move quickly in the event of a breach of the ECHR during the proceedings. Although the President of the Family Division has stated that the bringing of an application under the Human Rights Act 1998 does not fall within the duties of a child's guardian (*C* v. *Bury MBC* [2002] 2 FLR 868), there would appear to be no reason why the guardian could not initiate the application. Alternatively, another solicitor in the firm instructed by the guardian could act in that capacity.
- When instructed by a guardian, ensure that his/her reports filed in the proceedings address the issue of human rights and any possible breaches.

23.11 IMMIGRATION ISSUES

When acting in a case in which the parents are not British nationals, if possible obtain the child's birth certificate. Examine the parent's travel document/passport and identify if there is an entry visa. Also consider:

- What is the nationality of the parent(s) with parental responsibility?
- What is the status of the parents in the UK?
- Is the marriage of the parents recognised in this jurisdiction?
- What is the child's status in the UK? Does she have settled status?
- What were the circumstances of the child's arrival in the UK?

- Is the child dependent on the parent's claim or does she have a claim in her own right?
- Are there any outstanding applications to the Home Office?

If leave to remain has been granted, look at the document granting leave for confirmation of the type of leave granted.

Consider making enquiries of the Embassy/Consulate in the country of origin, but not if the person concerned has made an asylum application, since disclosure of this application might place him/her at risk.

The procedure set out in the President's Direction should be followed to obtain the relevant information.[6]

The Home Office will not usually disclose information about the basis for a parent's application. This will place the child at a disadvantage if there is a rift between them, and they refuse to disclose information which could support a claim by the child on her own account. Once the proceedings have concluded it may be impossible to obtain any information.

At the conclusion of the proceedings, consider what leave should be sought to disclose documents to the Home Office in connection with a pending claim.

Although the Home Office will usually follow an order of the court in relation to a child, and not seek to remove her during her minority, it is essential to ascertain who will take responsibility for pursuing any application for asylum/immigration status which may have been made, or should be made, otherwise the young person might be placed in an invidious position when she reached her majority.

If in doubt about the position, obtain advice from a specialist immigration practitioner during the course of the proceedings.

23.12   ATTENDANCE AT COURT

Under the Children and Young Persons Act 1969, the presence of a child over five years of age was required at court before a care order could be made. That requirement did not appear in the Children Act 1989, and indeed there has been considerable reluctance on the part of the judiciary to accept the presence or participation of children in legal proceedings: the general view has been that it should only be regarded as in the child's best interests in exceptional circumstances.[7] The Children Act Advisory Committee indicated that it did not agree with the principle of the child attending court: 'Except by the direction of the court, children should not attend a hearing'.[8]

The attendance of a child at a criminal trial is not in doubt. 'It follows from a notion of a fair trial that a person charged with a criminal offence should, as a general principle, be entitled to be present at the trial hearing' (*Ekbatani* v. *Sweden* (1988) 13 EHRR 504).

However, in civil cases European case law does not guarantee any right to be present. There is an implied right to be present where the proceedings involve an assessment of a party's general conduct/character/lifestyle (*Muyldermans* v. *Belgium* (1991) 15 EHRR 204, para.64). In the light of ECHR Article 6, there may now be a strong argument in favour of the competent child having a right to attend court where their civil rights and obligations are at issue (see *Colder* v. *UK* (1975) 1 EHRR 524 and the Special Educational Needs Tribunal Regulations 2001, SI 2001/600).

In 2000, Holman J proposed that children should have more access to the court,[9] although he did consider that the child should not normally be required to come into court if she does not wish to do so; should not be permitted to see her parents or other relatives or friends giving evidence, or see someone such as a social worker subjected to cross-examination, as the authority of a social worker should not be diminished by the court process; nor should allegations about parents or others be given in evidence or discussed whilst she is in court.

The fact that most children will not attend the hearing or meet the judge requires the solicitor and children's guardian to be very clear about how they explain the role of the judge, how the decision will be made and how seriously the child's views will be taken.

There is no reason why a guardian or a solicitor should not take a child to see the courtroom when the court is not sitting. The Children Act Advisory Committee regarded this as good practice.[10]

There are provisions governing the courts' powers to direct that the child shall or shall not attend court (Family Proceedings Courts (Children Act 1989) Rules 1991, SI 1991/1395, rule 16 and Family Proceedings Rules 1991, SI 1991/1247, rule 4.16). If there is no order, the solicitor should seek instructions from the guardian (or where appropriate the child) as to whether the child should attend court.

The Rules require that a party should attend a directions appointment if notified unless the court directs otherwise: the child has automatic party status and is rarely expressly directed not to attend, but the Rules permit the court to exclude the child if this is in her interests and where she is represented, provided there is an opportunity for the older child and children's guardian and solicitor to make representations.

The proceedings must take place in the absence of the child if the court considers it to be in her interests, having regard to the matters to be discussed or the evidence likely to be given; and she is represented by a guardian ad litem or solicitor (Family Proceedings Court (Children Act 1989) Rules 1991, SI 1991/1395, rule 16(2) and Family Proceedings Rules, rule 4.16(2)).

The courts generally do not encourage the child's presence. Where a 13-year-old child attended an appeal hearing, the judge stated that in the future a guardian should expect to justify supporting attendance of the child and 'it would be a pity if the presence of children as young as this . . . were to be allowed to develop unquestioningly into a settled practice' (*Re C (A Minor)* *(Care: Child's Wishes)* [1993] 1 FLR 832).

'The balance to be maintained between recognising and upholding the rights of children who are parties to Children Act litigation to participate and be heard and the need to protect children from exposure to material that might be damaging is a delicate one, and is essentially to be performed by the trial judge with a full perspective of the issues and the statements and reports, and at a relatively early stage in the proceedings' (Thorpe J in *Re A (Care: Discharge Application by Child)* [1995] 1 FLR 559).

23.13   THE CHILD GIVING EVIDENCE

There is no common view about children giving evidence which applies to all ages. The general principle is that, except by direction of the court, a child should not attend any Children Act 1989 hearing.[11] It follows that it is very unlikely that a court would allow a child to give evidence, even where she is instructing her solicitor on the basis that she has sufficient understanding to participate as a party to the proceedings (*Re O (Care Proceedings: Evidence)* [2004] 1 FLR 161). This will apply even where the child has made a written statement (*Re P (Witness Summons)* [1997] 2 FLR 447). However, it has also been held that fairness and the best interests of minors required the veracity of a 17-year-old girl's statements to be probed by some questioning (*R v. B CC, ex p. P* [1991] Fam. Law 313).

Where an adult party wishes the child to give evidence, the court has an inherent jurisdiction not to require the attendance of the child where it would be oppressive to do so (*R v. B. CC, ex p. P* [1991] Fam. Law 313). Where an application is made for a witness summons against a child, the child's welfare is relevant but the court is not bound to give consideration to the welfare test, as this is not a matter relating to the child's upbringing, and Children Act 1989, s.1(1) does not apply (*Re P (Witness Summons)* [1997] 2 FLR 447).

23.14   THE CHILD COMMUNICATING WITH THE JUDGE

The children's guardian and solicitor should always discuss with the child whether or not she wishes to communicate with the judge. This may be by a letter, a drawing or by seeing the judge. Since the views of the child will be communicated to the court through the children's guardian, it will be hard to persuade the court that the child should meet the judge. However, some children want to meet the person who is to decide their future, and their views should be respected. An application for such a meeting should be made ideally at the case management conference or at the pre-trial review. There must be good reason for the judge to see the child, and he/she must be satisfied that it is in the child's interests (*B* v. *B (Minors) (Interviews and Listing Arrangements)* [1994] 2 FLR 489). The interview will normally take place after the close of evidence and before closing submissions (*B* v. *B (Minors)* [1994] 2 FLR 489).

The child needs to understand that whatever she tells the judge will have to be relayed to the parties afterwards, and that nothing she says can be confidential (*H* v. *H (Child: Judicial Interview)* [1974] 1 WLR 595). She must be consulted about when she comes to court, e.g. at lunch time, and if so, what she wants to eat; whether she wants to bring a friend with her; whether she wants to meet her parents at court. Most importantly, she has to understand that her wishes will not necessarily be followed.

23.15   OTHER PROCEEDINGS

Private law proceedings

The child involved in private law proceedings will be treated in the same way as the child in public law proceedings in relation to giving evidence and seeing the judge. It has been held that justices were wrong to see a child when his wishes had been fully explored and dealt with in a report from the Court Welfare Officer (*Re M (A Minor) (Justices' Discretion)* [1993] 2 FLR 706).

Since the adult parties have a right to be present throughout the hearing, do children whose futures are being decided in such cases not enjoy the same right should they wish to exercise it?[12]

Special Educational Needs Tribunal

The child now has a right to attend the hearing, subject to controls by the Tribunal. A Protocol on the conduct of hearings involving children present is currently in preparation.

Immigration/asylum appeal hearings

The child appellant has the right to attend the hearing, and it is in the discretion of the judge whether or not to allow her to give evidence and, if he/she does, whether or not she should give evidence on oath.

23.16   APPLICATIONS IN RELATION TO HUMAN RIGHTS

The Legal Services Commission has indicated that it will not grant public funding for claims under the Human Rights Act 1998 unless all other channels of complaint have been attempted.[13]

Where a human rights point arises in the course of care proceedings, the correct approach is to raise the point within those proceedings under Human Rights Act 1998, s.7(1)(b). It is neither necessary nor desirable to transfer proceedings to a superior level of court merely because a breach of Convention rights is alleged (*Re V (Care Proceedings: Human Rights Claims)* [2004] 1 FLR 944).

Applications for transfer are to be strongly discouraged and may amount to an abuse of process.

Where an interim care order is in force, the court may make a direction under Children Act 1989, s.38(6) in relation to medical or psychiatric examination or other assessment of the child concerned, but there is no power to compel a local authority to fund therapeutic treatment for the parents, whether under the Children Act 1989 or the Human Rights Act 1998.[14]

The only Human Rights Act application reserved to the High Court is the making of a declaration of incompatibility under s.4.

It was held in *Re V* that whether the refusal of a local authority to fund treatment for the parents was a breach of their human rights was a matter to be determined within the care proceedings.

Habeus corpus proceedings are to be deprecated when care proceedings are on foot and where the purpose of the application is to challenge the exercise by a local authority of its powers. The proper forum is within care proceedings, not in the Administrative Court (*Re S (Habeus Corpus)*; *S* v. *Haringey LBC* [2003] EWHC (Admin) 2734).

23.17 COSTS

A failure to refer the judge to the relevant case law was held to be reprehensible and may lead to an order for wasted costs or the disallowance of fees at the conclusion of the case (*Re V (Care Proceedings: Human Rights Claims)* [2004] 1 FLR 944).

At the renewal of each interim care order, the court will be required to consider whether to grant a certificate of compliance with case management directions provided so far in the case. The penalty for non-compliance may be a wasted costs order.

23.18 POLICE AND FAMILY DISCLOSURE PROTOCOL

In December 2004 another protocol was piloted in five areas of the country: the Protocol for the Disclosure of Police Information in family proceedings. The objective is to establish a more effective and efficient way of dealing with the disclosure of relevant information held by the police. The procedure set out in the Protocol must be followed in every case in which it applies, except where real urgency makes it impossible to do so. It is expected that the Protocol will be implemented across England and Wales in the autumn of 2005.

The objectives are:

- to provide timely advance notice to the police of the existence of family proceedings and the level of information being sought;
- to enable the police to indicate in advance what evidential material is or may be available and highlight any difficulties with disclosure of the information required;
- to assist the court and the parties in framing workable, standard directions directed to the police without undue delay;
- to encourage early disclosure of full and frank information between the police, the parties and the court.

The request for information will be made on a standard form. In relation to a request for videotaped evidence of a child witness, there is a confidentiality undertaking at Annex A which must be signed by the solicitor making the request.

The Protocol and Explanatory Memorandum can be accessed on the website of the DCA at **www.dca.gov.uk/family/famfr7.htm**.

NOTES

1 *Practice Direction (Family Proceedings: Court Bundles)* [2000] 1 FLR 536.
2 President's Direction (Judicial Continuity) [2002] 2 FLR 367.
3 *Practice Direction (Children's Cases: Time Estimates)* [1994] 1 WLR 16.
4 LAC (84)3 and see Adoption Agencies Regulations 2005, SI 2005/389.
5 Included in *Good Practice in Child Care Cases*, Law Society (2004).
6 *Communicating with the Home Office*, President's Office, (1 December 2003).
7 See *Re CR (A Minor)*, *The Times*, 19 November 1992; Children Act Advisory Committee, *Annual Report* 1994/95.
8 *Handbook of Best Practice in Children Act Cases*, Children Act Advisory Committee (1997).
9 Holman J, 'Allowing Children into Court' (2000) 12 *Rep Ch* 336.
10 Children Act Advisory Committee, *Final Report* (June 1997).
11 *Handbook of Best Practice in Children Act Cases*.
12 R. Zentar, (2000) XIV *Practitioners Law Bulletin* no.3 (July/August).
13 LSC *Focus* 41 (March 2003).
14 But now there is some confusion following amendment to the Funding Code 2005 as a result of the decision of Ryder J in *Lambeth London Borough Council and LSC* [2005] EWHC Fam 776 v. *S, C, V and J* and pending the Court of Appeal of *Re G* to be heard in Autumn 2005.

CHAPTER 24

Disclosure and information-sharing

Key sources

- Local Government (Access to Information) Act 1985; Data Protection Act 1998; Freedom of Information Act 2000
- Children Act 2004, ss.12 and 29
- *Working Together* (1999) paragraphs 7.27–7.46
- *What to Do If You are Worried a Child is Being Abused*, DH (2003), App. 3
- *Pubic Sector Data Sharing: Guidance on the Law* (2003) and *A Public Sector Toolkit and Data Sharing* (2004), DCA
- ACPO Pilots: Police/Family Disclosure Protocol (2004)
- Guidance on Investigating Child Abuse and Safeguarding Children, ACPO and Centrex (2005), paras 1.6, 7.6, 8.3
- *Cross Government Guidance – Sharing Information on Children and Young People*, DfES consultation draft (August 2005)

24.1 INTRODUCTION

This chapter is designed to give an overview of the complexities of information-sharing within proceedings, against a background of changes to legislation and guidance and the outfall from various public inquiries (Climbie, Bichard, etc.)

A distinction must be drawn between:

- the duty of full and frank disclosure in Children Act 1989 proceedings;
- the duties and powers in child protection and children's services generally, including the sharing of information between agencies;
- the rights of data subjects to disclosure of information to them;
- the rights of adults and children to privacy of information and to confidentiality in a variety of circumstances.

This is a complex area, with no single source of law regulating the powers of public bodies to use and to share personal information. This has led to much uncertainty over what is, and what is not, permissible to disclose, which can inhibit data-sharing by public authorities to a child's detriment, or conversely constitute unwarranted intrusion into family and/or private life.

The main principles are derived from human rights law, the common law tort of breach of confidence, administrative law and the Data Protection Act 1998.

24.2 HUMAN RIGHTS

ECHR Article 6 requires 'that each party must be afforded a reasonable opportunity to present his case – including his evidence – under conditions that do not place him at a substantial disadvantage vis-à-vis his opponent'. This includes a right to disclosure of relevant documents (*Feldbrugge* v. *The Netherlands* (1986) 8 EHRR 425; *McGinley and Egan* v. *UK* (1998) 27 EHRR 1). Also, every party must have the opportunity to know about, and comment on, evidence of the other parties (*McMichael* v. *UK* (1995) 20 EHRR 205).

Entitlement to a fair trial under Article 6 is absolute, but does not mean an absolute and unqualified right to see all documents. Since the Human Rights Act 1998 came into force, it is no longer the case that the only interests capable of denying a litigant access to documents are those of the children involved in the litigation. The interests of anyone else who is involved whether as victim, party or witness and who can demonstrate that their ECHR Article 8 rights are sufficiently engaged could also have that effect.

It is essential that a parent should be placed in a position where she may obtain access to information which is relied on by the authorities in taking protective measures. This requires knowledge of the nature and extent of the allegations of abuse made by her child. It should not be the sole responsibility of the parent or lie at her initiative to obtain the evidence on which a decision to remove a child is based.

A local authority was in breach of Article 8 in having failed to disclose a video interview, in circumstances where it would have been apparent to the mother that allegations were not being made against her partner, as was assumed by the local authority. Her child had been removed from her for one year by the time the mother was able to see a transcript of the interview. Damages were awarded to the mother and child (Grand Chamber of the European Commission in *TP and KM* v. *UK* (Application No.28945/95) [2001] 2 FLR 549).

There was a breach of Article 8 when access to child care records was dependent on the contributor's consent (deemed to be acceptable) and no system of determining whether access should be granted when the contributor of the records was either not available or improperly refused consent. When a system of disclosure is operated by consent there should be an independent authority to decide whether access should be granted (*Gaskin*, Case No.2/1988/146/200 [1990] 1 FLR 167).

24.3 CONFIDENTIALITY AND DISCLOSURE OF INFORMATION AND DOCUMENTS

The local authority's safeguarding obligations (under Children Act 1989, s.17 to promote and safeguard the welfare of children, and see Children Act 2004) extend to information obtained as part of its legitimate role as a data processor for its partners, who also now have a safeguarding duty (see Chapter 4).

Compliance in information-sharing with the relevant law requires:

- clear protocols setting out the basis upon which information is shared and making clear the responsibilities and duties of individuals and organisations disclosing and receiving the information;
- standardised procedures for recording decisions, to maintain an audit trail;
- effective and secure arrangements for information transfer;
- understanding of the issues relating to consent, including limits to the principle.

Concern about breaking the law often leads to information being withheld from other professionals, even when it would be in the child's best interests to pass it on. Statutory duties in cooperation and information-sharing have now been extended under the Children Act 2004, and include education, health and police, and full guidance is due in December 2005.

24.4 LOCAL AUTHORITY DUTIES OF DISCLOSURE AND PUBLIC INTEREST IMMUNITY

General

Local authorities have a high duty in law, not only on grounds of general fairness, but also in the direct interest of a child whose welfare they serve, to be open in the disclosure of all relevant material affecting that child in their possession or power (excluding documents protected by established bounds of public immunity) which might be of assistance to the birth parents in rebutting charges against one or both of them of ill-treating the child.

The duty of the local authority to be objective, fair and balanced cannot be overemphasised. A social worker should include all the material upon which a judgment was based, both negative and positive, and be able to demonstrate that the judgment was objectively based on all the disclosed material (*Re JC (Care Proceedings Procedure)* [1995] 2 FLR 77).

The practitioner with otherwise privileged information must disclose it to the court and to all parties where it affects the welfare of a child, even though it is not in the interests of the client to do so: 'because children cases are in a special category and if all information is not disclosed, there is a risk that the court cannot uphold the welfare principle.' (*Re R (Minor) (Professional Privilege)* [1994] 1 FCR 225).

There is a need to encourage candor from all the people involved in the proceedings, not only the professionals, but also the parents themselves, who have the most relevant information to impart (*Cleveland CC v. F* [1995] 1 FLR 797).

Public interest immunity

Public interest immunity (PII) is a descriptive term for the reasons for refusing disclosure of relevant material at a trial. The public interest in confidentiality must be strong enough to compete with, and sometimes prevail over, the public interest in a fair trial and disclosure of all material that passes the relevant threshold test. Unless the documents are likely to be of real importance to the party seeking disclosure, they should not be disclosed (*Re M (A Minor) (Disclosure of Material)* [1990] 2 FLR 36).

Anyone claiming PII in respect of material held by a local authority should consider whether the material passed the threshold test, take advice, and set out with particularity the harm that it was alleged would be caused to the public interest by disclosure.

Overview of the duty to disclose

Standard disclosure requires a party to disclose only:

- the documents on which she relies; and
- the documents which adversely affect his/her own case adversely affect another party's case; or support another party's case; and
- the documents which s/he is required to disclose by a relevant Practice Direction.

A summary of guidance given by Charles J in *Re R (Care: Disclosure: Nature of Proceedings)* [2002] 1 FLR 755 is as follows.

(a) When seeking public law orders, the local authority should identify as soon as possible the allegations that it was seeking to establish, separately from the statements setting out its evidence, and ensure preparation of the statements is done by someone:

- with a proper understanding of the relevant legal principles, the case issues and the court procedures;
- who has made a proper examination of all the background material and all the relevant files;
- who has had a proper discussion with relevant witnesses to ensure their statements contain a full and proper account of the relevant

matters, including the central matter seen and heard, the sources of hearsay being recorded, and the relevant background to and circumstances in which the matter set out took place;

- who has properly considered what further information or material should be obtained.

(b) If this work were done properly by the legal advisers:

- experts would be instructed on a properly informed basis;
- statements would exhibit appropriate background material;
- there would be additional appropriate discovery.

(c) All respondents and their advisers, not merely the children's guardian, were under mirror duties and responsibilities, and should:

- check the decisions made as to the experts to be instructed and the terms of those instructed and thus the input they wish to have into those terms;
- consider whether it appeared that the local authority had performed its duties in preparing the case and as to disclosure;
- consider what further information or material should be obtained;
- pursue issues as to disclosure at interlocutory hearings if they had not been agreed.

The respondents and their advisers were under a duty to give a full account of their case and position, and thus to provide third party confirmation where it was available, which meant they could not adopt a stance of 'you prove it'. Respondents should give a full account of what they accepted and denied as soon as possible.

It is for the party seeking disclosure to show why the documents should be produced: but it is for the court to decide whether documents covered by PII should be disclosed.

Generally, confidentiality is not a valid reason for non-disclosure of material that passes the relevant threshold test for disclosure. Confidentiality is not a separate head of privilege but it may be a very material consideration to bear in mind when privilege is claimed on PII grounds (*Alfred Crompton Amusement Machines Ltd* v. *Customs and Excise Commissioners (No. 2)* [1974] AC 405 at 433H per Lord Cross).

If relevant documents appear to be protected by PII, the local authority should tell the other parties about their existence and prepare a précis of the information which would be disclosed if ordered.

Role of the children's guardian

The local authority should draw the attention of the children's guardian to any matters of concern within the documents. A guardian has a right at all times to examine and take copies of records held by a local authority or the NSPCC, compiled in the making or proposed making of any application under the Children Act 1989 with respect to the child (s.42). If in the course of inspecting social services files, the guardian found relevant records which had not been disclosed, she should invite disclosure. The guardian is not entitled to disclose documents covered by PII (*Re C (Expert Evidence: Disclosure: Practice)* [1995] 1 FLR 204).

The guardian is an officer of the court, and can be relied on to be well aware of her primary duty to safeguard the child's interests (*Re T (A Minor) (GAL Case Records)* [1994] 1 FLR 632).

24.5 DISCLOSURE OF DOCUMENTS

General

The court rules (Family Proceedings Rules 1991, SI 1991/1247, rule 4.23; Family Proceedings Court (Children Act 1989) Rules 1991, SI 1991/1395, rule 3(1)) prohibit disclosure, without leave, of any document filed in the proceedings, save for a court order, other than to:

- a party or her legal representative;
- a CAFCASS officer;
- the Legal Services Commission;
- an expert whose instruction has been authorised by the court.

Principles governing disclosure

Munby J in *Re X (Disclosure of Information)* [2001] 2 FLR 440 laid down the following principles.

Exercise of the judicial discretion in family proceedings requires consideration of a very wide range of factors. In the final analysis it involves a balancing exercise in which the judge has to identify, evaluate and weigh those factors which point in favour of the disclosure sought against factors which point in the other direction.

The child's interests are a major factor and very important, but they are not paramount.

In the typical case, the most important factor pointing against disclosure, other than the interests of the child concerned, is 'the importance of confidentiality in wardship proceedings and the frankness which it engenders in those who give evidence to the wardship court' (*Re D (Minors) (Wardship: Disclosure)* [1994] 1 FLR 346, 351A per Sir Stephen Brown).

Other principles

There is jurisdiction to hear an application from a body which is not a party to the care proceedings.

The welfare of the child is not paramount. No child is entitled to privacy or confidentiality.

Any right of confidentiality belongs to the court and is imposed to protect the proper functioning of the court (*Oxfordshire CC* v. *L and F* [1997] 1 FLR 235).

Disclosure to the police

Privilege against self-incrimination is given by Children Act 1989, s.98(2). In any proceedings in which a court is hearing an application for an order under Part IV or V, no person will be excused from (a) giving evidence on any matter, or (b) answering any question put to her in the course of her giving evidence on the ground that doing so might incriminate her or her spouse of an offence. A statement or admission made in such proceedings will not be admissible in evidence against the person making it or her spouse in proceedings for an offence other than perjury.

A social worker at a case conference disclosed information about a mother's admission of responsibility for injuries to her child, which had been made in the course of care proceedings. The police application for disclosure of this material was refused, on the ground that the balance was tipped towards the importance of maintaining frankness and confidentiality, notwithstanding the serious nature of the offence and the countervailing public interest in the pursuit of crime and interagency cooperation (*Re M (Care Proceedings: Disclosure: Human Rights)* [2001] 2 FLR 1316).

The court has discretion to disclose to the police material covered by s. 98 to enable them to shape the nature and range of enquiries they undertake in the investigation of an alleged criminal offence. Section 98 gives protection only against statements being admissible evidence in criminal proceedings. The judge must consider the following matters:

- the welfare and interest of the child concerned and of other children generally;
- the maintenance of confidentiality in children's cases and the importance of encouraging frankness;
- the public interest in the administration of justice and the prosecution of serious crime;
- the gravity of the alleged offence and the relevance of the evidence to it;
- the desirability of cooperation between the various agencies concerned with the welfare of children (now a statutory duty for police, probation, health, education and social care, Children Act 2004. s.10 (England) and s.25 (Wales));

- if s.98 applies, fairness to the person who had incriminated herself and any others affected by the incriminating statement;
- any other material disclosure which has already taken place (*Re EC (Disclosure of Material)* [1996] 2 FLR 725).

Practice issues

Before making an application for leave, consider the following.

Is leave required?

Only for disclosure of material held by the court and not, e.g. for notes made on the file prior to proceedings (*Re G (SW Disclosure)* [1996] 1 FLR 276). Note the following issues considered in *Oxfordshire CC and Another* v. *P* [1995] 2 All ER 22:

- Was a guardian entitled to disclose a mother's admission to a social services department?
- Was the social worker at liberty to report to police?
- Was the guardian at liberty to make a witness statement in criminal proceedings disclosing the admission without leave?

It was held that the privilege of confidentiality was that of the court, not of the guardian. The police should not have sought to make use of admissions and the guardian should not have made a statement. The appointment of the guardian was terminated.

What is the extent of the disclosure required?

There should be some selection process involved, to ensure that no more is disclosed than is necessary; depending on the reason for the disclosure, disclosure of the children's guardian's reports may be sufficient.

How can the disclosure be limited to those who need to have the information?

If disclosure is to take place to an organisation, as opposed to an individual, enquiries should be made to establish who will need to see the documents, and how the numbers can be limited.

Does the child/adult client agree to this disclosure?

If there is no consent to disclosure, whether during or after proceedings, the court must arrange for a hearing of which all parties to the proceedings are given notice. An application made after the proceedings have concluded will not be covered by the public funding certificate, and a fresh application for the freestanding application must be submitted.

Was the maker of each report and statement made aware that their evidence could be disclosed with leave of the court?

If not, they should be informed that an application to disclose the evidence is to be made, so that they have an opportunity to make any objections known.

What steps should be taken to ensure the material is returned?

Any person or establishment to whom material is sent must agree to return it on request without having taken a copy.

What is the purpose of the disclosure?

There are a number of situations in which a party may wish to disclose part, or all, of a document during the course of proceedings or after the proceedings have concluded. These may include disclosure to:

- a potential witness, for the purpose of obtaining comments on facts or allegations made;
- a multidisciplinary case conference;
- a family centre, or residential centre assessing a family;
- a residential establishment where a child is to be placed;
- a number of residential establishments to which initial referrals have been made;
- a criminal court;
- a professional body following findings of abuse;
- the Criminal Injuries Compensation Authority;
- a therapist;
- a Panel hearing an appeal following exclusion from school;
- the Home Office;
- prospective adopters.

The issue of disclosure will be considered at the case management conference and arguments on the need for disclosure and PII will be addressed at that hearing. At the final hearing, leave must be sought for disclosure where it may be required in the future. Once proceedings are at an end, the court controls the further distribution of the papers, including the report of the guardian (post-hearing: *Re C (GAL Disclosure of Report)* [1996] 1 FLR 61).

24.6   WITHHOLDING EVIDENCE FROM A PARTY

General principles

The elementary principle of natural justice, underpinned by ECHR Article 6, requires that cases are decided solely on the basis of evidence which is known to both parties (*Re S (A Child) (Family Division: Without Notice Orders)* [2001] 1 WLR 211). That principle is qualified in the context of cases in the Family Division by the principle that the receipt of evidence or information in private should only be undertaken by the judge with great circumspection (*Official Solicitor* v. *K* [1965] AC 201).

The current law on non disclosure can be summarised as follows (see Munby J in *Re B* [2001] 2 FLR 1017 at 1038).

Each party is entitled under Article 6 to a fair trial, and this is absolute. It cannot be qualified by the right of any other party, including the child concerned, under Article 8. However, that does not mean that she necessarily has an absolute and unqualified right to see all the documents (*Re B* [2001] 2 FLR 1017).

There is no longer any warrant for saying that the only interests capable of denying a litigant access to the documents in a proper case are the interests of the children involved in the litigation. There can be cases where a litigant's right to see the documents may have to give way not merely in the interests of the children involved but also, or alternatively, to the Article 8 rights of one or more of the adults involved, whether as victim, party or witness.

ECHR Article 8 guarantees only 'respect' for and not inviolability of private and family life; any restriction of a party's right to see the documents in the case must be limited to what the situation imperatively demands. Non-disclosure can be justified only when the case for doing so is, to use Lord Mustill's words, 'compelling' or where it is 'strictly necessary' (*Campbell and Fell* v. *UK* (1984) 7 EHRR 165).

Any difficulties caused to a litigant by a limitation on her right to see all the documents must be sufficiently counterbalanced by procedures designed to ensure that she receives a fair trial. At the end of the day, the court must be sure that whatever procedures are adopted, and whatever limitations on a litigant's access to documents may be imposed, everyone involved in the proceedings receives a fair trial.

The rights under Article 6 concern 'equality of arms' (*Dombo Beheer BV* v. *The Netherlands* (1994) 18 EHRR 213) for each party, which includes a right to disclosure of relevant documents (*Feldbrugge* v. *The Netherlands* (1986) 8 EHRR 425; *McGinley and Egan* v. *UK* (1998) 27 EHRR 1) and the opportunity to know about, and comment on, evidence of the other parties (*McMichael* v. *UK* (1995) 20 EHRR 205).

In any case concerning the welfare of a child, there is jurisdiction to order that material, disclosure of which might be damaging to a child, should not be disclosed to a party to the proceedings. Before making an order for non-disclosure, the court must satisfy itself that the disclosure of the evidence would be so detrimental to the child's welfare as to outweigh the normal requirements for a fair trial. The jurisdiction should only be exercised in exceptional circumstances and then only for the shortest period possible (*Re B (A Minor) (Disclosure of Evidence)* [1993] 1 FLR 191).

There was a breach of Article 6(1) in care proceedings where social services and medical reports were given to the court, but not disclosed to the parents, although the contents were made known to them (*McMichael* v. *UK* (1995) 20 EHRR 205).

The principle (set out in Chapter 1) that under Article 8(2) the child's interests prevail over those of her parent under Article 8(1) where there is a serious conflict between their respective interests, does not mean that a parent's rights under Article 6 are to be overridden. The paramount interests of the child must not prevent a parent being able effectively to participate in the decision-making process concerning a child (*L* v. *UK* [2000] 2 FLR 322 at 332G).

Application must be made to the High Court

Where a party seeks leave of the court to withhold information from another party, the question of principle involved is such that the proceedings should be transferred to the High Court.

The party against whom leave to withhold disclosure is sought should be served with notice of the application, even if the party consents to disclosure to her legal advisors only. An order authorising non-disclosure should never be made without giving notice.

The court should consider whether disclosure carries a real risk of significant harm to the child and, if so, whether the overall interests of the child would benefit from non-disclosure. Non-disclosure is the exception and not the rule. The court should be rigorous in its examination of the risk and gravity of the feared harm to the child, only ordering non-disclosure when the case for doing so is compelling (*Re C (Disclosure)* [1996] 1 FLR 797).

Information from police

A local authority received confidential information from police about a man living with a mother and her five children, the subject of interim care orders. Social workers were warned not to disclose the information to the mother, as this would prejudice the police operation and put an informer's life at risk. The authority was granted permission to disclose information from police to the mother and permitting the disclosure of all documents to her solicitors (per Wall J in *Re W (Care Proceedings: Disclosure)* [2003] EWHC (Fam) 1624). It was held that the mother had to be informed of the substance of allegations against her; non-disclosure of relevant information was the exception rather than the rule and should be ordered only when the case for it was compelling. The mother should be given the substance of the allegation only; her solicitors were to know of the series of applications made, and the wider picture, to satisfy themselves that the process had been fair.

Documents obtained in criminal proceedings

A party who is involved in both care and criminal proceedings is entitled to claim legal professional privilege in relation to her communications with experts instructed in the criminal proceedings. Unless she waives that privilege, she does not have to disclose the name of any expert, let alone any report obtained (*S CC* v. *B* [2000] 2 FLR 161).

Wardship proceedings

Parties in wardship proceedings have no absolute right to see confidential reports that have been lodged by the Official Solicitor as guardian ad litem to the child, since the welfare of the child rather than arbitration between interested parties is the paramount consideration. Disclosure must remain a matter for the judge's discretion, but the occasions when a judge will rule against disclosure will be rare; the welfare of the child must be balanced against the principle that a case should not be disclosed on information that a party has not seen and cannot challenge (*Official Solicitor* v. *K* [1963] 3 All ER 191).

Welfare report

In determining whether or not disclosure of a confidential welfare report should be withheld, the correct test to be applied is whether real harm would come from the disclosure, not the less stringent test of whether there was a significant risk of harm (*Re M (Minors) (Disclosure of Evidence)* [1994] 1 FLR 760).

Conciliation meetings

In proceedings under the Children Act 1989, statements made by either party in the course of meetings held or communications made for the purpose of conciliation are not admissible, given the public importance of conciliation, save in the very unusual case where a statement is made clearly indicating that the maker had in the past caused or was likely in the future to cause serious harm to the well-being of a child (*Re D (Conciliation: Privilege)* [1993] 1 FLR 932).

Videorecordings

Where a hospital sought a direction that videorecordings and written transcripts of interviews with a child should not be disclosed to the parents, it was held that there was no privilege attaching to the material in question. The child had no more right of confidence than anyone else coming before the court. She did have a right to have the matter decided in her best interests, but the court must take account of the need to do justice to the parents (*B* v. *B (Child Abuse: Evidence)* [1991] 2 FLR 487).

Contact disputes

In a contact dispute, the justices ordered medical reports to be filed on a schizophrenic father, not to be disclosed to any person save legal representatives, court officials and magistrates, without leave of the court. The mother successfully appealed. Her case could not be properly conducted without taking her instructions on the reports and it was essential in the interests of the child that she should be fully apprised of the father's condition (*Re NW (A Minor) (Medical Reports)* [1993] 2 FLR 591).

Disclosure of medical records

Disclosure of medical records is an area that causes great difficulty in practice, since patient confidentiality normally requires the patient's consent to such disclosure. There is no case directly on the point, and the usual rules of full and frank disclosure will apply, as indicated by the Court of Appeal in *Re B, R and C (Children)* [2002] EWCA Civ 1825; [2003] Fam Law 305, CA.

Social service records

The Local Government (Access to Information) Act 1985 provides for greater access to information held by local authorities. However, many if not all matters referred to social services committees are excluded from its provisions. The law relating to disclosure of documents held by social services departments is contained in the Data Protection Act 1998.

The 1985 Act adds Schedule 12A to Local Government Act 1972, which describes exempt information. Information exempt from the disclosure provision relates to the following:

- the adoption, care, fostering or education of any particular person (other than the authority);
- any particular applicant for, or recipient or former recipient of, any service provided by the authority;
- any particular occupier or former occupier of, or applicant for, accommodation provided by or at the expense of the authority.

These exemptions appear to completely exclude the obtaining of information from a local authority in relation to its duties under the Children Act 1989 and the Adoption Act 1976.

24.7 THE FUTURE

The Department for Constitutional Affairs issued a Consultation Paper in December 2004 on disclosure of information in family proceedings cases involving children. It intends to bring in Rules of Court which would specify the circumstances in which information should be able to be disclosed from such proceedings without the need for a court order authorising that disclosure. The changes will ensure that the courts retain their inherent power to authorise or restrict disclosure of information in any particular case, and nothing will allow the extension of disclosure of information from family proceedings to the media, or alter the arrangements for privacy of hearings.

CHAPTER 25

Expert evidence

Key Sources

- Children Act 1989
- Protocol for Judicial Case Management in Public Law Children Act Cases (2003), App. C
- LSC consultation paper: *The Use of Experts* (2004)
- Handbooks (see Appendix 1): Brophy (ed.) *Expert Evidence in Child Protection Litigation* (1999) and Wall and Hamilton, *A Handbook for Expert Witnesses in Children Act Cases* (2000)

25.1 INTRODUCTION

Before the Children Act 1989

Before the Children Act 1989, there was no widespread use of expert witnesses in public law proceedings. One of the major concerns[1] was how to ensure that the court had the benefit of professional opinion concerning the child's interests, expressed independently of the local authority and parents.

The period 1976 to 1984 saw the development of the 'independent social worker' who was increasingly used by practitioners to consider service provision and plans for children. The experts used had no right of access to local authority records, were frequently instructed for the parents and regarded as partial, and there was no disclosure duty on the party obtaining the report.

Position since implementation of the Children Act 1989

Significant changes were brought about with the implementation of the Children Act 1989 and the practice of appointing a guardian ad litem (GAL) in the majority of proceedings to safeguard the child's interests.

The child had a welfare representative who would be regarded as an expert in relation to matters of general child care and development, with a right of access to local authority records (Children Act 1989, s.42). Where care cases required specialist knowledge beyond the GAL's competence, it was hoped that a parent would accept an expert appointed by the GAL, instead of seeking to instruct their own.

Current trends

The Kennedy Report of the working group on sudden unexpected death in infancy[2] has recommended that:

- the Royal Colleges or speciality organisations should accredit experts;
- doctors should have special instruction on the role of the expert witness before holding themselves out as court experts;
- such instruction should be renewed at least every five years;
- before an expert gives evidence, the judge should establish the expert's credentials.

A pilot scheme is in operation in the northwest of England, where an established expert panel scheme based on nominations by lawyers and judges is already in use by the courts.

The Civil Justice Council Experts Committee established in 2003 is looking at accreditation, training, professional discipline and court control of experts as well as their fees and expenses.

The Legal Services Commission's Consultation Paper, *The Use of Experts* (2004) made proposals to address the quality and cost of experts' services. For Commission-funded cases it wishes to see:

- only accredited experts used;
- accreditation in the fields of psychiatry, psychology, pathology, independent social workers, accountancy;
- experts' fees subject to control.

For public law family proceedings, the LSC would like to work with the courts to find a way forward, but in the meantime where a case is subject to the Protocol for Judicial Case Management, the Commission will not take issue with an expert nominated by the court for a particular task.

25.2 HUMAN RIGHTS

A restrictive approach to the instruction of experts, both by the courts and the LSC (which may refuse to authorise an increase in a costs limitation to cover the fees), may lead to challenges under ECHR Article 6.

To date, ECtHR decisions have been in respect of decisions taken by other European courts with an inquisitorial system.

There is no obligation on the court to obtain an expert's report merely because one party seeks it (*H* v. *France* (1990) 12 EHRR 74). Where the court does appoint an expert, applicants must be given an opportunity to give instructions to the expert, and to see documents referred to in her report.

Where an expert has been jointly instructed, it will be difficult for a party against whom adverse comments are made to cross-examine that expert.

Where an application is made for that party to instruct her own expert following a joint report, there may be a breach of Article 6(1) if the application is refused (*Heinrich* v. *France* (1994) 18 EHRR 440). However, where there is a report from an expert there may be no violation if it is considered that 'proper steps were taken to obtain sufficient expert medical opinion for the purposes of the proceedings' (*Eriksson* v. *Sweden* (1989) 12 EHRR 183).

Where an applicant is allowed to read the report of an expert, but not keep a copy, the Commission did not exclude that such circumstances may prejudice an applicant's position before the court, so as to constitute a breach of Article 6 (*Hendriks* v. *The Netherlands* (1982) 5 EHRR 223). Where an applicant is not allowed to read the report of an expert, there may be a breach of Article 6 (*McMichael* v. *UK* (1995) 20 EHRR 205).

On the issue of court-ordered disclosure to the police of a report adverse to a mother, the ECtHR held unanimously that there was no deprivation of her rights to a fair trial, compulsory disclosure of an adverse report did not affect any issue of self-incrimination and there was no breach of Article 8(2) (*L* v. *UK (Disclosure of Expert Evidence)* [2000] 2 FCR 145).

25.3   GUIDANCE ON THE ROLE AND USE OF EXPERTS

Since at least 1991, a considerable amount of judicial guidance and directions have been produced on the instruction of experts.

Section 5 of the Handbook of Best Practice[3] on experts and the court summarised much of the previous guidance, urging advocates to consider an application for leave to instruct an expert at the earliest possible stage of the proceedings (*H* v. *Cambridgeshire CC* [1997] 1 FCR 569). It also referred practitioners to an Expert Witness Pack (from the Expert Witness Group) which included:

- several pro formas;
- draft letters of instruction and acceptance;
- checklist for solicitor and expert;
- guidelines and a model curriculum vitae for expert witnesses;
- a model format for expert's reports.

There is also Law Society guidance on the instruction of expert witnesses, an extensive Code of Guidance by the Academy of Experts,[4] the Expert Witness Pack for Use in Children Proceedings, Family Law (1997) and information available from the Expert Witness Institute.[5]

Appendix C of the Protocol for Judicial Case Management sets out the duties of the expert and the process for instruction which covers:

- preliminary enquiries;
- the expert's response;

- how the proposal is to be presented to the court at the case management conference;
- the content of the draft order;
- letter of instructions;
- the report;
- supplementary questions;
- expert's discussion;
- arrangements for the expert to attend court;
- post-hearing action.

What is an expert?

An expert is 'an expert . . . instructed to give or prepare evidence' for court proceedings (CPR rule 35.2), which covers any person with particular knowledge/experience of, or in connection with, a question to be determined by a court whose opinion on it would be admissible in evidence.

What is the expert's role?

It is the expert's duty to help the court on matters within his/her expertise (CPR rule 35.3(1)). This overrides any obligation to the person instructing and/or paying him/her (CPR rule 35.3(2)).

The law recognises that, so far as matters calling for special knowledge are concerned, judges are not necessarily equipped to draw the inferences from the facts stated by the witnesses. A witness is therefore allowed to state his/her opinion with regard to such matters provided s/he is expert in them.[6]

A witness's 'opinion on any relevant matter on which he is qualified to give expert evidence shall be admissible in evidence (Civil Evidence Act 1972, s.3(1)); and relevant matter 'includes an issue in the proceedings in question' (s.3(3)), including an opinion on what may be the ultimate issue in a particular case (*Re M and R (Child Abuse: Evidence)* [1996] 2 FLR 195).

The function of the expert is 'to inquire and report upon any question of fact or opinion not involving questions of law or of construction' (RSC Order 40 rule 1(1)).

When should an expert be used?

Consider:

- the qualifications and expertise of the professionals involved in the case, including the children's guardian;
- what aspects of the case require opinion evidence to be given;
- is there anyone already involved who can deal with these issues?
- are there gaps in the knowledge about the case, e.g. in relation to medical

or psychological matters, care planning, or cultural, which cannot be filled by those involved?

A local authority has a duty to make an assessment of a family in accordance with the Framework for Assessment.[7] Pressure on departments may result in a suggestion that an expert's report is needed, which in effect is to replace work that should be carried out by the local authority. Any such request should be considered very carefully – the LSC may refuse to fund such a report in these circumstances.

When there is no children's guardian, the appointed solicitor must consider the appointment of an expert to advise and report on welfare issues. The LSC has indicated that it will only consider funding for a specific piece of social work advice, and not on an ongoing basis to replace work that CAFCASS has a duty to provide.

What type is required?

In care cases experts may include:

- paediatrician: to carry out or comment on development, causation and dating of injuries, long-term prognosis;
- paediatric haematologist: to advise on the causes of bleeding;
- paediatric neuroradiologist, paediatric neurosurgeon, opthalmologist: to deal with head injuries;
- paediatric radiologist: to read the X-rays;
- paediatric metabolic consultant: to test for any metabolic disorder.

There is little consistency in the way that psychiatrists and psychologists are used: in some parts of the country it is invariably a psychiatrist who is brought in as an expert on parenting ability, attachment and contact issues; in others it is always a psychologist. However, they have different skills: a psychiatrist has expertise in terms of specialist knowledge of mental illness and personality disorders while a psychologist has expertise in general functioning and management of life's responsibilities.[8]

Where the age of a child is in dispute, it may be necessary to obtain an X-ray of the wrist bones and teeth for advice as to the correct age. However, paediatric reports of this kind are subject to a margin of error; it is 'extremely difficult to accurately assess the age of a child and almost impossible when the child is between the ages of 15 to 18'.[9]

Which expert?

Care must be taken in the choice of any expert. Questions to be addressed include:

- Does the CV indicate a relevant expertise in the particular field? e.g.
  - a doctor qualified as a physician may have acquired knowledge of the psychological aspects of the work, but would usually not be qualified to give a psychological or psychiatric opinion;
  - an adult psychiatrist will not usually be regarded as sufficiently expert in the field of psychological medicine to be called as an expert in that field;
  - a biochemist cannot give an opinion as a paediatrician.
- Has there been any reported judicial criticism of the proposed expert?
- Has s/he acknowledged a leaning towards a particular view?
- Does s/he usually get the report in on time?
- How difficult it is to arrange for him/her to attend court hearings for a block period?
- Whether the expert is suitable given case-sensitive issues such as allegations of sexual abuse, the gender of the child, ethnicity, language, religion, etc.

25.4 APPOINTMENT

Subject to the rules, an expert may be appointed by one party, jointly by the parties, or by the court.

There is considerable pressure on parties in family proceedings to agree joint instruction, with one solicitor acting as 'lead solicitor' for the purposes of the instruction. There are disadvantages to adopting this approach (see above regarding human rights).

Where a parent has a treating psychiatrist, it will usually be acceptable for that parent to commission a report. However, difficulties may arise where the parent is not willing to disclose a report containing material about which s/he is unhappy.

It has further been held that it was elementary for any professional working in the family justice system not to confuse the role of the expert to treat and the role of the expert to report. Forensic reports should always be impartial. Instructions where possible should be joint and agreed with the other side (per the Court of Appeal in *Re B (Sexual Abuse: Expert's Report)* [2000] 2 FCR 8).

Although rarely used in family proceedings, court Rules (RSC Order 40) enable the appointment of an independent expert to be appointed on the application of any party 'to inquire and report upon any question of fact or opinion not involving questions of law or construction'.

If the parties are unable to agree, the court nominates the expert, settles the question to be submitted to him/her and any instructions. The court also fixes the remuneration of the expert, which the parties are jointly and severally liable to pay.

25.5   OBTAINING LEAVE OF THE COURT

Leave to instruct the expert is required where disclosure of documents filed in the proceedings is required (Family Proceedings Rules 1991, SI 1991/1247 (as amended by SI 2002/821), rule 4.23 and Family Proceedings Court (Children Act 1989) Rules 1991, SI 1991/1395, rule 23): without leave, no evidence arising out of the assessment or examination of the child can be adduced. Leave is also required for an expert to examine or assess a child who is the subject of the proceedings (Family Proceedings Rules 1991, rule 4.18 and SI 1991/1395, rule 18(1)).

Leave is not necessary where one party wishes to obtain a report from an expert to whom it is not necessary to disclose papers filed in the proceedings, i.e. a treating psychiatrist.

Leave should be sought at the earliest possible stage in the proceedings and usually at the first directions hearing. Judicial guidelines for the instruction of experts were set out in 1994 by Wall J in *Re G (Minors) (Expert Witnesses)* [1994] 2 FLR 298.

The court has the power to limit expert evidence to given categories of expertise and to specify the number of experts to be called (*Re G (Minors) (Expert Witnesses)* [1994] 2 FLR 291).

Subject always to the requirements of the Protocol, the order should identify:[10]

- the particular expert;
- the area of expertise;
- the issues to be addressed;
- the date by which the letter of instruction is to be sent;
- the documents to be released to the expert;
- the date for filing the report with the court;
- make provision for experts of like discipline to communicate to agree facts and define issues, identifying who is to fix the agenda and chair the meeting;
- deal with the availability of the expert to give oral evidence, if required.

Where a report from a clinical psychologist was obtained in wardship proceedings, without leave of the court, and a family centre was criticised without foundation by the psychologist, the centre was awarded its costs of intervening against the father (*Re A (Family Proceedings: Expert Witnesses)* [2001] 1 FLR 723). It was for the court to decide what expert evidence should be obtained and was quite contrary to the spirit and letter of the established approach that one party should, without notice to the other party, commission a report from an expert about which neither the other party nor the court knew anything. It was essential that the experts were told explicitly that the court had given permission for their instruction and what the terms of the order were in relation to those instructions and was contrary to good practice to provide information in an anonymised form and bad practice for expert witnesses to accept anonymous instructions.

Where more than one expert is to be instructed, the court should consider appointing one of the parties to act as coordinator for the expert evidence (*Re C (Expert Evidence: Disclosure: Practice)* [1995] 1 FLR 204). Frequently, this will be the solicitor for the child.

25.6 LETTER OF INSTRUCTION

This should be drafted by the lead solicitor (usually the child's representative), then circulated to the other parties for agreement, within a timescale laid down at a directions hearing. It must follow the requirements detailed in Appendix C of the Protocol, and should contain (not necessarily in this order):

- details of the parties and their representatives;
- a chronology of events leading to the proceedings;
- a schedule of documents in the proceedings;
- the context in which instructions are being given;
- the specific questions for the expert to address;
- where relevant, a request to the expert to attend a meeting of experts appointed in the same field, and for that meeting to produce a statement of agreement and disagreement on the issues by a specified date.

The letter should contain a paragraph along the lines of the following:

it is expected that you will have meetings with the parents, children (if leave has been given), social workers and the children's guardian. You are also at liberty to discuss the case with any of the other experts instructed if you feel that would assist you in writing your report. It is, however, essential both to your role as an independent expert and to the parent's perception of your independent status, that when you do have informal discussions or correspondence with any of the professionals or the lay parties involved in the case, you should make an adequate note of all such discussions. You should also disclose the fact that you have had them when you write your report, and explain what influence if any such discussions have had upon your thinking and your conclusions.[11]

The letter of instruction, any subsequent letters of instruction, relevant correspondence with the expert and any relevant telephone notes, must form part of the court bundle.

25.7 KEEPING THE EXPERT UP TO DATE

The lead solicitor must ensure that the expert is provided with all evidence as it arrives, and is kept up to date with developments in the case. The expert should have available at the hearing all her contemporaneous notes; and a doctor who has clinical experience of a child before the commencement of the proceedings should have all clinical material such as X-rays and hospital records available for inspection by the other experts, the parties and the court.

25.8 GENERAL DUTIES OF THE EXPERT WITNESS

The general duties of the expert were set out by Cresswell J in *National Justice Compania Naviers SA* v. *Prudential Assurance Co. Ltd* [1993] 2 Lloyd's Rep 68. Expert evidence presented to court should be, and be seen to be, the independent product of the expert uninfluenced as to form or content by the exigencies of litigation. She should:

- provide independent assistance to the court by way of objective unbiased opinion in relation to matters within her expertise; in the High Court s/he should never assume the role of advocate;
- state the facts or assumptions on which the opinion is based, not omitting consideration of material facts detracting from that concluded opinion;
- make it clear when a particular question or issue falls outside his/her expertise;
- state where the opinion is not properly researched because she considers that insufficient data are available, with an indication that the opinion is no more than provisional;
- communicate any change of view on a material matter reached after exchange of reports to the other side without delay and when appropriate to the court;
- provide any photographs, plans, calculations, survey reports or other similar documents referred to, to the opposite party at the same time as the exchange of reports.

25.9 PARTICULAR DUTIES IN FAMILY PROCEEDINGS

There was a helpful judicial statement of principle by Cazalet J in *Re R (A Minor) (Experts' Evidence)* [1991] 1 FLR 291.

Such experts are in a privileged position; indeed only experts are permitted to give an opinion in evidence. Outside the legal field the court itself has no expertise and for that reason frequently has to rely on the evidence of experts. They must express only opinions which they genuinely hold and which are not biased in favour of one particular party. Opinions can, of course, differ and, indeed, quite frequently experts who have expressed their objective and honest opinion will differ, but such differences are usually within a legitimate area of disagreement.

Experts should not lead by omissions, but consider all the material facts in reaching their conclusions, and must not omit to consider the material facts which could detract from their concluded opinion.

If experts look for a report on factors which tend to support a particular proposition or case, their report should still provide a straightforward, not a misleading opinion, should be objective and not omit factors which do not support their opinion, and be properly researched.

Experts should indicate the opinion is provisional where there is insufficient data, as above.

In certain circumstances, experts may find that they have to give opinions adverse to the party instructing them. Alternatively, an expert must make it clear if the report seeks to promote a particular case, but such an approach should be avoided because it would (a) be an abuse of the expert's proper function and privilege and (b) render the report an argument, not an opinion.

The expert may express an opinion on the issues to be determined by the court, e.g. as to whether a child has suffered significant harm, but it is for the judge to finally decide (*Re CB and JB (Care Proceedings: Guidelines)* [1998] 2 FLR 211).

25.10   MEETINGS OF EXPERTS

Before a meeting is arranged, its purpose must be identified. If clarification on some aspects of the report is required, this may be obtained conveniently through the lead solicitor.

A meeting of experts may take place either following agreement between the parties or following a direction by the court in accordance with Appendix C of the Protocol.

It may take place prior to a causation hearing, or following that, to discuss the care plan and it will usually fall to the child's solicitor to organise it. Issues to be addressed beforehand include:

- its purpose;
- issues for discussion; these should be agreed with the other parties in advance, and sent to the experts for their consideration;
- venue;
- whether a face-to-face meeting is required, or whether the issues can be satisfactorily addressed through a video/telephone conference;
- who will chair the meeting;
- who will minute the meeting;
- who should attend; apart from the experts, a legal representative for each party should attend and the children's guardian;

- how much time is required; the meeting should neither be rushed, nor open-ended;
- who is paying for the attendance of the experts, and minute-taker?

The outcome of the meeting should be a statement of agreements and disagreements between the experts. If possible, the experts should sign a note to this effect at the meeting. In any event, the minutes of the meeting should be sent out for approval and amendment to all participants. The final version will form part of the experts' section of the court bundle. Any further subsequent questions should be sent to the lead solicitor, who can seek a response from each expert.

Unless all parties agree that lawyers should attend, they should not do so. The role of the lawyers at such a meeting should be established prior to the meeting; for example, should they merely observe, save for answering questions put to them by the experts or advising them on the law?

The principle of the lawyer's attendance at an experts' meeting was considered by the Court of Appeal in *Hubbard* v. *Lambeth Southwark and Lewisham Health Authority* [2001] All ER 11.

The advantages were considered to be:

- it would give clients confidence;
- lawyers would be able to assist on law and facts if there was some misunderstanding;
- lawyers would be able to assess the real effect of the experts' debate.

The disadvantages were considered to be:

- it added unnecessarily to the costs if lawyers had to stay out of the debate;
- there was a real risk that they would influence the experts.

25.11   JUDICIAL ASSESSMENT OF EXPERT EVIDENCE

A judge is at liberty to depart from the opinion of expert witnesses, e.g. on issues of future placement and parent-child attachment, but could not reject evidence concerning the personality and instability of a parent on the basis of impressions while the parent was in the witness box. If a judge wishes to depart from the experts, s/he must explain his/her departure fully (*Re M (Residence)*, *The Times*, 24 July 2002; *Re B (Care: Expert Witness)* [1996] 1 FLR 667, CA; *Re J (Children) (Residence: Expert Evidence)* [2001] 2 FCR 44).

25.12   JUDICIAL ASSESSMENT OF NON-EXPERT WITNESSES

A judge must assess the credibility and reliability of non-expert witnesses. It did not follow because the witness was credible that her evidence necessarily reflected the child's true experience. If she had not satisfactorily explained the basis on which she decided a child's allegations were reliable, on the balance of probability (noting that an expert child psychiatrist had assessed the chance of their reliability at 25 per cent) her findings of facts could not stand (per the Court of Appeal in *Re R (Children) (Sexual Abuse: Standard of Proof)* [2001] 1 FLR 86).

25.13   PAYMENT OF THE EXPERT'S FEES

Public funding implications

The expert will usually charge an hourly rate for:

- reading papers;
- interviewing/examining the client;
- preparation;
- writing the report;
- travel time;
- preparation for the hearing, including additional reading time;
- attendance at court (usually charged by the half day).

The following areas of work will usually not be included in the fee estimate: for attendance at an experts' meeting (prior to or post a causation hearing), a professionals' meeting or a secure review meeting, a separate estimate must be obtained.

There may be cancellation fees for late cancellation of meetings or court attendances.

It is advisable to include very clear guidance on the payment of fees in the letter of instruction, and to request that one copy is signed and returned to the solicitor before work commences.

A failure to pay the expert in accordance with the agreement could lead to a complaint to the Consumer Complaints Service, an action for recovery of fees and a refusal to carry out further work for that solicitor.

Following decisions in *Calderdale MBC* v. *S* [2004] EWHC 2529 and *Lambeth* v *S, C, V* and *J and LSC* [2005] EWC (Fam.) 776, the LSC has published guidance on the payment of fees for experts in public law proceedings and the costs of treatment, therapy or training. This appears in *Focus 48* (August 2005) and will appear at Part D (Narrative and Guidance) in the next release in the LSC *Manual*, vol. 1.

Under the new unified procedure, the lead solicitor can apply for apportioned payments on account for all the solicitors acting for publicly funded clients. The apportioned payment on account is made directly to each solicitor who can then deal with it according to the court direction or agreement made between the parties.

NOTES

1 See Field Fisher Report into the death of Maria Colwell (1974).
2 Convened by the Royal College of Pathologists and the Royal College of Paediatrics and Child Health and chaired by Baroness Helena Kennedy QC.
3 *Handbook of Best Practice in Children Act Cases*, Children Act Advisory Committee (1997).
4 **www.academy-experts.org**.
5 **www.ewi.org.uk**.
6 *Cross and Tapper on Evidence*, 8th edn, Butterworths (1995).
7 Framework for Assessment of Children in Need and their Families, DH, Home Office and DfEE (2000).
8 See an article by Dr K.S. Carstairs, [2005] Fam Law 40, about the value of psychometric testing.
9 Letter from BMA to AVID, 28 May 1998 (see Chapter 17).
10 *Handbook of Best Practice in Children Act Cases.*
11 Wall J and I. Hamilton, *A Handbook for Expert Witnesses in Children Act Cases*, Jordans (2000), p. 27; and see *Handbook of Best Practice in Children Act Cases* and the Expert Witness Group draft letter of instruction.

CHAPTER 26

Outside court and after proceedings

Key sources

- Children Act 1989, ss.24D and 26 (as amended by Adoption and Children Act 2002); Children Act 2004, s.53
- Representations Procedure (Children) Regulations 1991, as amended by Advocacy Services and Representation Procedure (Children) (Amendment) Regulations 2004
- *The Right to Complain: Practice Guidance on Complaints Procedures in Social Services Departments*, DH, SSI (1991)
- National Standards for the Provision of Children's Advocacy Services 2002, DH
- *Get It Sorted*, DfES (2004)
- *Good Practice in Child Care Cases*, Law Society (2004), paras 3.8, 4.14 and 5.9

26.1 INTRODUCTION

This chapter looks first at avenues of redress before, during and after proceedings, secondly at the all-important task of achieving appropriate closure once proceedings have ended and overlaps with Chapter 11.

26.2 PRINCIPLES

Access to appropriate forms of redress is a right principally afforded by ECHR Article 6. However, children in particular face obstacles when they wish to make complaints or challenge aspects of safeguarding and care and are at the mercy of their own levels of awareness and adult assistance in the pursuit of their rights. The English Children's Commissioner cannot take up individual cases (the Welsh Commissioner can, and has done so). The roles of independent reviewing officers (under the Adoption and Children Act 2002, s.118) and the Children's Rights Director in the inspectorate system are therefore crucial, particularly for looked after children, who should be given as much information as possible (see Chapter 11).

The way in which the end of proceedings is handled, however difficult the case has been, can make a considerable contribution to good outcomes.

26.3 REPRESENTATIONS AND COMPLAINTS

Local authorities are required to have (and publicise) procedures for considering any representations, including complaints, made about the exercise of their functions under Part III of the Children Act 1989 by:

- a child who is looked after or is in need;
- the child's parent or person with parental responsibility;
- a local authority foster carer;
- anyone else whom the local authority considers to have sufficient interest in the child's welfare;
- specified categories of care leavers, i.e. a relevant child under Children Act 1989, s.23A or s.23c or someone who qualifies under s.24B.

The following definitions are found in the Representations Procedure (Children) Regulations 1991, SI 1991/894, reg. 2(1).

Representation: this is not necessarily critical and includes inquiries and statements about such matters as availability, delivery and nature of services.

Complaint: this is a written/oral expression of dissatisfaction or disquiet in relation to an individual child, decision-making services or delay or non-delivery.

But, as has emerged from various inquiries, inspections and consultations,[1] these procedures are not always readily accessible and independent, may vary and can prove lengthy and complex. Children in particular still experience serious barriers to making complaints about services.[2] Regulations set out the procedure to be followed and the information to be provided.[3] It is particularly important that local authorities actively promote the procedures and raise children's awareness, particularly those in foster care.

Advocacy

Local authorities must arrange advocacy services for children and care leavers wishing to make complaints (Advocacy Services and Representations Procedure (Children) (Amendment) Regulations 2004, SI 2004/719). Formal complaints procedures normally used are not the most appropriate way for children to air grievances and *Get It Sorted* stresses that the arrangements for these services should ensure effective provision in particular for children placed ouside the authority or in foster care and those who use other forms of communication or whose first language is not English. Statutory national standards apply and the *Get it Sorted* guidance sets out the principles, including an emphasis on:

- early detection and resolution so that concerns and problems are put right quickly and effectively, with procedures devised and operated in a wider context of encouraging children to speak out and decision-makers to hear their views;

- provision of services through agencies that can be seen as independent of the local authority, with advice on how to maintain the advocate's independence;
- provision of independent and confidential information, advice, representation and support, noting the good practice of some advocacy services in routinely visiting children to foster relationships, seen as an important issue by children themselves.

There are 10 National Standards for Advocacy that must be followed, including advocacy that is:[4]

- led by the wishes and views of children, champions their rights and needs and listens to them;
- well-publicised, well managed, accessible and responsive;
- operated to a high level of confidentiality;
- based firmly on policies that promote equality.

Local authorities must also have a designated complaints office with over-arching responsibility for coordinating the system. Some have children's complaints officers and Part 3 of *Get it Sorted* (DfES, 2004) sets out their role. In early 2005 new regulations (see Children Act 1989, s.26(2A)) were being proposed to allow for further consideration of representations by the Commission for Social Care Inspection, with referral to an independent panel.

26.4   COURT CHALLENGES

Judicial review

Public bodies who act outside the scope of their powers can be challenged via judicial review (brought under CPR Part 54), e.g. for a lack of opportunity to present information or an account of events (*R* v. *Lewisham BC, ex p. P* [1991] 2 FLR 185), a denial of a right to participate in decision-making processes, or local authority failure to plan and provide jointly funded services in complex cases (Wall J in *Re T (Judicial Review: Local Authority Decisions concerning Child in Need)* [2003] EWHC Admin 2515, [2004] 1 FLR 601).

Arguing that local authority complaints and appeals procedures provide appropriate remedies (see *R* v. *RB Kingston-upon-Thames ex p. T* [1994] 1 FLR 798), the courts have stressed that these should be exhausted first and that judicial review should be resorted to rarely, and may result in only limited relief (Court of Appeal in *R* v. *Hampshire CC ex p. H* [1999] 2 FLR 359). It is not appropriate where the argument is about the right to be given an indication of allegations in order to rebut them (*R* v. *Harrow LBC ex p. D* [1990] 1 FLR 79) or to try to prevent commencement of emergency protection or care proceedings (unless exceptional) (*Re M (Care Proceedings: Judicial Review)* [2003] 2 FLR 171).

The advantages and disadvantages of judicial review include:

- the need to get leave for an application, the strict time limits and the restricted scope for oral evidence;
- success will only require the public body to revisit the process using the correct criteria, rather than reviewing the merits;
- potentially faster listing in the Administrative Court than in the Family Division.

Human Rights Act 1998

Human rights issues should normally be raised in the course of proceedings (applications under CPR Part 8) and judicial guidance sets out how these should be handled (Court of Appeal in *Re V (Care Proceedings: Human Rights Claims)* [2004] 1 FLR 944; reaffirmed by Munby J in *Re S; S* v. *Haringey LBC* [2004] 1 FLR 590). Any allegation that a local authority has breached Convention rights should be dealt with in the care proceedings by the court hearing those proceedings (pursuant to Human Rights Act 1998, s.7(1)(b)). Applications for transfer up are strongly discouraged and may amount to an abuse of process.

But freestanding human rights challenges are being made on a wide variety of issues outside care proceedings, including children in young offenders institutions (see *R (Howard League for Penal Reform)* v. *Secretary of State for the Home Department* [2002] EWHC (Admin) 2497, [2003] 1 FLR 484 and *R (BP)* v. *Secretary of State for the Home Department* [2003] All ER (D) 310), separation of mothers in prison and their babies (see *CF* v. *Secretary of State for the Home Department* [2004] 2 FLR 517; *Islington LBC* v. *TM* [2004] EWHC (Fam) 2050), and immigration cases (see *Re A (Care Proceedings: Asylum Seekers)* [2003] EWHC Fam 1086, [2003] 2 FLR 921).

The test is one of proportionality and necessity, rather than the *Wednesbury* test of irrationality. But the substantive principles to be applied are precisely the same (Munby J in *CF* v. *Secretary of State for the Home Department* [2004] 2 FLR 517), with e.g. more scope for oral evidence and cross-examination than in judicial review.

Cases involving children should be heard by a Family Division High Court judge who is also a nominated judge of the Administrative Court (the same applies to judicial review).

Scope for future challenge includes children's Article 6 rights, a largely untested area, but there are both opportunities and limitations.[5]

26.5   AFTER PROCEEDINGS HAVE ENDED

The 'outfall' from a case can reverberate long after practitioner involvement has ceased: final advice and support is vital and can sometimes make a good deal of difference to outcomes, even if the practitioner is unaware of this.

The case and the client relationship should be ended on the basis of sound advice, enabling clients to move on with their lives, at least in the foreseeable future. Relationships between child, family and professionals may be subject to considerable pressure during proceedings: it is important not to undermine these further nor damage prospects of future re-establishment. Practitioners should, wherever possible, put advice in writing, confirm the outcome of proceedings and, where available, return any original documents which the clients have provided, and remind clients about the continuing confidentiality of the case and any relevant documents.

Practitioners and professionals should try and ensure that all parties:

- do not feel they or anyone else have 'won' or lost';
- have details of appropriate and future help and support, not merely those provided during the case (counselling and therapy may be particularly important);
- are encouraged to focus on progressing matters for the child and on rebuilding any relationships under pressure;
- have access to redress including appeals, contact complaints and representation, without further undermining relationships important to the child.

Child or young client

It is important to remain accessible, sympathetic but professional and discourage overdependence by either preparing the child for the end of the client relationship, and/or exercising care over continuing contact, otherwise future representation may be compromised.

You should ensure future access to information about safeguarding, the care plan, complaints, independent reviewing officers (see Chapter 11), returning to court and the guardian and not undermine family/carer and professional relationships. Provide all information personally and confirm all matters in a final letter for the child to refer to later.

The Family Law Protocol advises that practitioners should consider with their clients how the child is to be told the results of private law proceedings, particularly where the court has not accepted her views. In public law proceedings, this should be discussed with the children's guardian.

The child who is to be looked after should be given details of sources of information and support for the future.

Adult clients

Social workers

Local authority lawyers should focus particularly on the final, court-approved care plan, stressing its significance, the importance of its main provisions and the need to keep a copy on file as the basis for future care planning, to discuss any significant departure, or intention to depart, from it as soon as possible with the child, family and carers, and to seek legal advice (this applies in particular to the contact arrangements set out in the plan and in any orders made under Children Act 1989, s.34).

They should comply with the restrictions on changing the child's name or removing her from the jurisdiction (Children Act 1989, s.33(7)), consider any claim to the Criminal Injuries Compensation Agency or civil proceedings for compensation on behalf of the child, and review time-limited orders (e.g. supervision orders) and consider applying for extensions before they expire.

Feelings can often run high if the court did not approve the local authority's plan. The lawyer should ensure that the client understands the importance of remaining focused on the child and implementing the plan that has been approved without delay.

Parents and other adult parties

Practitioners should explain contact with a child who is not returning to the adults' care, and if contact set out in the care plan is changed or not offered, seek legal advice. If the child is to be placed for adoption, practitioners should explain the importance for the child of the parent participating in the 'life story' work. They should give details of any counselling and support/specialist services which may help the client address problems that led to the child's removal; where adoption is the plan, explain the client's entitlement to adoption support services; and give advice on the local authority's future responsibilities to them and the child: even if no order was made, the child may still be a child in need and entitled to services under Children Act 1989, s.17.

The importance of the care plan should be emphasised and the client advised on:

- parental rights to be invited to meetings which seek to make fundamental changes where a child is subject to a care order;
- documentation and information on the child which they should receive;
- attendance at statutory reviews to assist the process, being alert to breaches and raising any omission of discussion of contact and discharge of the care order;

- retaining all future documentation and information of potential future importance;
- the mechanism for review of the court's decisions and the circumstances in which it would be appropriate to apply for discharge of a care order or for variation of contact;
- the steps the local authority will take in considering whether to apply to extend a supervision order on its expiry.

Documents: safekeeping, confidentiality and destruction

Retention of documents to the child's twenty-fourth birthday or until the youngest child who is the subject of the proceedings reaches 18 is advisable.[6]

Where an undertaking has been given on, e.g. safekeeping of documents, practitioners should seek to have this discharged at the end of proceedings.[7]

NOTES

1   See e.g. Joint Inspectors Report, *Safeguarding Children*, DH (2002) commenting on implementation of the recommendations of Sir W. Utting, *People Like Us: The Report on the Safeguards for Children Living Away from Home* (1997) and the Report of the North Wales Tribunal of Inquiry, *Lost in Care*, DH/Welsh Office (2000).

2   Joint Inspectors Report, *Safeguarding Children*, p.65 at **www.safeguarding children.org.uk**.

3   Representations Procedure (Children) Regulations 1991, SI 1991/894, as amended.

4   The National Standards for the Provision of Children's Advocacy Services, DH (2002) is statutory guidance issued under Local Authority Social Services Act 1970, s.7.

5   For analysis see Munby J's speech, ALC Conference 2004, ALC Newsletter (February 2005).

6   *The Guide to the Professional Conduct of Solicitors 1999*, Law Society (**www.guide-online.lawsociety.org.uk**).

7   *Family Law Protocol*, Law Society (2002).

APPENDIX 1

Bibliography

BOOKS AND PRICED PUBLICATIONS

Brophy, J. (ed.) *Expert Evidence in Child Protection Litigation: Where do We Go from Here?* The Stationery Office (1999).

Campbell, J., Sharps, P. and Glass, N. (2000) 'Risk Assessment for Intimate Partner Homicide' in *Clinical Assessment of Dangerousness: Empirical Contributions*, Pinard G. and Pagani, L. (eds), Cambridge University Press.

Daniel, B., Wassell, B. and Gilligan, R. (1999) *Child Development for Child Care and Protection Workers*, Jessica Kingsley.

Department of Health (1989) *An Introduction to the Children Act 1989: A New Framework For The Care And Upbringing Of Children*, The Stationery Office.

—— (1990) *The Care of Children Principles and Practice in Regulations and Guidance*, The Stationery Office.

—— (1991) Children Act 1989 Guidance and Regulations, vols 1–10, The Stationery Office.

——, Social Services Inspectorate (1991) *The Right to Complain: Practice Guidance on Complaints Procedures in Social Services Departments*, The Stationery Office.

—— (1995) *The Challenge of Partnership in Child Protection: Practice Guide*, The Stationery Office.

——, Plotnikoff and Wilson (1996) *Reporting to Court under the Children Act: Handbook for Social Services*, The Stationery Office.

——, Department for Education and Employment and Home Office (2000) *Framework for Assessment of Children in Need and their Families*, The Stationery Office (pack).

Jones, D. (2003) *Communicating with Vulnerable Children*, Gaskell (Royal College of Psychiatrists).

Legal Services Commission, *LSC Manual*, The Stationery Office (looseleaf, online and CD subscription).

Hague Conference on Private International Law Permanent Bureau (2003) *Guide to Good Practice of 25 October 1980 under the Hague Convention on the Civil Aspects of International Child Abduction*, Parts 1 and 2, Jordans.

Law Society (1999) *The Guide to the Professional Conduct of Solicitors 1999*, 8th edn, Law Society.

—— (2002) *Family Law Protocol*, Law Society (2nd edn due 2005).

——, with the Association of Lawyers for Children, the Child Care Law Joint Liaison Group and the SFLA (2004) *Good Practice in Child Care Cases*, Law Society.

Wall, J. and Hamilton, I. (2000) *A Handbook for Expert Witnesses in Children Act Cases*, Jordans.

Wilson, C. and Powell, M. (2001) *A Guide to Interviewing Children*, Routledge.

RESEARCH, GUIDANCE AND GOVERNMENT PUBLICATIONS

See *Appendix 2 for details of websites where many of these publications can be found. Some useful links are given below, although government sites are reorganised regularly.*

Association of Chief Police Officers (February 2001) *Asylum Seekers Policing Guide.*
—— and Department for Constitutional Affairs (2004) 'ACPO Pilots: Disclosure of Information in Family Proceedings: Police/Family Disclosure Protocol'.
—— and Centrex (2004) *Guidance on Investigating Domestic Violence.*
—— and Centrex (2005) *Guidance on Investigating Child Abuse and Safeguarding Children.*
Association of Council Secretaries and Solicitors and Solicitors in Local Government Child Care Joint Liaison Group (2004) *Arrangements for Handling Child Care Cases.*
Barnardo's, Family Rights Group and NCH (2002) *Family Group Conferences: Principles and Practice Guidance* (**www.frg.org.uk/fgc/FamilyGConference.pdf**).
Brophy, J., Jhutti-Johal, J. and Owen, C. (2003) *Significant Harm: Child Protection Litigation in a Multi-cultural Setting*, Lord Chancellor's Department.
Commission for Racial Equality (2003) *The Law, the Duty and You – The Race Relations Act and the Duty to Promote Race Equality: A Guide for Public Employees* (**www.cre.gov.uk/downloads/Lawdutyou.rtf**).
Crown Prosecution Service (November 2001, revised February 2005) *Policy for Prosecuting Cases of Domestic Violence* (at **www.cps.gov.uk/publications/docs/ DomesticViolencePolicy.pdf**).
——, Association of Chief Police Officers, Local Government Association of England, and Association of Directors of Social Services (September 2003) *A Protocol between the Crown Prosecution Service, Police and Local Authorities in the Exchange of Information in the Investigation and Prosecution of Child Abuse Cases.*
Department for Constitutional Affairs (February 2003, revised November 2004) Domestic Violence: A Guide to Civil Remedies and Criminal Sanctions (at **www.dca.gov.uk/family/dvguide04.pdf**).
—— (November 2003) *Public Sector Data Sharing: Guidance on the Law* (**www.dca.gov.uk/foi/sharing/toolkit/lawguide.htm**).
—— (May 2004) *A Public Sector Toolkit on Data Sharing* (**www.dca.gov.uk/foi/ sharing/toolkit/index.htm**).
Department for Education and Skills (October 2001) Guidance on the education of school age parents (DfES/0629/2001 and **www.dfes.gov.uk/schoolageparents**).
—— (2001) Special Educational Needs Code of Practice (DfES/581/2001).
—— (2001) SEN Toolkit (**www.teachernet.gov.uk/wholeschool/sen/ teacherlearningassistant**).
—— (2004) *Get it sorted: Guidance – Providing Effective Advocacy Services for Children and Young People Making a Complaint under the Children Act 1989* (**www.dfes.gov.uk/childrensadvocacy/docs/GetitSorted.pdf**).
—— (2004) Independent Reviewing Officers Guidance: Adoption and Children Act 2002 (**www.dfes.gov.uk/adoption/pdfs/IRO.pdf**).
—— (September 2004) Safeguarding Children in Education' (DfES 0027/2004 and **www.teachernet.gov.uk/childprotection/guidance**).
—— (September 2004, revised May 2005) *Who Does What: How Social Workers and Carers Can Support the Education of Looked After Children.*
—— (January 2005) *Guidance for Local Authorities and Schools – PRUs and Alternative Provision* (LEA 0024–2005).
—— (July 2005) *Lead Professional Good Practice Guidance for Children with Additional Needs.*

—— (August 2005) *Guidance on the Children and Young People's Plan.*

—— (August 2005) *Statutory Guidance on Inter-Agency Co-operation to Improve the Well-being of Children: Children's Trusts.*

—— (August 2005) *Statutory Guidance on the Role and Responsibilities of the Director of Children's Services and the Lead Member for Children's Services.*

—— (August 2005) *Statutory Guidance on Making Arrangements to Safeguard and Promote the Welfare of Children under section 11 of the Children Act 2004.*

—— (consultation July–October 2005) *Working Together to Safeguard Children Draft For Public Consultation* including Chapter 3, 'Local Safeguarding Children Boards'.

—— (consultation August–November 2005) *Cross-Government Guidance – Sharing Information on Children and Young People.*

—— (September 2005) *Every Child Matters: Change for Children – An Overview of Cross Government Guidance* (overview of recent guidance and signposting to individual documents at **www.everychildmatters.gov.uk/strategy/guidance**).

Department of Health and Welsh Office (1998) 'Mental Health Act 1983: Memorandum on Parts I to VI, VIII and X'.

—— and Welsh Office (1999) 'Mental Health Act 1983: Code of Practice'.

——, Home Office and Department for Education and Employment (1999) *Working Together to Safeguard Children: a guide to inter-agency working to safeguard and promote the welfare of children*, and see supplementary guidance (May 2000) *Safeguarding Children Involved in Prostitution* and (August 2002) *Safeguarding Children in Whom Illness is Fabricated or Induced.*

—— (March 2000) *Domestic Violence: A Resource Manual for Health Care Professionals.*

—— (2001) *Getting it Right: Good Practice in Leaving Care* (resource pack).

—— (March 2001) *Planning and Providing Good Quality Placements for Children in Care.*

—— (2002) *Children's Homes National Minimum Standards, Children's Homes Regulations.*

—— (November 2002) *National Standards for the Provision of Children's Advocacy Services.*

—— (2002) *Protocol on Advice and Advocacy for Parents (Child Protection)* (Lindley, B. and Richards, M. Centre for Family Research, University of Cambridge at **www.sps.cam.ac.uk/cfr/advocacyprotocol.pdf**).

—— (May 2003) *What to Do If You Are Worried A Child is Being Abused: Children's Services Guidance.*

—— and Refugee Council (June 2003) *Caring for Dispersed Asylum Seekers: A Resource Pack.*

—— and DfES (October 2004, updated January 2005) 'National Service Framework for Children, Young People and Maternity Services'.

Disability Rights Commission (2002) 'Disability Discrimination Act 1995 Part 4: Code of Practice for Schools' (**www.drc-gb.org**).

Home Office Crime Reduction Unit, 'Anti-Trafficking Toolkit' (**www.crimereduction. gov.uk/toolkits**).

Home Office, Crown Prosecution Service and Department of Health (2001) *Provision of Therapy for Child Witnesses Prior to a Criminal Trial: Practice Guidance* (**www.homeoffice.gov.uk/docs/therapybook.pdf**).

—— (2003) *Complex Child Abuse Investigations: Inter-Agency Issues.*

——, Lord Chancellor's Department, CPS, Department of Health and Welsh Assembly (January 2002) *Achieving Best Evidence in Criminal Proceedings: Guidance for Vulnerable or Intimidated Witnesses, including Children.*

Housing Corporation (August 2004) *Anti-Social Behaviour: Policy and Procedure – Guidance for Housing Associations* (**www.together.gov.uk** under 'Working in Partnership, Landlords').

Immigration Law Practitioners' Association (November 2004) *Working with Children subject to Immigration Control: Guidelines for Best Practice.*

Law Society (June 1997) Family Law Committee Guidance: 'Attendance of solicitors at child protection conferences' (see Family Law specialism section at **www.lawsociety.org.uk**).

—— (October 2003) 'Guidance on acting in the absence of a children's guardian – Notice to children panel members: Representation of children in public law proceedings'.

—— and CAFCASS (March 2004) 'Guidance on working relationship between Children Panel solicitors and Children's Guardians'.

—— (June 2005) 'Children Panel: Criteria and Guidance Notes' (**www.lawsociety.org.uk/professional/accreditationpanels.law** under Children Panel).

Lord Chancellor's Department (June 2003) 'Protocol for Judicial Case Management in Public Law Children Act Cases' (at **www.hmcourts-service.gov.uk/docs/protocol-complete.pdf**).

Lord Chancellor's Advisory Committee (June 2003) 'Statement of Good Practice in the Appointment of Solicitors Where it Falls to the Court to Do So in Specified Proceedings'.

Office of the Deputy Prime Minister (July 2002, revised Chapter 15 January 2005) *Homelessness Code of Guidance for Local Authorities.*

Refugee Women's Legal Group (July 1998) *Gender Guidelines for the Determination of Asylum Claims in the UK.*

Resolution (2002) (formerly Solicitors' Family Law Association) *Guide to Good Practice for Solicitors Acting for Children*, 6th edn (issued free to members).

Royal College of Paediatrics and Child Health (November 1999) *The Health of Refugee Children: Guidelines for Paediatricians.*

—— and Association of Police Surgeons (April 2002, revised September 2004) *Guidance on Paediatric Forensic Examinations in Relation to Possible Child Sexual Abuse.*

—— (April 2004) *Child Abuse and Neglect: The Role of Mental Health Services* (council report).

—— and Royal College of Pathologists (September 2004) *Sudden Unexpected Death in Infancy: A Multi-Agency Protocol for Care and Investigation* (Baroness Helena Kennedy QC).

Royal College of Psychiatrists (June 2002) *Patients as Parents* (council report CR105).

Save the Children/UNHCR (3rd edn 2004) 'Separated Children in Europe Programme – Statement of Good Practice' (**www.separated-children-europe-programme.org**).

UNHCR (1972, revised 1992) *Handbook on Procedures and Criteria for Determining Refugee Status* (can be found at **www.hrea.org/learn/tutorials/refugees/Handbook/hbtoc.htm**).

Welsh Assembly (September 2001) 'Children (Leaving Care) Act 2000: guidance'.

—— (2002) 'Special Educational Needs Code of Practice for Wales' (**www.learning.wales.gov.uk**).

—— (February 2003) *National Standards for the Provision of Children's Advocacy Services.*

—— (2003, amended November 2004) *All Wales Child Protection Procedures.*

—— (May 2004) *Independent Reviewing Officers Guidance Wales.*

DEPARTMENT FOR EDUCATION AND EMPLOYMENT CIRCULARS

Chief Inspector Letters

CI (95)2: Arrangements for Inter-authority Recoupment after 1 April 1995 (March 1995).

CI (96)14: Supporting pupils with medical needs in school (October 1996).

DEPARTMENT OF HEALTH CIRCULARS

Most letters and circulars published by the Department of Health/Department for Education and Skills can be found at **http://www.dh.gov.uk/ PublicationsAndStatistics/fs/en.**

Local authority social services letters

LASSL(2001)2: The children and family court advisory and support service (CAFCASS) and complaints about the functioning of child protection conferences (May 2001).

LASSL(2002)4: Guidance on accommodating children in need and their families (March 2002).

Local authority circulars

LAC (86)15: Mental Health Act 1983 approved social workers (November 1986).

LAC(92)13: The Children (Secure Accommodation) Amendment Regulations 1992 (September 1992).

LAC(94)9 (also DFE Circular 9/94): The education of children with emotional and behavioural difficulties (May 1994) (currently being revised).

LAC (98)20: Adoption achieving the right balance (August 1998).

LAC (99)11: Mental Health Act 1983 revised code of practice (March 1999).

LAC (99)25: Implementation of further provisions under Part III of the Disability Discrimination Act 1995: Implications for social services authorities (July 1999).

LAC (99)29: Care plans and care proceedings under the Children Act 1989 (August 1999).

LAC (2000)13: Guidance on the education of children and young people in public care (12/5/2000); see also *Guidance on the Education of Children and Young People in Public Care* (DH and DfES, May 2000).

LAC (2002)16: Children Act (Miscellaneous Amendments) (England) Regulations 2002: new guidance on promoting the health of looked after children (November 2002).

LAC (2003)12: New arrangements for intercountry adoption and adoption support services (May 2003) (see also *Intercountry Adoption Guide,* Department of Health, 2003).

LAC (2003)13: Guidance on accommodating children in need and their families (June 2003).

LAC (2004)11: Regulations and guidance on providing effective advocacy services for children and young people making a complaint under the Children Act 1989 (April 2004).

LAC (2004)14: The independent review mechanism (April 2004).

LAC (2004)24: The Community Care Assessment Directions 2004 (August 2004).

LAC (2001)22: National Adoption Standards for England (August 2001).

LAC (2001)27 (also Health Service Circular 2001/019, DfES 0732/2001): Access to Education for Children and Young People with Medical Needs (November 2001).

LAC (2000)3: After-care under the Mental Health Act 1983: section 117 after-care services (February 2000).

HOME OFFICE CIRCULARS

Home Office Circular 20/2003: Healthcare professionals in custody suites – Guidance to supplement revisions to the Codes of Practice under the Police and Criminal Evidence Act 1984 (including National Protocol on Custody Care) (April 2003).

Home Office Circular 44/2003: The duties and powers of the police under the Children Act 1989 (revised September 2003, replaces HO Circular 54/1991, can be found at **www.homeoffice.gov.uk**).

Immigration and Nationality Directorate

Asylum Policy Instructions (APIs) and National Asylum Support Service (NASS) Policy Bulletins (PBs) can be found at **www.ind.homeoffice.gov.uk**.

Immigration Rules (a consolidated version of the current Immigration Rules can be found at **www.ind.homeoffice.gov.uk** under 'Laws and Policy').

APPENDIX 2

Useful contacts

For reasons of space, the following is just a sample of the many organisations offering advice, information and support. However, several websites provide a wealth of links to other sources of information.

EMERGENCIES

Emergency powers

Family Division Lawyer
President's Chambers, Royal Courts of Justice,
Strand
London WCA 2LL
Tel: 020 7947 7197
Fax: 020 7947 7274

Police National Ports Office: Heathrow Airport
Tel: 020 7230 4800 (24-hour advice line)

Domestic violence and victim support

Cardiff Rape Crisis Line
Tel: 029 2037 3181 (Mon and Thurs 7–10pm)

Rape Crisis
www.rapecrisis.org.uk/contact.htm (for list of local rape crisis group helplines)

Refuge
Tel: 0808 2000 247 (24–hour helpline, run in partnership between Women's Aid and Refuge)
www.refuge.org.uk

Rights of Women
Tel: 020 7251 6575 (administration), Advice line: 020 7251 6577 (open Tues to Thurs 2–4pm, Fri 12–2pm)

Sexual violence legal advice line: 020 7251 8887
www.rightsofwomen.org.uk

Samaritans
Tel: 08457 909090
Email: jo@samaritans.org.uk
www.samaritans.org.uk

Victim Support National Office
Tel: 020 7735 9166 (administration), 0845 3030900 (Victim Support helpline)
www.victimsupport.org.uk

Welsh Women's Aid
Tel: 0808 80 10 800 (domestic abuse helpline)
www.welshwomensaid.org

Women's Aid Federation of England
Head Office
PO Box 391
Bristol BS99 7WS
Tel: 0117 944 4411 (office), 0808 2000 247 (helpline)
www.womensaid.org.uk

Worst Kept Secret
Tel: 0800 028 3398 (Merseyside domestic violence confidential helpline)
www.worstkeptsecret.co.uk

Black and ethnic minority groups

Newham Asian Women's Project
661 Barking Road

London E13 9EX
Tel: 020 8472 0528 (general), 020 8552 5524 (advice line)
www.nawp.org

Southall Black Sisters
21 Avenue Road
Southall
Middlesex UB1 3BL
Tel: 020 8571 9595
Fax: 020 8574 6781
www.southallblacksisters.org.uk

Families and children

Childline
Tel: 0800 1111 (helpline for children and young people)
www.childline.org.uk

Gingerbread
Tel: 0800 018 4318 (helpline Mon to Fri 10am–4pm)
www.gingerbread.org.uk

National Society for the Prevention of Cruelty to Children (NSPCC)
Tel: 0808 800 5000 (child protection helpline), 0808 100 2524 (Wales)
Textphone: 0800 056 0566 (English only)
www.nspcc.org.uk

Parentline Plus
Tel: 020 7284 5500
Helpline: 0808 800 2222
Textphone: 0800 783 6783
www.parentlineplus.org.uk

GENERAL

Adoption and fostering

Adoption UK (support group)
46 The Green, South Bar Street
Banbury
Oxon OX16 9AB
Tel: 01295 7522540
Helpline: 0870 7700 450
www.adoptionuk.org.uk

British Agencies For Adoption And Fostering (BAAF)
Skyline House
200 Union Street

London SE1 0LX
Tel: 020 7593 2000
www.baaf.org.uk

Fostering Network (formerly National Foster Care Association)
87 Blackfriars Road
London SE1 8HA
Tel: 020 7620 6400 (London office)
Tel: 029 2044 0940 (Wales office)
www.thefostering.net

General Register Office
Adoptions Section, Room C201
Trafalgar Road
Southport PR8 2HH
Tel: 0151 471 4830
Email: adoptions@ons.gsi.gov.uk

National Organisation for Counselling Adoptees and their Parents (NORCAP)
112 Church Road
Wheatley
Oxford OX33 1LU
Tel: 01865 875000
www.norcap.org.uk

The Post Adoption Centre
5 Torriano Mews
Torriano Avenue
London NW5 2RZ
Tel: +44 (0) 207 284 0555
www.postadoptioncentre.org.uk

Advice

Advicenow
www.advicenow.org.uk (information on rights and legal issues)

Advisory Centre For Education
Tel: 0808 800 5793 (advice line Mon to Fri 2–5pm)
Tel: 020 7704 9822 (24–hour exclusion information line)
www.ace-ed.org.uk

Anti-bullying campaign
Tel: 020 7378 1446
www.show.scot.nhs.uk/fpct/mhweb/abc.htm

Bullying Online
Email: help@bullying.co.uk
www.bullying.co.uk

Children's Legal Centre
Tel: 01206 872 466
Tel: 0845 456 6811 (education law
advice line)
E-mail: clc@essex.ac.uk
www.childrenslegalcentre.com

Education Otherwise
Tel: 0870 730 0074 (helpline for families
of children educated outside school,
open 8am–8pm)
www.education-otherwise.org

Family Rights Group
Tel: 0800 731 1696 (advice and support
for families whose children are involved
with social services)
www.frg.org.uk

*Grandparents' Association (formerly
Grandparents' Federation)*
Tel: 01279 428040 (office)
Helpline: 01279 444964 (information
for grandparents, families and professionals on contact and residence issues)
www.grandparents-federation.org.uk

*National Association of Citizen's Advice
Bureaux*
www.nacab.org.uk (nearest CAB)
www.adviceguide.org.uk (CAB information online)

*National Youth Advocacy Service
(NYAS)*
Tel: 0151 649 8700 (general)
Young person's helpline: 0800 616101
(Mon to Fri 8am–8pm, Sat 10am–4pm)
Email: main@nyas.net
www.nyas.net

Shelter
Tel: 020 7505 4699
Helpline: 0808 800 4444 (housing
advice)
www.shelter.org.uk

Asylum and immigration

Asylum Aid
Tel: 020 7247 8741 (advice)
www.asylumaid.org.uk

Asylum and Immigration Tribunal
Tel: 0845 6000 877
Minicom: 0845 6060 766

Fax: 01509 221699
www.ait.gov.uk

Immigration Advisory Service
3rd Floor, County House
190 Great Dover Street
London SE1 4YB
Tel: 020 7967 1200
Fax: 020 7403 5875
www.iasuk.org

Immigration and Nationality Directorate
www.ind.homeoffice.gov.uk

*Joint Council for the Welfare of
Immigrants*
Tel: 020 7251 8708
Fax: 020 7251 8707
Email: info@jcwi.org.uk
www.jcwi.org.uk

Disability

Council for Disabled Children
Tel: 020 7843 1900
www.ncb.org.uk/cdc

Disability Alliance
Tel: 020 7247 8776
Email: office.da@dial.pipex.com
www.disabilityalliance.org

*Disability, Pregnancy and Parenthood
International*
Tel: 0800 018 4730 (information serv-
ices Mon to Fri 9.30am–5.30pm)
Textphone: 0800 018 9949
www.dppi.org.uk

Disability Rights Commission
Tel: 08457 622 633 (helpline 8am–8pm)
www.drc-gb.org

Disability Wales
Tel: 029 2088 7325
Fax: 029 2088 8702
www.disabilitywales.org

Disabled Parent's Network:
Tel: 08702 410 450 (parent-to-parent
helpline)
www.DisabledParentsNetwork.org.uk

Royal National Institute for the Deaf
Tel: 0808 808 0123 (information line)
Textphone: 0808 808 9000 (information
line)

Email: informationline@rnid.org.uk
www.rnid.org.uk

*Special Educational Needs and
Disability Tribunal*
SEN helpline: 0870 241 2555
(9am–5pm Mon to Fri)
Discrimination helpline: 0870 606 5750
(9am–5pm Mon to Fri)
www.sendist.gov.uk

PRACTICE

Commissioners and ombudsman

*Children's Commissioner for England
(Prof Al Aynsley-Green)*
Tel: 020 7273 5559
Email: support@childrenscommis
sioner.org

*Children's Commissioner for Wales
(Peter Clarke)*
Tel: 01792 765600
Email: post@childcomwales.org.uk
www.childcom.org.uk

*Children's Rights Director (CSCI) (Dr
Roger Morgan OBE)*
Tel: 0800 528 0731 (freephone)
www.rights4me.org.uk

*Commission for Social Care Inspection
(CSCI)*
Tel: 0207 979 2000, 0845 015 0120
(helpline)
Email: enquiries@csci.gsi.gov.uk
www.csci.org.uk

Commission for Racial Equality
Tel: 020 7939 0000 (England), 02920
729 200 (Wales)
www.cre.gov.uk

*Parliamentary and Health Service
Ombudsman*
Tel: 0845 015 4033
Email:
phso.enquiries@ombudsman.org.uk
www.ombudsman.org.uk

Government departments

Department for Constitutional Affairs
www.dca.gov.uk

Department for Education and Skills
www.dfes.gov.uk/childrenandfamilies/
www.dfes.gov.uk/youngpeople/

Department of Health
www.dh.gov.uk

National Assembly for Wales
www.wales.gov.uk

Law Society of England and Wales

113 Chancery Lane
London WC2A 1PL
Tel: 020 7242 1222
DX 56 London/Chancery Lane
www.lawsociety.org.uk

Children Panel
Tel: 0870 606 2555
Email: panels@lawsociety.org.uk
www.panels.lawsociety.org.uk
www.lawsociety.org.uk/documents/dow
nloads/panelscpmemblistchildrep.pdf
(list of members)

Professional Ethics
Tel: 0870 606 2577
www.guide-on-line.lawsociety.org.uk

Legal

*Association of Lawyers for Children
(ALC)*
Tel: 020 8224 7071
Email: admin@alc.org.uk
www.alc.org.uk

CAFCASS
Tel: 020 7510 7000
www.cafcass.co.uk

Community Legal Service Direct
www.clsdirect.org.uk
Tel: 0845 345 4345 (referrals to local
specialist legal adviser/solicitor)

Crown Prosecution Service
www.cps.gov.uk

Education Law Association
Tel: 01189 669866
Email: secretary@educationlawassocia-
tion.org.uk
www.educationlawassociation.org.uk

Family Law Bar Association
Tel: 020 7242 1289
Fax: 020 7831 7144
www.flba.co.uk

Legal Aid Practitioners Group
Tel: 020 7960 6068
www.lapg.co.uk

Legal Services Commission
www.legalservices.gov.uk

Liberty (formerly National Council for Civil Liberties)
21 Tabard Street
London SE1 4LA
Tel: 020 7403 3888
Fax: 020 7407 5354
info@liberty-human-rights.org.uk
www.liberty-human-rights.org.uk

National Association of Guardians ad Litem and Reporting Officers (NAGALRO)
Tel: 01372 818504
www.nagalro.com
Email: nagalro@globalnet.co.uk

Office of the Official Solicitor
Tel: 020 7911 7127
Email: enquiries@offsol.gsi.gov.uk
www.offsol.demon.co.uk

Resolution (Solicitors' Family Law Association)
Tel: 01689 820 272
Fax: 01689 896 972
Email: info@resolution.org.uk
www.sfla.org.uk
www.carelaw.org.uk (guide for young people)

Medical

Royal College of General Practitioners
www.rcgp.org.uk

Royal College of Paediatrics and Child Health (RCPCH)
www.rcph.ac.uk

Royal College of Physicians
www.rcplondon.ac.uk

Royal College of Psychiatrists
www.rcpsych.ac.uk

Mental health

Institute of Mental Health Act Practitioners
www.markwalton.net

Medical Foundation for the Care of Victims of Torture
Tel: 020 7697 7777; 0161 236 5744
www.torturecare.org.uk

Mental Health Act Commission
www.mhac.org.uk

Mental Health Foundation
Tel: 020 7803 1100
Email: mhf@mhf.org.uk
www.mentalhealth.org.uk

Mental Health Lawyers Association
www.mhla.co.uk

Mental Health Review Tribunal
www.mhrt.org.uk

MIND
Tel: 020 8519 2122 (legal advice service), 0845 766 0163 (Info Line)
Email: contact@mind.org.uk
www.mind.org.uk

National Institute for Mental Health in England (NIMHE)
www.nimhe.org.uk

Together (formerly the Mental After Care Association)
Tel: 020 7061 3400
Email: contactus@together-uk.org
www.together-uk.org

Young Minds
Tel: 020 7336 8445
Parents Information Line: 0800 018 2138 (Mon and Fri 10am–1pm, Tue to Thur 1–4pm, Wed 6–8pm)
www.youngminds.org.uk

Policy and services

Barnardo's
www.barnardos.org.uk

Children in Wales
Tel: 029 2034 2434
www.childreninWales.org.uk

Joseph Rowntree Foundation
www.jrf.org.uk

National Association for the Care and Resettlement of Offenders (NACRO)
Tel: 020 7582 6500
www.nacro.org.uk

National Children's Bureau
Tel: 020 7843 6000
www.ncb.org.uk
www.childpolicy.org.uk (information on policy and legislation)

National Society for the Prevention of Cruelty to Children (NSPCC)
www.nspcc.org.uk

Voice for the Child in Care (VCC)
Tel: 020 7833 5792
www.vcc-uk.org

Who Cares Trust
Tel: 0207 251 3117
www.thewhocarestrust.org.uk

RESEARCH AND REFERENCE

Legal reference

The Stationery Office
Tel: 020 7873 9090
www.tsoshop.co.uk

British and Irish Legal Information Institute (BAILII)
www.bailii.org

Casetrack (transcripts of judgments)
www.casetrack.com

DCA Human Rights Unit
www.humanrights.gov.uk

European Court of Human Rights portal (HUDOC)
www.echr.coe.int/echr

Family Law Journal
www.familylaw.co.uk

House of Lords judgments
www.parliament.the-stationery-office.co.uk/pa/ld199697/ldjudgmt/ldjudgmt.htm

HM Courts Service
www.hmcourts-service.gov.uk

Lawtel
www.lawtel.co.uk

Legislation
www.opsi.gov.uk/legislation/index.htm

University research

Centre for Evidence-Based Social Services (1997–2004)
www.ripfa.org.uk/aboutus/archive/

Centre for Research on the Child and Family (CRCF)
University of East Anglia
www.uea.ac.uk/swk/research/centre

Centre for the Study of the Child, the Family and the Law
University of Liverpool
www.liv.ac.uk/law/cscfl

Centre for the Study of Safety and Wellbeing (SWELL)
University of Warwick
www2.warwick.ac.uk/fac/soc/shss/swell

Social Science Information Gateway
www.sosig.ac.uk

Index

Practical Education Law

Angela Jackman, Deborah Hay and Pat Wilkins

Education has become the focus of intense legal activity over the past decade, resulting in the development of a comprehensive package of rights for pupils and their parents. However, the legal position is now so complex that the lay or unrepresented parent of a school-aged child may struggle to gain any access to the system.

This book provides a comprehensive yet accessible guide to the law and procedures relevant to the school system, including admissions, exclusions, special educational needs, negligence and transport. The authors present a clear analysis of the statutory framework, case law and government guidelines and give practical and detailed step-by-step guidance on the areas most commonly in dispute. It features:

- case summaries, precedents, letters and checklists
- detailed analyis of the law and practice
- practical guidance on procedures, strategies and client care issues.

Available from Marston Book Services:
Tel. 01235 465 656.

1 85328 816 0

280 pages
£39.95
October 2005

The Law Society